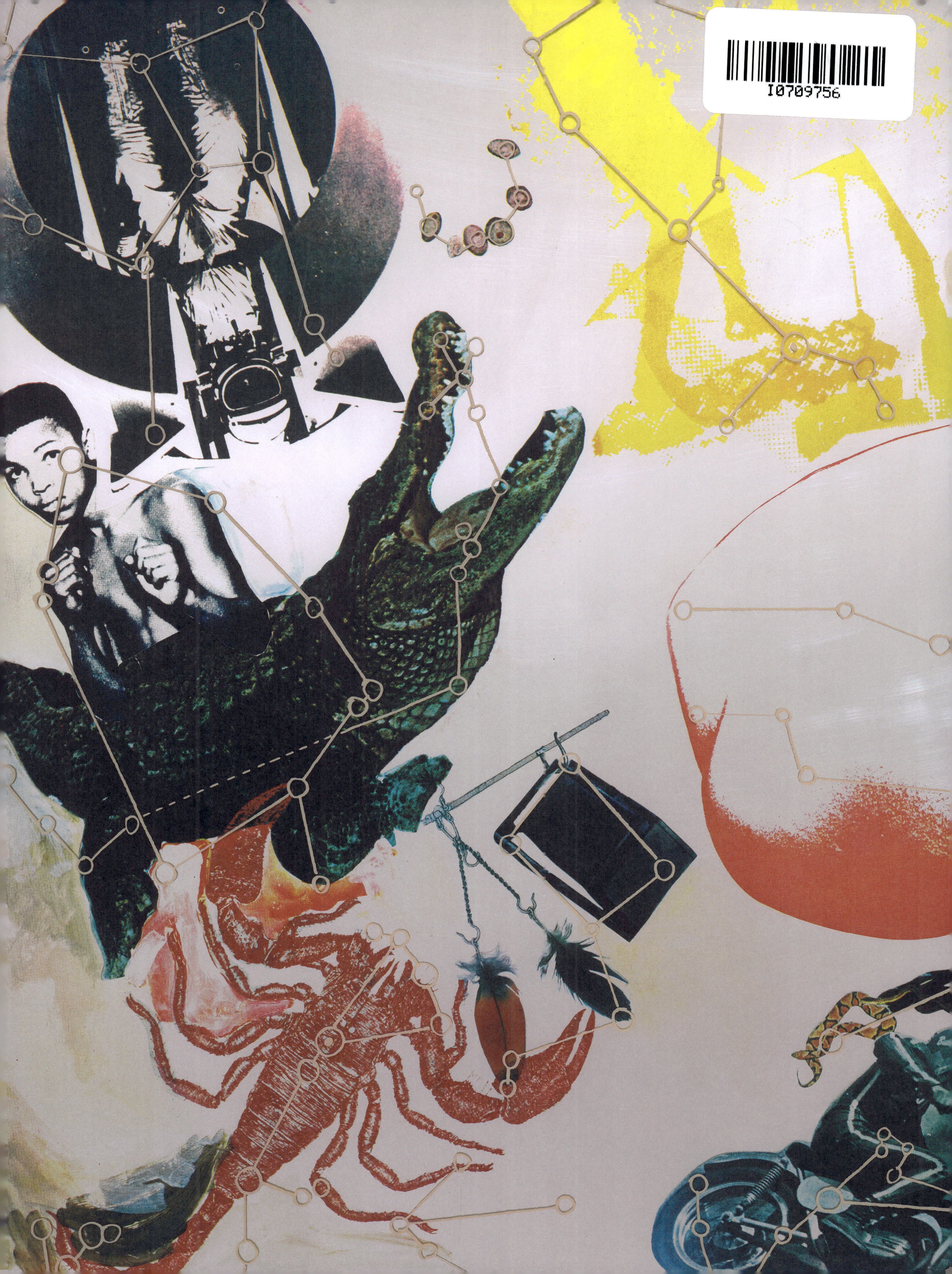
I0709756

The Ascent of Rauschenberg

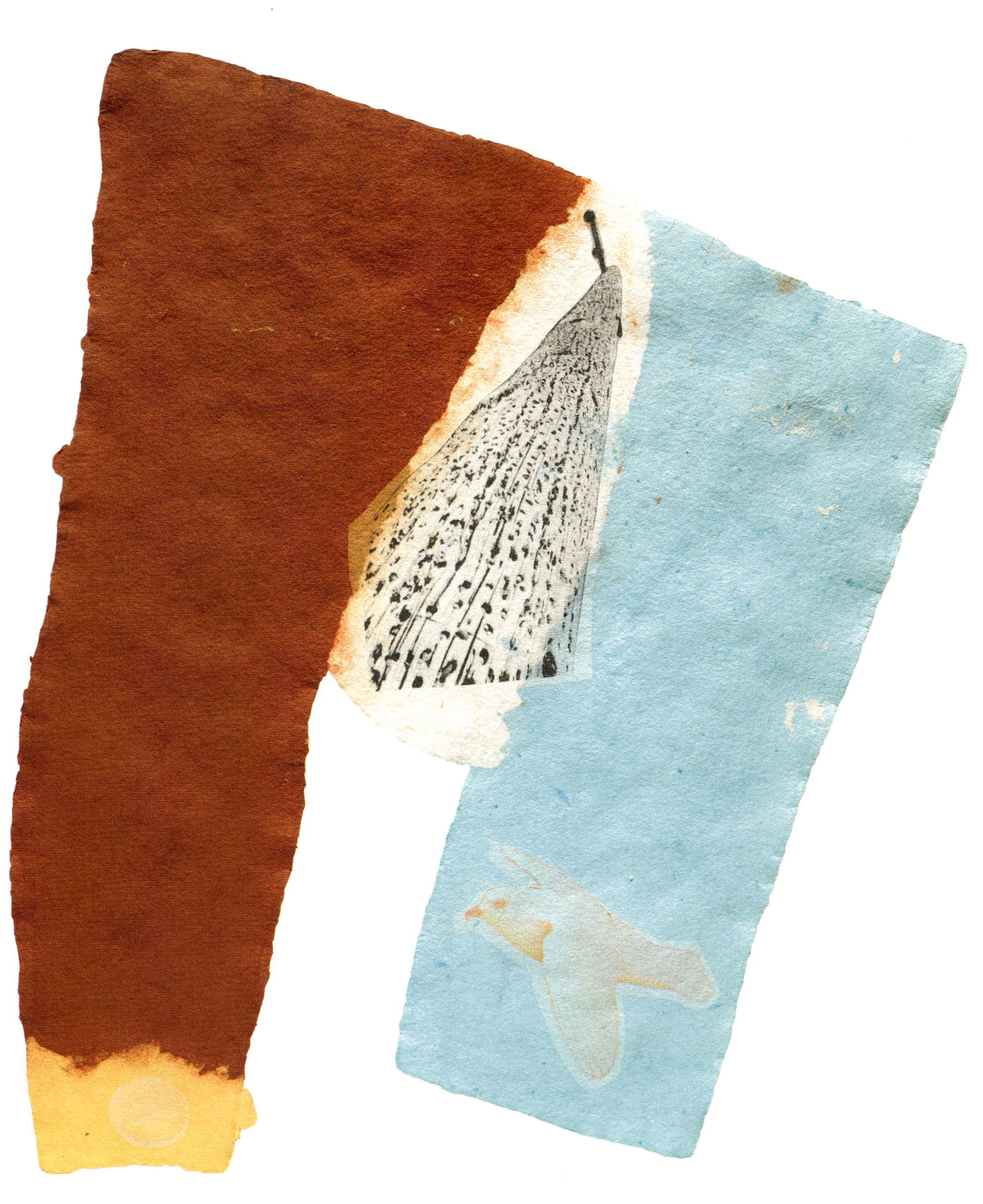

The Ascent of Rauschenberg

Reinventing the Art of Flight

Carolyn Russo

Foreword by Alexander Nemerov

Smithsonian Books
Washington, DC

Published by Smithsonian Books
Smithsonian Books
PO Box 37012, MRC 513
Washington, DC 20013
smithsonianbooks.com

Director: Carolyn Gleason
Senior Editor: Jaime Schwender
Digital Imaging Technician: Bill Whitcher
Edited by Tom Fredrickson
Designed by Anjali Pala

This book may be purchased for educational, business, or sales promotional use. For information, please write to the Special Markets Department at the address or website listed above.

Library of Congress Cataloging-in-Publication Data

Names: Russo, Carolyn author
Title: The ascent of Rauschenberg : reinventing the art of flight / Carolyn Russo ; foreword by Alexander Nemerov.
Description: Washington, DC : Smithsonian Books, [2025] | Includes bibliographical references and index.
Identifiers: LCCN 2025009980 | ISBN 9781588347992 hardcover
Subjects: LCSH: Rauschenberg, Robert, 1925-2008--Criticism and interpretation | Flight in art | Space flight in art
Classification: LCC N6537.R27 R87 2025 | DDC 709.2--dc23/eng/20250429
LC record available at https://lccn.loc.gov/2025009980

Printed in Hong Kong, not at government expense
29 28 27 26 25   1 2 3 4 5

Frontispiece: **Link (Fuses)**, 1974

Endsheets: **Star Quarters I-IV**, 1971

Contents

Leaving the Ground . . . for a While

Alexander Nemerov

Robert Rauschenberg was the John Joseph Montgomery of art. Montgomery (1858–1911) was an aviation pioneer who invented and flew heavier-than-air gliders starting in the early 1880s, first outside San Diego and later in the hills around San Jose. Traveling six to eight hundred feet at an altitude of about twenty feet, he made some fifty-five flights in October 1911 on the *Evergreen*, his most advanced glider. But that Halloween he died when the *Evergreen* stalled and fell to earth. Having failed, Montgomery succeeded in the most beautiful way, as did Robert Rauschenberg.

Art is designed not to work. It cannot really get off the ground for very long. It can simulate flight, make a show of it, but the rest is up to our imagination. For that reason, art's lift can be more exciting than those successful flights that gain a thrilling but prosaic separation from Earth. Rauschenberg lived for that kind of lift, the imaginative kind. And Montgomery, for all his aeronautical expertise, was perhaps too much of an artist to top the mechanical Wright brothers. The beauty of the *Evergreen* recalls Leonardo da Vinci's flying machines more than the airplanes of the twentieth century.

Clouds come to earth in many forms. Bernini's St. Teresa sits in a rocky grotto of cumulus. Correggio's Jupiter wraps a foggy paw around Io. The puffs in Rauschenberg's *American Pewter with Burroughs I* (1981) flutter like awnings in the wind. But no cloud is so persuasive as an idea, a bubble in the artist's mind, born of spontaneity and foresight, plan and chance. The ship of dreams fails because it is made of the clouds it would surmount. Yet this is not all bad. Never realized, the dream lives.

How does the dream start? In the least likely places. A figment of the mind, the dream comes from leftovers, remains, a dump like the one Rauschenberg and his wife, Susan Weil, enjoyed visiting, looking for treasures among the trash. To scavenge is not to repair broken and discarded things. It is to regard uselessness in a new light. The grocery bag in Rauschenberg's *Killdevil Hill* (1975) is its own cloud, a sack of wind, the very gusts of winter that blew the Wright brothers' plane at Kitty Hawk.

As any artist will tell you, the creation of useless things is a higher calling. It recalls what children do when they play, carrying themselves to giddy and dangerous heights. In a Lewis Hine photograph of 1909, waifs on a Boston playground rock on ladders that look like propellers, ascending to the same blank sky that drew Orville and Wilbur Wright and, for a few moments, John Joseph Montgomery. Art is perilous; play is too. Both are founded on nothing, what Rauschenberg called "zero."

Art finds value where none seems to exist. In another Hine photograph taken at the same site in Boston, we see that the plain is not a plain but a dump (as its caption makes clear). As some kids dig for treasure, others swing into the sky; the two activities become one. Rummaging for junk and achieving a momentary elevation are the same adventure. If Rauschenberg was famously a junk artist—if his work stood for the mind "as dump, as reservoir, switching center," as the art historian Leo Steinberg wrote in 1972—then he, like Montgomery, paired the thought with the achievement until the thought *was* the achievement.

Is the mannequin of Montgomery riding the *Evergreen* at the San Diego Air & Space Museum really Rauschenberg? In a way, yes. Art is a temporary leap that remains up in the air.

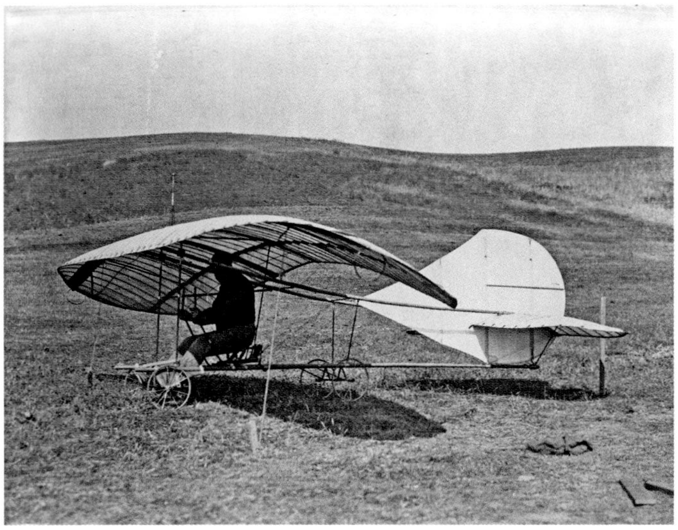

The 1911 Montgomery *Evergreen* Glider.

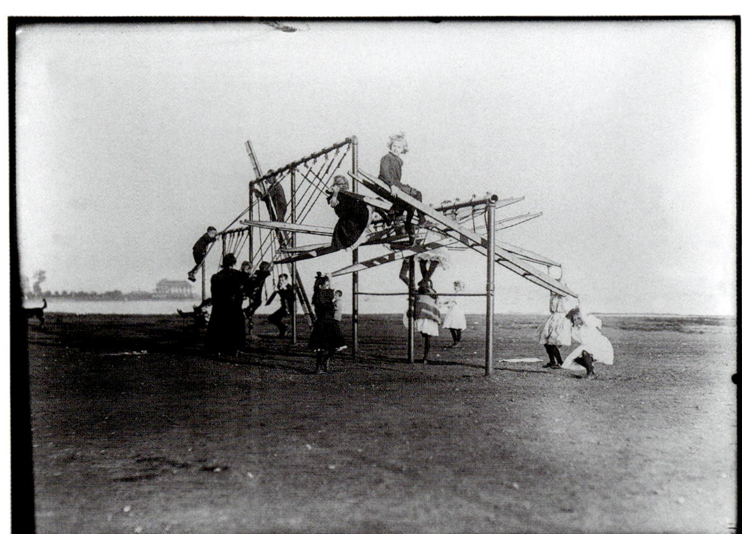

Lewis Wickes Hine (1874–1940), *The Dumps Turned Into A Children's Play Ground*, 1909. Photographic print made from glass negative, 5 × 7 inches (12.7 × 17.78 cm). Library of Congress, Washington, DC

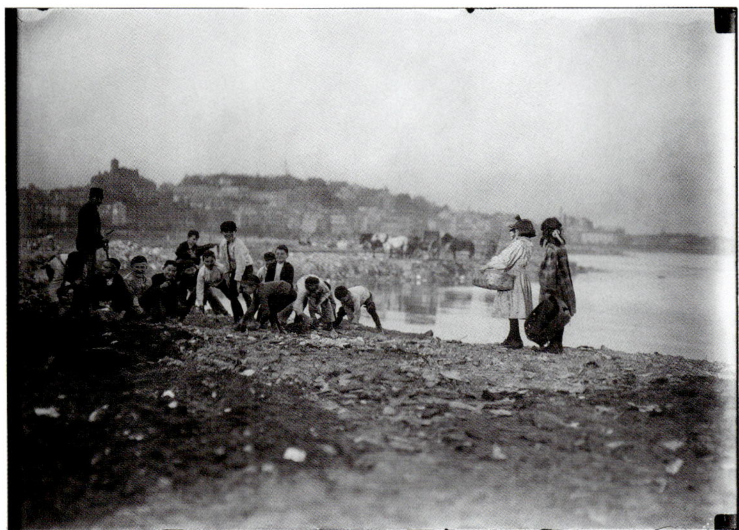

Lewis Wickes Hine (1874–1940), *Boys and Girls Working on the Dumps*, 1909. Photographic print made from glass negative, 5 × 7 inches (12.7 × 17.78 cm). Library of Congress, Washington, DC

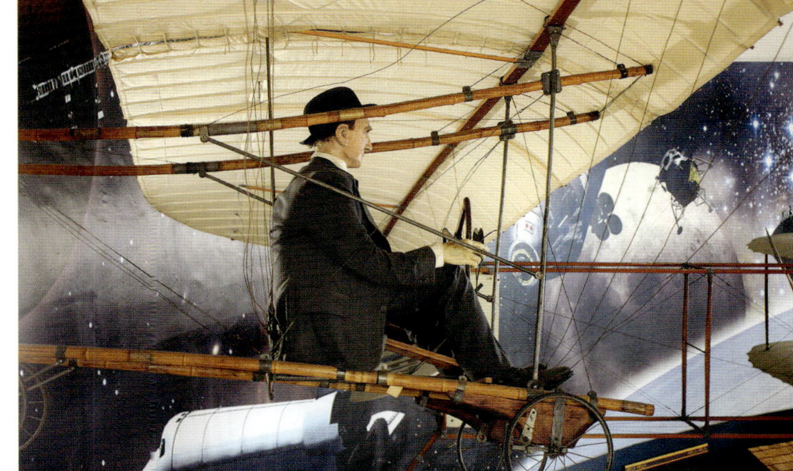

Smithsonian National Air and Space Museum's 1911 Montgomery *Evergreen* Glider at the San Diego Air & Space Museum, California.

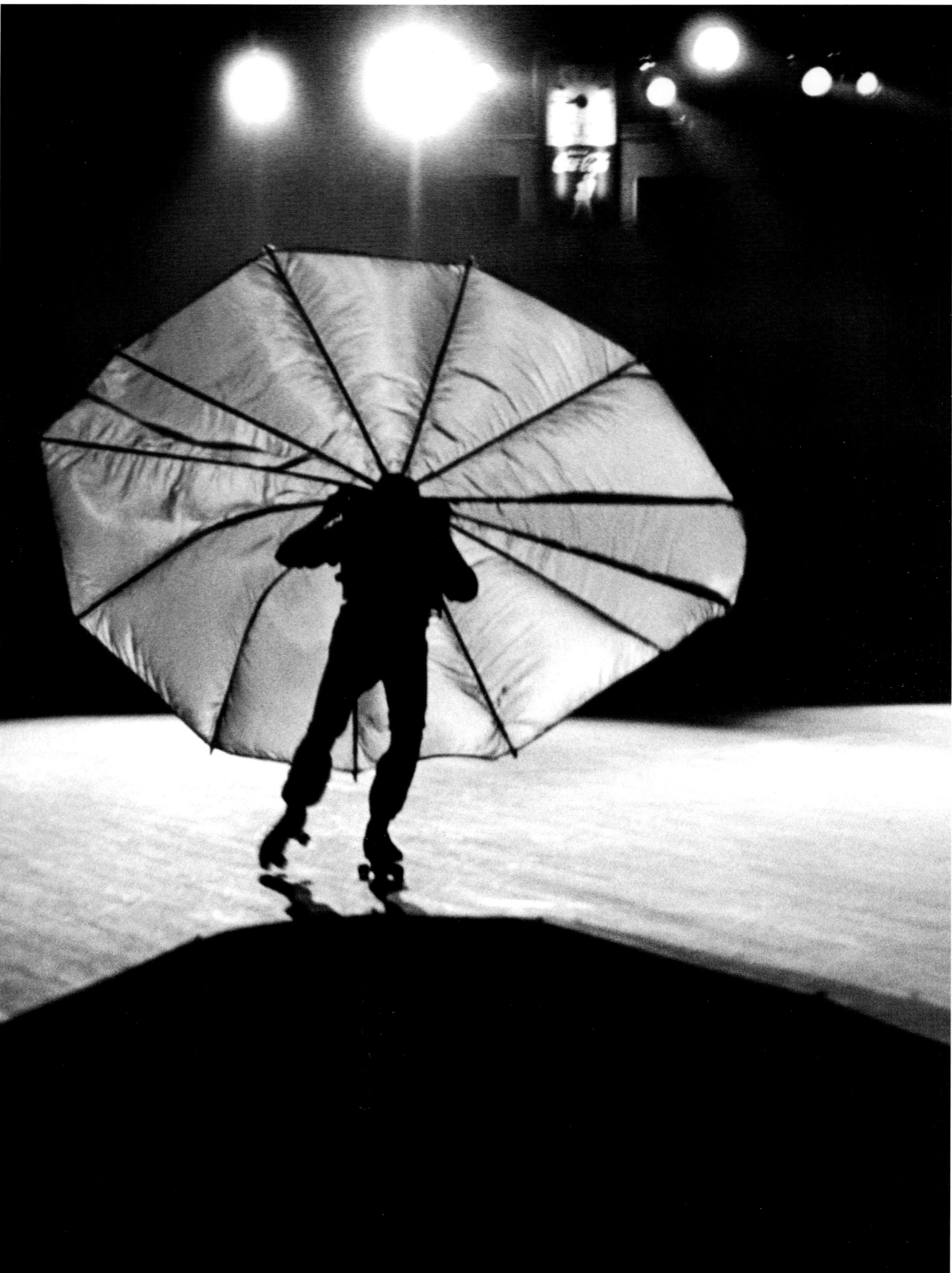

Introduction

I always liked Leonardo so much, because he had a curiosity that was boundless. I thought I had the curiosity of the Wright brothers.

—Robert Rauschenberg[1]

In 1996 a writer in *Artforum* posed a thought-provoking question to contemporary artists: What is one work of art (other than your own) that you wish you had created, and why? The American artist Robert Rauschenberg (1925–2008) answered, "I would have liked to have been around to help the Wright brothers work on their concept of flying bicycles."[2] When asked in 1987 about a favorite artist that was most influential in another interview, he replied, "I really loved Leonardo da Vinci ... he wasn't pinned down in fixed form."[3] Leonardo da Vinci, a visionary of the Renaissance, seeded the possibility of human flight in his meticulous studies in the *Codex on the Flight of Birds* (1505–06). This inspired the Wright brothers to achieve the dream of heavier-than-air powered flight in 1903. It is no surprise that Rauschenberg, profoundly influenced by these inventors, engaged deeply with themes of innovation and experimentation and the synergy between art, nature, and technology.

Rauschenberg's early experimentation was initially shaped by his time at Black Mountain College in North Carolina (1948–49, 1951–52), where he collaborated with fellow art students and influential teachers. Among these were the modern dance choreographer Merce Cunningham and the avant-garde composer John Cage, who, in summer 1952, played crucial roles in redefining conventional norms in the performing arts. Their impact on the young artist was significant, setting the stage for his innovative approach to art.

In New York City during the 1950s, Rauschenberg challenged himself not to mimic such Abstract Expressionist heavyweights as Jackson Pollock, Mark Rothko, and Willem de Kooning. Instead, Rauschenberg created new ways of making and defining art by literally incorporating the outside world in works across a diverse array of media: drawing, painting, sculpture, photography, collage, screenprint paintings, and theatrical stage sets and costume designs. It was his groundbreaking Combines (1954–64), however, that truly set him apart and captivated the public

and art critics alike. These innovative works masterfully fused elements of sculpture and painting with printed reproductions, fabrics, and an eclectic mix of found objects ranging from soda bottles to a taxidermied goat and birds. Bursting onto the American art scene in the late 1950s, Rauschenberg achieved international acclaim in 1964, becoming one of the very few Americans to win the prestigious International Grand Prize in Painting at the Venice Biennale.

Rauschenberg's art occupies a territory in art history between Abstract Expressionism and Pop Art, and he is sometimes associated with Neo-Dada due to his connection to the principles of Dada artists.[4] However, the space he claimed is distinctively his own, which he aptly defined as "that gap between" life and art, and his contributions significantly altered the trajectory of art history.[5] While some scholars seek to unravel the layers of meanings within his seemingly indecipherable works, others focus on his varied processes or his collaborations with fellow artists, printmakers, dancers, scientists, and engineers. Rauschenberg's distinctive style within an all-encompassing oeuvre that spanned nearly sixty years presents endless opportunities for exploration and interpretation.

Engaging with Rauschenberg's artwork presents both stimulating and challenging experiences, akin to interpreting complex literary works—particularly the Combines and *Silkscreen Paintings* (1962–64) that incorporate ostensibly unrelated imagery and may overwhelm viewers. The artworks themselves are seemingly open-ended, with viewers bringing their own experiences and perspectives to the process of finding meaning.[6] This publication explores Rauschenberg's art through the framework of various themes related to flight, and that is the driving force behind the interpretations that follow.

Scholars have explored the connections between flight and Rauschenberg's art, focusing on identifiable imagery and relevant aspects of his biography to draw out links to this theme.

Rauschenberg performing *Pelican* (1963) at the Rollerdrome, Culver City, California, 1966.

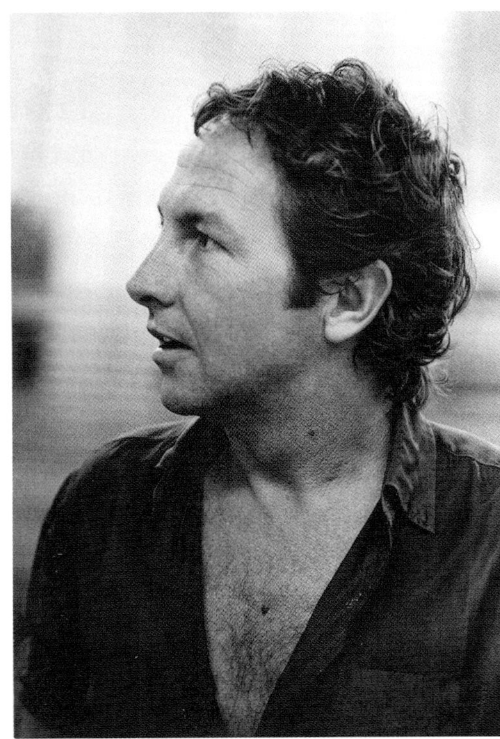

Rauschenberg during the *Stoned Moon* project
(1969–70) at Gemini G.E.L., Los Angeles, 1969.

The insights of Thomas Crow, Roni Feinstein, Mary Lynn Kotz, Robert Mattison, Barbara Rose, Calvin Tomkins, Lisa Wainwright, and others are invaluable. By examining some of the initial arguments such as Mattison's insights that bicycles, umbrellas, and parachutes symbolize flight in Rauschenberg's work, this publication builds upon their understandings and further enriches the dialogue with new research and interpretations.[7]

While this catalogue does not claim to encapsulate the entirety of Rauschenberg's extensive oeuvre concerning flight within a single volume, it's the first to gather more than 80 works related to flight across his career, with supporting archival documents from the Robert Rauschenberg Foundation and the Smithsonian's National Air and Space Museum's art curatorial files. Rather than adhering to a rigid chronological timeline or organizing the content thematically by medium, this collection invites readers to engage in a more exploratory approach through flight-themed groupings while investigating biographical details about the artist. This method also fosters a deeper understanding and appreciation of the artworks within their historical context. Furthermore, the nine essays that follow offer a thematic guide highlighting subtleties that might otherwise be easily overlooked.

Rauschenberg frequently integrated into his works imagery of aircraft, rockets, and other aeronautical devices, as well as references to the sensory experiences associated with flight, such as weightlessness and the feeling of the wind rushing by.

The first essay, "Embodying Flight" (pp. 16–25), examines the theme of flight through an autobiographical lens, addressing both literal and metaphorical aspects. Works such as *Autobiography* (1968), which serves as a three-part representation of Rauschenberg's life at the age of forty-three, incorporate significant elements that reference air and space. These include a zodiac chart based on constellations visible in the night sky as well as a photographic representation of the artist resembling a bird and equipped with a parachute as "wings." This image is derived from his inaugural choreographed dance, *Pelican* (1963).

Throughout his career, Rauschenberg consistently incorporated avian and insect motifs into his prints, paintings, and sculptures while also employing both found imagery and objects within the three-dimensional constructs of his Combines. The essay "Birdland" (pp. 26–47) commences with some of his earliest works, created in 1952 and 1953 during his travels with the artist Cy Twombly across Europe and North Africa. Works of this period include *North African Collages* (1952) and *Scatole Personali* (1952–53), Italian for "personal boxes," which feature remnants of a bird as a decorated treasure, and other untitled works that integrate exotic feathers and images of flying insects. His Combines—a synthesis of sculpture, painting, and collage—place birds at the forefront, as illustrated in works such as *Odalisk* (1955/58) and *Canyon* (1959). The representation of avian subjects in Rauschenberg's artwork allows for a multifaceted range of interpretations, encompassing the traditional symbolism of freedom linked to flight, allusions to mythology, and the artist's personal commitment to wildlife and environmental issues.

"Aerial Meditations" (pp. 48–71) examines themes related to humanity's aspiration for flight and the pioneering spirit embodied by artists and early aviators. Rauschenberg drew

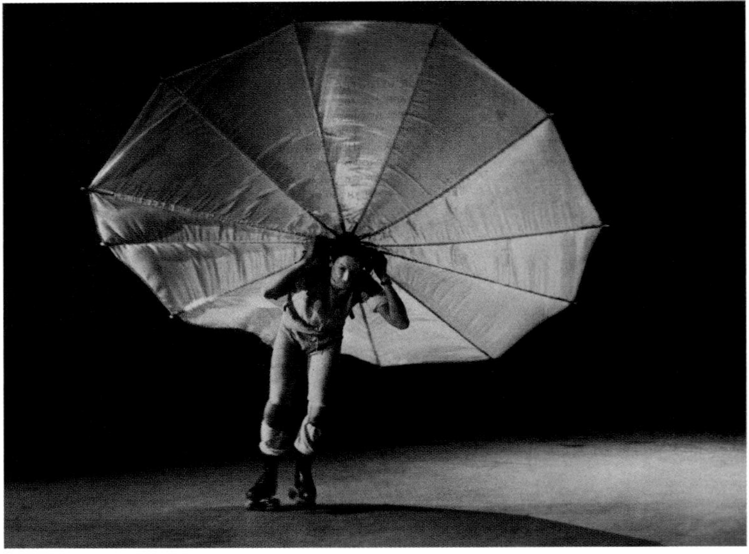

Rauschenberg performing *Pelican* (1963) during
the First New York Theater Rally, former CBS studio,
Broadway and Eighty-First Street, New York, 1965.

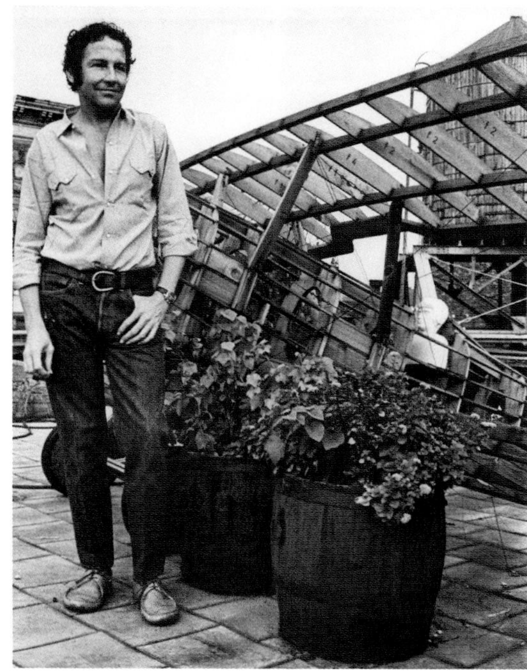

Rauschenberg with model airplane on the roof
of his home and studio at 381 Lafayette Street,
New York, 1968.

inspiration from the Wright brothers, whose technological innovations lay the groundwork for works such as *Kitty Hawk* (1974) and *Killdevil Hill* (1975). In these works, Rauschenberg employed bicycle imagery as a tribute to the Wright brothers, who built and sold bicycles from their shop in Dayton, Ohio, and accomplished their first successful powered flight at Kill Devil Hills, North Carolina.

Additionally, Rauschenberg contextualized his work within the broader heritage of aviation, acknowledging notable figures such as Charles Lindbergh. His exploration encompasses a variety of aviation-related themes and technologies, including military helicopters and commercial flight, as well as the ethereal qualities of the sky and what it means to defy gravity, as demonstrated in the large sculptural work *Sor Aqua (Venetian)* (1973).

Floating volumetric cubic forms are prevalent throughout his work. Remain attentive to these boxes! Upon acquiring an understanding of these forms, as well as Rauschenberg's regular use of them with arrows pointing toward flight-related content, they will inevitably be perceived in a new light.

In July 1969 Rauschenberg participated in a four-day program at the Kennedy Space Center in Florida as one of a select group of artists invited by the National Aeronautics and Space Administration (NASA) to observe and document various facets of the space program. During this period, he witnessed the preparations and lift-off of Apollo 11 and astutely followed the historic mission that resulted in the first human landing on the Moon on July 20, 1969. The essay "NASA Inception" (pp. 72–89) addresses his experiences within the program and incorporates archival documents highlighting his introduction to new artistic source materials through the support of a NASA ally, James Dean, the director of the NASA Art Program. Notably, Rauschenberg not only expressed interest in becoming one of the first civilian participants during the Space Shuttle program but also sought to find space-related materials and Moon dust to incorporate into his works.

Rauschenberg's initial interest in space predated the 1960s, and is reflected in his early *Silkscreen Paintings*, where he appropriated imagery of the early space program from magazines such as *Life*, *National Geographic*, *Time,* and *Newsweek*.[8] In these early works, painterly gestures are applied over certain imagery, a technique that serves to erase explicit references, thereby obscuring any specific meaning. After Rauschenberg witnessed space launches through the NASA Art Program, his perception of the program saw a dramatic shift as he became more personally involved. "Constructing Space" (pp. 90–113) analyzes these space-related works in light of the new visual vocabulary he realized through NASA.[9] New source materials from NASA and experiments with lithography at the Gemini G.E.L. workshop in Los Angeles spawned Rauschenberg's *Stoned Moon* series. These thirty-three lithographic prints, created in 1969 and 1970, raise questions about the impact of technology in relation to nature, prompting new considerations of the ethical and philosophical implications of space exploration for the sake of scientific progress. At the same time, the artist viewed the space program through the lens of the era, acknowledging the achievements of the Moon landings while grappling with pressing issues like the Vietnam War, racial and gender inequality, and the loss of cultural icons.

Also discussed in this essay is Rauschenberg's collaboration with several contemporary artists—including Forrest Myers, Andy Warhol, and Claes Oldenburg, among others—to create *Moon Museum* (1969), which was smuggled onto the lunar module of Apollo 12 and allegedly still sits on the Moon. The endeavor was not authorized by NASA, and therefore no official acknowledgment exists of the project or its final destination on the lunar surface. Recent findings from the Robert Rauschenberg Archives, however, shed new light on this event, potentially providing evidence for the project's realization.

From the start, Rauschenberg incorporated found objects in his work. "Reinventing Flight" (pp. 114–25) explores his readymades, a term coined by Dada artist Marcel Duchamp,

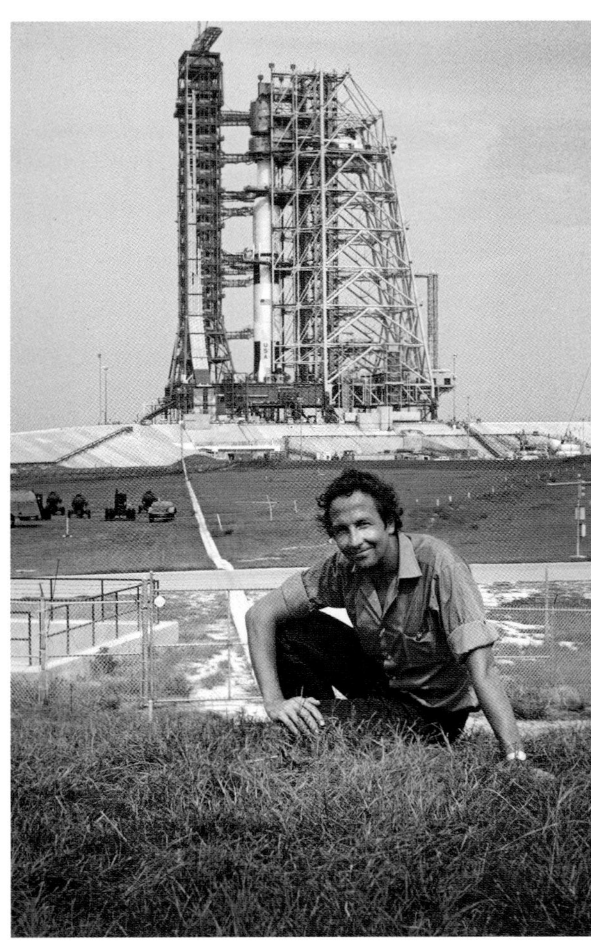

Rauschenberg at Cape Kennedy as a NASA Art Program artist in 1969, with the Apollo 11 launch site in the background. The photo was taken by James Dean, the program director.

which involved turning ordinary objects into works of art.[10] For example, *Prehistoric Rose Spore (Kabal American Zephyr)* (1981), consisting of a faux propeller affixed to a wooden stool, exists in direct conversation with Duchamp's *Bicycle Wheel* (1913), a bicycle wheel mounted to a kitchen stool. The *Gluts* (1986–89/1991–94) series further explored the readymade, as Rauschenberg used found aircraft parts and distilled them into sculptures, in the process rediscovering the history in these objects.[11] He encouraged interactive play in *Twin Bloom / ROCI TIBET* (1985), a small sculpture made of fan blades and bicycle pedals that resembles a winged bug. Such works exemplified the nature of *ROCI TIBET* (1985), a project of the Rauschenberg Overseas Culture Interchange inspired by and exhibited in Tibet. The blending of aircraft parts and "propelled" concepts speaks to the influence of the mechanics of flight, resulting in innovative art forms.

In 1989 Rauschenberg received an invitation from the Goethe Institute to construct a kite and participate in a kite festival held in Himeji, Japan. This experience prompted him to explore the kinetic characteristics of the form and led him

"to create a painting that would not be art if nature would not accept it," thereby establishing a measure for the ultimate success of the artwork.[12] "Seated in the Sky" (pp. 126–41) focuses on the domestic imagery found in the kites, specifically *Sky House I* and *Sky House II* (both 1988), and explores the significance of placing imagery of chairs in the sky. The earlier *Hoarfrosts* (1974–76), works made mainly from unstretched fabric, draw connections to early flight pioneers through the images of hang gliders and the fabric's materiality. The unconventional presentation of the *Hoarfrosts* and the kite works challenge traditional art display methods by involving the wind itself. The themes of wind and sky also serve as powerful metaphors for exploring environmental issues and the nuances of the human experience.

As an advocate for environmental and human rights causes, Rauschenberg used art as a means for change. He designed and contributed the poster for the inaugural Earth Day on April 22, 1970, which features an eagle. This initiative was inspired by a significant oil spill off the Southern California coast in 1969, underscoring the need for urgent action. "Down to Earth" (pp. 142–53) reflects on Rauschenberg's views on globalization and the environment. In many of the works featured here, the environment is portrayed from an aerial perspective or incorporates references to the air and sky.

"Interpreting the Night Sky" (pp. 154–79) takes us on a voyage through the stars and planets, which Rauschenberg reimagined through inspiration from contemporary sources. In *Star Quarters I–IV* (1971), he incorporated pop culture symbols and icons from the 1960s and early 1970s in a reinterpretation of constellations and signs of the zodiac, demonstrating his

Rauschenberg working on the *Stoned Moon* series (1969-70) at Gemini, Los Angeles, 1969.

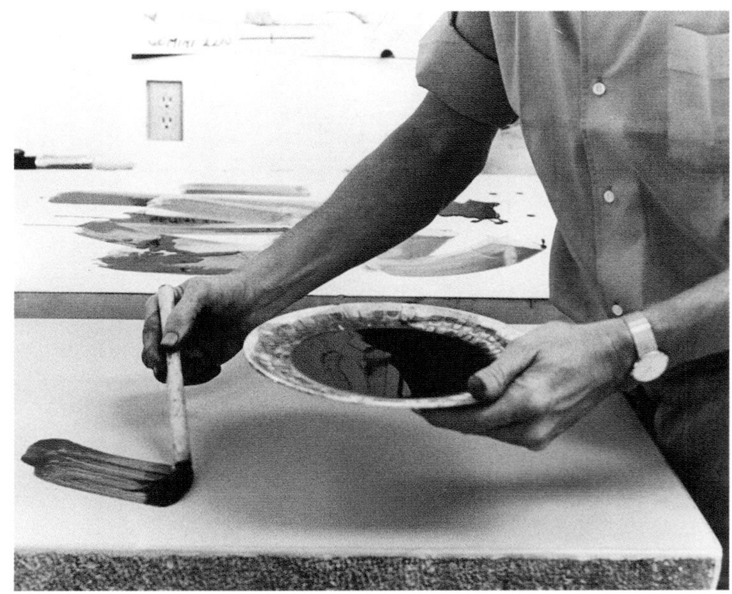

Rauschenberg working on the *Stoned Moon* series (1969–70) at Gemini G.E.L., Los Angeles, 1969. The artwork visible in the background is a proof of *Ape* (1970).

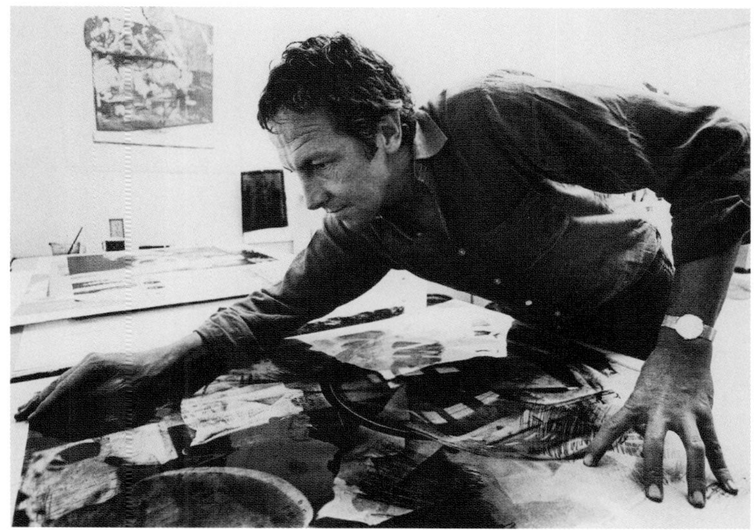

ability to bridge past and present. One constellation employs a photograph by American photographer Diane Arbus to designate the Gemini twins, and another features the boxer Muhammad Ali as Hercules. Although the arrangement may seem disorienting, the constellations are in fact carefully positioned using star charts and other reference materials. From the celestial aura of the night sky, Rauschenberg's work elevates into the heavens with angel wings and a commissioned work by the Vatican.

Rauschenberg's personal papers and collections convey a wide array of flight-themed sources, including photographs, advertisements, news clippings, and books on the history of flight, weather, math, astronomy, and astrology. One intriguing news clipping from the *Los Angeles Herald* bears the headline "Students May Fly with Both Feet." The article covers a student project to construct an experimental aircraft with a thirty-six-foot wingspan, a fuselage, and a propeller powered by a ten-speed bicycle: "Pedaling moves chains, which rotate pulleys, ultimately spinning the propeller."[13] Sound familiar? This innovative project echoes Rauschenberg's obsession with bicycles, his admiration for the Wright brothers, and his undeniable appetite for exploring the many concepts of flight.

In the summer of 1976 Rauschenberg visited the newly opened Smithsonian National Air and Space Museum in Washington, DC, and met with his friend James Dean, who had assumed the role of art curator there. We can imagine Rauschenberg's feelings when he was in the presence of significant aeronautical and space artifacts such as the 1903 Wright Flyer, the *Spirit of St. Louis*, and the Apollo 11 Command Module, all of which are represented in his oeuvre. The purpose of their meeting was to discuss a potential performance of *Pelican* (1963) at the Museum to coincide with Rauschenberg's upcoming retrospective exhibition at the Smithsonian National Collection of Fine Arts (now the Smithsonian American Art Museum).[14] Walter Hopps, the curator of twentieth-century painting and sculpture there, declared the artist the ideal subject for an exhibition in the nation's capital during its bicentennial year: "Rauschenberg is overwhelmingly the obvious choice for such a celebration.... Beyond the extraordinary range of artwork, he embodies the notion of citizen and artist, involved in secular life, through politics and philanthropy, with an insatiable curiosity."[15] The exhibition of about 150 works exhibited in reverse chronological order (beginning with his most recent works) ran from

October 1976 to January 1977. Subsequently, the exhibit toured four major museums across the United States.[16] Also in 1976, the Hirshhorn Museum and Sculpture Garden mounted an exhibition of twenty-nine lithographs from the *Stoned Moon* series to mark the opening of the National Air and Space Museum.[17]

To celebrate the nation's 250th anniversary and the centennial of Robert Rauschenberg's birth, the National Air and Space Museum's Flight and the Arts Center will debut an exhibition featuring works by Rauschenberg from the collections of the Smithsonian, the National Gallery of Art, and the Robert Rauschenberg Foundation. *The Ascent of Rauschenberg* seeks to deepen the connection visitors have with Rauschenberg's artwork, particularly those who have explored the Museum's renowned aviation and spaceflight artifacts that fueled his enduring curiosity about flight. The accompanying publication provides fresh insights and discusses how the theme of flight is intricately embedded throughout Rauschenberg's body of work. It examines his fascination with human achievement and the interplay between people, aviation and space technologies, and the natural world. This publication aims to reintroduce Rauschenberg's art to both seasoned admirers and new audiences, using the lens of flight to offer a richer understanding of his innovative techniques, sustained legacy, and his unique perspective on all things that fly.

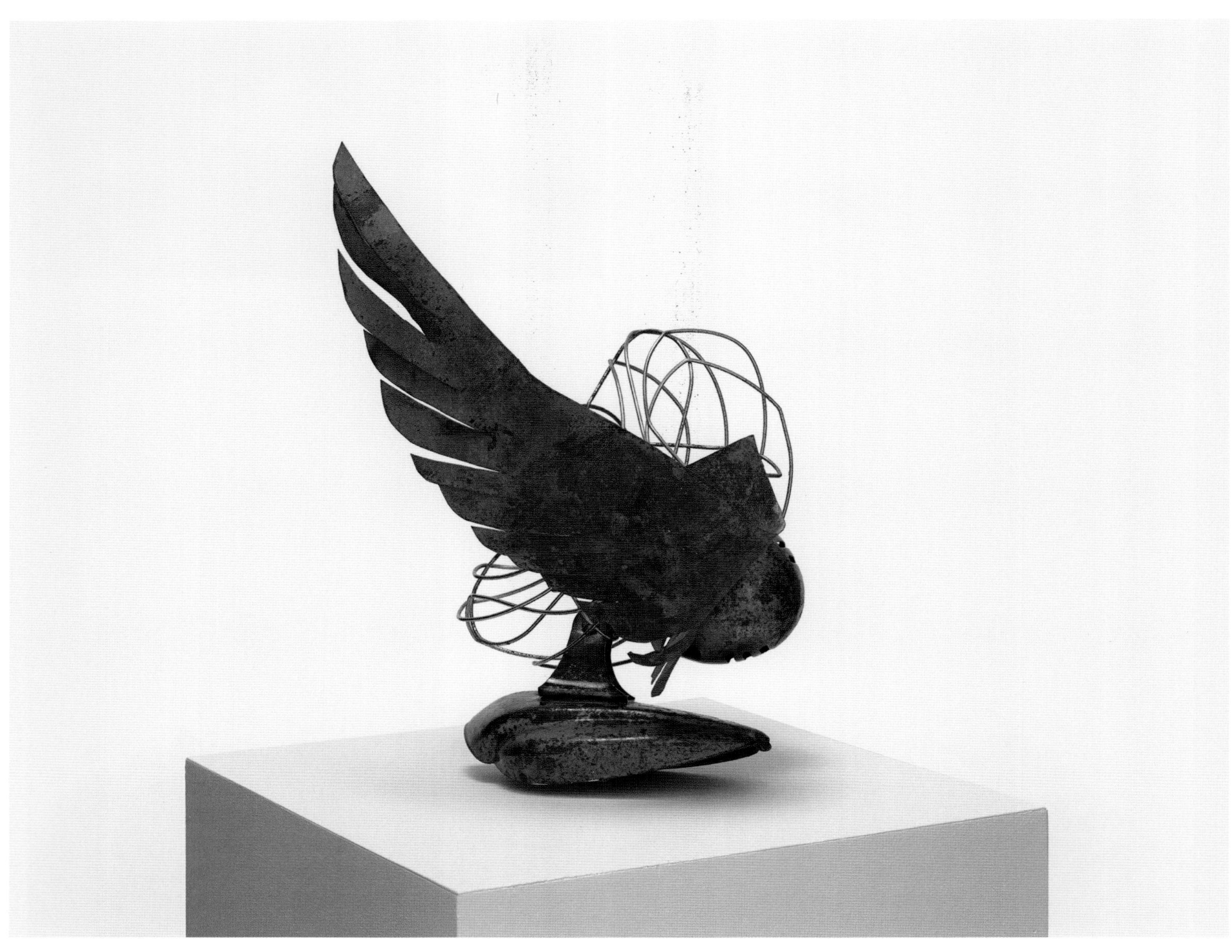

Mercury Zero Summer Glut, 1987
Assembled metal
10⅝ × 17½ × 8½ inches (27 × 44.5 × 21.6 cm)
Robert Rauschenberg Foundation

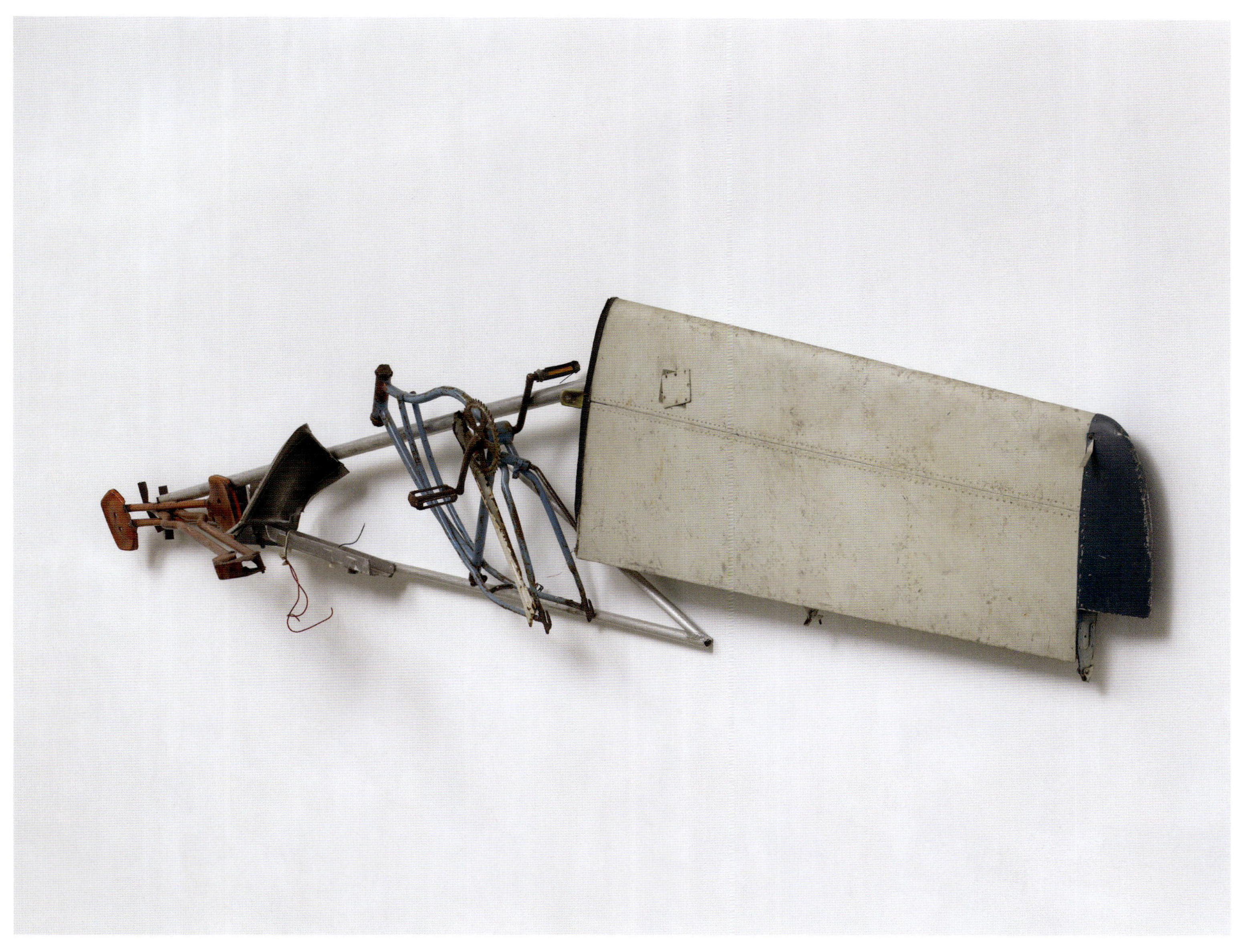

Nagshead Summer Glut Sketch, 1987
Assembled metal
33 × 184 × 19 inches (83.8 × 467.4 × 48.3 cm)
Robert Rauschenberg Foundation

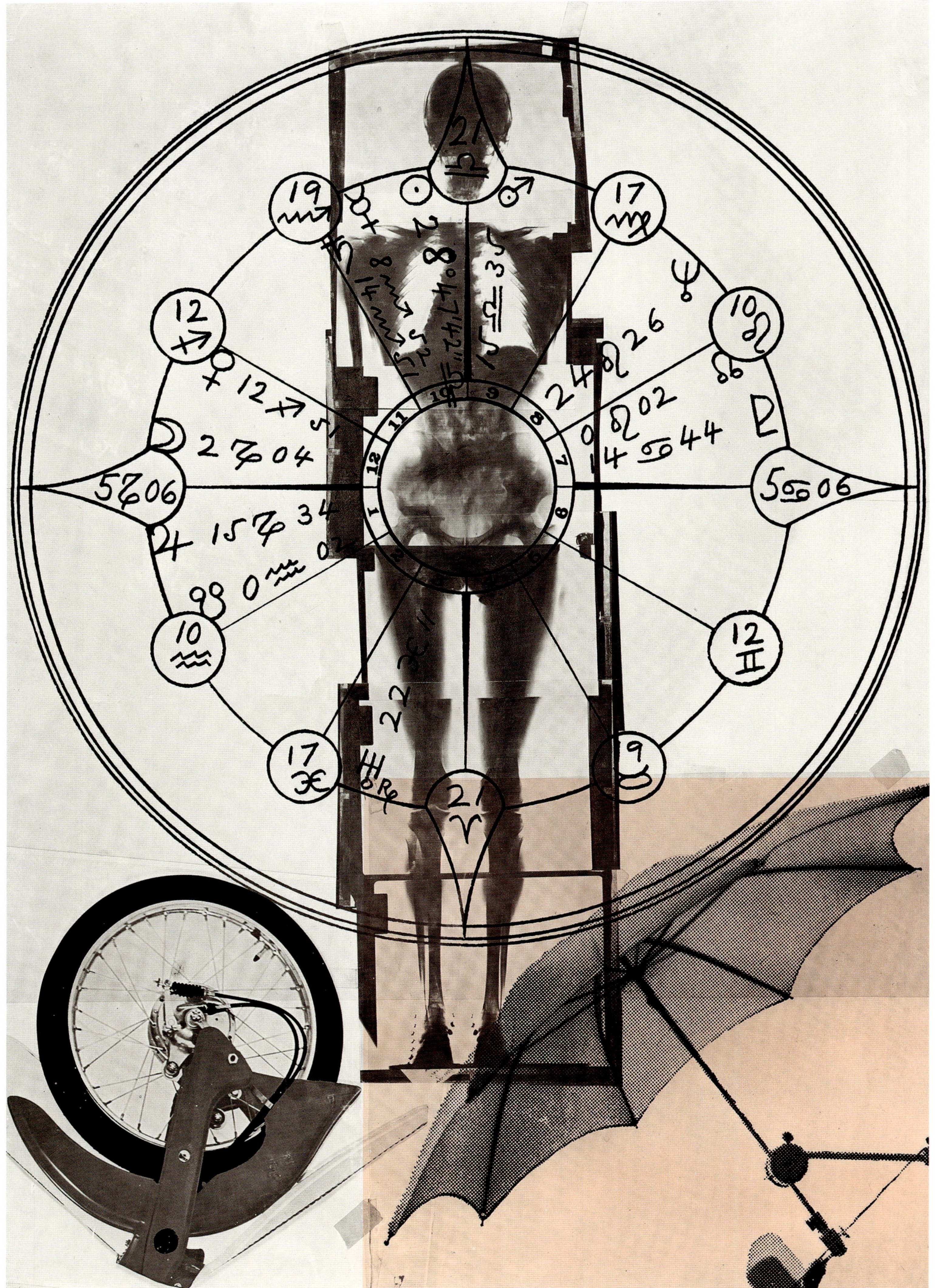

1

Embodying Flight

**In the Sky
I am Walking
A Bird
I Accompany**

—Chippewa dream song quoted in Rauschenberg's *Opal Gospel* (1971)[1]

Robert Rauschenberg's exploration of the theme of flight was both extensive and profoundly autobiographical, encompassing both its literal representations and significant metaphorical implications. Throughout his body of work, Rauschenberg skillfully intertwined himself thematically with the subject of flight—spanning birds in nature, aviation, and the vastness of space. This introspective approach is particularly evident in several works where he identified himself with flight through self-portraiture, drawing on experiences from various phases of his life. At the same time, he forged a strong connection between his art and the pioneering spirit behind the achievements in aviation and space exploration, thus establishing a rich personal narrative.

Astrological Musings

During the late 1960s, while residing in New York City, Rauschenberg sought guidance from celestial bodies. In an interview with the art historian Barbara Rose, he mentioned consulting the prominent astrologist Zoltan Mason and discovering a misalignment in the cosmos: "I found out that I had five of my most troublesome stars in conjunction with each other in my horoscope. The advice was to not ever go to the mountain … and to head for the sun and sea."[2] This horoscope reading prompted Rauschenberg's decision in 1968 to purchase property in Captiva Island, Florida, and his eventual relocation from New York to Florida in 1970.

Rauschenberg's interest in astrology plays a significant role in his three-panel self-portrait *Autobiography* (1968). The first panel boldly displays a near life-size X-ray of Rauschenberg overlaid with an astrological chart. Just below it, a wheel and an umbrella appear as aerial references. The wheel serves as a

tribute to the Wright brothers and their origins as mechanics and owners of a bicycle shop. Robert Mattison notes that the umbrella is "parachute-like," emphasizing Rauschenberg's deep fascination with those devices. Their unique blend of user control and vulnerability to unexpected winds perfectly captures the essence of the "flights of fantasy" and serendipitous discoveries that permeate Rauschenberg's artistic vision.[3]

The second panel presents a photograph of Rauschenberg as a child with his parents in a boat framed by a red volumetric box and an arrow pointing down. (We'll explore the significance of the box in "Aerial Meditations," pp. 48–71.) Surrounding the image is text, meticulously arranged in concentric circles that mimic the lines of a fingerprint, providing an account of significant events in the artist's life. It begins with his birth in Port Arthur, Texas, on October 22, 1925. The text mentions his family members, ancestry (Dutch, Swedish, German, and Cherokee), education and military service, influential relationships, the birth of his son, artistic endeavors, and major exhibitions.

The Artist Spreads Wings

Among the achievements catalogued in the fingerprint pattern is Rauschenberg's pioneering choreographed performance *Pelican* (1963), a photograph of which dominates the entire third panel of *Autobiography*. The piece featured Rauschenberg and the Swedish artist Per Olof Ultvedt gracefully gliding on roller skates to mimic the ethereal movements of birds. Wearing parachutes on their backs, they created a stunning visual representation of wings in flight. In 1965, Rauschenberg performed *Pelican* with the dancer Alex Hay, prompting the journalist and film critic Erica Abeel to write, "It's a bird, it's a plane, it's

Detail of **Autobiography**, 1968

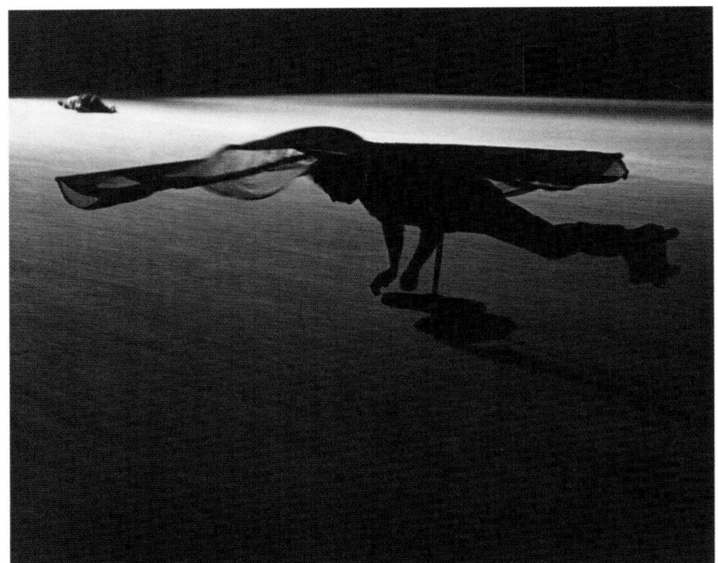

Rauschenberg performing *Pelican* (1963) at the
Rollerdrome, Culver City, California, 1966.

Rauschenberg and Hay zooming around the Eighty-first Street
TV studio with monster parachutes strapped to their shoulders!
It's the Pop vision of Kitty Hawk! It's Batman on wheels! Daedalus at the Rollerdrome! It's *Pelican*."[14] The pair navigated around
Carolyn Brown, a founding member of Merce Cunningham's
troupe, who, adding a dynamic contrast, danced en pointe. The
combination of parachutes simulating wings and roller-skating
evokes the imaginative spirit of the early aviation pioneers, and,
indeed, Rauschenberg dedicated *Pelican* to the Wright brothers.[5] The prominence of *Pelican* in *Autobiography* reinforces a
theme already evident in its bicycles, umbrellas, and astrological
signs, capturing the essence of flight and providing a rich
portrayal of his multifaceted life.[6]

As the designer of stage sets, costumes, and lighting,
collaborating with the likes of Merce Cunningham and John
Cage, Rauschenberg embraced the concept of flight. For the
ambitious *Minutiae* (1954), he envisioned a groundbreaking set
design that floated on helium balloons. When that approach
didn't pan out, he created a striking free-standing sculpture—
among his earliest Combines—for dancers to engage with.
Additionally, he cleverly suspended certain sets above the
stage, providing dancers ample space to express themselves.
For the Trisha Brown Dance Company performance *Set and
Reset* (1983) he created the hanging fabric sculpture *Elastic
Carrier (Shiner)* (1983), which resembled a floating pyramid or
ship from outer space.[7] Rauschenberg articulated these theatrical concepts by stating, "I chose to fly what could be assumed
as a set in the sky above, leaving the dancers room to move."[8]
In so doing, he conceptualized stage sets as all-encompassing
spaces that allowed the potential for aerial props and flight
within the performance realm.

Flying themes in dance and music carried over into
Rauschenberg's personal background; he believed his paternal
grandmother was Cherokee.[9] This influence is explicit in *Opal
Gospel* (1971), an interactive acrylic "book" containing ten
translucent printed inserts.[10] Viewers engage with the piece by
rearranging the acrylic pages, which feature evocative words
from nine Native American songs and stories that celebrate
elements of the sky and nature, including a loon, dark clouds,
the interplay of male and female rain, a rainbow, celestial bodies,
and even a total solar eclipse. The cover features a line from a
Chippewa dream song: "In the Sky / I am Walking, A Bird / I
Accompany."[11] Through this integration of words and imagery,
Rauschenberg illustrated his connection to the sky and embodied the spirit of flight with elegance and intention.

Tracks

Beginning in 1969, Rauschenberg's involvement with the NASA
Art Program opened new avenues of artistic expression, enriching his work with innovative source materials and firsthand
experiences. Rauschenberg was invited by NASA to visit the
Kennedy Space Center to work alongside other artists in the
NASA Art Program to capture the essence of space exploration
through art and document the technical advancements of the
era. An untitled drawing from 1969 encapsulates various aspects
of the Apollo 11 mission, including a rocket, parachutes used
for the capsule's return, a photograph of Wernher von Braun
(1912–77), the pioneering aerospace engineer and architect of
the Saturn V rocket, and images of the three astronauts.[12] The
inclusion of a chimpanzee at the upper left corner serves as a
reminder of the early contributions that primates made to space
exploration. The work communicates the astronauts' commitment to peace, prominently featuring a plaque that states, "We
came in peace for all mankind," which was placed on the lunar
lander. Rauschenberg included an outline of his left foot as a
symbolic gesture to Neil Armstrong's first step on the Moon,
but it was also a way of placing himself at the center of the
Moon-landing narrative and reflects his personal experiences
as an artist within NASA.[13]

Another instance of Rauschenberg's foot tracks is found in
Lawn Combed (1954). In this early work, he traced his feet over a
sample of Standard Swan White fabric, retaining the original tag
with its swan logo and the manufacturer's printed swan logos on
the fabric within the outline of his left foot. The art critic Blake

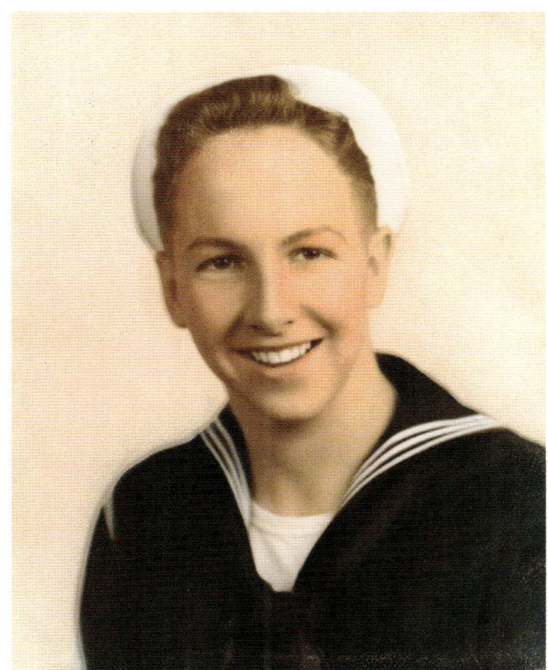

Portrait of Rauschenberg in his US Navy uniform, 1944.

Gopnik interprets this action through the lens of queer theory, positing a connection between Rauschenberg's footprint over two swans as a reference to his sexuality. "No 'real' man at that homophobic moment could possibly have been seen swanning about in a bird-printed textile. He would want to trample it underfoot. Whereas Rauschenberg seems to take an unmanly stand for delicacy and delight."[14] Alternatively, Rauschenberg may have attributed different meanings to the tracing, perhaps nodding to his personal affection for birds and the concept of flight. Or maybe the term "Airedale" on the label (the swatch of fabric was the product of Airedale Worsted Mills in Woonsocket, Rhode Island) piqued his interest. In the 1940s, "Airedale" was used to refer to US Navy aviators, a designation with which Rauschenberg would have been familiar.[15]

Rauschenberg served in the Navy from 1944 to 1946 and worked in naval hospitals as a neuropsychiatric technician. This experience likely influenced his decision to incorporate a Navy figure in another self-referential work entitled *Arena II (Stoned Moon)* (1969). In this lithograph, the Russian cosmonaut Adrian Nikolayev is prominently featured amid celestial blue imagery interspersed with American iconography, including Charles Lindbergh at the top and an American sailor to the left. The artwork underscores the performative aspects of the space program while highlighting the international significance of space exploration. Furthermore, it reflects the artist's personal connection to the realm of space as a former service member, his association with both aviation and space icons, and his introspective exploration of the events related to his role as an artist.

E. A. T. Model Airplanes

As a founding member of Experiments in Art and Technology (E.A.T.), alongside engineers Billy Klüver and Fred Waldhauer and artist Robert Whitman, Rauschenberg played a key role in promoting collaborations between art, science, and technology. In June 1967, Rauschenberg hosted a fundraiser in his studio at 381 Lafayette Street in New York to support the organization. This event featured a "Giant Model Airplanes" exhibition and auction that saw Claes Oldenburg and Patty Mucha bidding on airplanes from opposite sides of the room. The airplane they purchased ended up in their living room and was decorated with Christmas lights that never came off.[16] Rauschenberg's own purchase from the auction—a biplane that eventually found a spot parked on his rooftop—serves as a testament to his early philanthropic endeavors in support of the arts and sciences as well as his affection for airplanes.[17]

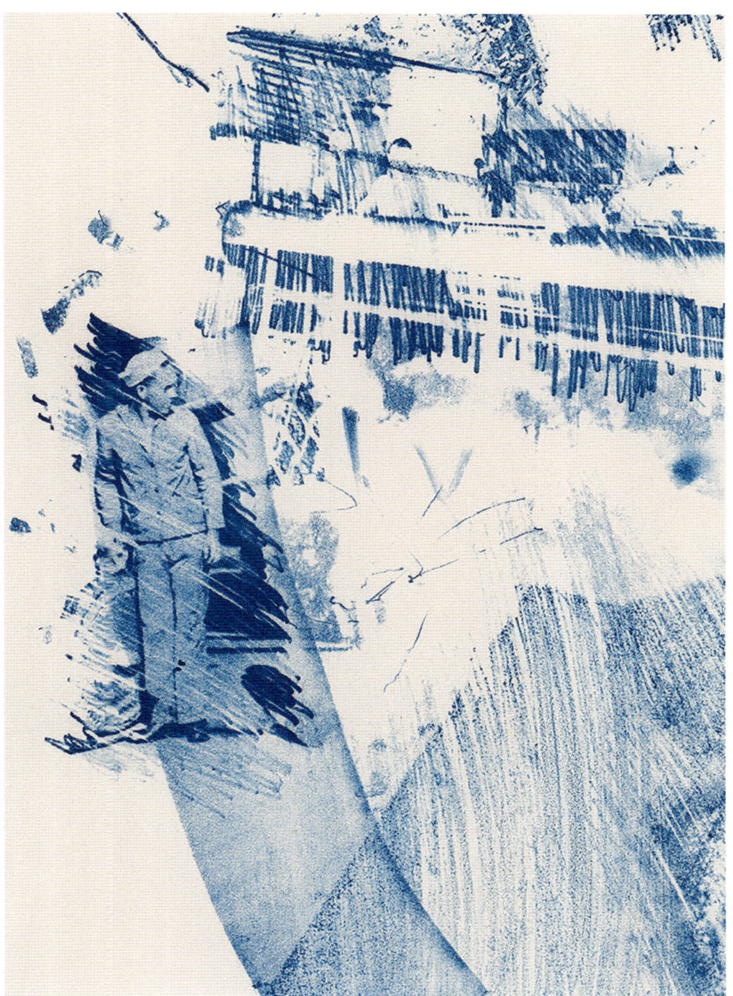

Detail of **Arena II (Stoned Moon)**, 1969

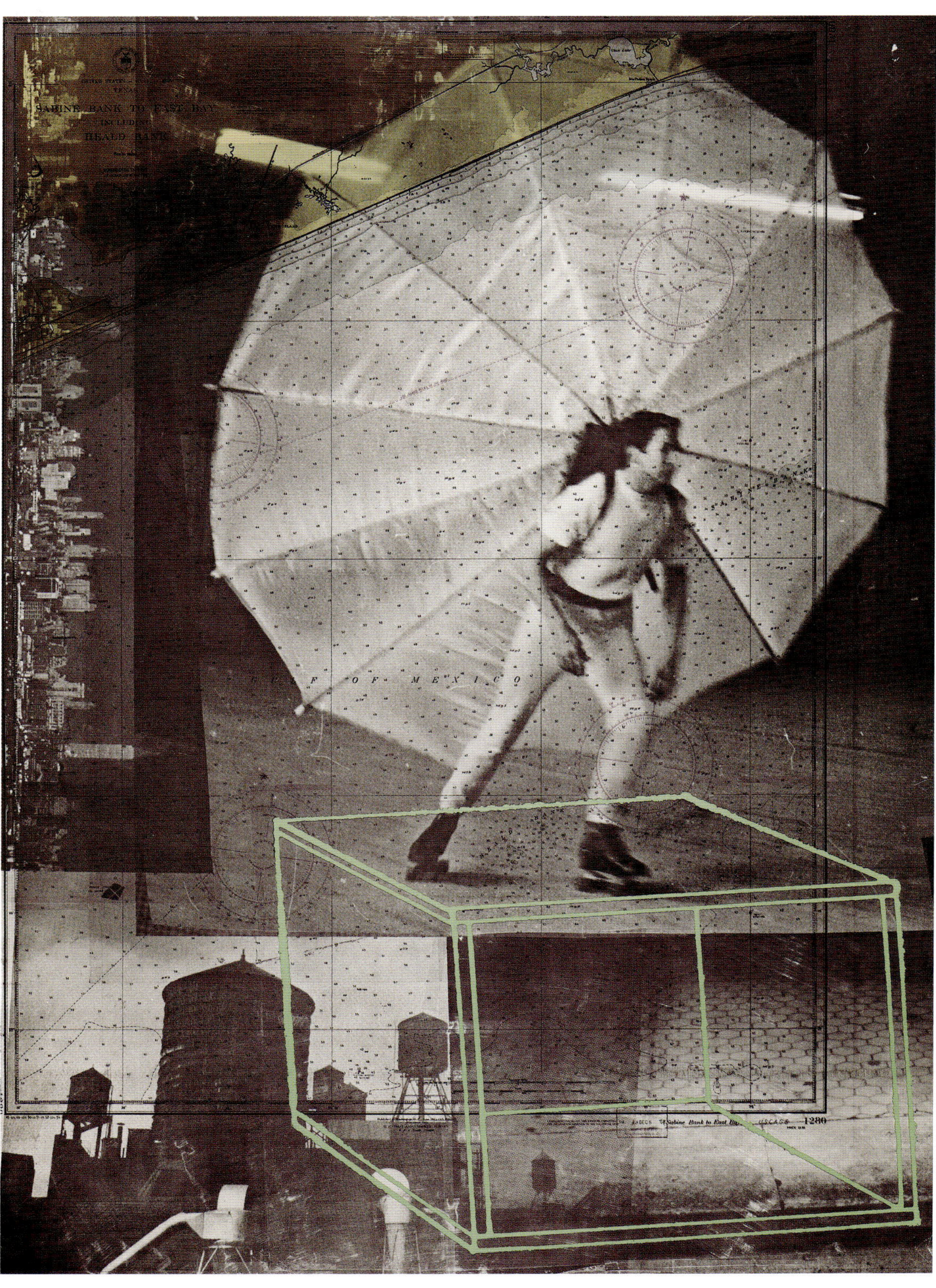

Detail of **Autobiography**, 1968

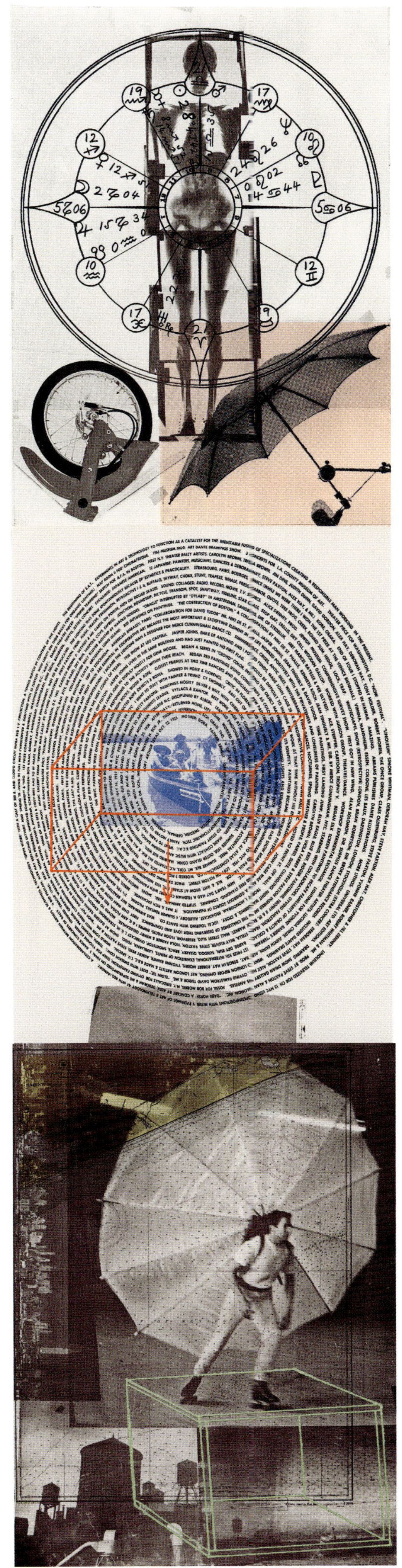

Autobiography, 1968
Offset lithograph on three sheets of paper
198¾ × 48⅝ inches (504.8 × 123.5 cm) overall
National Gallery of Art, Washington, DC

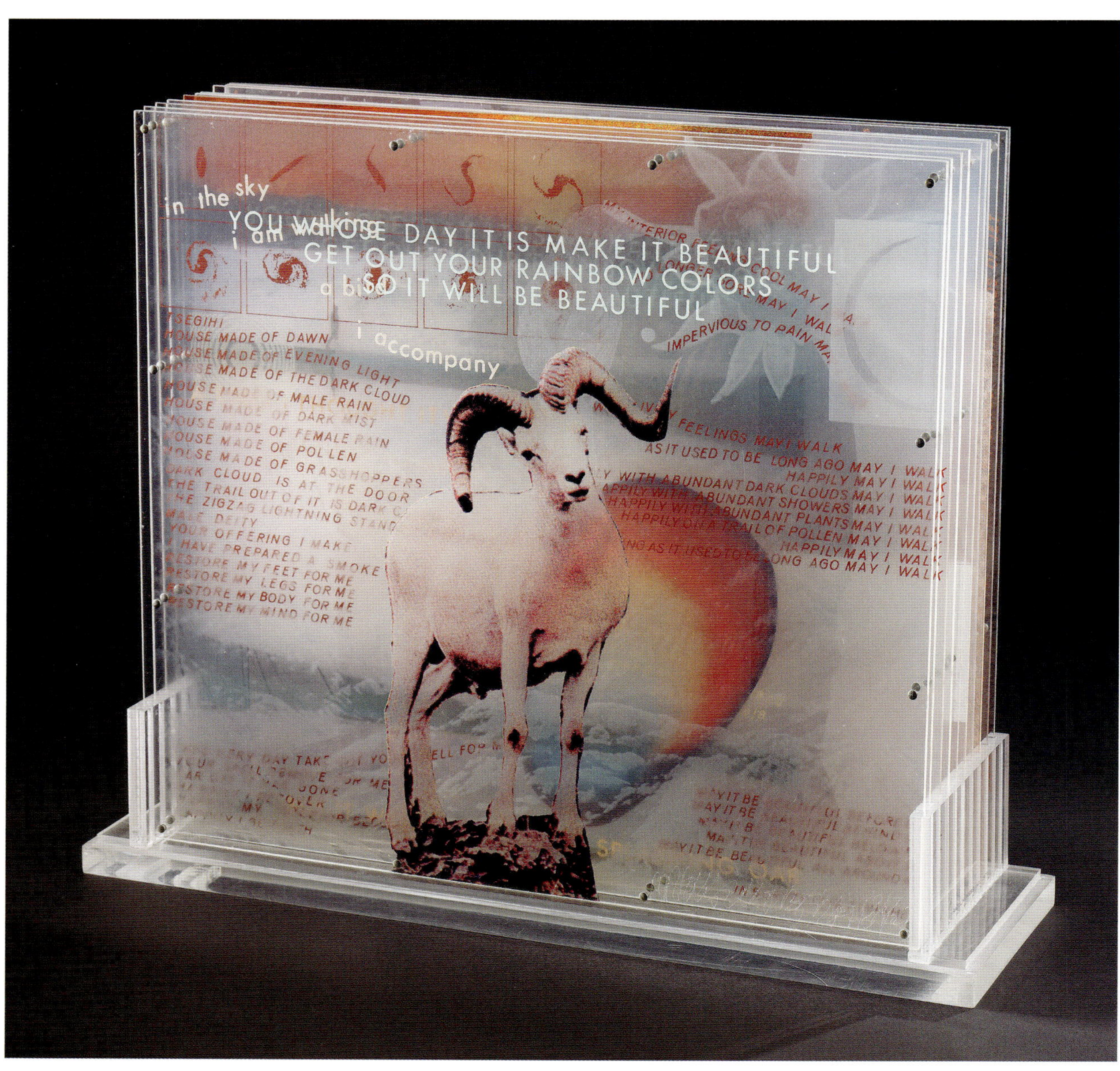

Opal Gospel, 1971
Screenprint on ten Plexiglas sheets in Lucite base, with stainless-steel cover
21 × 23 × 7 inches (53.3 × 58.4 × 17.8 cm)
Minneapolis Institute of Art

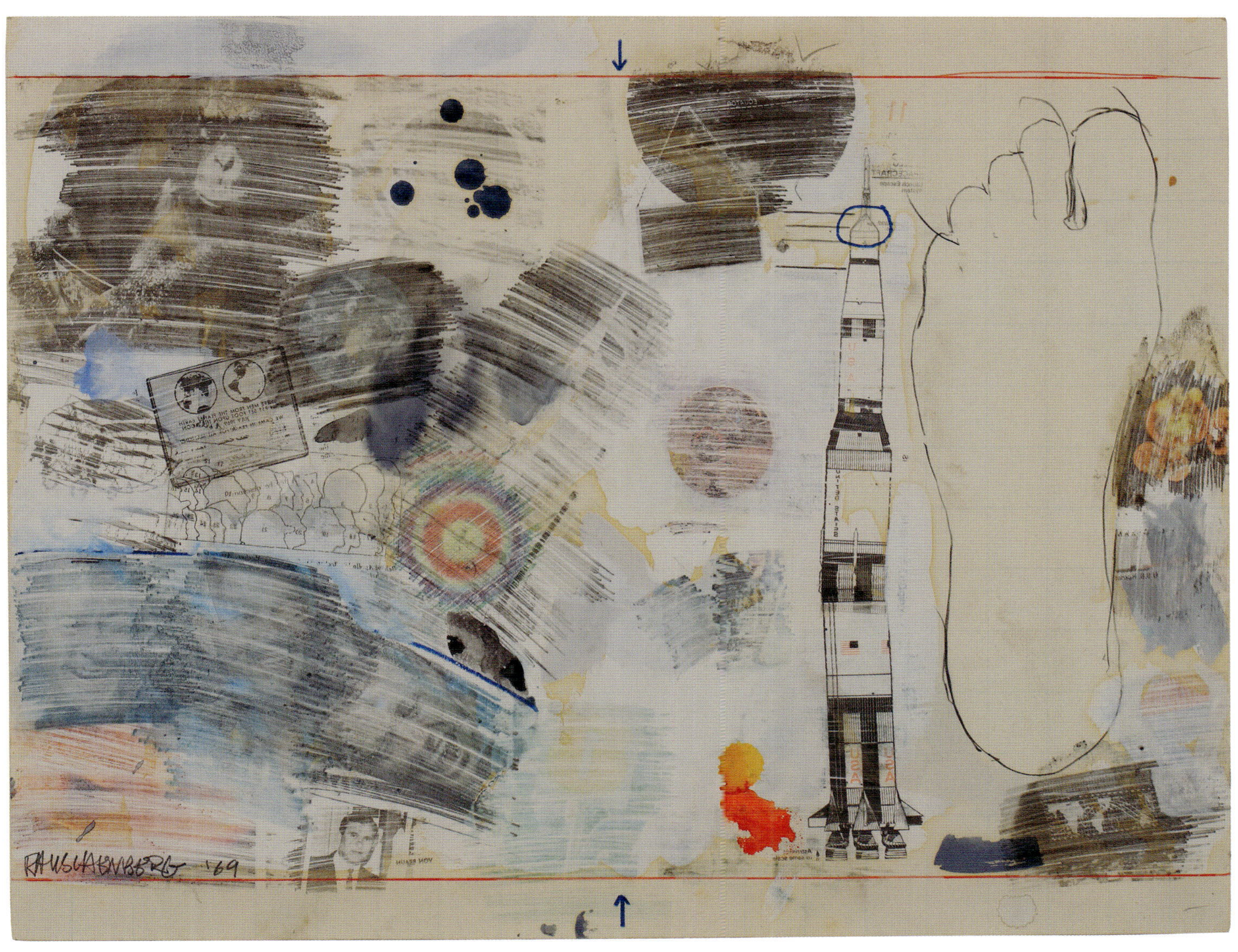

Untitled, 1969
Solvent transfer with watercolor, gouache, graphite, and colored pencil on paper
15 × 20 inches (38.1 × 50.8 cm)
Private collection

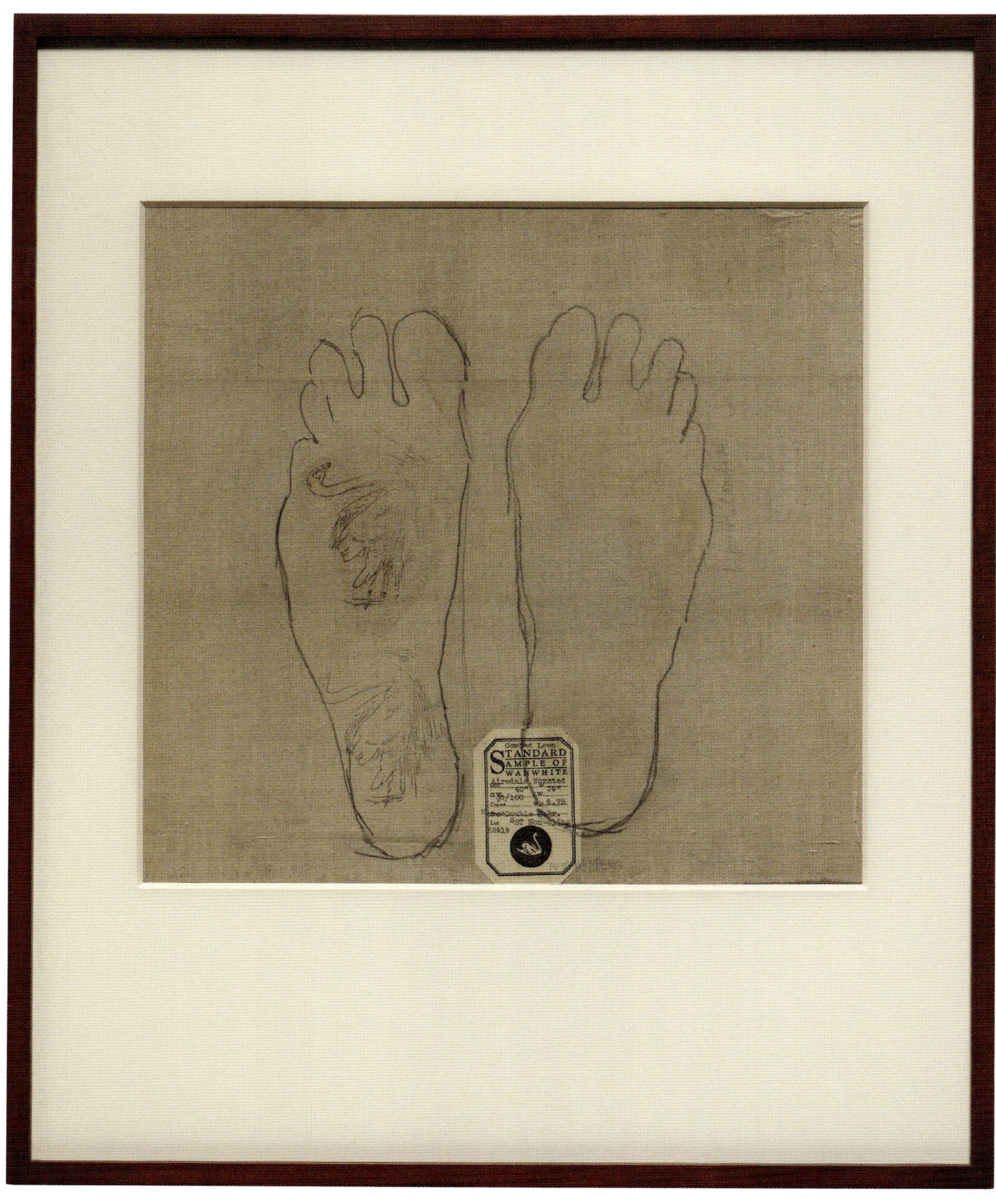

Lawn Combed, 1954
Graphite body tracing on found fabric
14½ × 15½ inches (36.8 × 39.4 cm)
Robert Rauschenberg Foundation

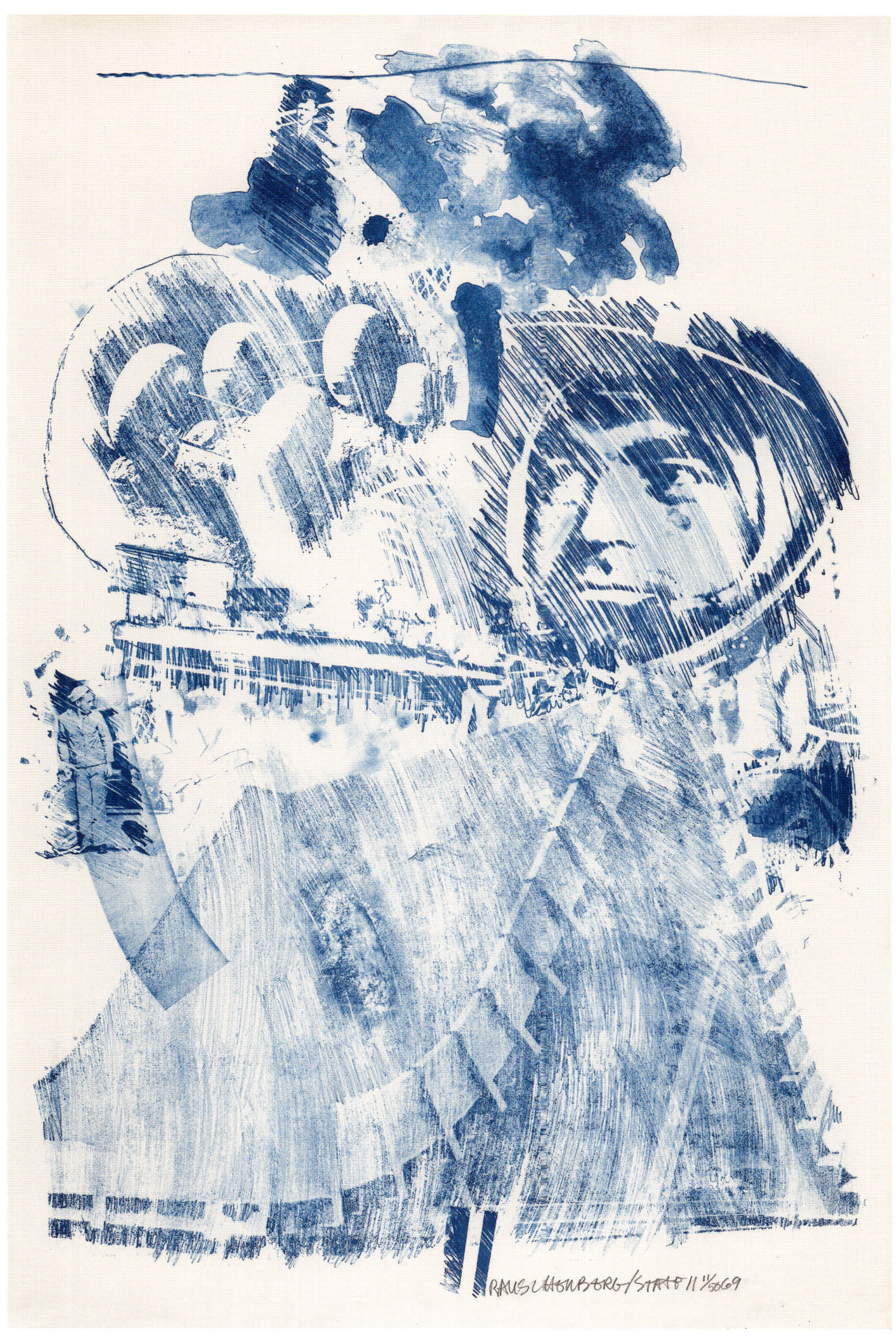

Arena II (Stoned Moon), 1969
Lithograph
47 × 32 inches (119.3 × 81.3 cm)
Hirshhorn Museum and Sculpture Garden

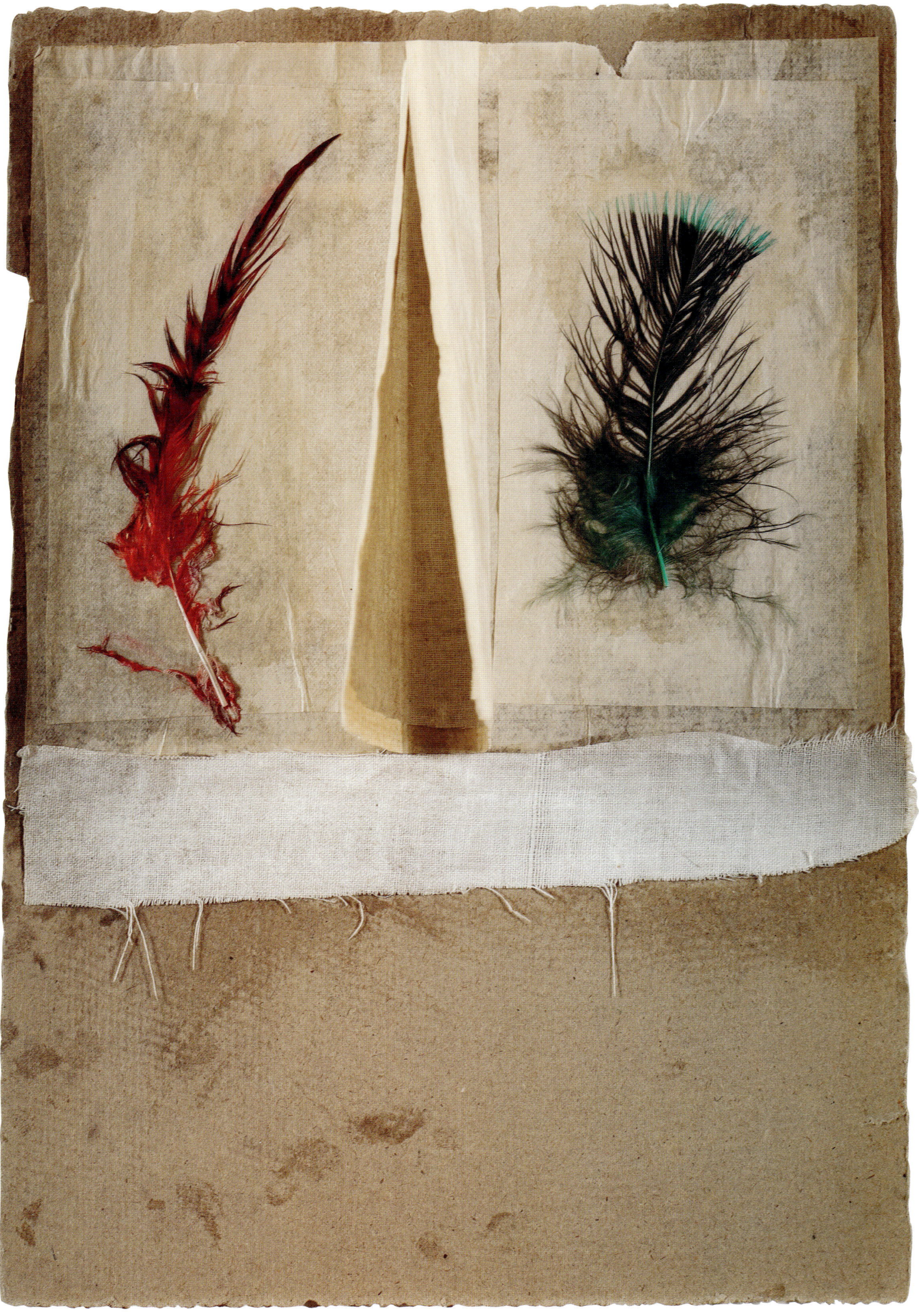

2

Birdland

**It was a place on Sixth Avenue—a real old-fashioned taxidermy place.
I bought the chicken for ... *Plymouth Rock*, and the chicken for *Odalisque* there.
There were all kinds of different stuffed animals all over the place.**

—Robert Rauschenberg[1]

Leonardo da Vinci called birds one of nature's wonders, creatures whose form and function was characterized by a harmonious balance in which "nothing is wanted and nothing is superfluous."[2] Rauschenberg examined the intricate relationship between nature and artistry, effectively capturing the essence of flight inherent in the natural world across various mediums. Throughout his career, he integrated the imagery of birds and flying insects into his artworks, even including taxidermied fowl within his Combines. These motifs reveal Rauschenberg's personal commitment to wildlife and environmental causes, often draw on mythology, and explore the notion of flight and freedom.

Ab Ovo

Some of Rauschenberg's earliest works associated with nature and flight are found in a series of small assemblages, collages, and intricate wooden boxes made in Italy and North Africa during his travels with Cy Twombly in 1952 and 1953.[3] This trip represented a pivotal moment in Rauschenberg's artistic development, with artworks such as *North African Collages* (1952) and *Scatole Personali* (1952–53) serving as predecessors to the Combines for which he is renowned. The collages and assemblages were made from cardboard inserts from laundered shirts and found materials such as etchings and decorative embellishments gathered from flea markets and books stalls.[4]

One of the *North African Collages*, Untitled [pictographs and feathers], features two exotic feathers—one red and one green alluding to the national colors of Italy—arranged on an off white background and positioned beneath two side-by-side folded paper flaps. On the flaps concealing the feathers, Rauschenberg pasted prints containing Egyptian hieroglyphics, which include two avian representations: a duck and another bird that evokes characteristics associated with raptors. These elements suggest a nuanced exploration of the cultural heritage of both Italy and North Africa and may also reflect Rauschenberg's association of flight with a journey of self-discovery and artistic evolution.

Other works from the same time evolve the theme. In Untitled [insects and pod], the image of a multitiered flower pod joins two pieces of paper, with the gap between them creating the appearance of a long stem. At the base of this "stem" sit two flies and two beetles; below them, a spherical flower radiates rays like the sun. The juxtaposition of the insects with the sunlike flower evokes the Egyptian sun god, Ra, while the extreme verticality of the composition recalls the obelisks Rauschenberg surely encountered on his travels and the intertwined themes of death and resurrection associated with those ancient monuments. These themes are echoed in Untitled [insects], which features a variety of insects, some with outspread wings suggesting flight, others resembling scarabs—powerful symbols of transformation and rebirth in Egyptian mythology.

A series of *Scatole Personali*, or personal boxes, reinforces themes of metamorphosis through flight and the quest for new artistic identities that permeate Rauschenberg's body of work. One example consists of a wooden box containing the skull of a bird that is adorned with string, feathers, a bell, and a rhinestone on its beak, denoting both the preciousness of and a reverence for the deceased creature. The box is decorated with a print of a bird and recalls a miniature casket a child might craft for a deceased pet.

In 1953 Rauschenberg exhibited works such as these in Florence and Rome to uncomprehending audiences. One critic said the works should be thrown into the Arno River. While some

Detail of **Untitled [pictographs and feathers]**, ca. 1952

boxes sold and helped pay for his trip back to the United States, Rauschenberg heeded the critic's advice and destroyed others. Little did they know that these miniature treasures were precursors to the influential Combines.[5]

Ode to Ornithology

As a child, Rauschenberg kept a variety of pets, including dogs, a goat, and chickens. Several of these early companions were later revisited as thematic elements in artworks, notably *Monogram* (1955–59), which features a stuffed goat, and early Combines that incorporate birds. In *Odalisk* (1955/58), a stuffed rooster sits atop an open-sided box. The box rests on a wooden furniture leg, which in turn sits on a pillow. The exterior of the box is covered with a variety of found imagery, including a reclining nude woman that makes explicit the work's evocation of the odalisque—a slave or concubine in a harem—as a subject in art history. Counterbalancing this is the dominating "male" presence of the rooster.[6] Graham Smith has explored the associations present in this work and noted that its erect structure (and the unique spelling of the title) recalls the obelisks that Rauschenberg would have encountered during his travels.[7] In this light, we can see *Odalisk* as harking back to his earlier works featuring birds and flying insects. And given that the open-sided box recalls a stage or theater, it's possible to view *Odalisk* as a precursor to Rauschenberg's first choreographed performance, *Pelican* (1963), where he mimicked a bird in flight.

In *Satellite* (1955), a pheasant perches on a rectangular Combine brimming with fabric, patterned wallpaper, lace doilies, and an eclectic mix of imagery: fruit, a comic strip featuring Popeye, and a black arrow pointing down toward a pair of socks. The superior position of the bird, juxtaposed with the mundane socks below, suggests its elevated status in Rauschenberg's world. Tucked within this composition are additional references to flight, including a comic strip featuring a futuristic spaceship, which underline the interplay of sky and ground, up and down, while exploring the themes of domesticity and advancing frontiers of technology and space exploration.

In *Canyon* (1959), a stuffed golden eagle stretches its powerful wings and appears to fly directly at the viewer as if breaking free from the confines of the artwork. Rauschenberg acquired the eagle from the artist Sari Dienes, who discovered it outside a neighbor's residence. The original owner was reportedly one of Teddy Roosevelt's Rough Riders during the Spanish-

American War (1898); he probably captured the eagle before the practice became illegal.[8] *Canyon* also features a photograph of Rauschenberg's son, Christopher, as a baby, reaching skyward. The eagle recalls the Roman myth of Zeus disguising himself as an eagle in order to abduct the youthful Ganymede.[9] Rauschenberg expanded on this association in *Pail for Ganymede* (1959), a work that references Rembrandt's painting *Ganymede in the Claws of the Eagle* (1635). That painting shows an infant being pulled upward by an eagle and urinating mid-flight out of fear, with the pail in Rauschenberg's sculpture an allusion to catching the stream of urine. The art historian Leah Dickerman describes *Pail for Ganymede* as an exploration of the force of gravity and the fear of flight.[10] Other imagery in *Canyon* includes the child's arm raised toward the sky, a photograph of the Statue of Liberty in front of a blue sky, a starry night scene, and an image of a rooster—all allusions to ascent according to curator Lawrence Alloway.[11] Eagles appear repeatedly in Rauschenberg's early *Silkscreen Paintings*, including *Tracer* and *Kite* (both 1963), and in later works such as *Earth Day* (1970) and *7–UP (Shales)* (1994).

Birds remained a prominent feature in Rauschenberg's *Silkscreen Paintings*, lithographs, and other paper works within his Combines. Flying birds appear in several pieces, such as *Overdrive* (1963) and *N.Y. Bird Calls for Öyvind Fahlström* (1965). While the images remain consistent, the surrounding visuals change. In *Overdrive*, four birds are depicted with their wings in various positions. Surrounding them is an upside-down photograph of the Statue of Liberty with clouds in the background alongside various technical drawings and a number of traffic signs, including a cluster from the intersection of Nassau and Pine Streets in New York City, sourced from a photograph by Phillip Harington in *Look* magazine.[12] In this context, the "freeze-frame" images of the birds surrounded by stop signs (stopping their motion) recalls Harold Edgerton's experiments with hummingbirds and strobe photography at the Massachusetts Institute of Technology in the 1930s.[13] The one-way signs are arranged at disorienting angles, enhancing the feeling of flying through an upside-down city. This dizzying arrangement reflects the natural aerobatic movements of the birds, especially hummingbirds, which fly upside down and backwards as they navigate through the air.

In 1964 Rauschenberg published an essay on the Swedish artist Öyvind Fahlström that highlights their shared embrace of randomness and sensitivity to imagery laden with profound meaning.[14] Fahlström's work also addresses birds, with notated birdcalls appearing in his painting *Sunrise* (ca. 1962). In a gesture to his fellow artist, Rauschenberg created his own interpretation of the theme in *N.Y. Bird Calls for Öyvind Fahlström*. Here, the birds that appeared in *Overdrive* expand into a formation of eleven birds that fly upright and upside down at the top of the canvas. Scattered throughout are photographs of clouds, urban street scenes, beach umbrellas (signifying flight), and water towers. Rauschenberg enriched the painting by affixing metal letters, numbers, and eclectic objects such as a hockey stick and springs to the canvas. A small wooden block attached to the canvas by a chain features a silkscreened photograph of a worker precariously perched on a skyscraper ledge, with a dizzying view of the ground far below.

In the *Cardbird* series, editioned works published by Gemini G.E.L., Los Angeles, in 1971, Rauschenberg created print facsimiles of found cardboard components to construct new avian forms. In *Cardbird III* (1971) he transformed a discarded cardboard box bearing the word "Turkeys" into a whimsical edition representing a bird, complete with a head, wings, tail, and an eye. This playful approach and its punning title aptly convey Rauschenberg's humor and fascination with flight.

A Mixed Flock

Working with Gemini G.E.L. in Los Angeles, Rauschenberg stretched the bounds of printmaking with the *Horsefeathers Thirteen* series (1972–73), which combines embossing, collage, and lithography, among other techniques. Each print within the series is unique yet draws on a common cast of fixed shapes and images. *Horsefeathers Thirteen V* (1972) includes a little owl (*Athene noctua*), a dab of white paint, a red circular object at the bottom resembling a wheel, and a photograph of a vast cloud-scape on the right among its fixed images; interchangeable elements include a circle representing the sun and a beach scene depicting a scientist seemingly surrounded by salps, gelatinous marine creatures that use a natural jet-propulsion system for movement. Other variations in the *Horsefeathers Thirteen* series include imagery such as moonwalkers' legs, an engine turbine, an airplane, additional clouds, and an aerial map, creating rich visual narratives on celestial activities.

The combination of handmade molded paper with the screenprint process in *Link (Fuses)* (1974) creates tactile imagery that appears to float or fly.[15] A feather-like image alongside a seagull flying toward a circular form alluding to the sun evokes pop-literature and mythological themes. This composition resonates with Richard Bach's narrative in *Jonathan Livingston Seagull*, which chronicles a seagull's journey in pursuit of freedom, flight, and transformation. The novel opens, "It was morning, and the new sun sparkled gold across the ripples of a gentle sea."[16] The juxtaposition of the sun and bird inevitably suggests the story of Daedalus, who invents wings made of feathers and wax for himself and his son, Icarus. Despite his father's warnings, Icarus flies too close to the sun and falls to his death when the wax melts and the wings disintegrate.

In *Back-Up (Borealis)* (1991), two blue herons stand side by side, one white and the other dark—mimicking light and shadow. The distinctive coloring in this series was achieved through chemical reactions resulting from tarnishing agents applied to reflective metal substrates, or panels. The series title alludes to the northern lights, with their bursts of color dancing across the night sky. Asked about the origins of the series, Rauschenberg explained that he was first experimenting with rainbow corrosions when "I was on my way to Sweden, and saw my first borealis."[17]

Rauschenberg's final body of work before his death in 2008 are the *Runt* paintings (2006–08), which feature inkjet prints of color photographs transferred to a polylaminate panel. *Ibis Review (Runt)* (2007) presents a white panel adorned with a series of white Floridian ibises. The varied poses of the birds evoke the pioneering photographic studies of Eadweard Muybridge that captured animal locomotion. These birds, however, are juxtaposed with images of a white cottage and a detail of the cottage window. They depict the Waldo Cottage, located on Rauschenberg's property on Captiva Island, which originally served as a cabin for people working in the surrounding citrus groves. It's possible Rauschenberg envisioned himself as the ibis and set the bird before the historic workers' building in a kind of review of his life's labors.

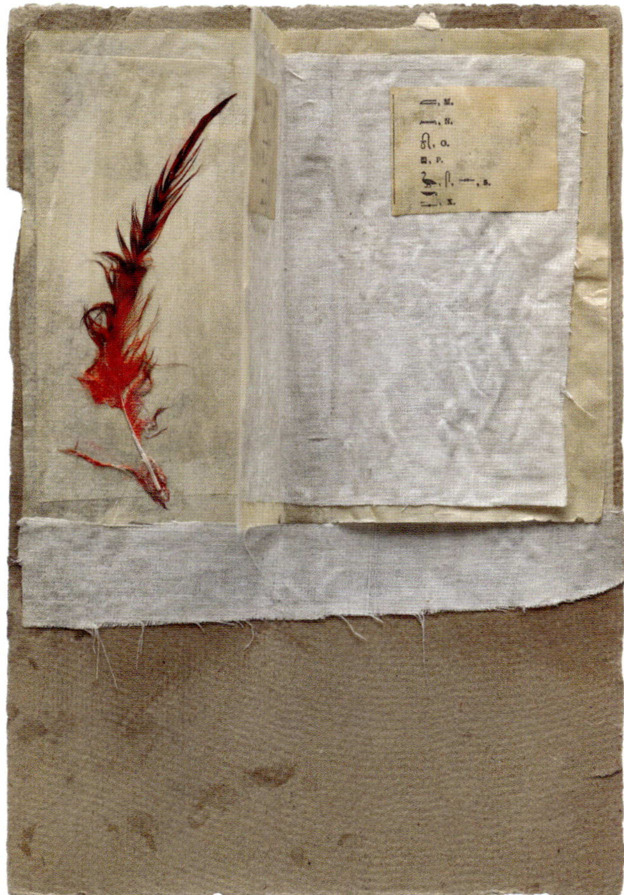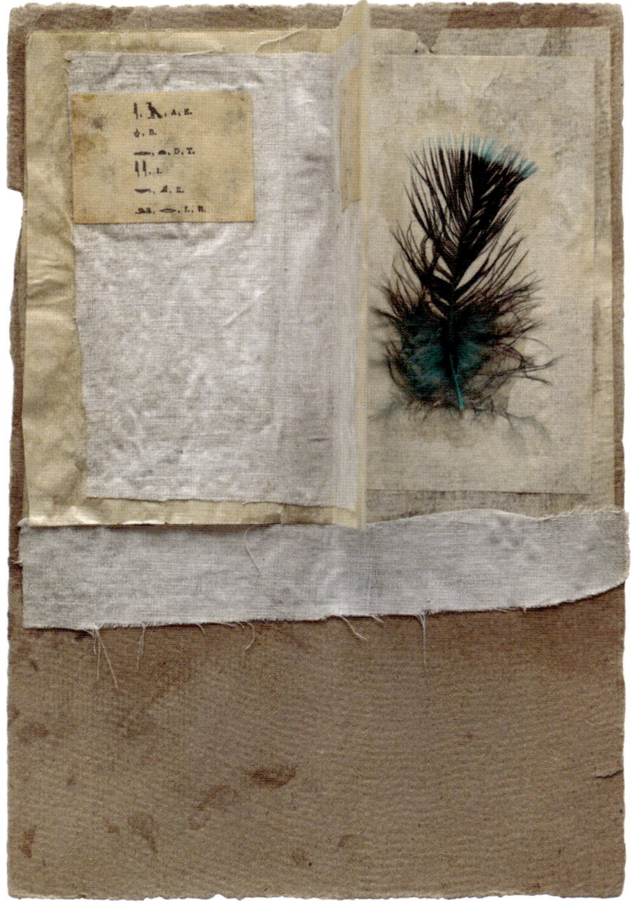

Untitled [pictographs and feathers], ca. 1952
Feathers, printed paper, and fabric on paper, mounted on paperboard with two central hinged panels
10 × 6⅞ inches (25.4 × 17.5 cm)
Robert Rauschenberg Foundation

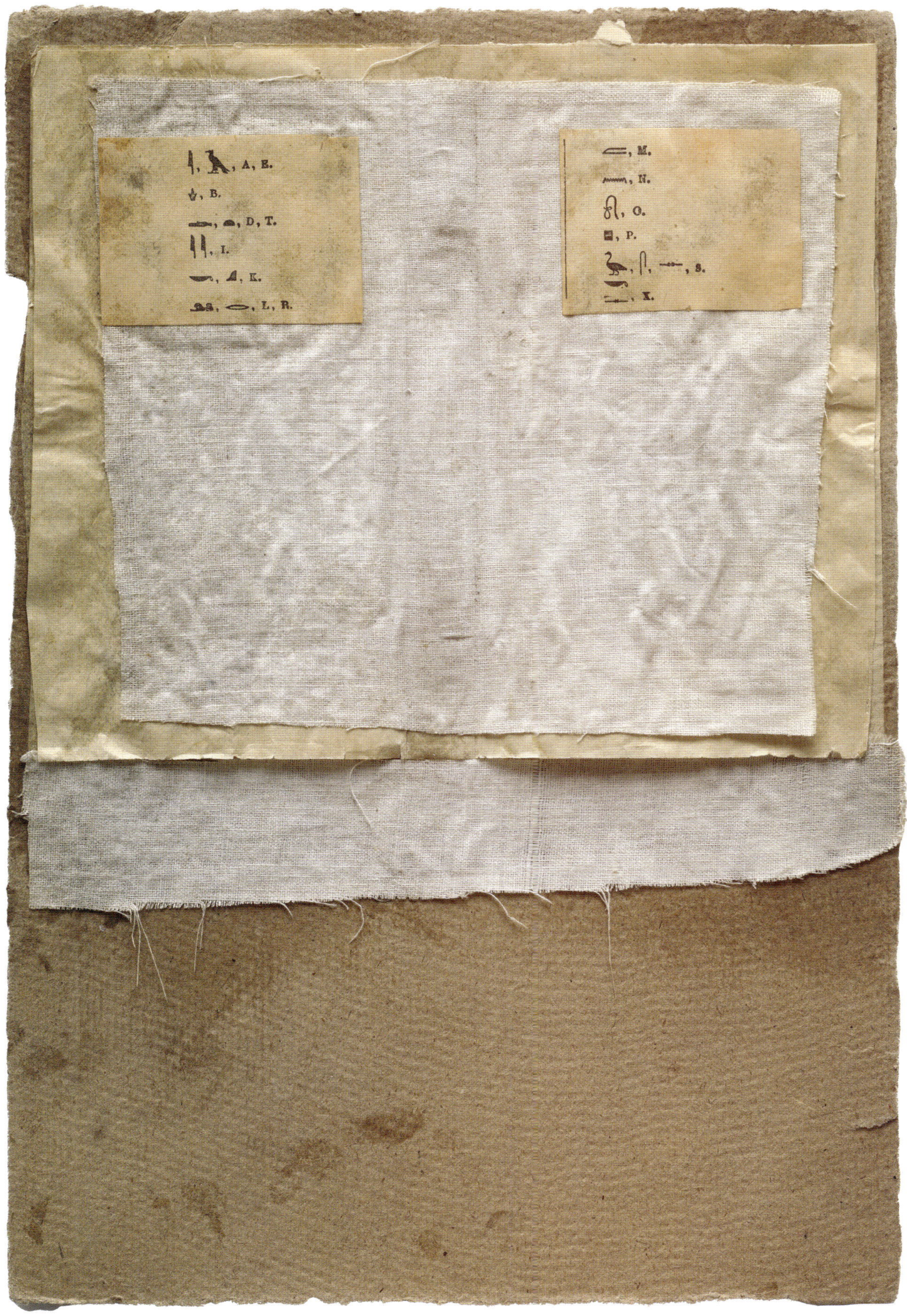

Alternate view of **Untitled [pictographs and feathers]**, ca. 1952

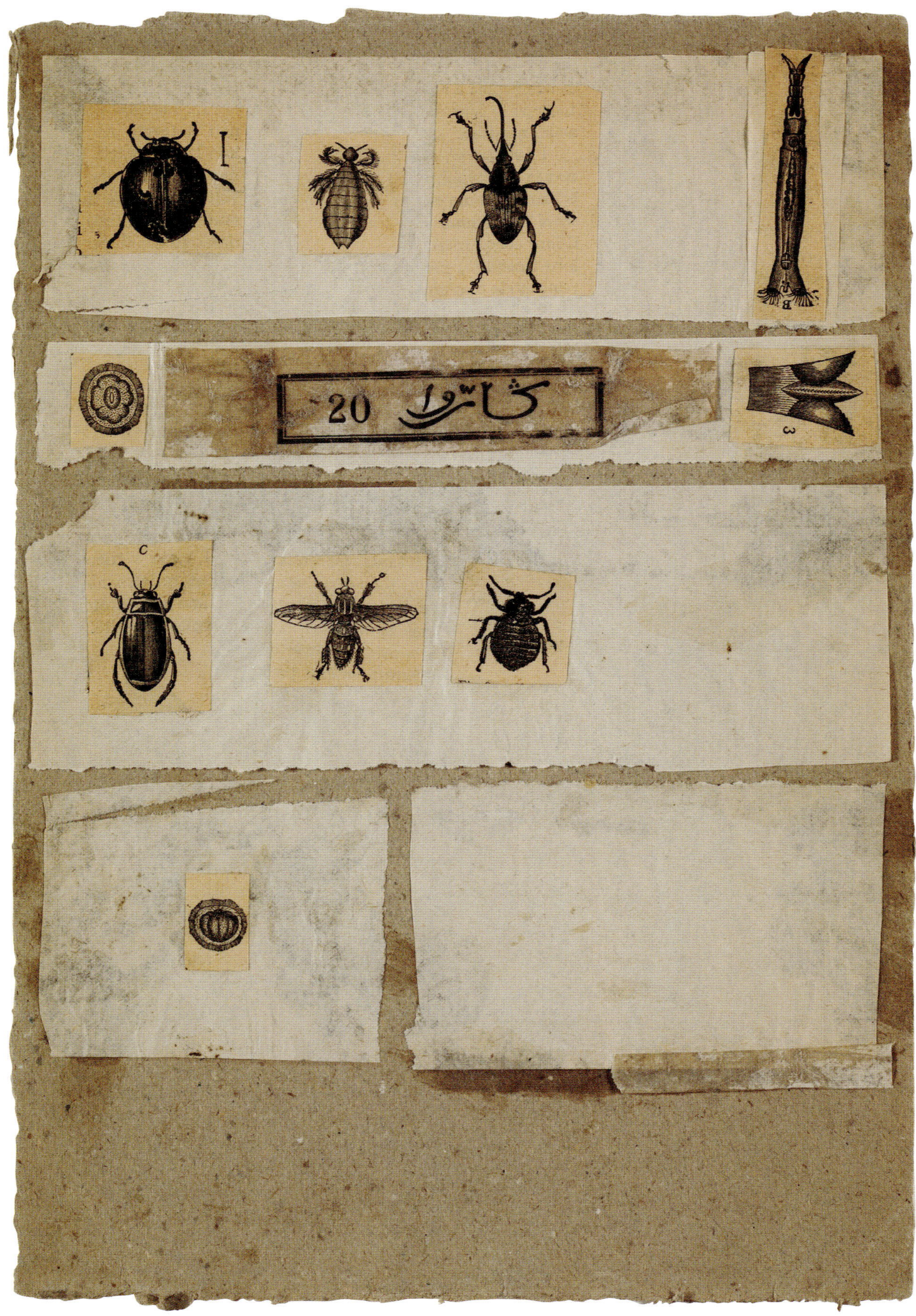

Untitled [insects], ca. 1952
Engravings, printed paper, and glue on paper, mounted on paperboard
10 × 7 inches (25.4 × 17.5 cm)
Private collection

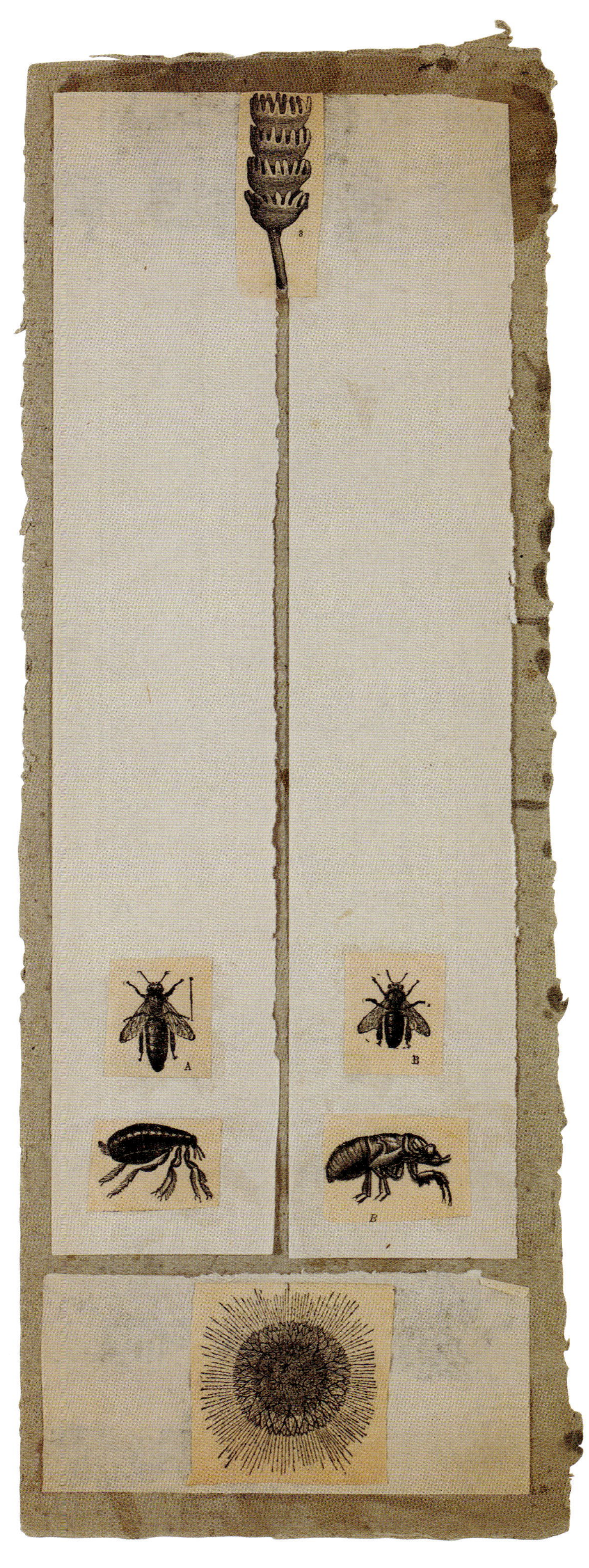

Untitled [insects and pod], ca. 1952
Engravings and paper, mounted on paperboard
14 × 5 inches (35.6 × 12.7 cm)
Private collection

Untitled (Scatole Personali), ca. 1952
Painted wood box with lid, containing printed reproductions, paper, fabric,
bird skull with rhinestone, thread, twine, feathers, and metal bell
2⅛ × 4⅝ × 2⅛ inches (5.4 × 11.9 × 5.4 cm)
Menil Collection

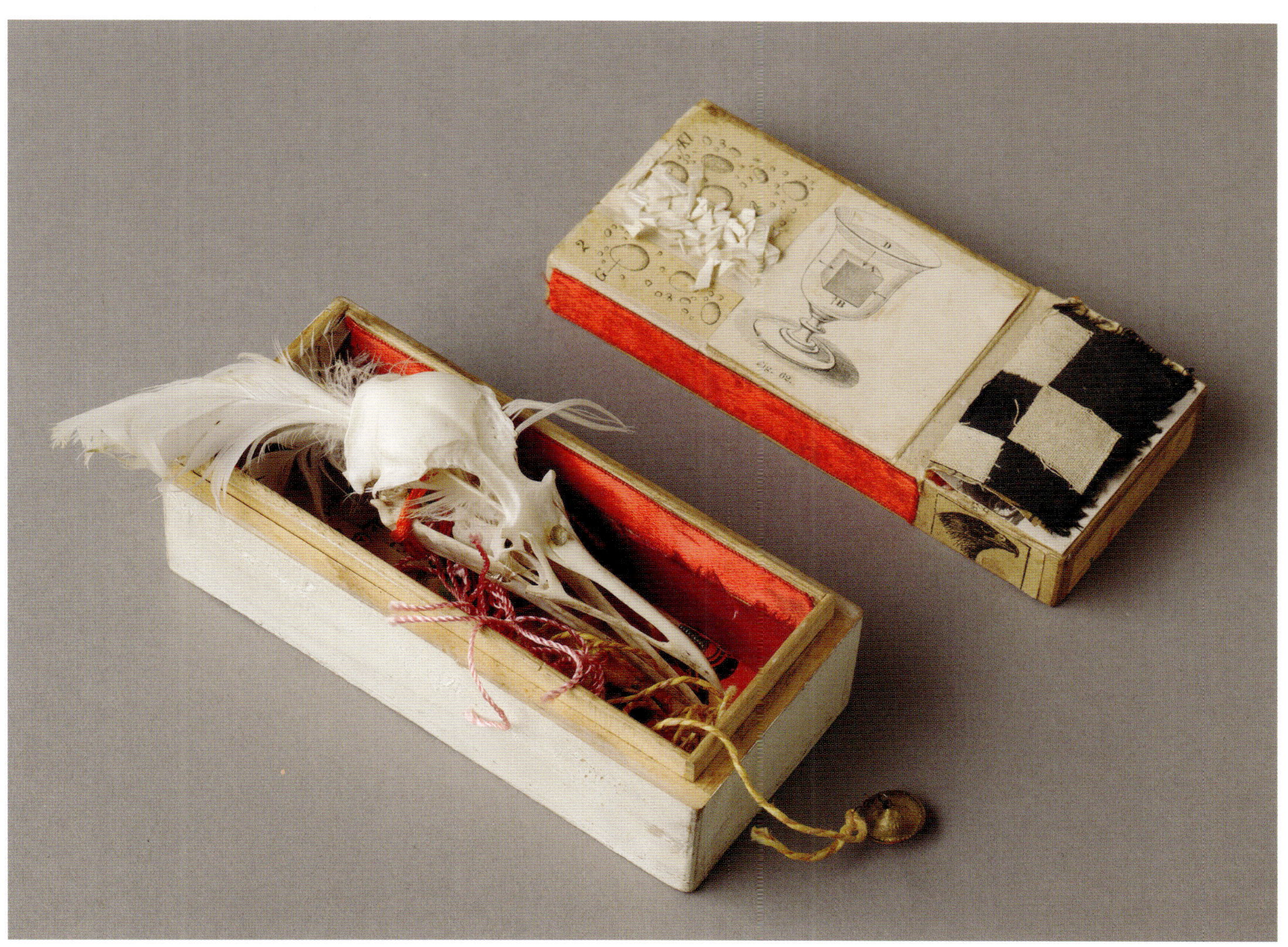

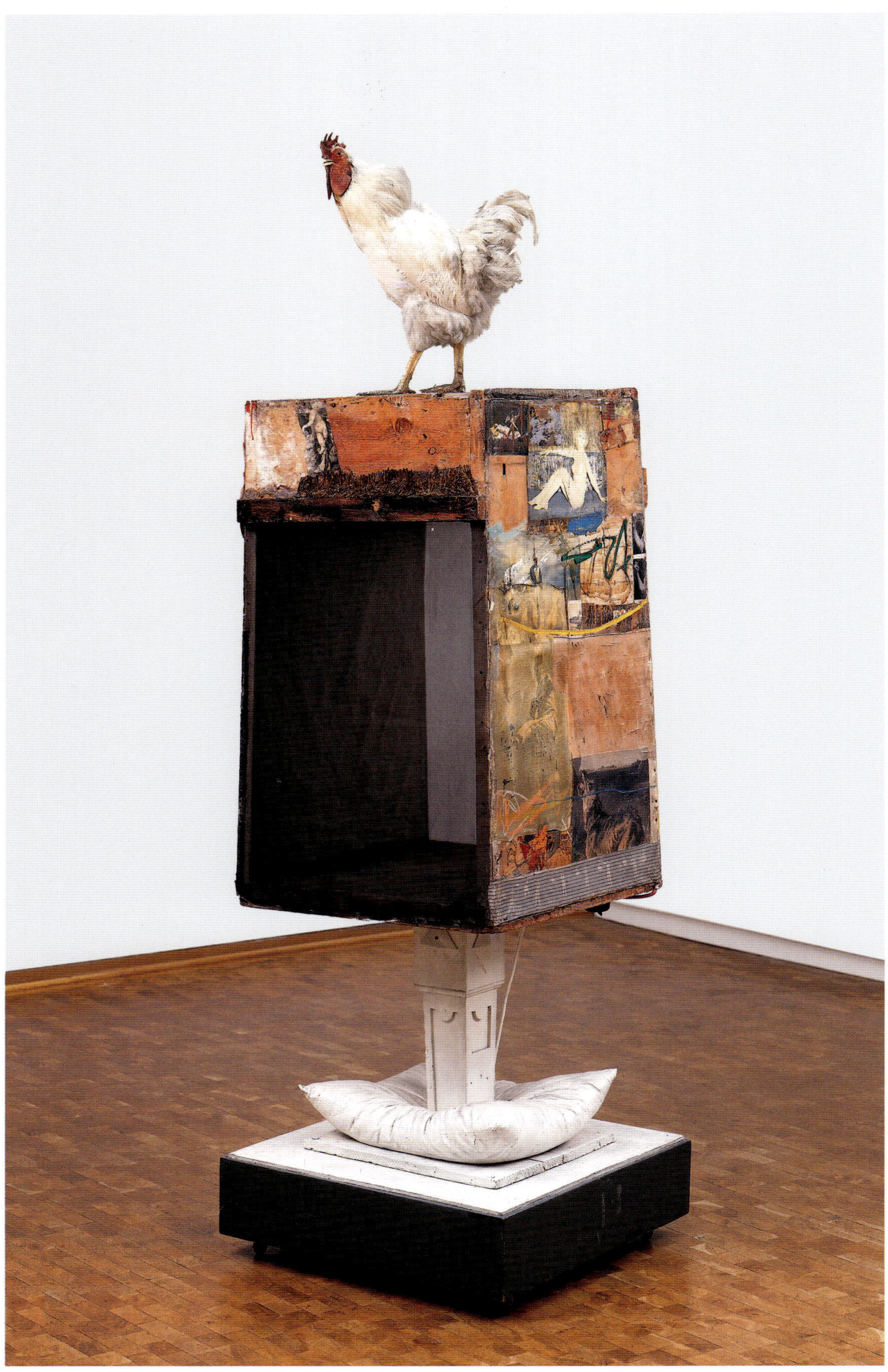

Odalisk, 1955/58
Combine: oil, watercolor, graphite, crayon, paper, fabric, photographs, printed reproductions, miniature
blueprint, newsprint, metal, glass, dried grass, and steel wool with pillow, wood post, electric lights, and rooster
on wood structure mounted on four casters
83 × 25¼ × 25⅛ inches (210.8 × 64.1 × 63.8 cm)
Museum Ludwig, Cologne

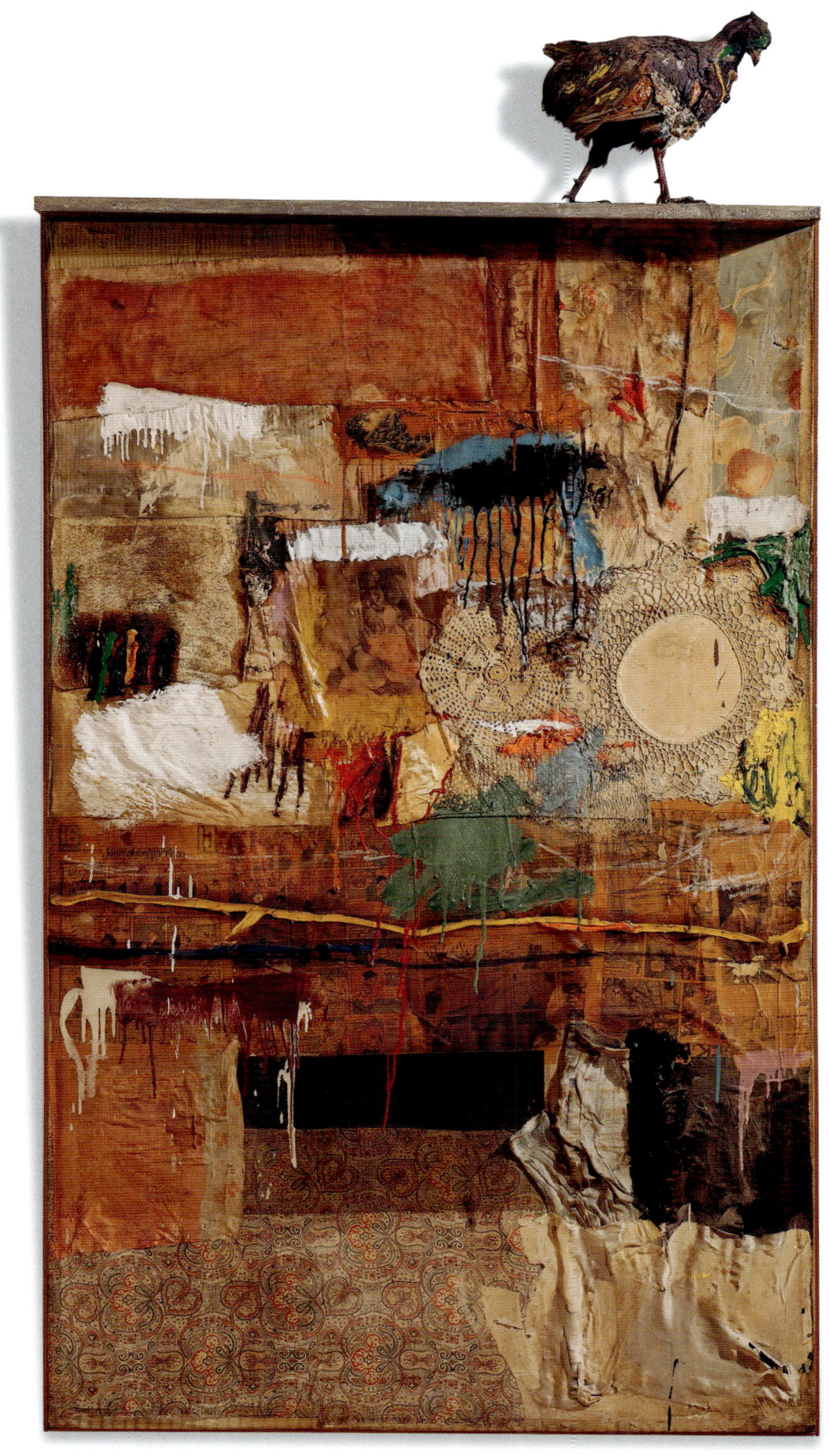

Satellite, 1955
Combine: oil, fabric, paper, and wood on canvas with taxidermied pheasant
79⅜ × 43¼ × 5⅝ inches (201.6 × 109.9 × 14.3 cm)
Whitney Museum of American Art

Canyon, 1959
Combine: oil, pencil, paper, fabric, metal, cardboard box, printed paper, printed reproductions, photograph, wood, paint tube, and mirror on canvas with oil on taxidermied golden eagle, string, and pillow
81¾ × 70 × 24 inches (207.6 × 177.8 × 61 cm)
The Museum of Modern Art

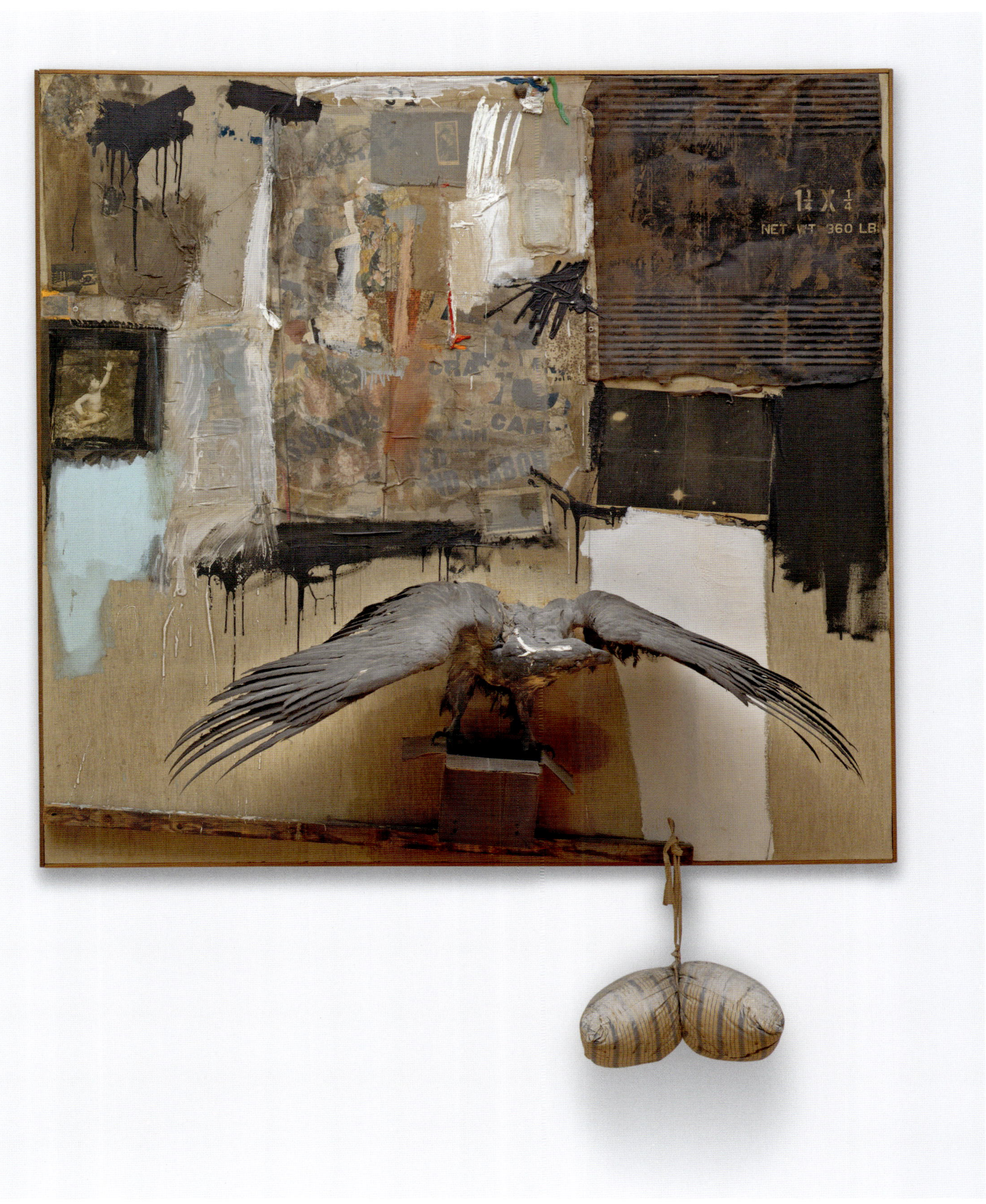

1¼ X ¼
NET WT 360 LB

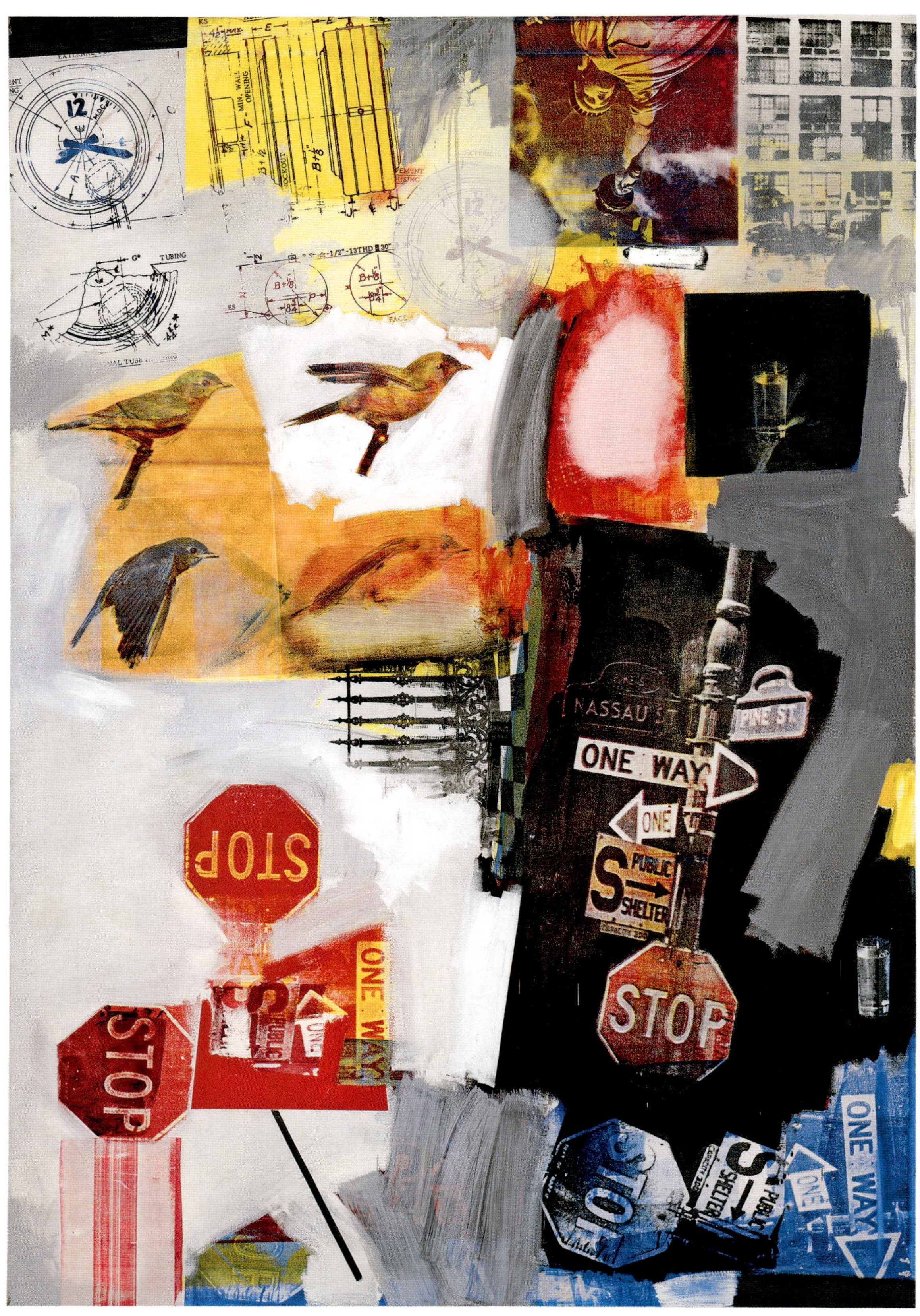

Overdrive, 1963
Oil and silkscreen ink on canvas
84 × 60 inches (213.4 × 152.4 cm)
The Museum of Modern Art

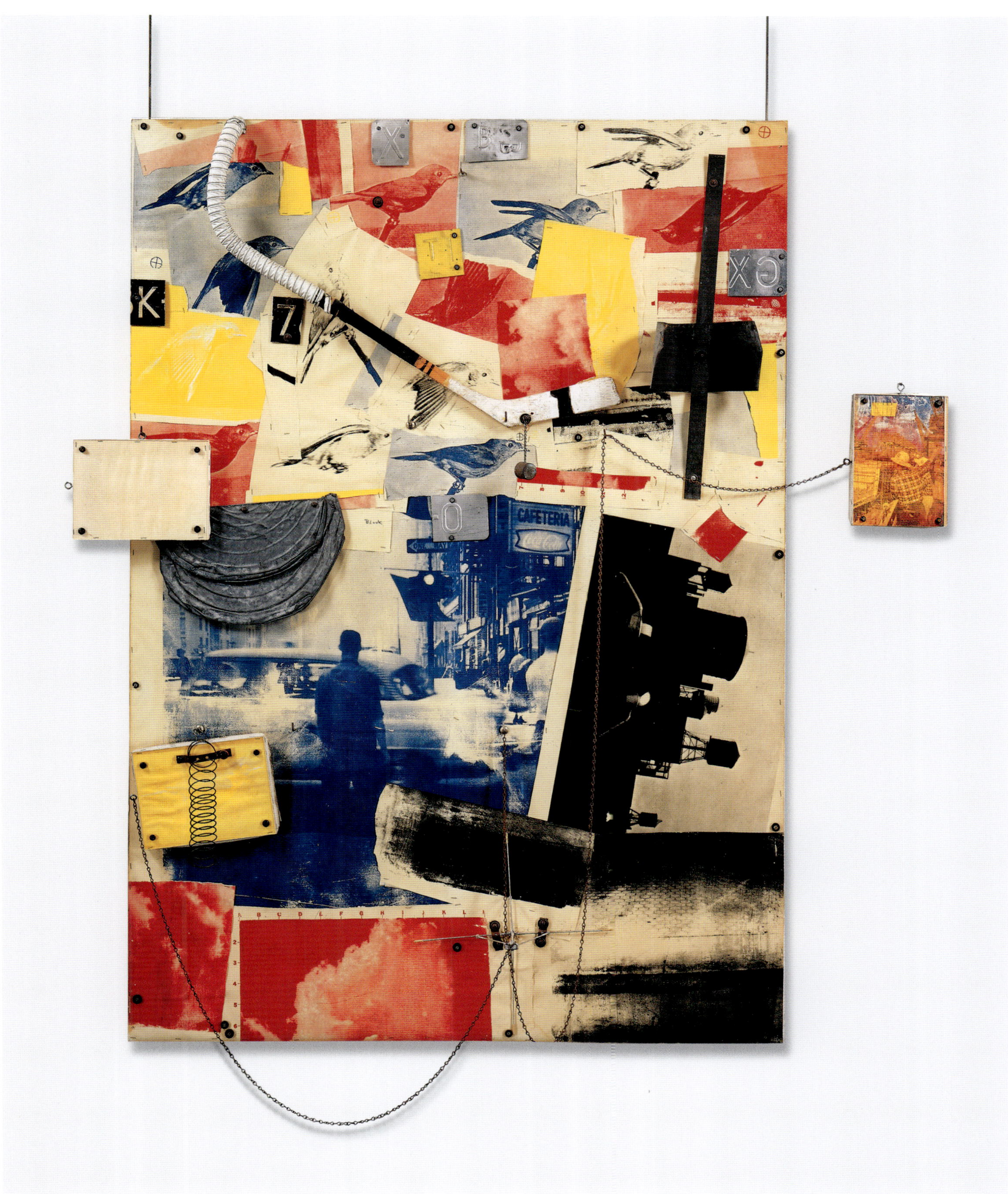

N.Y. Bird Calls for Öyvind Fahlström, 1965
Silkscreen ink on cut-and-torn papers stapled to canvas and covered with Plexiglas, with hockey
stick, hose, metal garbage-can lid, antenna, metal, spring, film canister, and chains
84 x 60 x 11 inches (213.4 x 152.4 x 27.9 cm), variable
Private collection

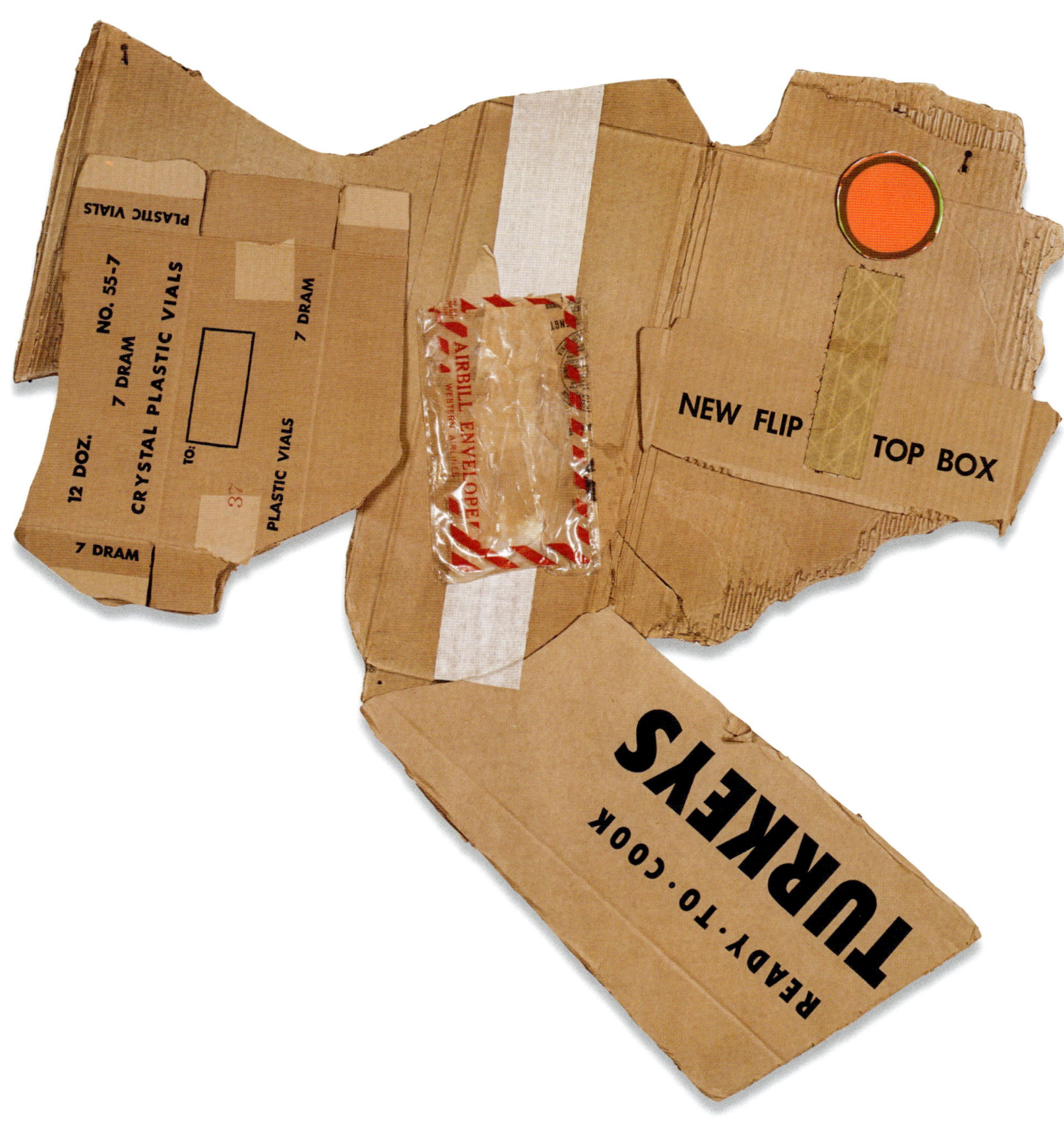

Cardbird III, 1971
Photolithograph and screenprint on paper with tape and plastic bag on cardboard
36 × 36 inches (91.4 × 91.4 cm)
Robert Rauschenberg Foundation

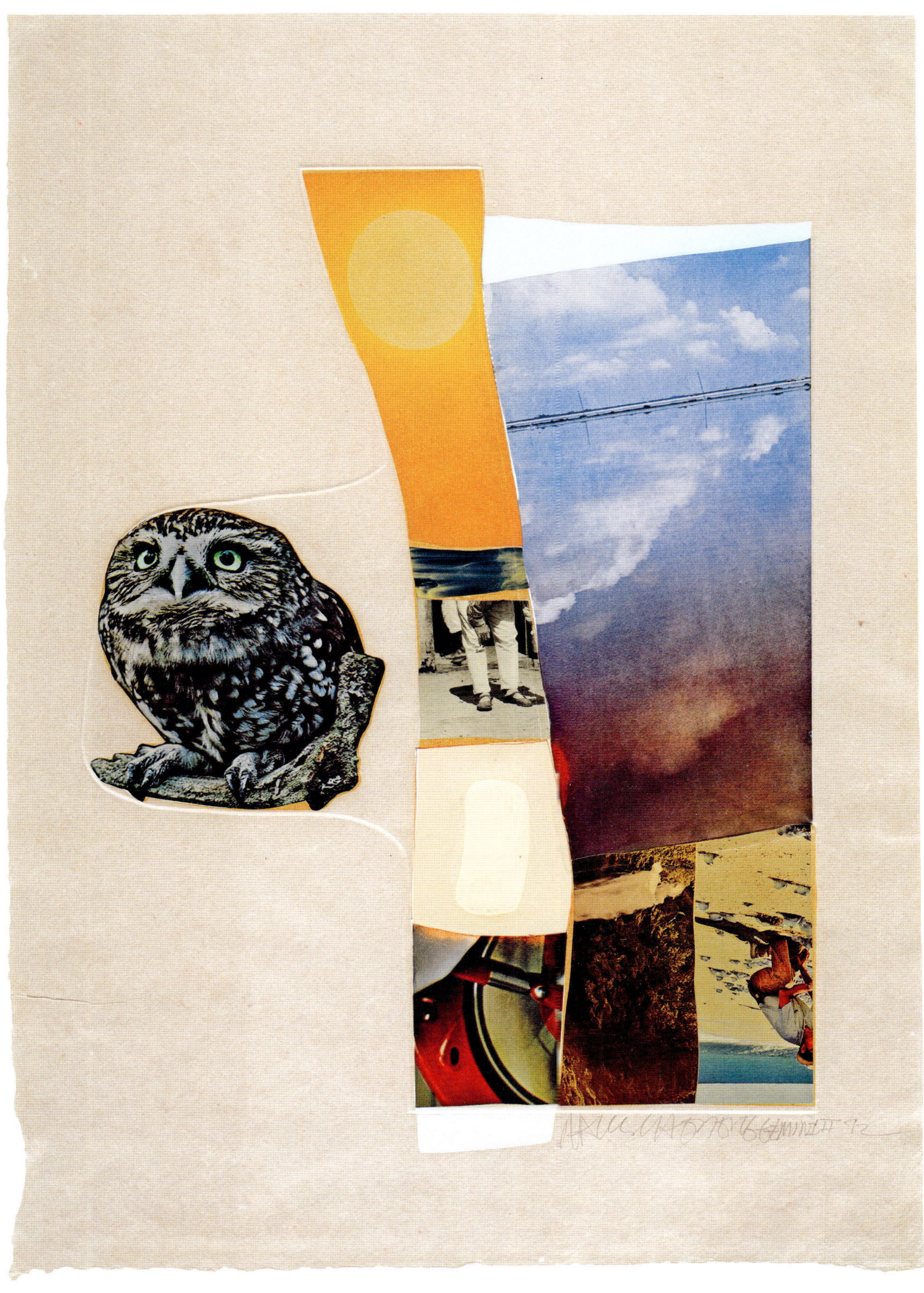

Horsefeathers Thirteen V, 1972
Lithograph, screenprint, pochoir, printed reproductions, and embossing on paper
24⅛ × 17¾ inches (61 × 45.1 cm), Gemini II apart from edition of 76
Walker Art Center, Minneapolis

Link (Fuses), 1974
Screenprint on tissue paper on handmade paper
23⅞ × 19½ inches (60.64 × 49.53 cm)
National Gallery of Art, Washington, DC

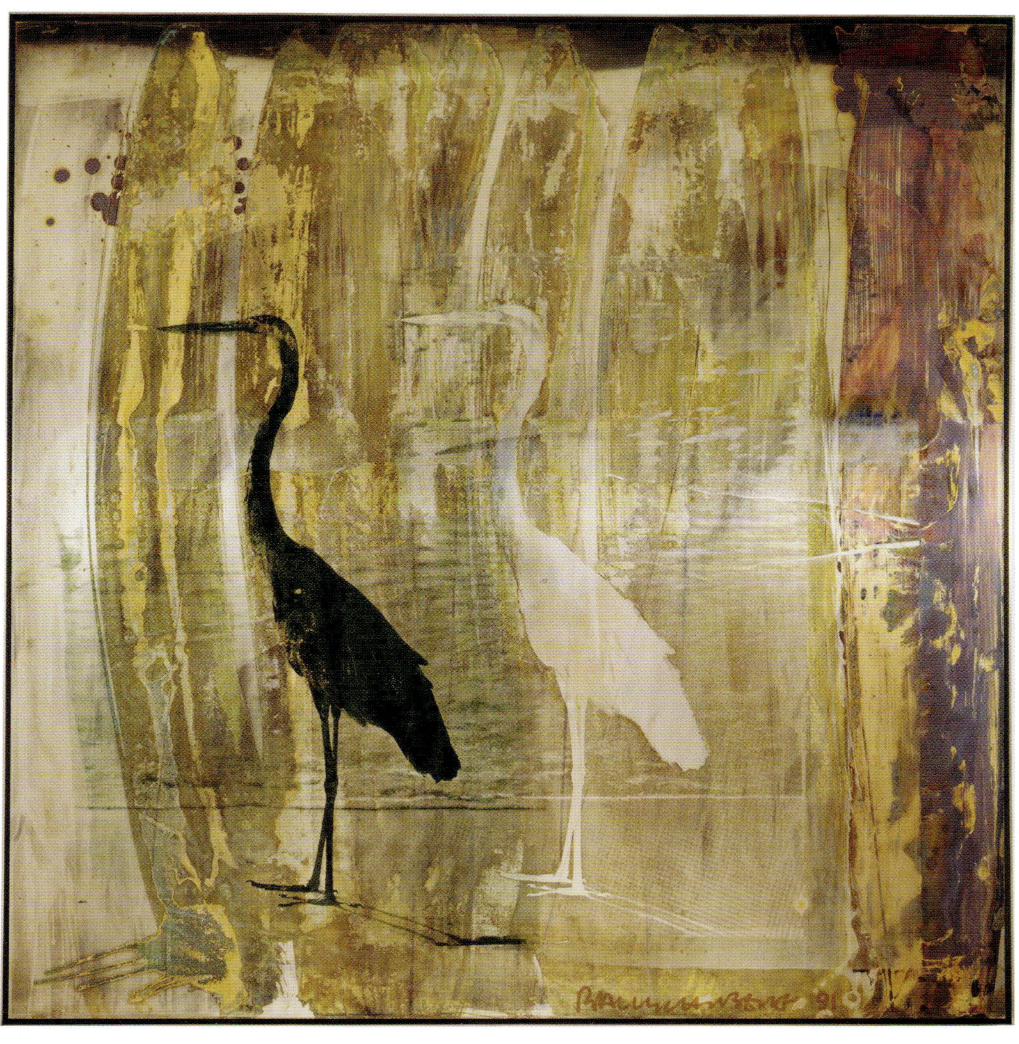

Back-Up (Borealis), 1991
Tarnish and silkscreen ink on bronze
48 × 48 inches (121.9 × 122 cm)
Private collection

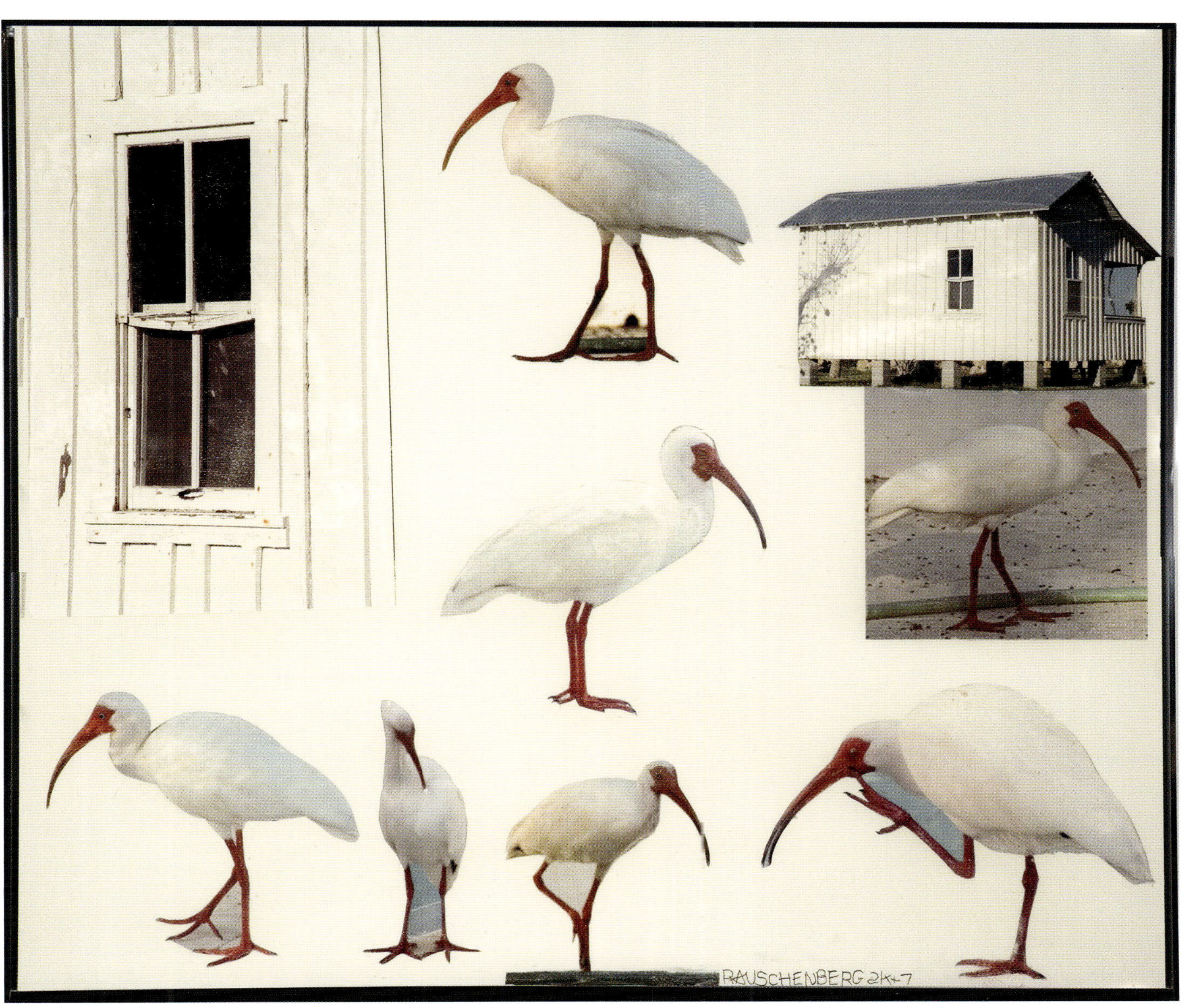

Ibis Review (Runt), 2007
Inkjet pigment transfer on polylaminate
61 × 73½ inches (154.9 × 186.7 cm)
Robert Rauschenberg Foundation

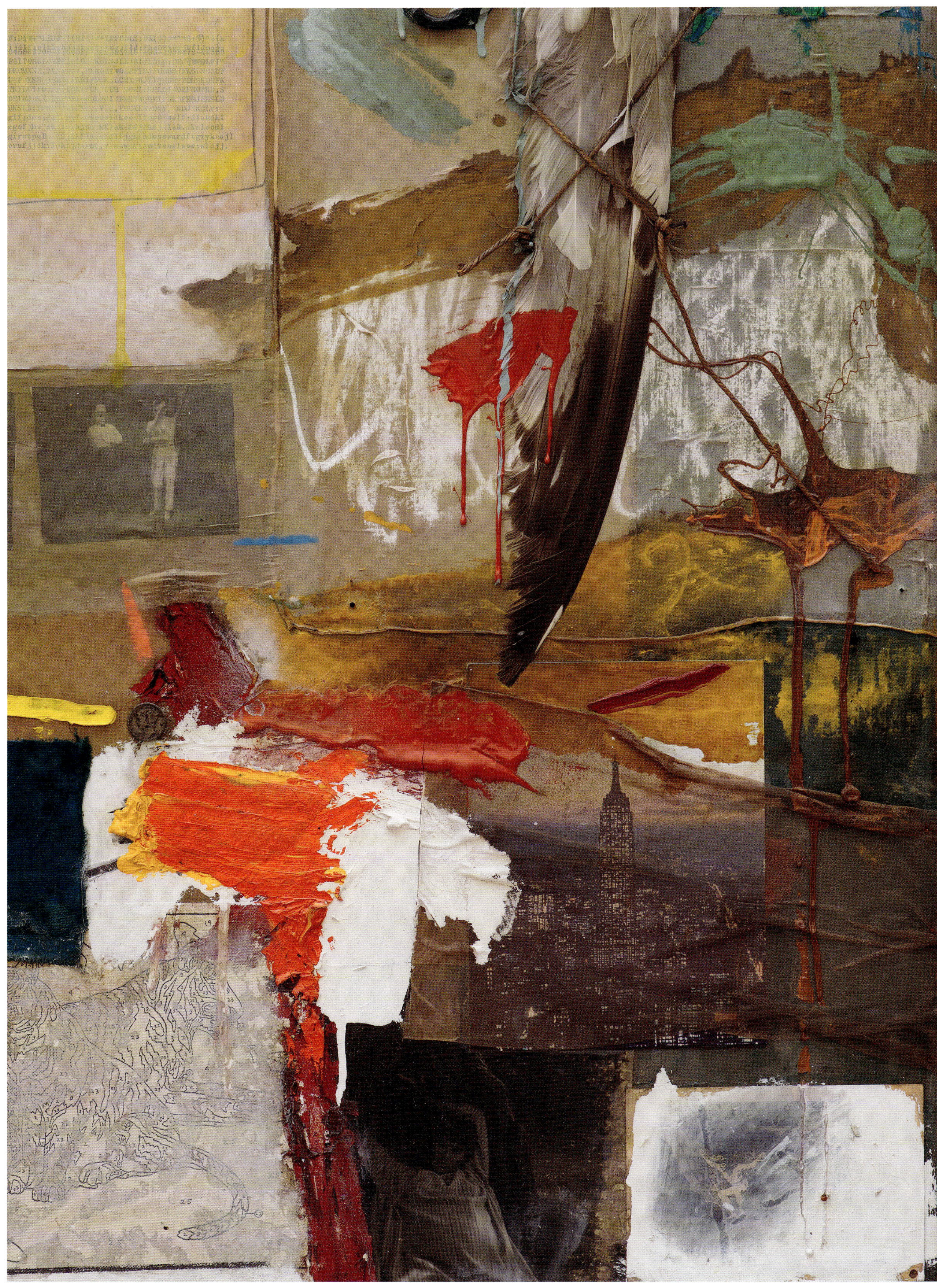

3

Aerial Meditations

**The absurdity and success of teaching a bicycle to fly . . .
it's just the phenomena of what people are capable of doing.**

—Robert Rauschenberg[1]

Viewing Rauschenberg's oeuvre through the lens of flight reveals a rich tapestry of concepts that span various media and subjects over time. Many of his untitled early drawings were given descriptors that were mistakenly reproduced as titles, until the artist titled the works in 1986.[2] These titles expand on his transferred imagery. Take, for example, four works from 1958. He transformed a solvent-transfer print that vividly depicts a flying goose on its flight path from "duck" to *Course*. "Airplane" was reimagined as *Trans-Plant*, and the Cessna it features conveys not just movement but also the transplantation of something or someone. "Small partridge" became *Spinner + Game*, referring to the act of hand-feeding a bird (spinning) while hinting at bird hunting. Additionally, the artwork includes baseball players signaling "three strikes, and you're out!" "Owl" was aptly updated to *Quiz*, capturing the essence of a wise owl.

Birdmen

In *Painting with Grey Wing* (1959), a feathered bird's wing is affixed to the painting with twine, creating an unexpected visual representation of a departed object held in place. Yet, the true essence of the work lies in the tiny reproduction at the lower right of Francisco Goya's *Modo de volar* (A way of flying) from the series *Los disparates* of 1815–23. In his etching, Goya rendered innovative mechanical devices to portray human flight. Strings are attached to a figure's hands and feet, and muscular arms facilitate the flapping of wings. Rauschenberg emphasized the central figure in the reproduced print, establishing a direct connection between Goya's winged man and the bird's wing in his own artwork. The art historian Thomas Crow offers a seminal interpretation of this work that highlights themes of ascent and descent and draws attention to less overt references to flight, such as the skyscraper in the background, which may not be

immediately apparent to viewers encountering the work for the first time [3]

Similarly, an untitled Combine from circa 1955 prominently features the theme of human flight, string play, and a metaphor for escape through the depiction of a toy parachute. Like Goya's flying men, the absent parachutist in this piece is the driver of its flying destiny. The small, deployed chute is positioned toward the bottom of the composition near a pasted sock. At the top of the piece, a landscape with a cow pasture is depicted. Crow interprets the parachute as representing a soft landing, with the sock suggesting "some lift from gravity's ultimate grip."[4] Alternatively, the artwork may allude to parachutists bailing out of a plane and becoming entangled in trees—another reality within the realm of flight.

As noted earlier, a prevalent theme in Rauschenberg's oeuvre is the bicycle, which evokes the concept of flight in

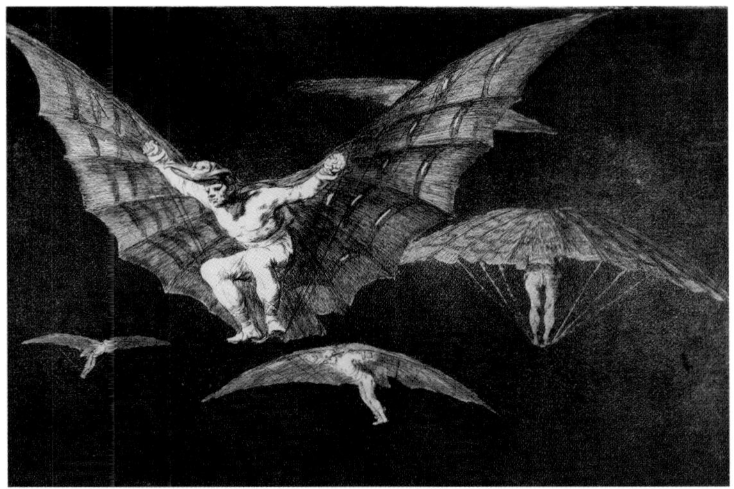

Francisco de Goya y Lucientes (1746–1828), *Los disparates (No. 13: Modo de volar)*, 1815–23. Etching on paper, 8½ × 13¼ inches (21.6 × 33.7 cm). Smithsonian National Air and Space Museum.

Detail of **Painting with Grey Wing**, 1959

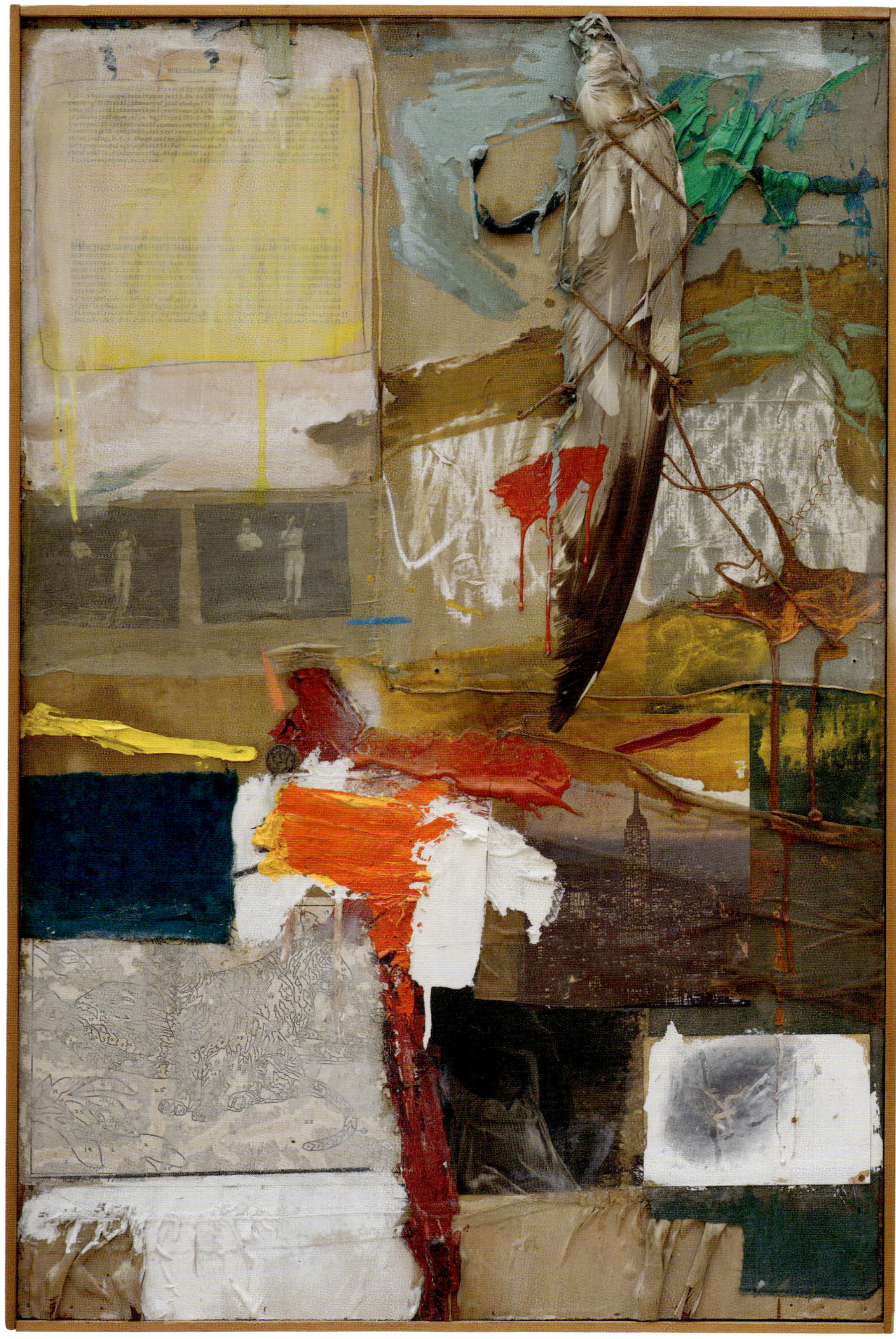

Painting with Grey Wing, 1959
Combine: oil, printed reproductions, unpainted paint-by-number board, typed print on paper,
photographs, fabric, stuffed bird wing, and dime on canvas
31 × 21 × 2½ inches (78.7 × 53.3 × 6.4 cm)
The Museum of Contemporary Art, Los Angeles

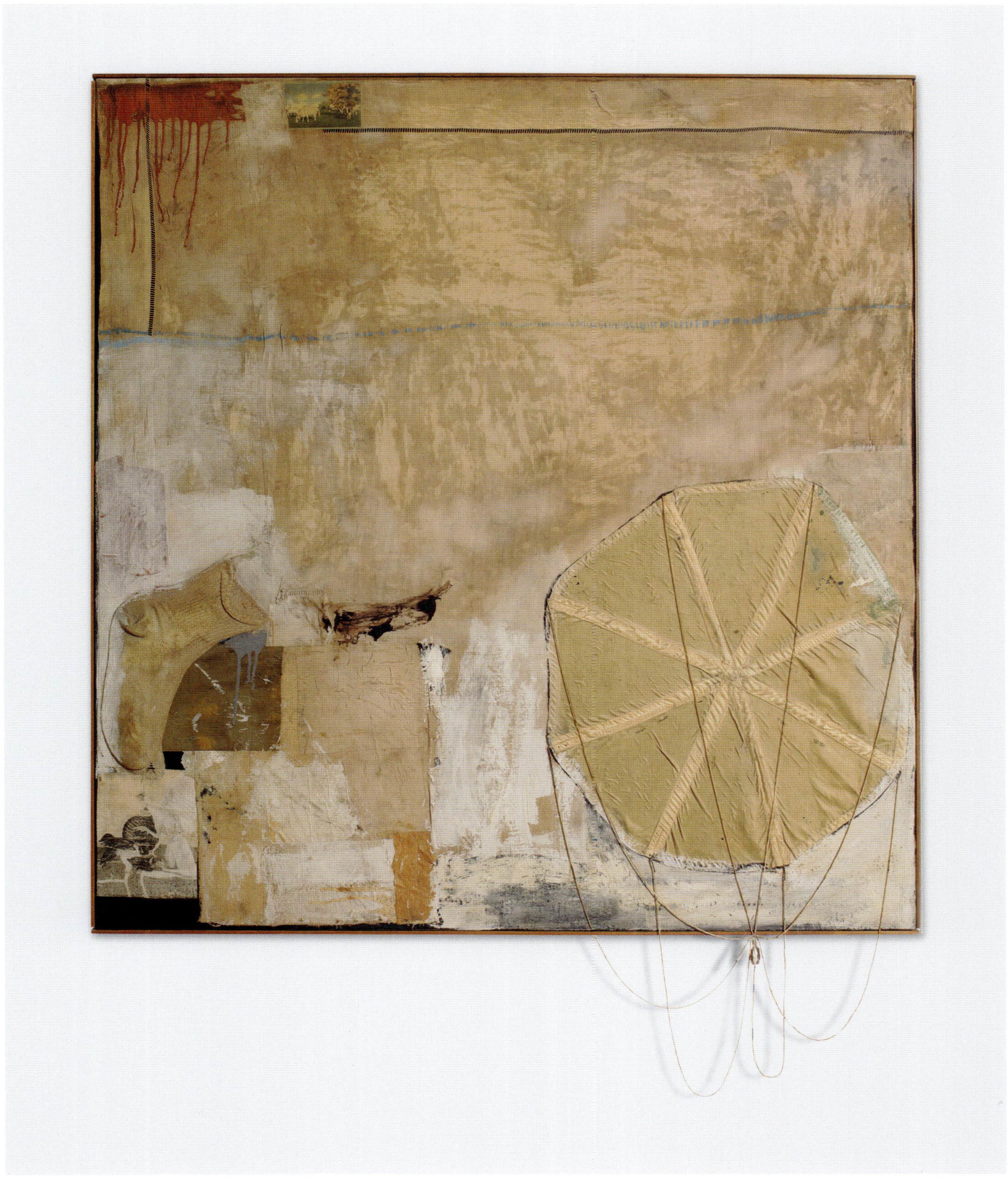

Untitled, ca. 1955
Combine: oil, house paint, paper, fabric, and printed reproductions, with sock and parachute on canvas
68 × 55 inches (172.7 × 139.7 cm)
The Art Institute of Chicago

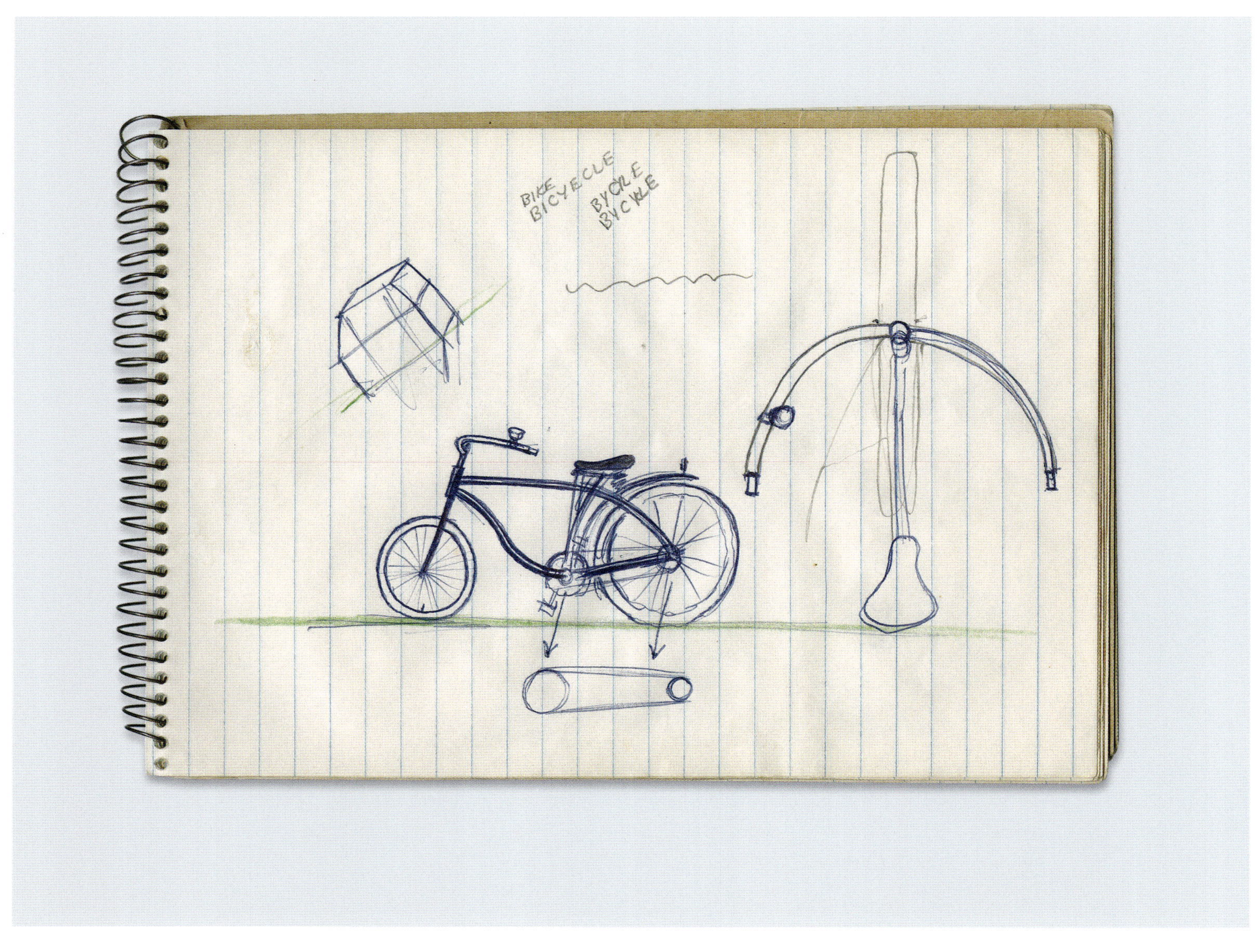

Page from Rauschenberg's blue steno notebook with a sketch of a bicycle, n.d. The motif of the bicycle is prominently featured in his works. Notably, the word *bicycle* is misspelled in this sketch. Rauschenberg contended with dyslexia, a learning disorder that affects reading and writing abilities. He explained, "I spell phoenetically [phonetically], the way things ought to be—with a Southern accent."[5]

works such as *Kitty Hawk* (1974) and *Killdevil Hill* (1975). The titles of these works pay homage to the Wright brothers, owners of a bicycle shop in Dayton, Ohio, who achieved the pioneering feat of powered flight, but not without trial and error. Their aircraft, the 1903 Wright Flyer, was constructed from fabric, wood, wire, and string. With a transmission inspired from a bicycle's chain-and-sprocket, it took its inaugural flight on the sandy dunes of Kill Devil Hills near Kitty Hawk, North Carolina, on December 17, 1903. After three attempts, their last and most successful flight on that day lasted fifty-nine seconds and covered 852 feet—giving birth to the world's first successful piloted heavier-than-air flight.[6]

The lithograph entitled *Kitty Hawk* presents images of bicycles arranged in unexpected orientations, creating the impression of aerobatic flight across the sky. In the lower left corner, beneath a suspended bicycle, a swath of blue resembles a scene of the ocean and horizon that functions as a boundary between terrestrial and celestial realms. The black ink on brown Kraft paper imparts an antique quality to the image, further enhancing its connection to the early twentieth-century invention.

Rauschenberg reused the same imagery in *Killdevil Hill* but presented it in a reconfigured arrangement. The patriotic color scheme of red, white, and blue evokes a tribute to American innovation. Additionally, the inclusion of a Shop-Rite bag, featuring the words "Brand is the Answer," reinforces the thematic exploration of early twentieth-century technology in America and the branding of inventions as a pathway toward modernity. The composition features depictions of a coal mine and a mule, effectively linking the imagery of flight and the bicycle to broader concepts of transportation and cargo conveyance. A central blue patch suggests water and serves as a focal point that anchors the overall composition, while a solitary bicycle, its front wheel rising, indicates a sense of readiness for ascent and recalls the Wright brothers inaugural flight. By positioning the bicycles as he did in both prints, Rauschenberg almost seemed to grant them the power of flight.

Pioneering themes continue in *Test Stone 2 (Booster Study)* (1967), which features depictions of civil and military aviation heroes. Positioned in the upper left corner is Charles Lindbergh, captured prior to his historic 1927 solo transatlantic flight (embarking from New York on May 20, he successfully landed in Paris approximately thirty-three and a half hours later, on May 21). Adjacent to this American icon Rauschenberg created a moving tribute to other heroes of the air: the airmen who served in the

Vietnam War. While Lindbergh received widespread acclaim and ticker-tape parades, participants in the war in Vietnam were rarely celebrated. The work includes the image of a flag-draped casket being unloaded from an Air Force aircraft. A spherical object resembling a peach appears above the scene—perhaps an allusion to the children's novel *James and the Giant Peach*, whose author, Roald Dahl, served as a fighter pilot and acting wing commander in the Royal Air Force during World War II. In the book, a colossal peach, fastened by string and aided by birds, becomes the means for a young boy to embark on a transformative journey.

Flying Bananas

The helicopter emerged as a symbol in Rauschenberg's work in 1963—specifically, the Army H-21 Shawnee helicopter, colloquially known as the "Flying Banana" due to its elongated shape. The artist sourced the image from a *Life* magazine article titled "We Wade Deeper into Jungle War," published on January 25, 1963, which documents the initial stages of US involvement in Vietnam.[7] The photographs featured in the article were captured by the British photojournalist Larry Burrows, who covered the Vietnam War for nine years and tragically lost his life while covering the conflict in 1971. The *Life* article marked the first time the Vietnam War was depicted using color film, enhancing the immediacy and impact of the imagery. The photographs starkly portray the realities of war, including scenes of Vietnamese prisoners with ropes around their necks and deceased individuals in the jungle and surrounding swamps. At that juncture, US involvement in Vietnam was characterized primarily by the utilization of aircraft, machinery, and advisers. The article presents an unembellished view of the situation: "The fighting in South Vietnam, where each hour deepens the US commitment, is many things. It is the whirl of helicopter blades in the steaming air; it is the stench of cloying jungle mud, teeming with parasitic infestation; it is monotony punctuated by songs of insects; it is the closeness of an invisible enemy who strikes out of green ambush with the suddenness of crackling death."[8]

The art historian Roni Feinstein has discerned an antiwar message in Rauschenberg's *Silkscreen Paintings*, *Kite* and *Archive* (both 1963), based on his personal sentiments about war and his use of the image of the helicopter from *Life*.[9] A bald eagle sits at the top of *Kite* overlooking a patch of light blue sky. Below it, a helicopter hovers above a black-and-white image of a

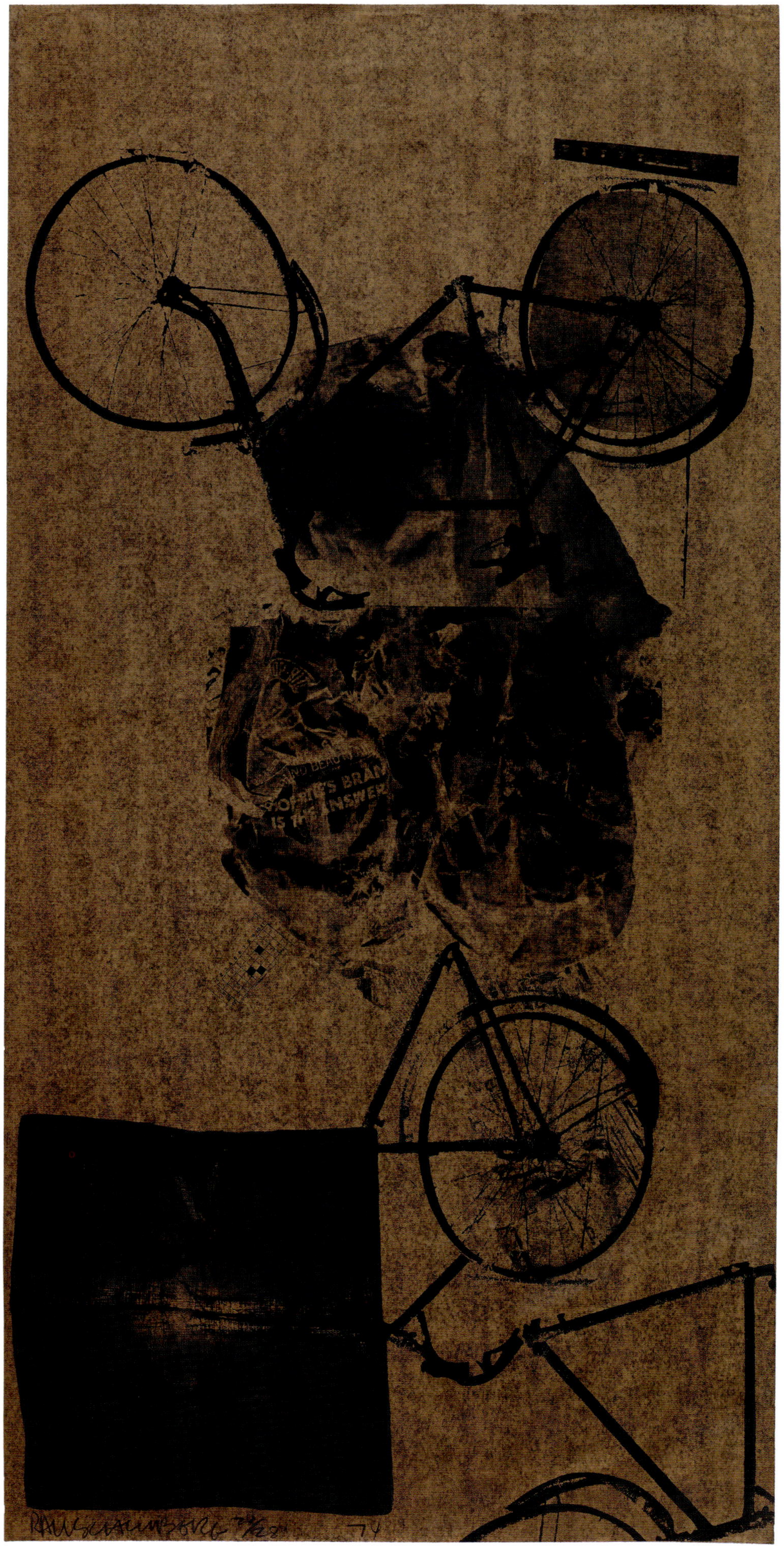

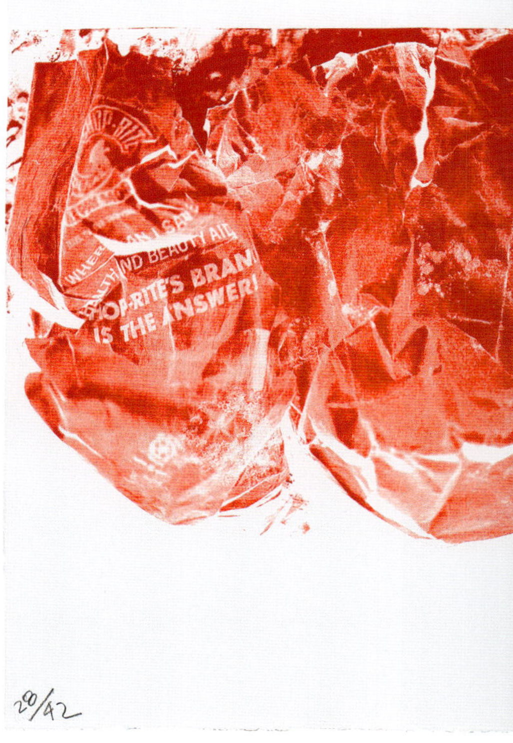

Kitty Hawk, 1974
Lithograph on Kraft brown wrapping paper,
edition 26/28
79 × 40 inches (200.7 × 101.6 cm)
The Museum of Fine Arts, Houston

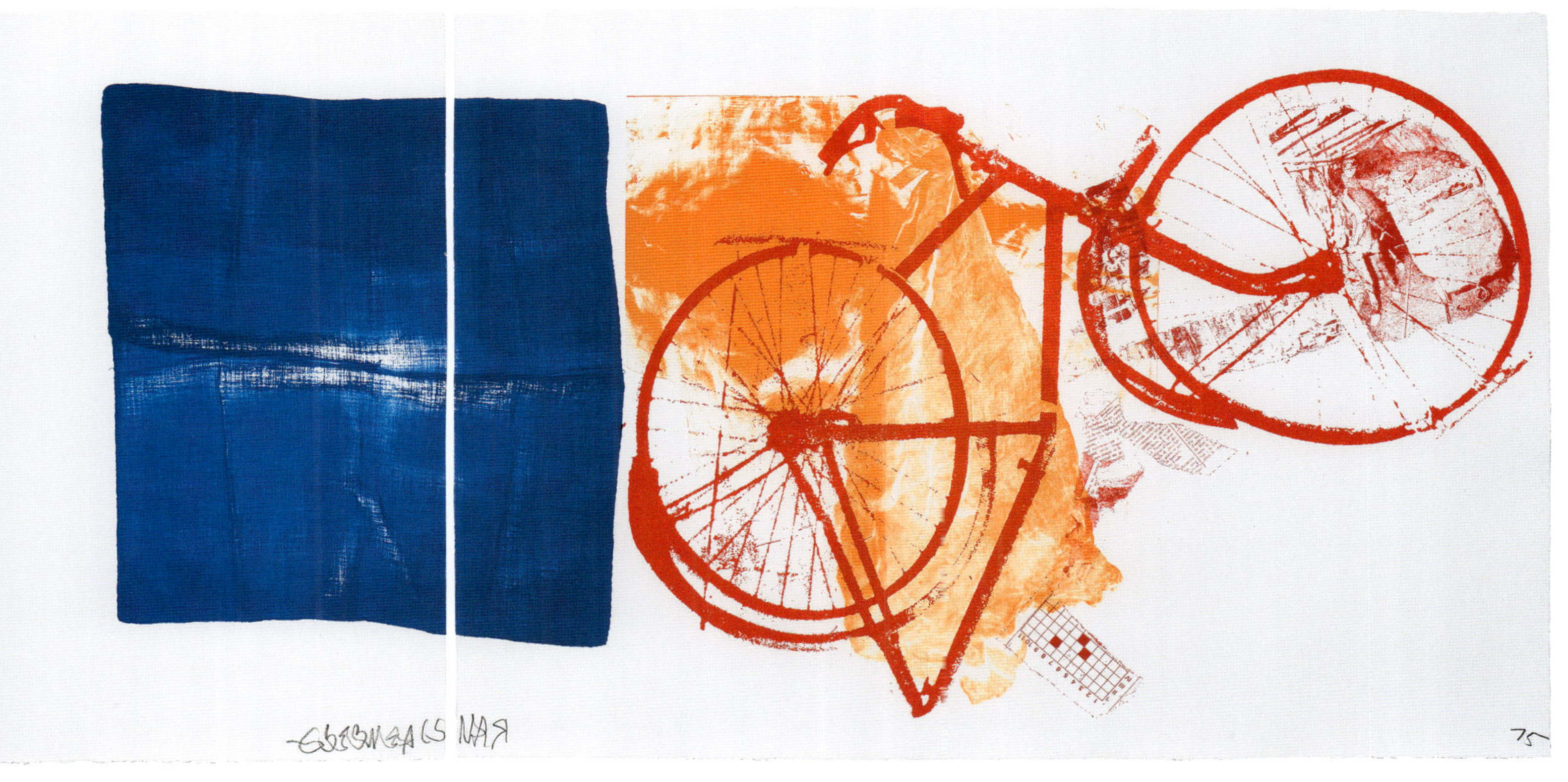

Killdevil Hill, 1975
Lithograph on two sheets of paper,
edition 28/42
26⅞ × 80¼ inches (68.4 × 203.7 cm)
The Museum of Fine Arts, Houston

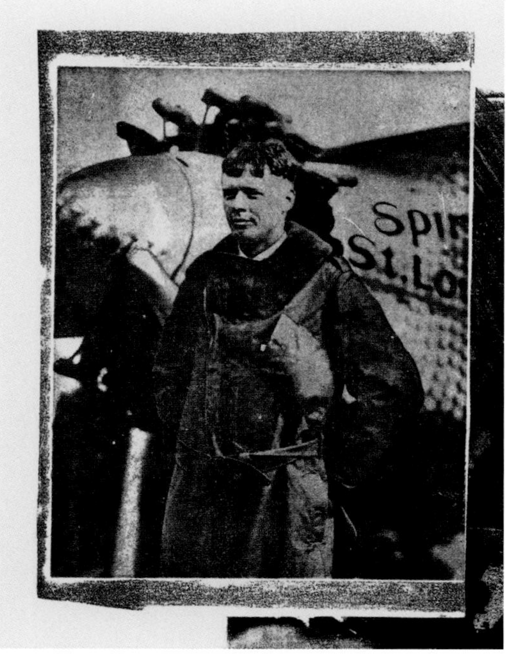

In this detail from *Test Stone 2 (Booster Study)* (1967), Lindbergh is shown standing in front of the *Spirit of St. Louis* in San Diego in 1927.

parade with uniformed men waving American flags. Feinstein draws attention to the national symbols of the eagle and the flag and contrasts them with an image of beachgoers under umbrellas, conveying a sense of leisure, at the right edge of the painting. This juxtaposition, says Feinstein, "argues against American Imperialism and militarism" and critiques "unthinking patriotism and unconcerned pleasure-seeking."[10]

Archive uses the same image of the helicopter twice, once flying straight and level and once turned on its side. Here, the photograph of the parade appears in color, and the beach scene is multiplied by four. The eagle is replaced with a red circle, and the entire right side of the *Silkscreen Painting* is devoted to an aircraft instrument panel. A photograph of the fence protecting Jean-Antoine Houdon's statue of George Washington in the Virginia State Capitol appears upside down, which Feinstein likens to the pointed tips of spears prodding the beachgoers out of their selfish complacency.[11]

While this analysis must be considered, it's also important to remember Robert Mattison's interpretation of umbrellas as signifiers of flight—how umbrellas are parachute-like and are used as open canopies as if "floating in the air."[12] Instead of focusing on umbrellas for beachgoers, we see Rauschenberg's use of them in these works combined with other flight imagery, such as helicopters, an instrument panel, and an eagle, as well as American flags. Perhaps we can see these elements as emblems of American air power, honoring the duty, courage, and the complexities of aerial combat and possibly even empathy for the soldiers and pilots engaged in the Vietnam conflict.

In *Tracer* (1963) the H-21 helicopter and the bald eagle appear again in a color field of light blue, as if in the sky. Two helicopters are placed side by side at the top of the painting, as if to mirror each other. Rauschenberg doubled down on the mirroring with an image of *Venus in Front of a Mirror* (ca. 1614–15) by Peter Paul Rubens. Just below, two caged birds mirror the goddess's voluptuous buttocks. Also doubled in this silkscreen painting is a sketch of a cube. (We'll address this significant "box" detail in a moment.) By mixing an Old Master with new technology, perhaps Rauschenberg was reflecting on his role as an artist enamored with flight.

Dry Cell (1963) is an interactive sculpture that combines a microphone and a toy motor within a structure formed by a folding metal camp stool. These elements are tied to a piece of Plexiglas on which an image of the H-21 Shawnee helicopter has been silk-screened. The work is an example Rauschenberg's interest in technology and was a collaborative effort with engineers Per Biorn and Harold Hodges from Bell Labs, who contributed their expertise to the sound-activated rotor. The connection between the helicopter image and the device lies in its interactivity: when a person speaks into the microphone, the sound activates the toy motor, causing a small propeller to spin around.[13] From an aeronautical perspective, the metal frame resembles the bracing found between the wings of biplanes. In addition to the recurring theme of helicopters, *Tracer* and *Dry Cell* both display a box or cube. In *Dry Cell*, the helicopter is integrated within the "box" of a metal folding camp stool, whereas in *Tracer*, a cube is rendered beneath the helicopters, with an arrow oriented upward toward the airborne objects. Additionally, a segment of a box flies off the right-hand edge of the canvas.

Roni Feinstein suggests these "space boxes" reflect the influence of Rauschenberg's former teacher at Black Mountain College Josef Albers, specifically his *Homage to the Square* paintings (1950–79) and similar geometric "space" squares in *Pair D* (1958).[14] Robert Mattison says the cubes are akin to the Necker cube, an optical illusion developed by the Swiss crystallographer Louis Albert Necker (1786–1861) that "floats magically in space like a vessel from another planet."[15] Rosalind Krauss, meanwhile, calls the floating-box motif a "volumetric cube signal" that she relates to the perspective approaches of Renaissance artists such as Leon Battista Alberti and Piero della Francesca, who viewed these forms as having sides that serve as absolute limits.[16]

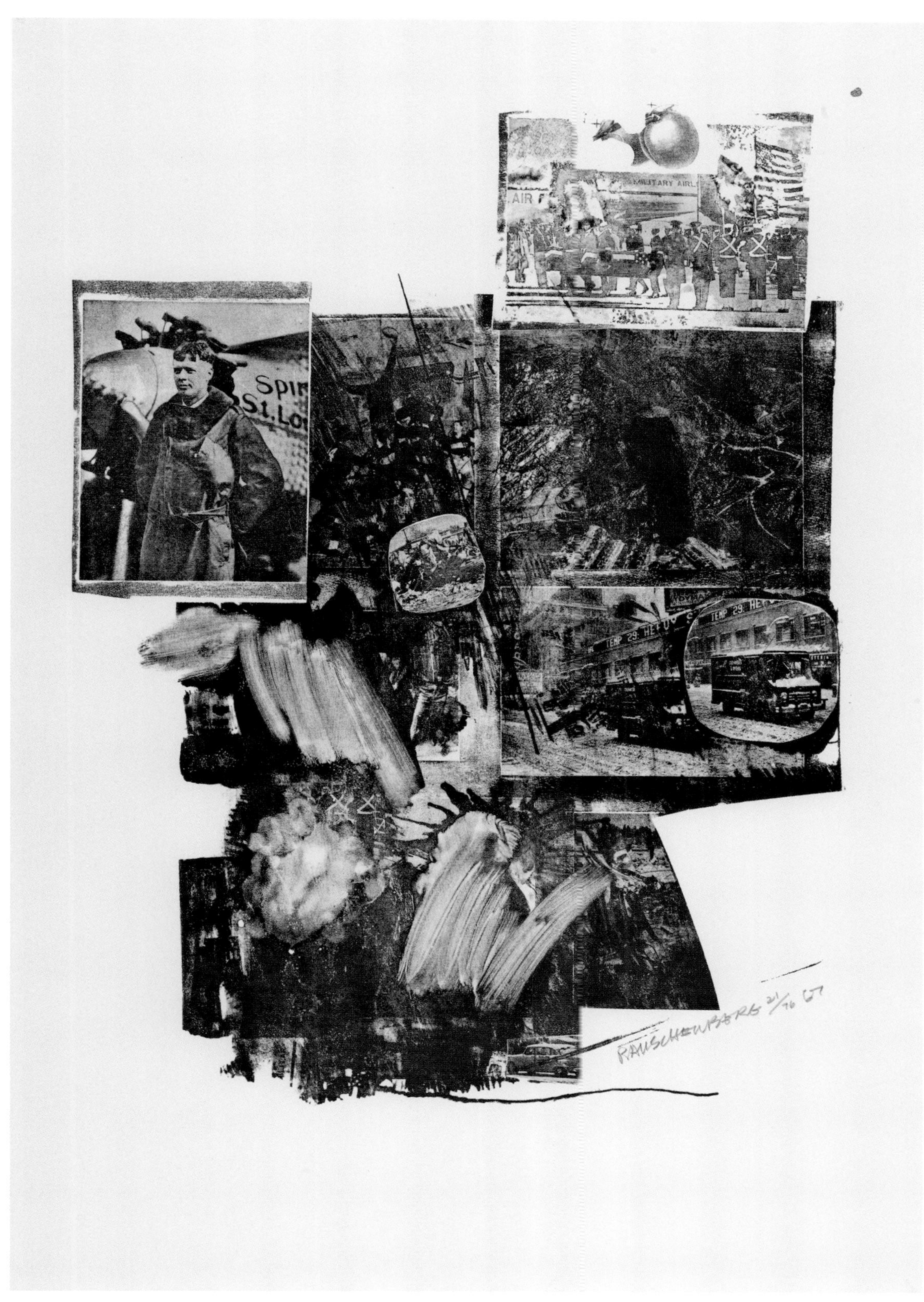

Test Stone 2 (Booster Study), 1967
Lithograph on paper
41 × 30 inches (104.1 × 76.2 cm)
Smithsonian American Art Museum

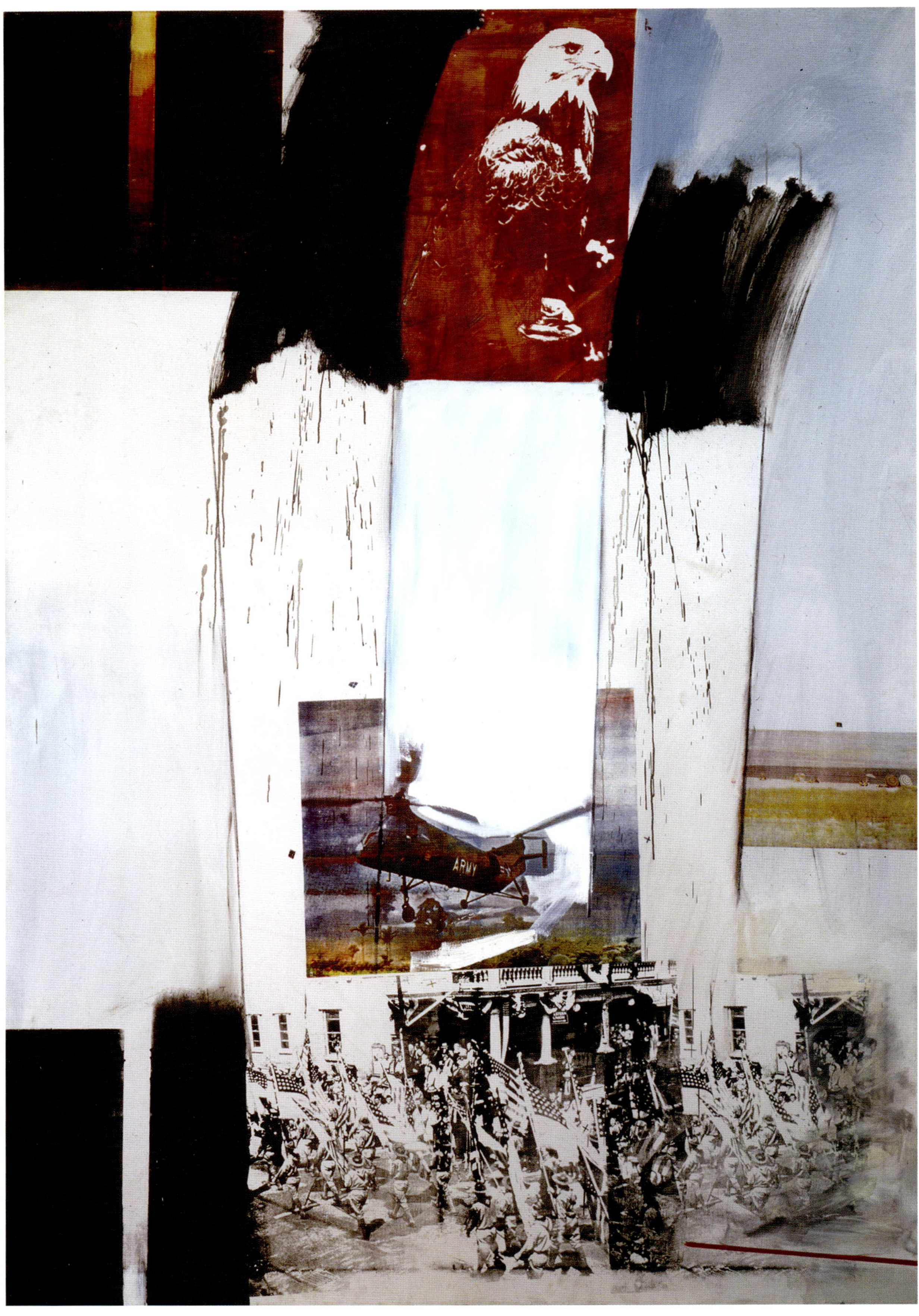

Kite, 1963
Oil and silkscreen ink on canvas
84 × 60 inches (213.4 × 152.4 cm)
The Sonnabend Collection Foundation

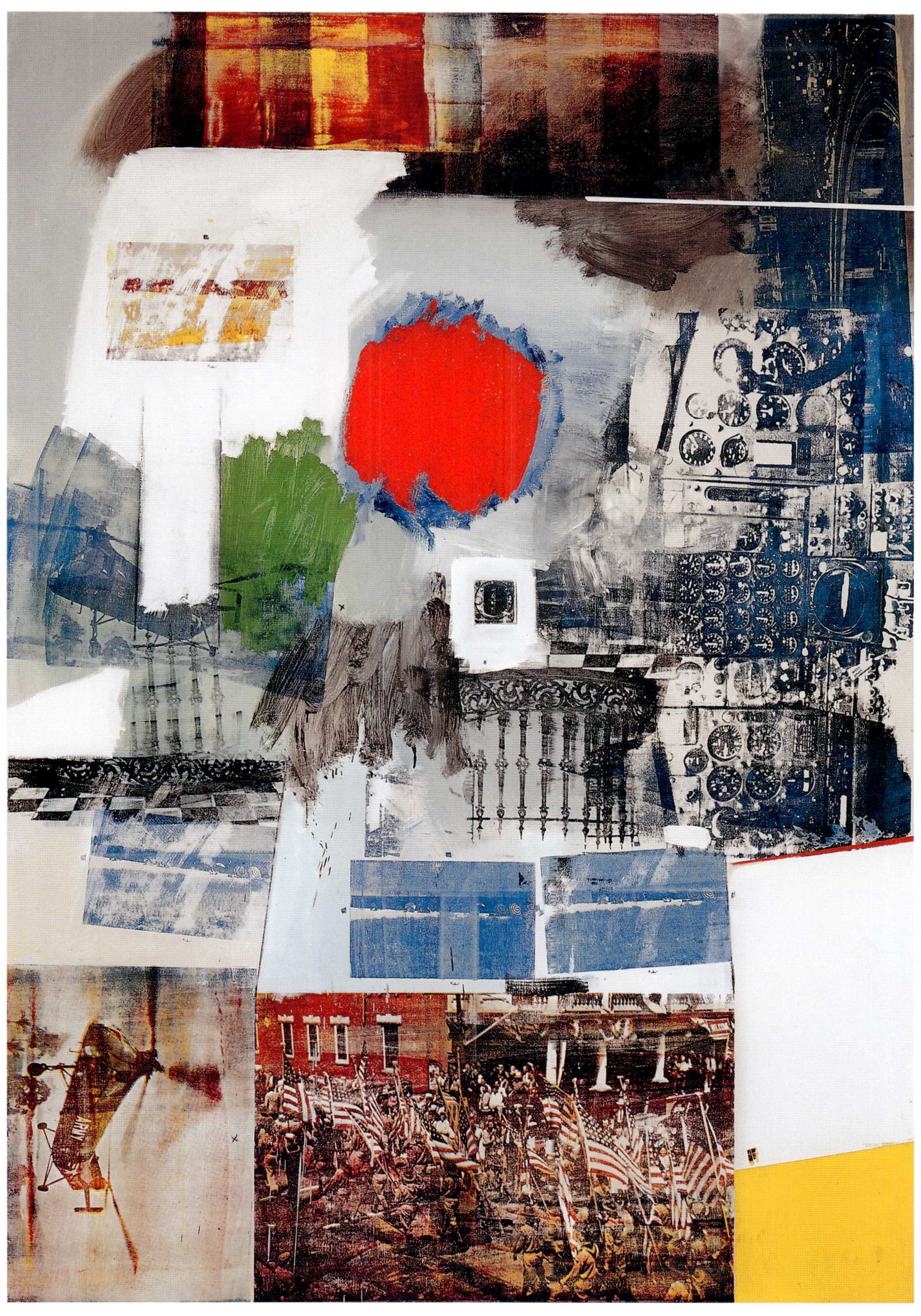

Archive, 1963
Oil and silkscreen ink on canvas
83⅞ × 60 inches (213 × 152.4 cm)
Collection of the Robert and Jane Meyerhoff Modern Art Foundation

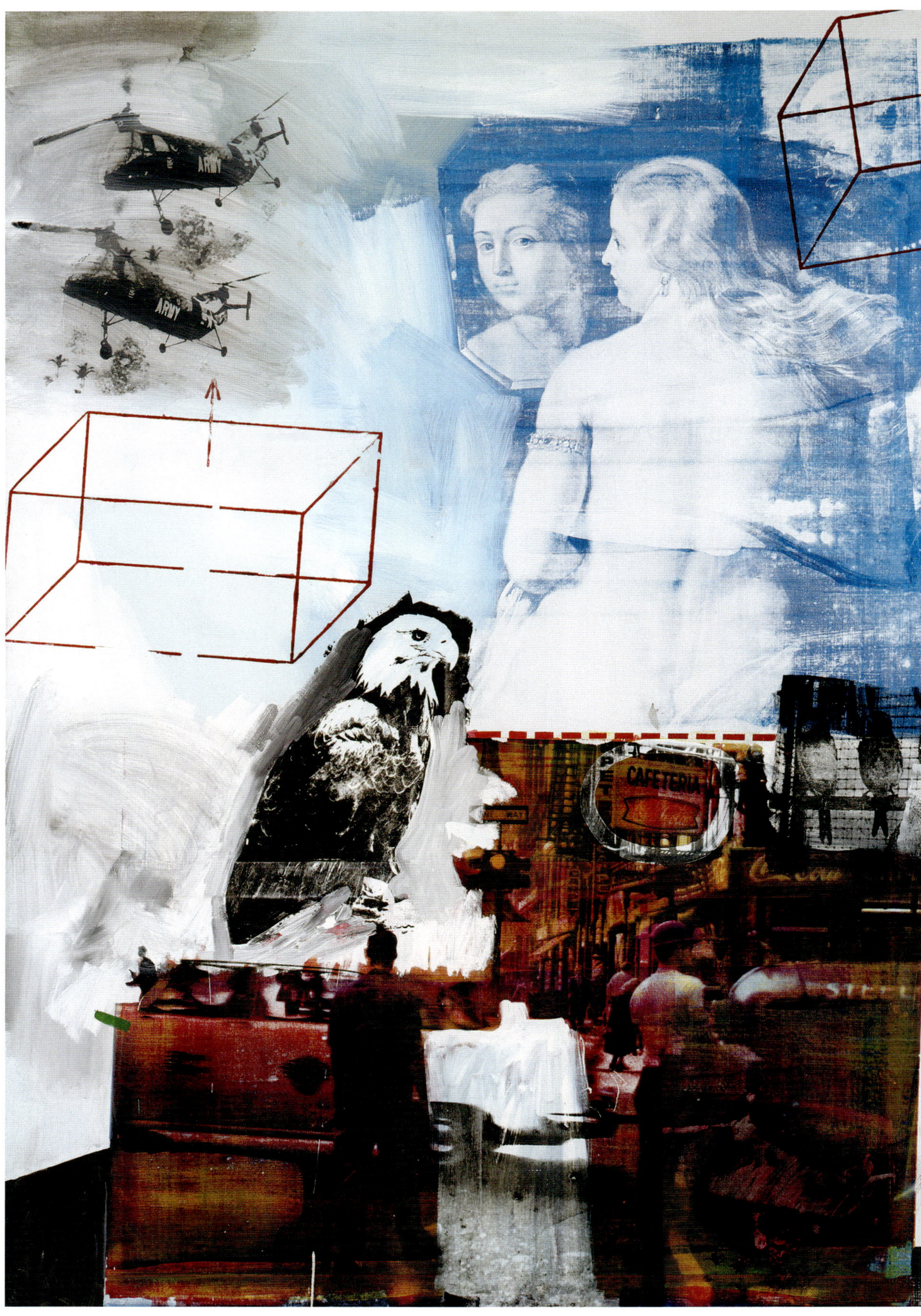

Tracer, 1963
Oil and silkscreen on canvas
84⅛ × 60 inches (213.7 × 152.4 cm)
The Nelson-Atkins Museum of Art

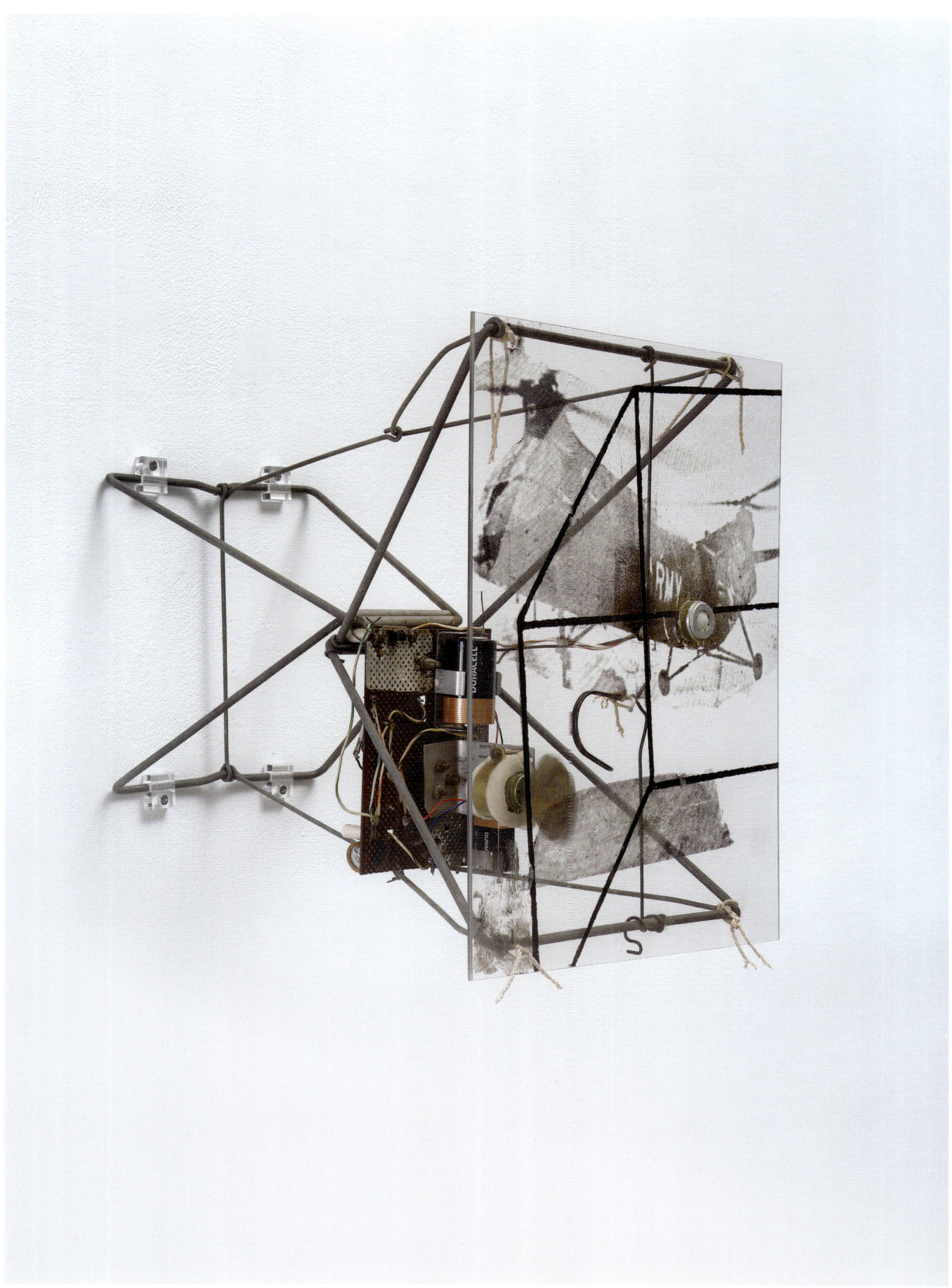

Dry Cell, 1963
Silkscreen ink and oil on Plexiglas, with metal coat hanger, wire, string, sound
transmitter, circuit board, and battery-powered motor on metal folding camp stool
15 × 12 × 15⅜ inches (38.1 × 30.5 × 39.1 cm)
Robert Rauschenberg Foundation

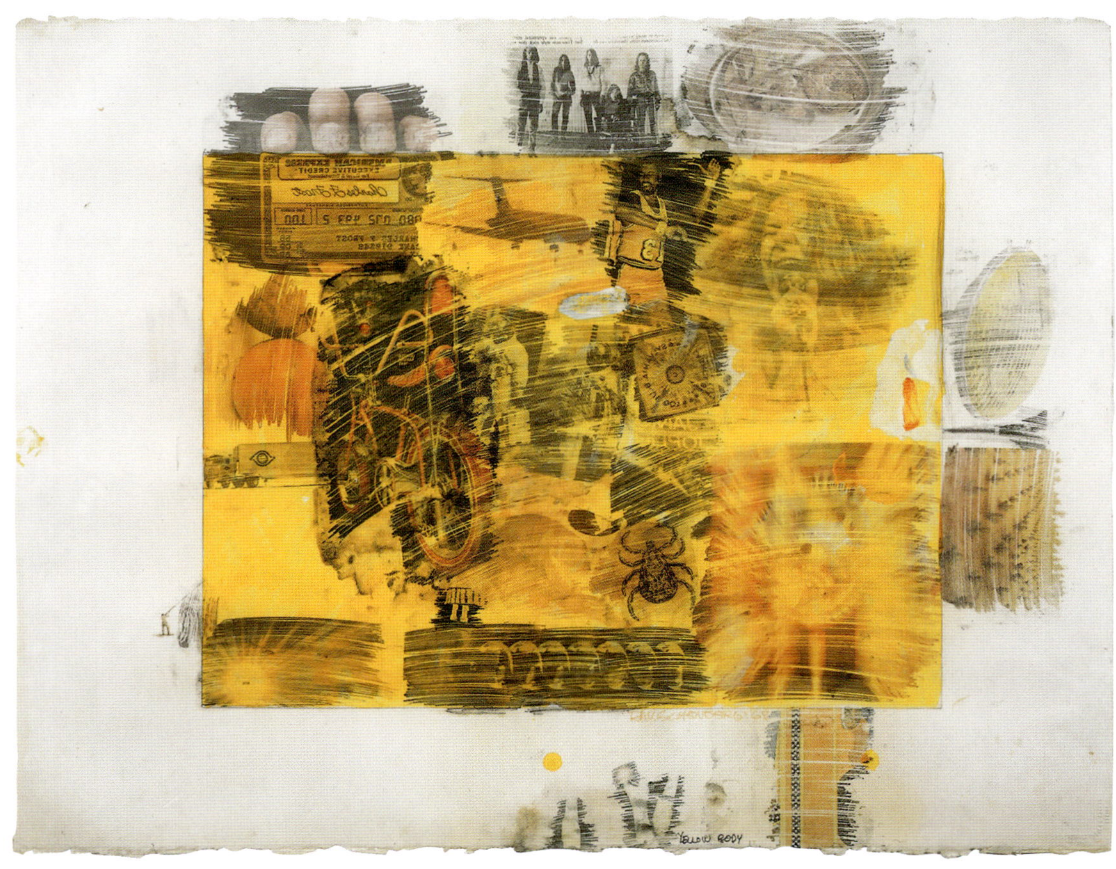

Yellow Body, 1969
Solvent transfer on paper with graphite, watercolor, gouache, and wash on paper
22½ × 30 inches (57.2 × 76.2 cm)
Solomon R. Guggenheim Museum, New York

A further—and, in the present discussion, more relevant—explanation of the boxes can be found in the aerobatic box: an area of airspace in which aerobatic competitions take place. It is a cube measuring 1,000 meters (3,281 feet) on each side, with a ceiling of 3,500 feet. This airspace serves as a perimeter within which a pilot is evaluated on their skill to remain within established boundaries while ensuring safety for spectators on the ground.[17] In Rauschenberg's *Autobiography* (1968), two-thirds of the print is dedicated to themes of air and space, and in the middle panel a box is superimposed over the spiraling account of Rauschenberg's life. An arrow points down from that box toward the photograph of the artist performing in *Pelican* (1963). In this light, the boxes in Rauschenberg's art can be seen as a metaphor for the airspace (life, art) he travels through and the various dimensions of flight he explores.

Jet-setting

In the *Currents* project (1970), Rauschenberg combined collage and screenprinting techniques using only black-and-white images and text sourced from US newspapers. One iteration showcases all thirty-six artworks as a comprehensive fifty-four-foot print. Contemporary news on commercial aviation is prominently featured in at least two of the screen prints. In *Features (from Currents) 73,* excerpts from newspapers are arranged like the body of an airplane: a fuselage in the center bounded by wings. In bold capital letters, the headline on the right wing reads, "Arabs Boast: We Bombed Jet, 47 Die in Israel-Bound Plane," referring to the February 21, 1970, bombing of Swissair Flight 330 from Zurich to Tel Aviv.[18] Below this, another headline—"Nixon Adds Toxins to Banned Weapons"—is placed next to the cropped image of a missile. The layout of the text here is reminiscent of the calligrams of the French writer and poet Guillaume Apollinaire, who arranged typeset letters and words to create a form of free verse with layered meanings.[19] Rauschenberg's spatial awareness and arrangement of the newspaper headlines conjures the visual poetry in Apollinaire's *Calligrammes: Poems of Peace and War* (1918), where words are shaped into objects. Here, Rauschenberg created an airplane and commented on commercial aviation as an aspect of terrorism and war.

The main image in *Features (from Currents) 63* is a cutaway illustration of a Boeing 747, a commercial jet that had recently been added to TWA's fleet of aircraft. Alongside it is a clipping concerning the phases of the Sun and the Moon and a feature story about Apollo 8 astronaut Frank Borman. Borman was the first astronaut to circumnavigate the Moon, and the feature discusses his plans to leave NASA and join a venture headed by the Texas businessman Ross Perot, who, as explained in the article, "recently attempted without success to deliver by chartered aircraft Christmas packages to the American prisoners held in North Vietnam." Works in the *Currents* series address the diverse social and political implications of commercial air travel.

The solvent-transfer drawing *Yellow Body* (1969) features a yellow-and-black color scheme with images that are unmistakably associated with flight. These include astronauts from the early Apollo program, a bicycle (always a symbol for flight for Rauschenberg), and a DC-9 aircraft designed for short-to-medium range commercial travel. The artwork also includes two images of Janis Joplin—who, like Rauschenberg, was originally from Port Arthur, Texas, and had little good to say about it. Calvin Tomkins recounts Rauschenberg receiving a handwritten note from the singer that said, "We're the only two people who ever got out of Port Arthur, Texas."[20] After this initial connection, Rauschenberg and Joplin became good friends whose flight from their creatively repressive hometown represented the ultimate escape. This combination of elements, notably the bicycle outfitted with a banana seat, recalls the song "Yellow Bird," which was popular in the late 1950s and 1960s and whose lyrics suggest unattainable romance and escapism.[21]

The song also connects to the title *Yellow Body* through the imagery of the yellow main section, or body, of the DC-9 and the metaphorical relationship between airplanes and birds. Rauschenberg was a frequent flyer, traveling to international destinations throughout his career. Handwritten notes on a ticket envelope from a July 1988 flight on Continental Airlines into Newark, New Jersey, reveal his mindset during the journey. He calls himself a "Cloud Correspondent," suggesting a role of observing from above, and writes, "It isn't important to think love can only be understood by lon[e]liness"— a possible reflection on the experiences of solo travel and a sentiment that again echoes the song "Yellow Bird."[22] As a self-proclaimed "Cloud Correspondent" and admirer of clouds, Rauschenberg named one of his dogs "Cloud." Furthermore, he established a company dedicated to managing the logistics of ROCI, which he aptly titled "Cloud Management."[23]

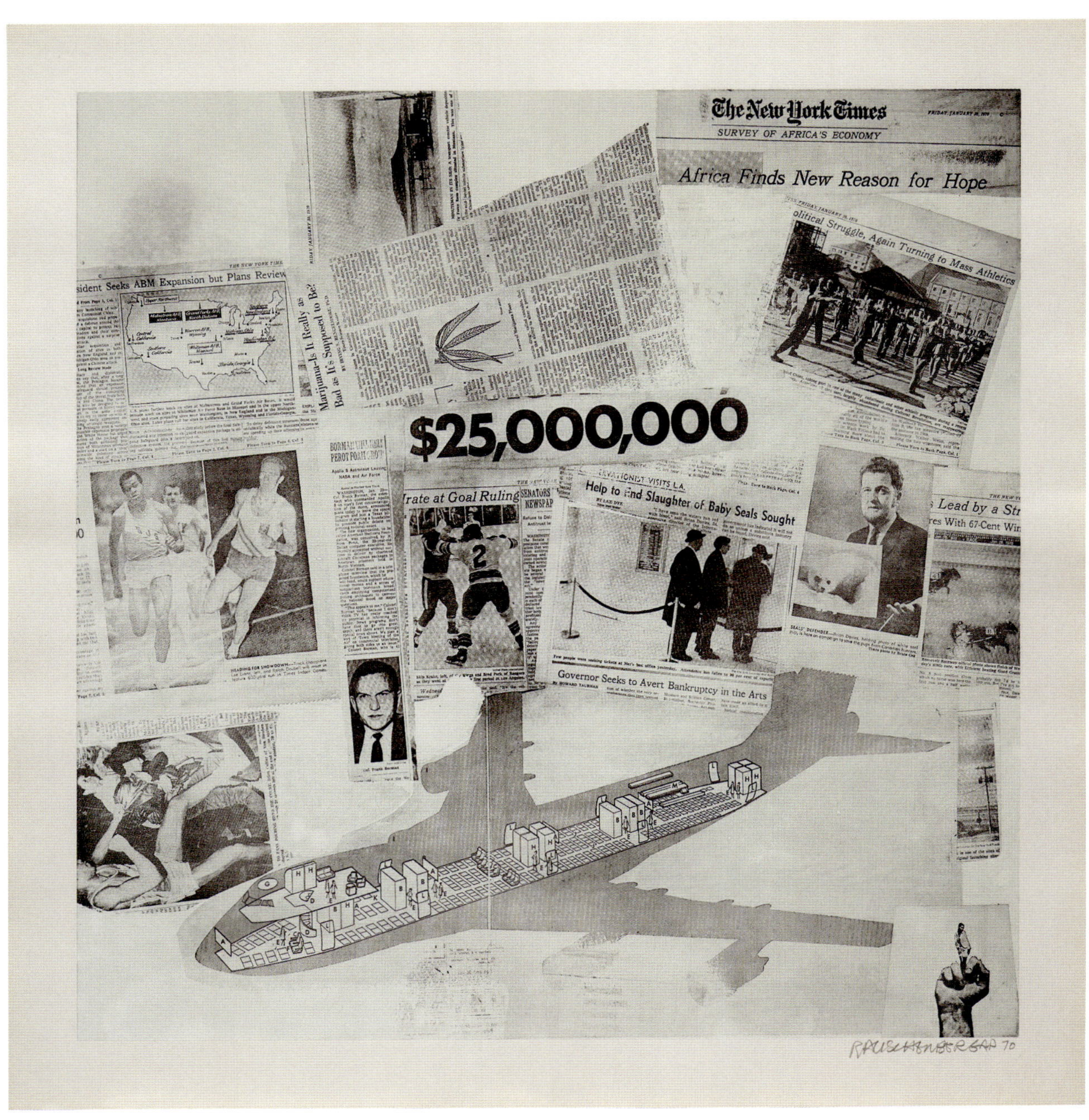

Features (from Currents) 63, 1970
Screenprint
40 × 40 inches (101.6 × 101.6 cm)
Robert Rauschenberg Foundation

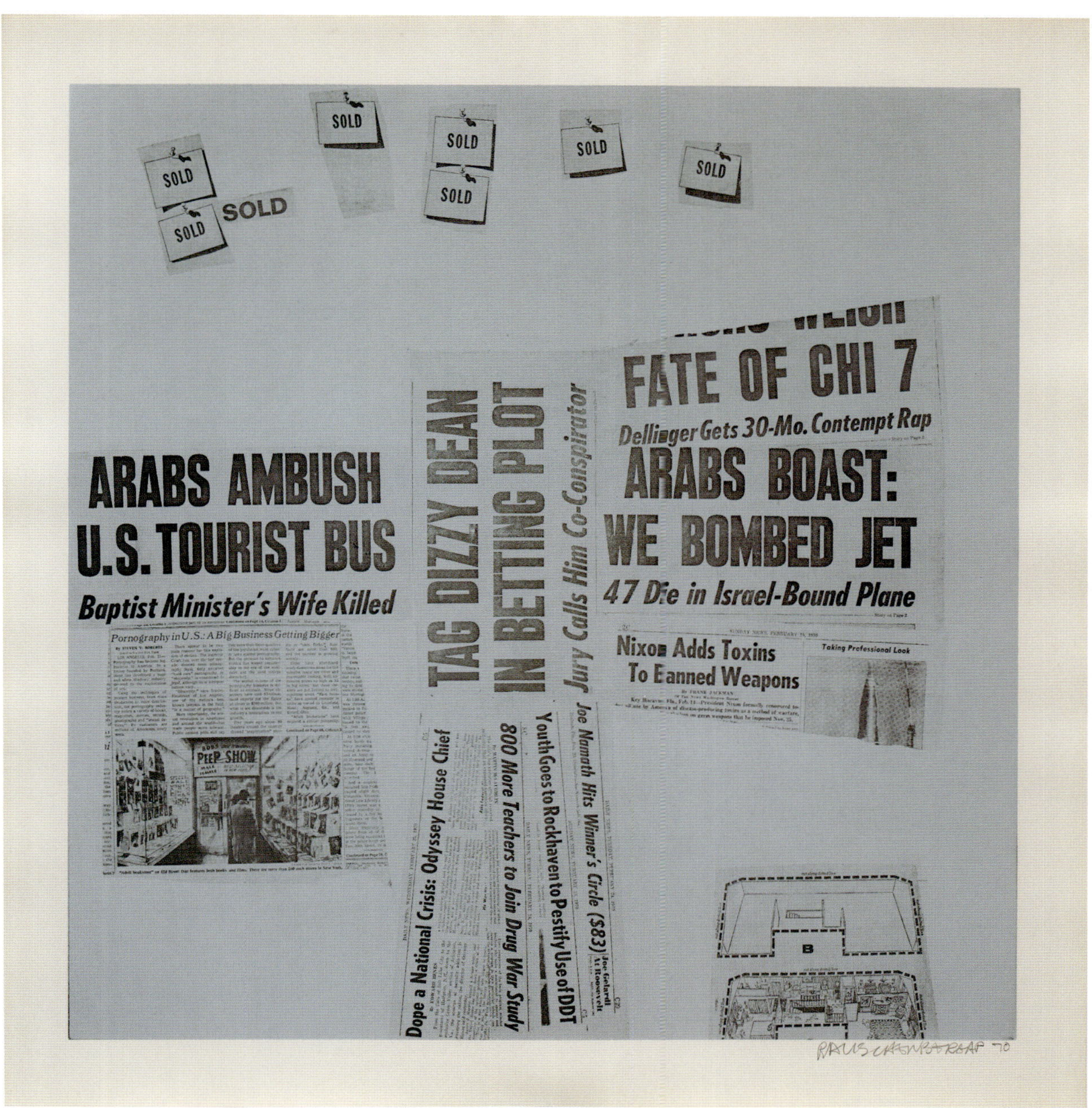

Features (from Currents) 73, 1970
Screenprint
40 × 40 inches (101.6 × 101.6 cm)
Robert Rauschenberg Foundation

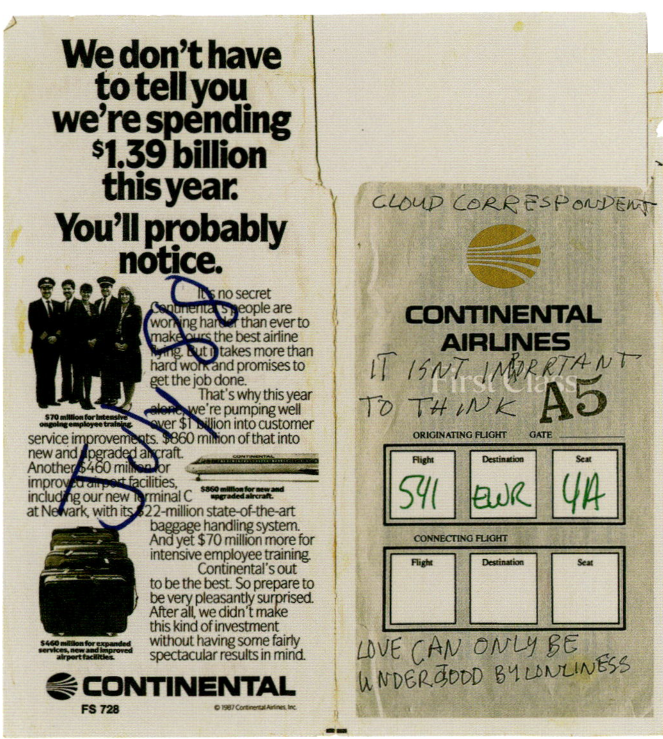

Clouded Visions

Rauschenberg considered gravity-free flight environments in an array of artworks depicting clouds and atmospheric conditions. *Patrician Barnacle (Scale)* (1981) takes the form of an inverted V-shaped box propped up by a wooden stepladder, which creates a top-heavy form. One side of the box features solvent-transferred photos of flowers, horses, and an airplane between dual images of smoke pouring from an industrial site that resembles cloud formations. Behind the stepladder is an image of the airplane ascending from the industrial plume. The ladder symbolizes a pathway to the upper half of the box, representing an opportunity for ascent and a connection to the celestial realm, illustrated by the presence of horses in the clouds and associations with their mythological counterpart, Pegasus. The other side of the box presents a more somber narrative, with images of men on ladders engaging in highwall mining. It also includes representations of several parachute jumpers grasping one another as they descend from the sky. This combination of imagery evokes themes of striving for new heights, spiritual ascension, and the intricate connections between the terrestrial and celestial realms.[24]

The sculpture *Sor Aqua (Venetian)* (1973) consists of a tangle of corrugated metal wrapped around a length of wood

that is suspended above a water-filled bathtub; a rope tethered to a glass jug connects the two elements. The work recalls the time Rauschenberg made history as one of the few Americans to win the Golden Lion (then referred to as the International Grand Prize for Painting) at the 1964 Venice Biennale and had to transport his artworks by barge through the city's canals. In this sense, the bathtub represents the barge, and the metal above represents the grandeur of the Venetian architecture seemingly floating on water. Moreover, the title *Sor Aqua* suggests the image of water soaring like clouds. Curator Pontus Hultén describes the hovering metal as a cloud or thunderstorm, tethered to a floating anchor.[25] The contrast of the bathtub and the metal floating above it also reflects a theme of gravity defiance, akin to planes soaring through the sky despite their weight.

Rauschenberg's interest in clouds is also evident in his black-and-white photograph *Boston, Massachusetts* (1980). The image features the very top of a streetlamp and a large cumulus cloud that dominates the space above it. About two-thirds of the photograph is occupied by an expansive, empty sky, which effectively isolates the cloud, while the streetlamp serves as an anchor to the human world. This juxtaposition emphasizes the separation between technology and nature, illustrating the contrasting realms of human invention and the natural environment. The composition also invites contemplation of the layers of the sky beyond clouds.

The archive of Rauschenberg's source materials from the 1960s provides further evidence of his consuming interest in all things celestial. One image comes from an ad by the Otis Elevator Company that offers a twist on a scientific chart of the layers of the Earth's atmosphere. Above the New York skyline actual layers are labeled "Ionosphere," "Stratosphere," and "Troposphere," with the fictional "Otisphere" placed just above the tallest skyscrapers—a sales pitch illustrating the remarkable heights Otis elevators can reach.[26] This particular ad was featured in his *Revolver VI* (1967), an artwork comprised of round screenprinted Plexiglas disks that rotate on a motorized base. Another Otis ad features the slogan, "The sky's the limit." Rauschenberg's work reveals a complex interaction between human creations and the natural dynamics of flight and the atmosphere, prompting critical reflection on how society navigates the relationship between these two domains.

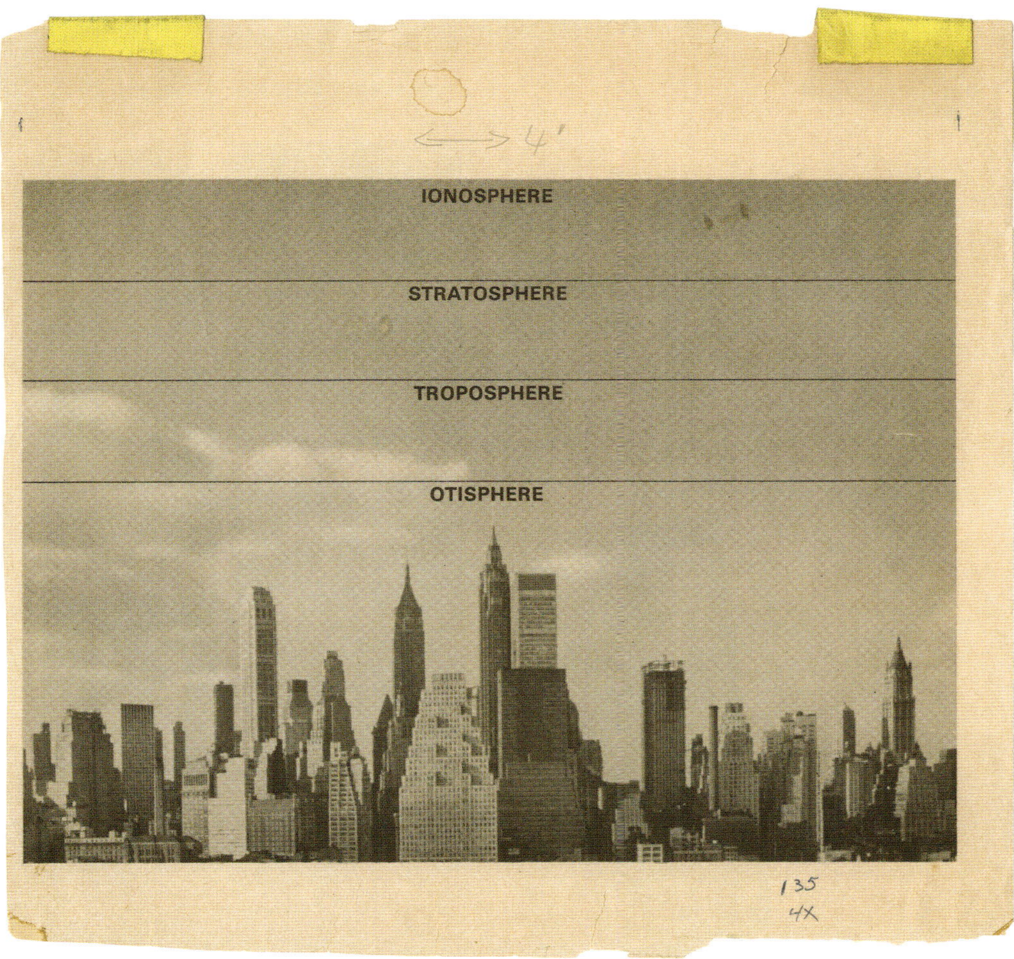

Otis Elevator Company 1960s advertisement illustrating the fictional "Otisphere" level in the atmosphere above the New York City skyline from Rauschenberg's studio files, now part of his archives.

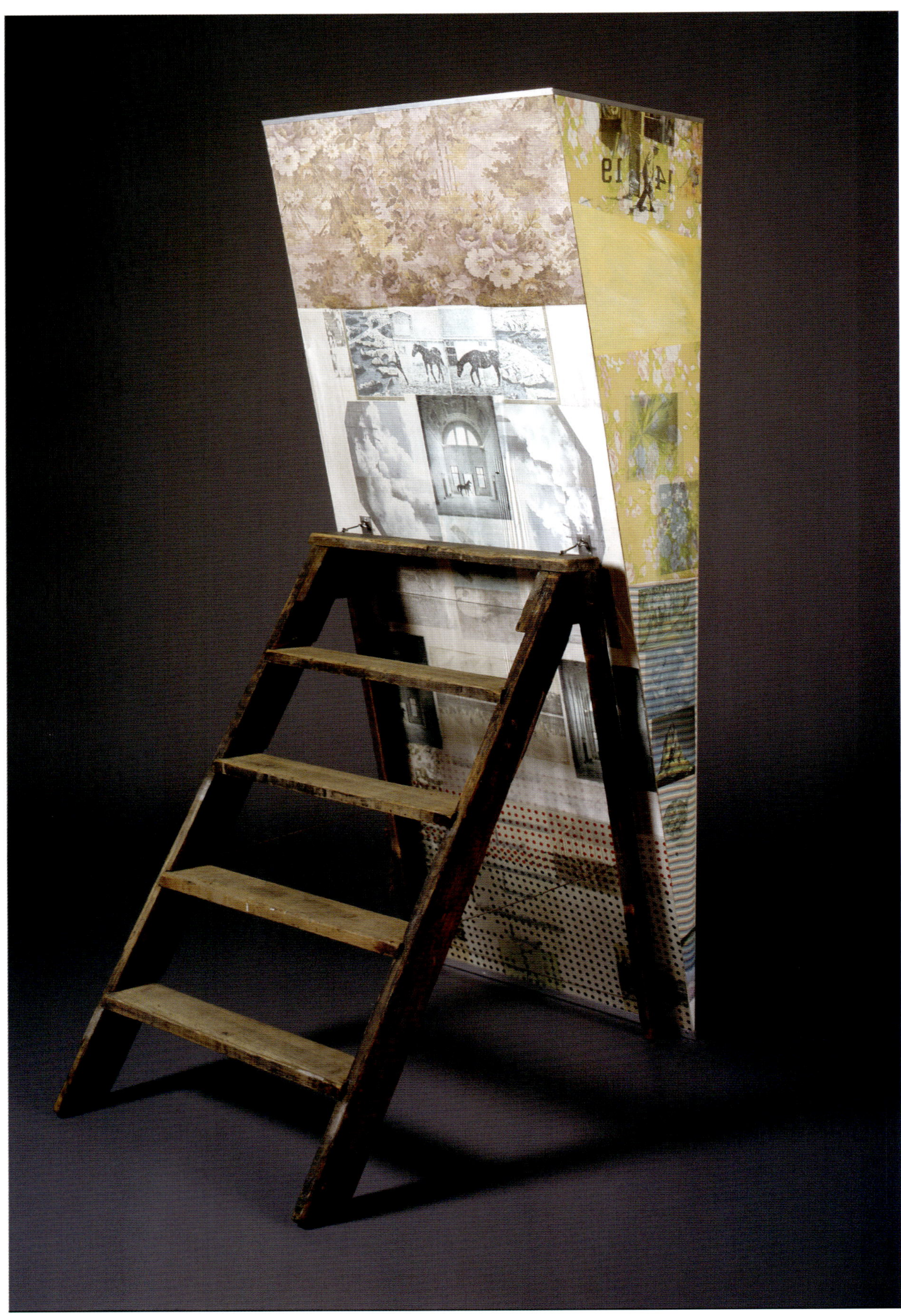

Patrician Barnacle (Scale), 1981
Solvent transfer, acrylic, and fabric on wood with mirrored Plexiglas, safety reflector, and wood stepladder
94 × 37 × 55 inches (238.8 × 94 × 139.7 cm)
Portland Museum of Art

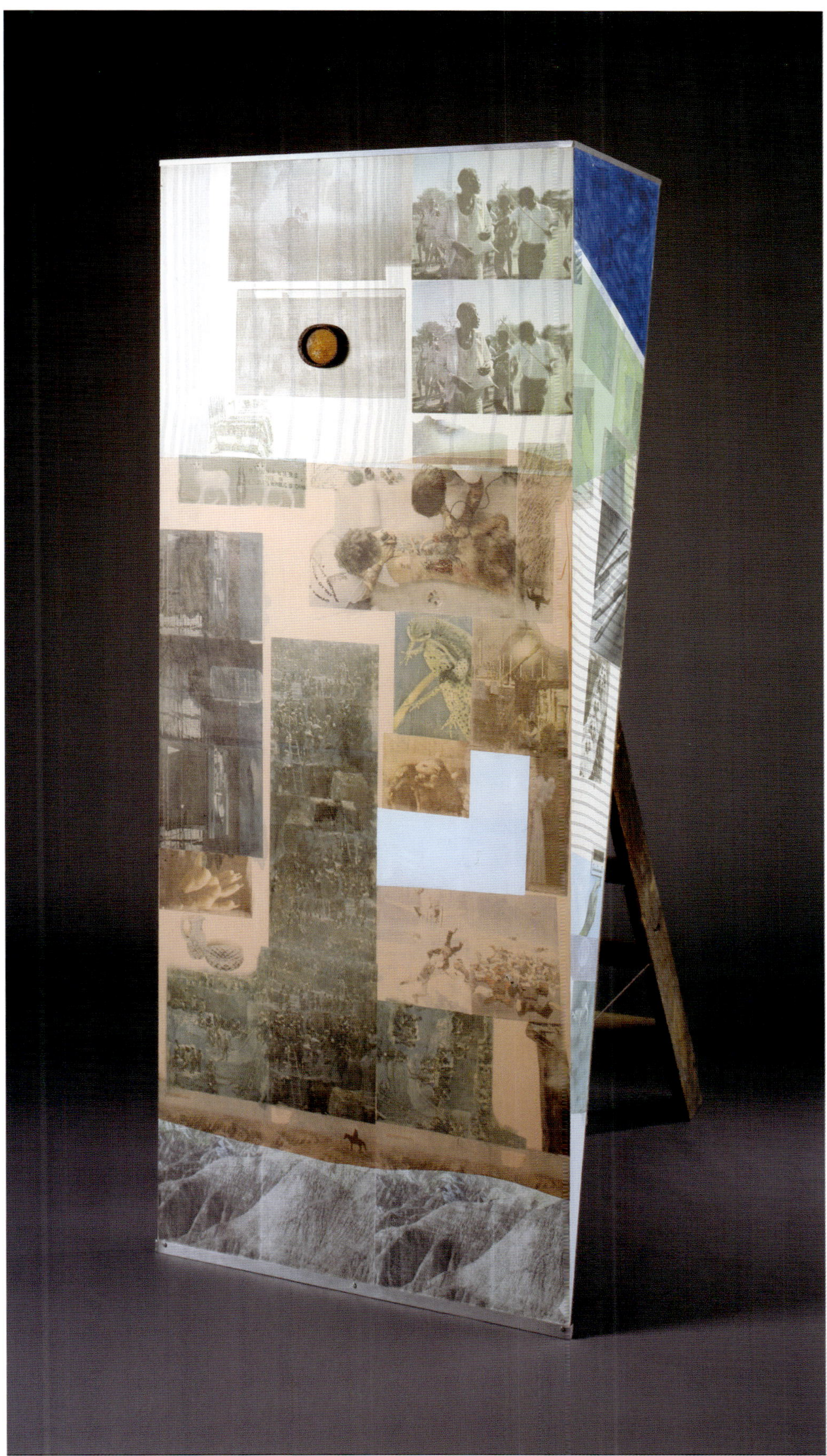

Alternate view of **Patrician Barnacle (Scale)**, 1981

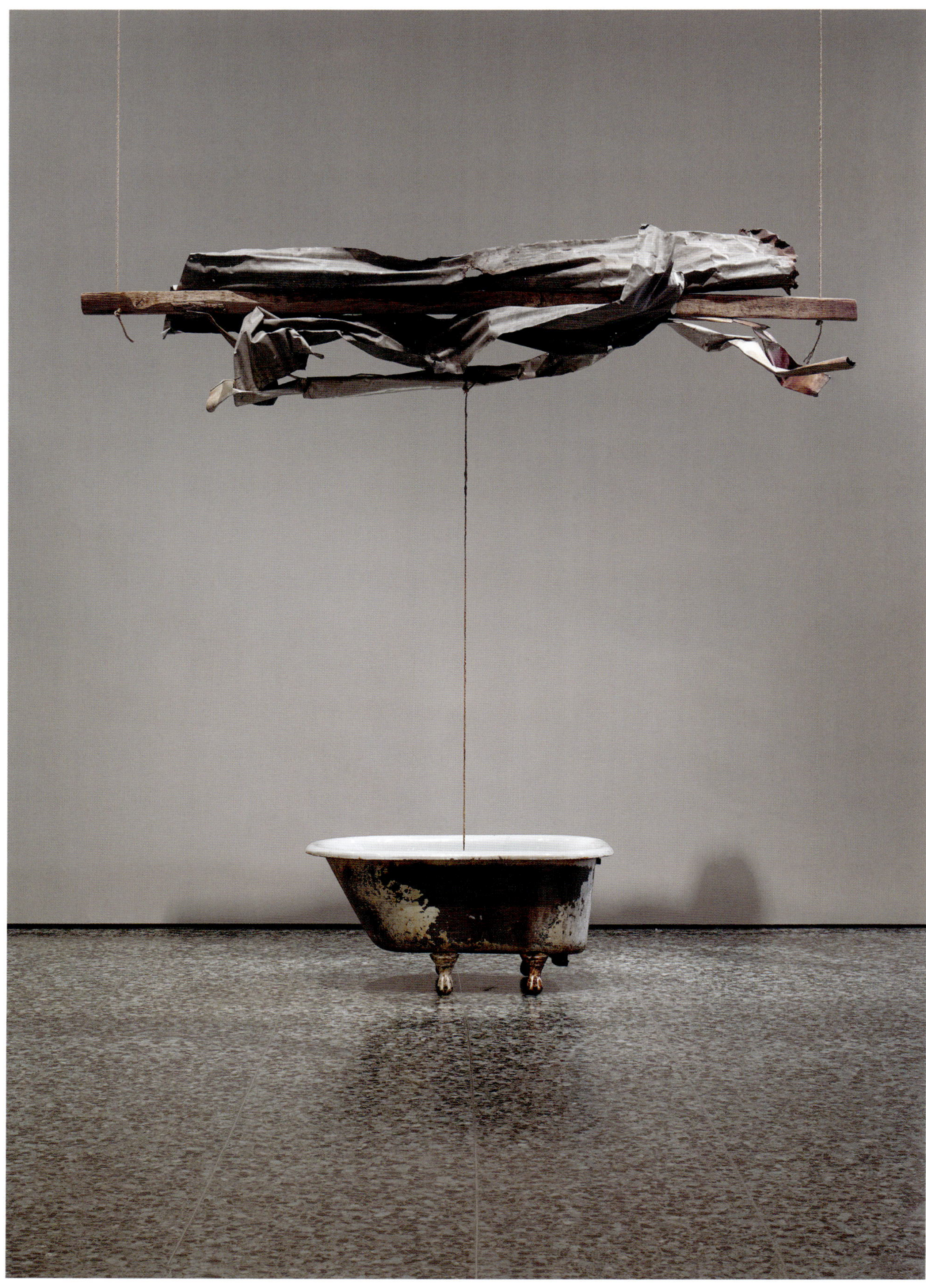

Sor Aqua (Venetian), 1973
Water-filled bathtub, wood, found metal, rope, and glass jug
120¼ × 120⅛ × 33⅞ inches (305.5 × 305 × 86 cm)
Museum of Fine Arts, Houston

Boston, Massachusetts, 1980
Gelatin silver print
19 × 13 inches (48.3 × 33 cm)
Museum of Fine Arts, Houston

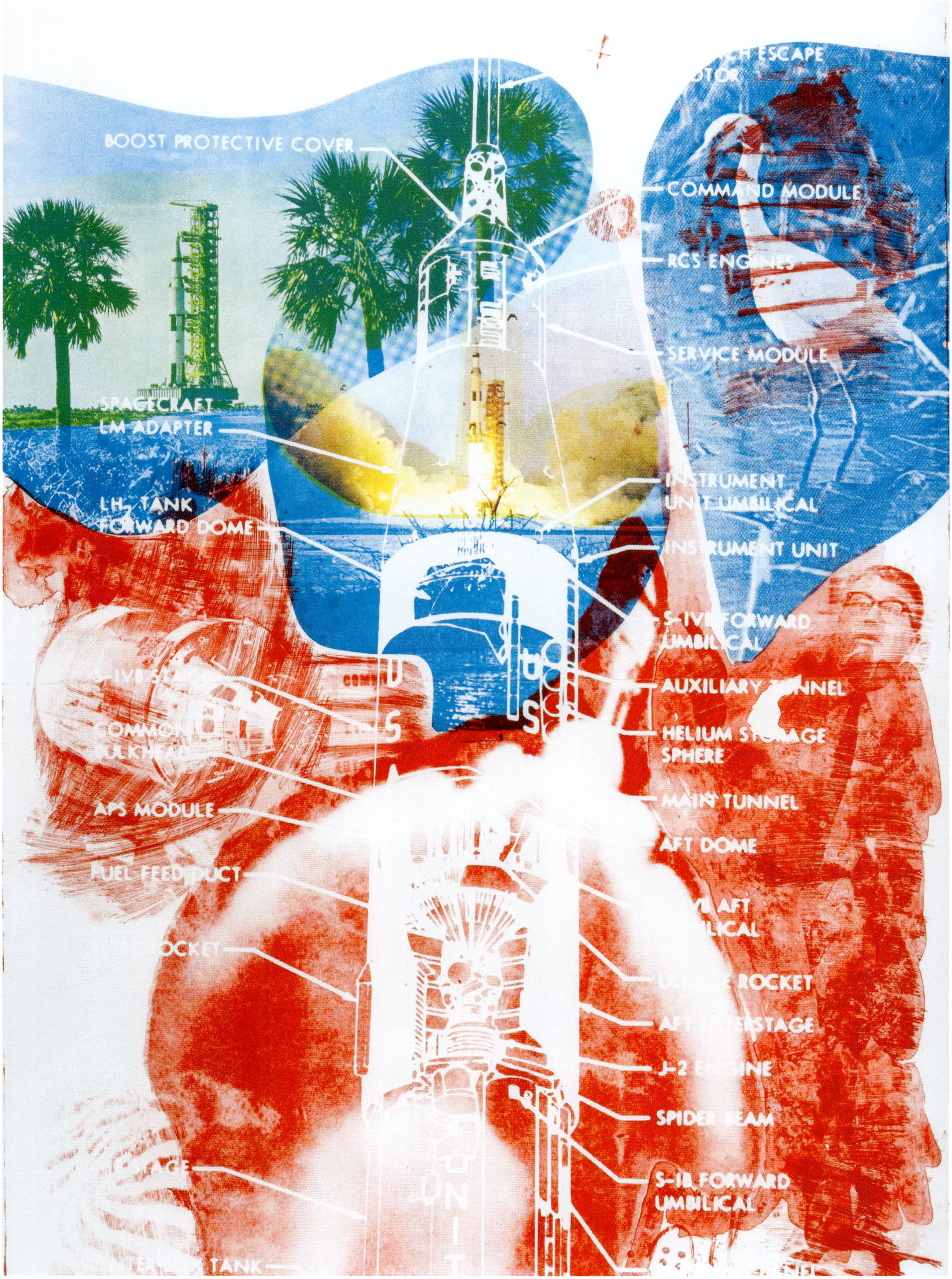

BOOST PROTECTIVE COVER
LAUNCH ESCAPE MOTOR
COMMAND MODULE
RCS ENGINES
SERVICE MODULE
SPACECRAFT LM ADAPTER
INSTRUMENT UNIT UMBILICAL
INSTRUMENT UNIT
LH2 TANK FORWARD DOME
S-IVB FORWARD UMBILICAL
AUXILIARY TUNNEL
S-IVB STAGE
HELIUM STORAGE SPHERE
COMMON BULKHEAD
MAIN TUNNEL
APS MODULE
AFT DOME
AFT UMBILICAL
FUEL FEED DUCT
ULLAGE ROCKET
RETRO ROCKET
AFT INTERSTAGE
J-2 ENGINE
SPIDER BEAM
S-II FORWARD UMBILICAL
STAGE
TANK

4

NASA Inception

My head said for the first time Moon was going to have company and knew it.

—Robert Rauschenberg[1]

In July 1969 Robert Rauschenberg received an invitation from NASA to observe and document the space program alongside a cohort of artists. During his four-day stay at the Kennedy Space Center, he watched the preparations for the Apollo 11 launch and witnessed the groundbreaking mission that culminated in the first human landing on the Moon on July 20, 1969. He first heard of the program through his friend Lane Slate in February 1969: "A friend of mine is in charge of the of the NASA Cape Kennedy Art Program. He says, would Rauschenberg like to come and watch an Apollo shoot?"[2] Naturally, Rauschenberg was interested. He had been following the space program from the beginning. By April, he was formally invited by NASA.

The NASA Art Program was conceived in 1962, under the leadership of NASA Administrator James Webb, and aimed to give artists unprecedented access to document the achievements of the space program. James Dean, the director of the program, and Hereward Lester Cooke, curator of paintings from the National Gallery of Art, selected artists for the program. Since NASA was not an art institution, Cooke was brought in as an adviser for the project and helped set guidelines for the artists. He said, "I am sure that it is good policy to leave the artist alone.… We are commissioning not only the artist's skill, but also his perception and his imagination, and for best results neither should be dictated or forced; therefore you are free to use whatever style you wish."[3] In exchange for their art and a front-row seat, most of the artists were given a meager stipend of $800, often barely enough to cover their transportation to Florida.[4] Other artists participating in the program included Jaime Wyeth and Norman Rockwell (who was there on a commission from *Look* magazine but was managed through the NASA Art Program), but Rauschenberg was the sort of major figure Dean and Cooke were hoping to attract to the program, and they were delighted with his participation.[5]

An Ally at NASA

In his first letter to Rauschenberg, inviting him to join other artists for the Apollo 11 launch, Dean included Apollo 8 lunar flight maps, writing, "I thought you might find them interesting," and suggested there would be more from where those came from.[6] It was an early indication of Dean's admiration for the artist and his willingness to serve as a collaborator. Dean bestowed on Rauschenberg enriching and sometimes unprecedented source materials that ended up in the *Stoned Moon* lithograph series (1969–70).

In the days leading up to the launch, Rauschenberg was escorted to the different facilities within the Kennedy Space Center. Despite the fact that Cooke had urged artists to make sketches on site ("Every drawing made on site, regardless of how slight, must be saved and eventually added to the permanent archive. The reason for this is that the on-the-spot sketches often have an impact and immediacy which finished works of art lack."[7]), Dean recalled that Rauschenberg simply sat quietly in front of the gigantic rocket, chewing on a blade of grass, taking in the sounds and sights around him.[8] There were no sketches to be had. Instead, the artist gathered source materials for his upcoming series from NASA photographs and other resources provided by Dean.[9]

Rauschenberg had long been interested in the space program, as evidenced by his works from the early 1960s, including *Overcast I* (1962) and *Retroactive II* (1963), which incorporated imagery of rockets, astronauts, and celestial bodies. However, as the art historian Noah Randolph states, the experiences he gained in the NASA Art Program gave Rauschenberg a "new visual vocabulary" with which to interpret the space program.[10] The artist's enthusiasm surrounding the Apollo 11 launch not only generated new opportunities for work but also spilled over into his personal life: He called the puppies

Detail of **Sky Garden (Stoned Moon)**, 1969

12 Feb 69

NATIONAL EDUCATIONAL TELEVISION
10 COLUMBUS CIRCLE • NEW YORK, NEW YORK 10019 • JU 6-0055

Dear Bob — a friend of mine is in charge of The NASA–Cape Kennedy art program. He says: would Rauschenberg like to come watch an apollo shoot? They pay $800.00 & expenses and hope "you would make something" for them. Are you interested at all? Call me — or have somebody call me — at 262-5566.

Regards,
Lane Slate

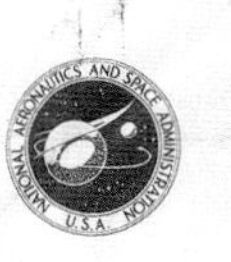

NATIONAL AERONAUTICS AND SPACE ADMINISTRATION
WASHINGTON, D.C. 20546

IN REPLY REFER TO:

4-11-69

Dear Mr. Rauschenberg:

Lester Cooke tells me he spoke with you yesterday and that you would be willing to go to Cape Kennedy with us for the lunar landing flight in July. That is very good news. It is scheduled for July 16 and we usually get there 2-3 days before. I will keep you posted.

I have enclosed some lunar flight maps that I thought you might find interesting. We used them on Apollo 8 and will probably use something similar on Apollo 11.

Look forward to meeting you.

Sincerely,
James Dean

Tel. 202/9623477

Letter dated February 12, 1969, from Rauschenberg's friend Lane Slate informing him about the NASA Art Program.

Letter dated April 11, 1969, from James Dean inviting Rauschenberg to participate in the NASA Art Program.

<table>
<tr><td colspan="4"></td><td>PAGE 1 OF 1 PAGES</td></tr>
</table>

PURCHASE ORDER-INVOICE

THIS NUMBER MUST APPEAR ON ALL PACKAGES AND PAPERS RELATING TO THIS ORDER. ▶

PURCHASE ORDER NO.
W-12,888 A/1

REQUISITION NO./PURCHASING AUTHORITY
No Change

CONTRACT NO.

DATE OF ORDER
4/10/69

ISSUED BY
No Change

BUREAU VOUCHER NO.
N/A

MAIL INVOICE TO
No Change

BUREAU SCHEDULE NO.
N/A

SHIP TO
National Aeronautics and Space Administration
Code FA
Washington, D.C. 20546

TO: *(Contractor and Address)*
Mr. Robert Rauchenberg
381 Lafayette St.
New York, N. Y. 11201

ACCOUNTING CLASSIFICATION
No Change

DATE OF DELIVERY

DELIVERY FOB □ DESTINATION □ OTHER

DISCOUNT TERMS

TYPE OF ORDER
☒ PURCHASE

IN ACCORDANCE WITH YOUR ___ OF ___ PLEASE FURNISH THE FOLLOWING ON THE TERMS SPECIFIED ON BOTH SIDES OF THIS ORDER AND ON THE ATTACHED SHEETS, IF ANY, INCLUDING DELIVERY AS INDICATED. THIS PURCHASE IS NEGOTIATED UNDER AUTHORITY OF 10 U.S.C. 2304(a) ( ).

□ DELIVERY

THIS DELIVERY ORDER IS SUBJECT TO INSTRUCTIONS CONTAINED ON THIS SIDE ONLY OF THIS FORM AND IS ISSUED ON ANOTHER GOVERNMENT AGENCY OR IN ACCORDANCE WITH AND SUBJECT TO THE TERMS AND CONDITIONS OF THE ABOVE NUMBERED CONTRACT.

TYPE NAME AND TITLE OF PURCHASING/CONTRACTING OFFICER
J. Ronald Jeshow, Contracting Officer

SIGNATURE

ITEM NO.	DESCRIPTION	UNIT	UNIT PRICE	QUANTITY ORDERED	AMOUNT	QTY. SHIP'D	AMOUNT BILLED
	The Basic Purchase Order W-12,888 is amended to add the following:						

1. Further information regarding the time of departure, reservations, etc., will be provided by Mr. James Dean, Code FA, NASA Headquarters, Washington, D.C. 20546 (telephone AC 202/962-3477).

2. It is understood that all paintings and drawings delivered by the artist under this order are the sole property of the Government, and the artist agrees not to assert any rights at law or equity in such articles or to obtain or assert any copyrights in such articles.

3. A partial payment of the total sum specified on this order will be made for transportation and travel expenses upon presentation of an itemized invoice of such expenses.

PAYMENT RECORD: □ PARTIAL □ FINAL

TOTALS No Change

VOUCHER AUDIT

NASA FORM 177W (REV. AUG. 65)
JUNE 61 ED. MAY BE USED UNTIL SUPPLIES ARE EXHAUSTED: EARLIER EDITIONS ARE OBSOLETE.
1. ORIGINAL ORDER - VENDOR'S COPY

Purchase order dated April 10, 1969, from NASA to Rauschenberg formalizing his participation in its art program.

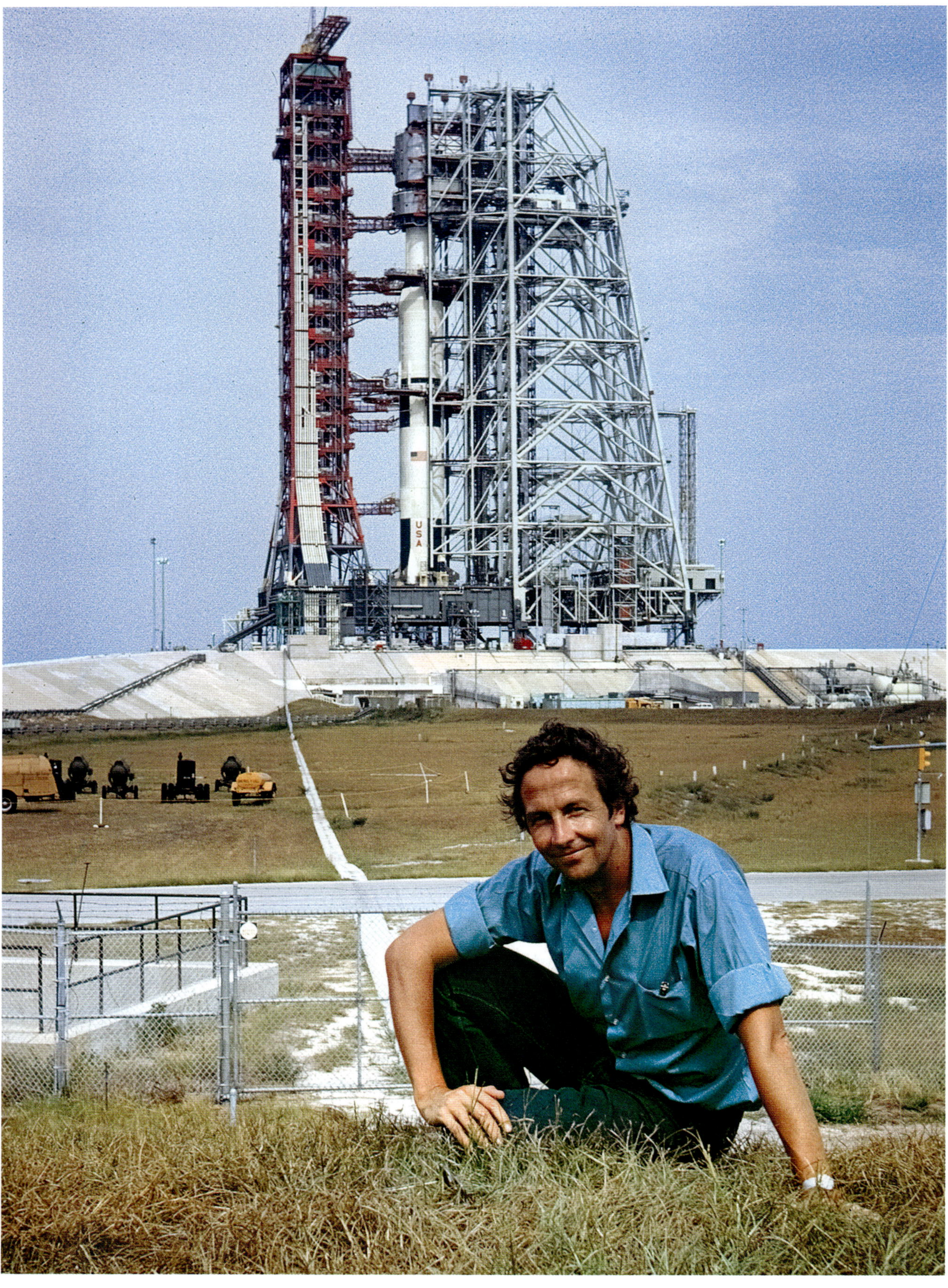

Rauschenberg at Cape Kennedy as a NASA Art Program artist in 1969, with the Apollo 11 launch site in the background. The photo was taken by James Dean, the program director.

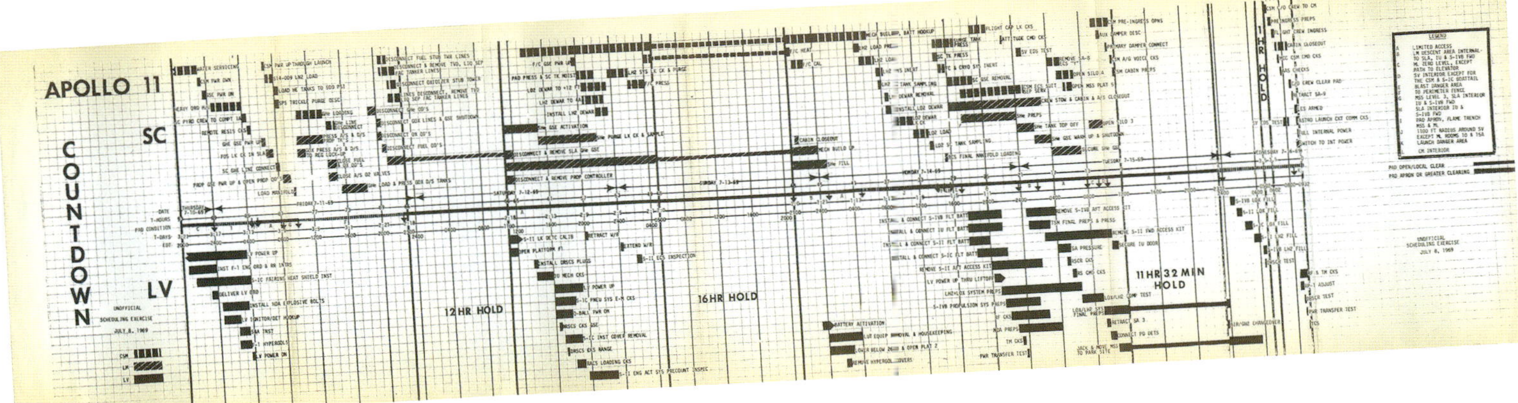

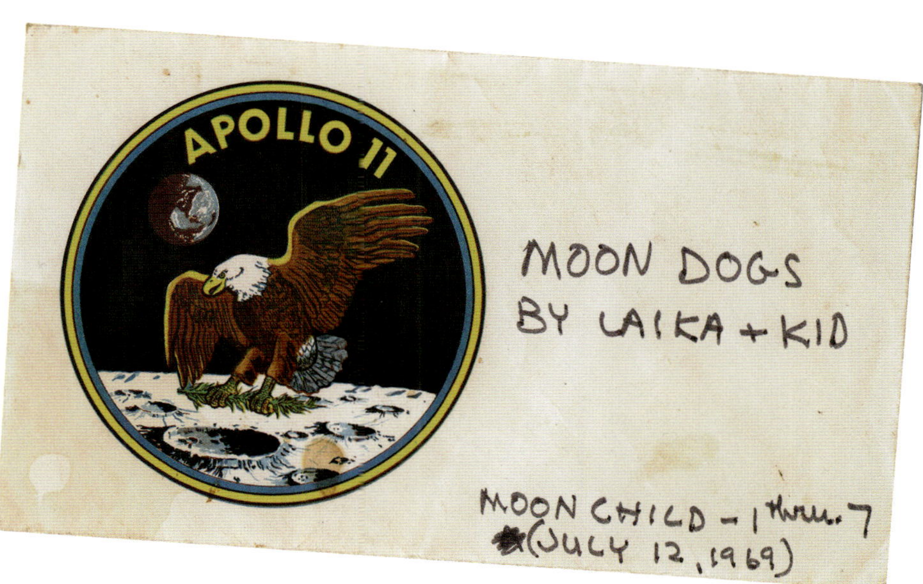

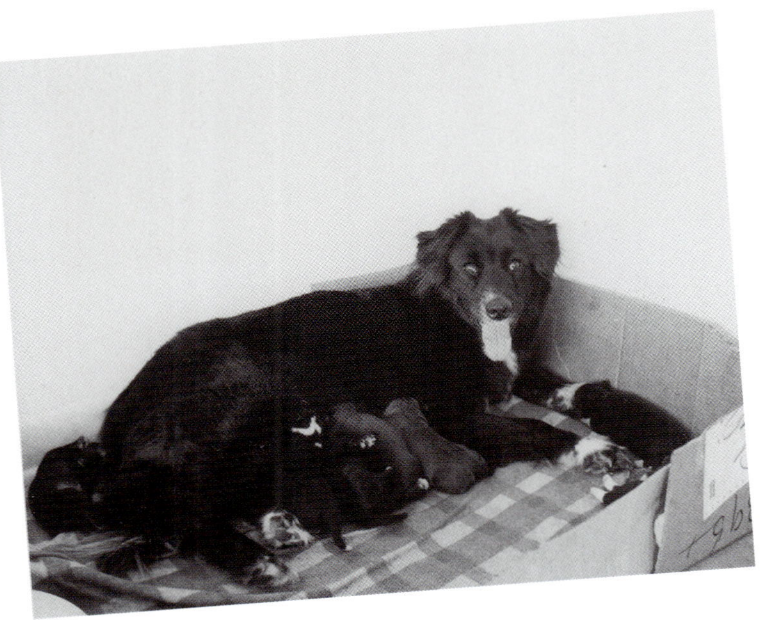

NASA Apollo 11 Countdown chart provided by Dean to Rauschenberg as source material for the *Stoned Moon* series (1969–70).

Handwritten note by Rauschenberg captioning an Apollo 11 mission patch envelope with the names of his dogs Laika and Kid and their puppies, Moon Child 1 through 7, 1969.

Rauschenberg's dog Laika with her puppies, born July 12, 1969, four days before the launch of Apollo 11.

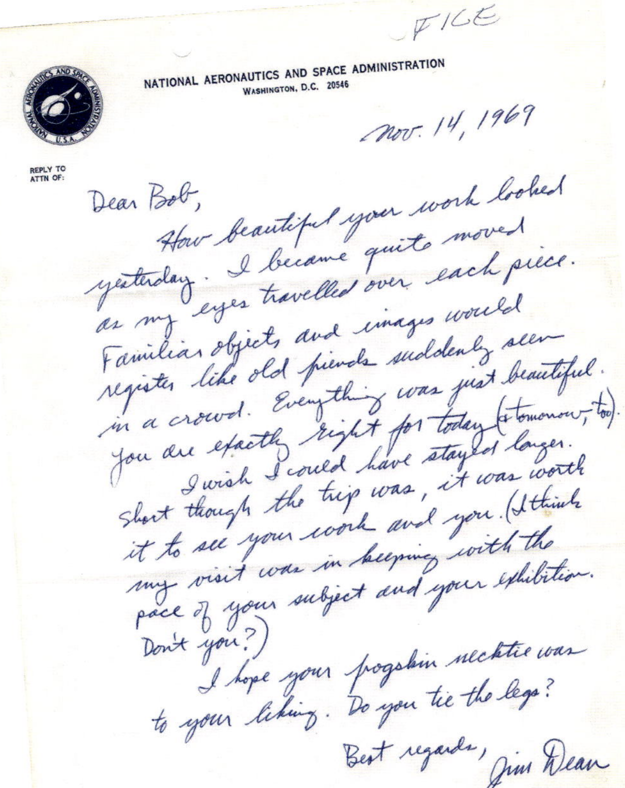

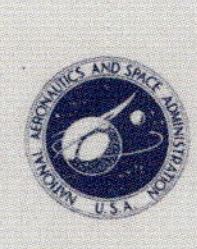

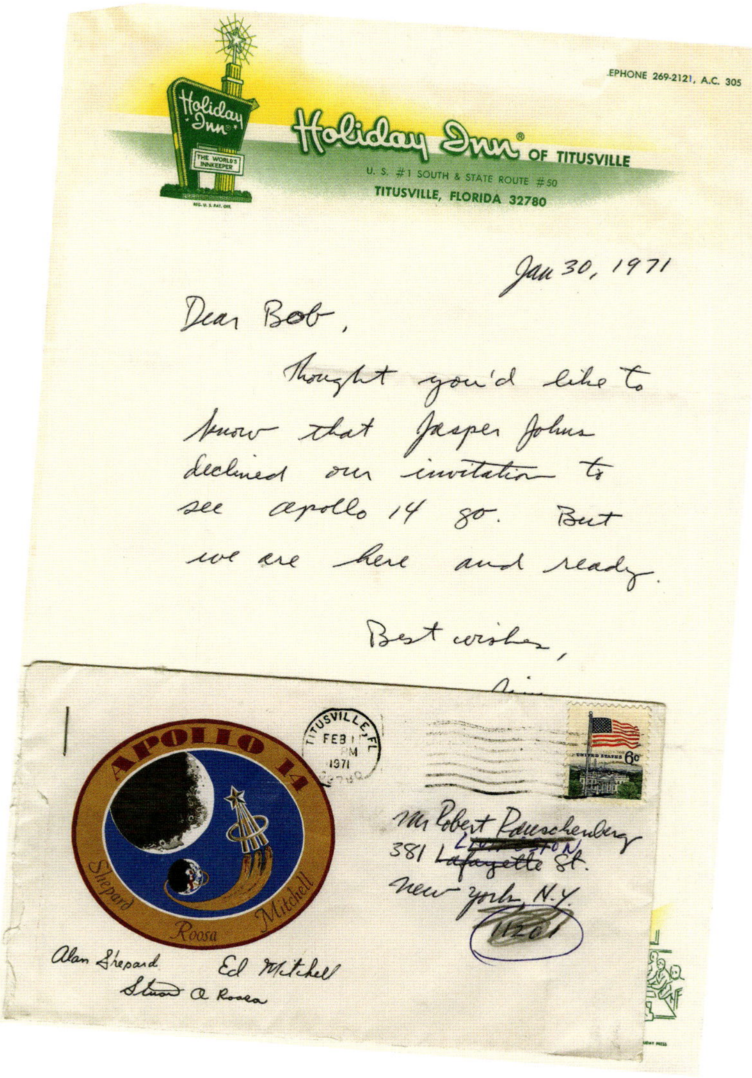

Letter from Dean to Rauschenberg, dated November 14, 1969, praising the *Stoned Moon* series (1969–70) after a visit.

Letter from Dean to Rauschenberg dated July 2, 1970, regarding payment for Rauschenberg's participation in the NASA Art Program.

Letter from Dean to Rauschenberg dated January 30, 1971, regarding Jasper Johns's decision to decline an invitation to the Apollo 14 launch.

Note from Dean to Rauschenberg dated November 18, 1970, regarding saved newspaper clippings on Rauschenberg's exhibition in Washington, DC.

Copy of *This Island Earth* edited by Oran. W. Nicks, given to Rauschenberg by Dean to use as reference material.

Note from Dean to Rauschenberg accompanying the book *This Island Earth*, offered as reference material. This date 1971 would have been too late for *Stoned Moon* series (1969–70).

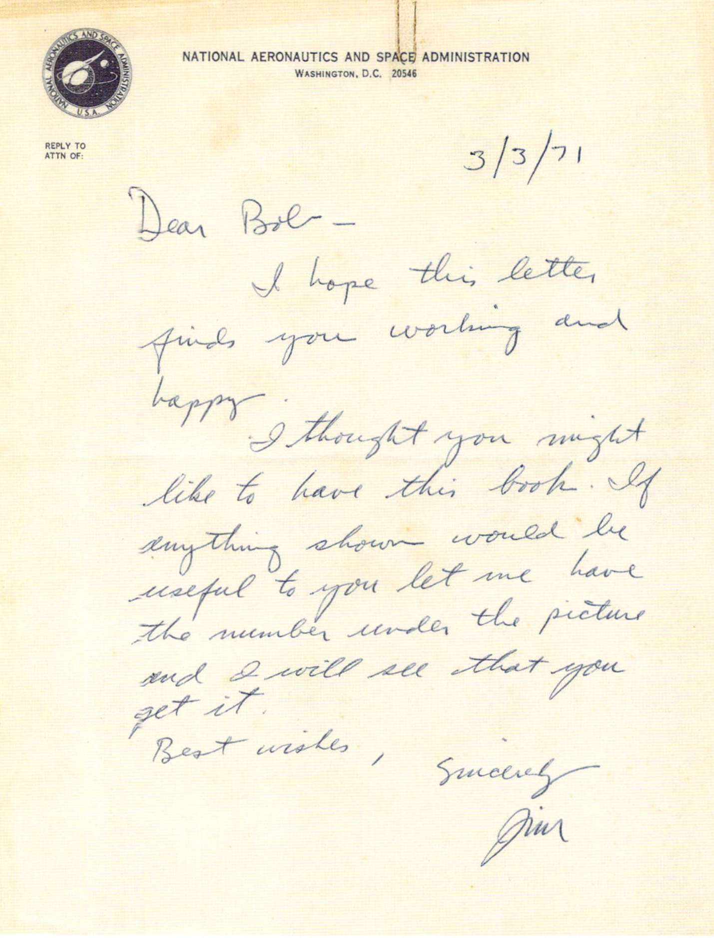

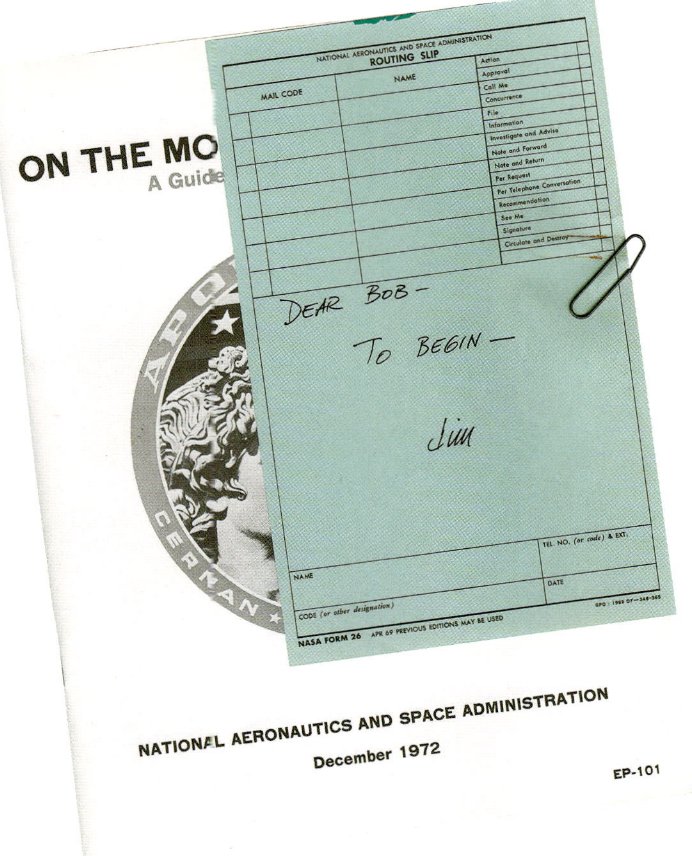

Note from Dean to Rauschenberg along with NASA's official guidebook for the Apollo 17 mission.

Letter from Dean to Rauschenberg dated July 26, 1973, regarding NASA's equipment junkyard.

Clearance and visitor's pass to the Kennedy Space Center for Rauschenberg, granting him access to the Apollo 17 launch in 1972.

Rauschenberg (right) at the entrance of the Smithsonian's National Air and Space Museum in August 1976 with James Dean, the first art curator of the museum (1974–80). Dean served as the director of the NASA Art Program from 1963 to 1974.

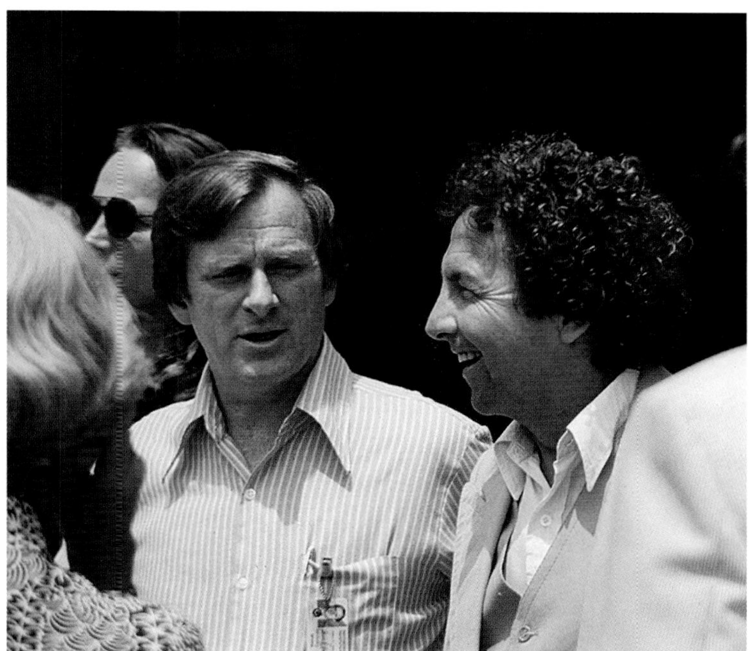

of his dog Laika (named for the dog who perished aboard Sputnik 2 in 1957), who were born on July 12, 1969, Moon Child 1 through 7.

After the Apollo 11 launch, Dean continued to correspond with Rauschenberg, expressing enthusiasm for the *Stoned Moon* series and providing source materials that included a lunar trajectory chart, books, and an unofficial Apollo 11 schedule for the astronauts leading up to the launch. In one letter, Dean offered Rauschenberg access to photograph the NASA junk-yard: "There is one thing you might like—it's the NASA excess equipment junk yard. It looks like your yard after you took apart the Datsun—but BIG!! You'd need to make photos but it's here if you want to see it."[11] In a letter of July 2, 1970, he said, "A year ago this month our 'Apollo–Moon' relationship began." That missive ends with: "What are you working on now? I have started to accumulate all kinds of things in my office should you decide to return to Space."[12] Dean's generosity bespoke the support and enthusiasm of an enthralled fan; Rauschenberg was the NASA Art Program's champion contemporary artist.

A New Sky

Rauschenberg began the *Stoned Moon* series shortly after the Apollo 11 launch. It incorporated many source materials from NASA, ranging from photographs of astronauts in training and in space, rockets, and graphic schematics. The prints were made at Gemini G.E.L. in Los Angeles, a lithography workshop run by master printer Kenneth Tyler and a stable of artists and printers. Describing the collaboration between Rauschenberg and the printers and the pace at which they were working, the art historian Robert Mattison says, "Rauschenberg likened his working process with the printmakers at Gemini to the cooperative endeavors of the scientists at NASA."[13]

The title of the *Stoned Moon* series is derived from the stone used in lithography—and is also perhaps a knowing nod to altered states of mind especially prevalent in the late 1960s. The series would ultimately comprise thirty-three lithographs. One of the first prints in the series was the largest hand-pulled lithograph at that time: *Sky Garden (Stoned Moon)* (1969). In vivid hues of red, blue, green, and turquoise, the gigantic print almost ninety inches tall is a collage of technology and nature, showing a diagram of a Saturn 1B, SA-205 rocket (not the Saturn V rocket used for Apollo 11), a launch tower, a space capsule, a footprint on the lunar surface, Wernher von Braun, and support crew from

mission control involved in the Moon landing. Juxtaposed with the natural surroundings of the Kennedy Space Center, Rauschenberg addressed the balance of technology and nature and the impacts of space exploration on our planet.

Rauschenberg attended the last launch to the Moon— Apollo 17—in 1972; the conclusion of human activity on the lunar surface also brought a pause to the NASA Art Program. James Dean left NASA in 1974 and joined the staff at the Smithsonian's National Air and Space Museum as the first official art curator. Michael Collins, the command module pilot for Apollo 11, became the Museum's first director and oversaw the grand opening in 1976. Together, they arranged the transfer of about 2,000 works from the NASA Art Program to the Museum's art collection, including NASA's special print of *Sky Garden (Stoned Moon)*. Dean continued to communicate and collaborate with Rauschenberg during his time at the Museum and well into his retirement. An amusing letter from Rauschenberg's assistant Terry Van Brunt to Dean requested information on whether heat tiles from the Space Shuttle could be obtained, adding that "Bob is still interested in owning a Moon rock.… Also, is there any 'Moon dust?'"[14] Obviously, Dean couldn't help with this request.

After Apollo

Following the 1975 reboot of the NASA Art Program under Robert Schulman, Rauschenberg was invited back to NASA in 1981 as one of the first eight artists to witness the launch of the Space Shuttle *Columbia*.[15] In response, he created the print *Hot Shot* (1983), which features photographs of the Space Shuttle, its

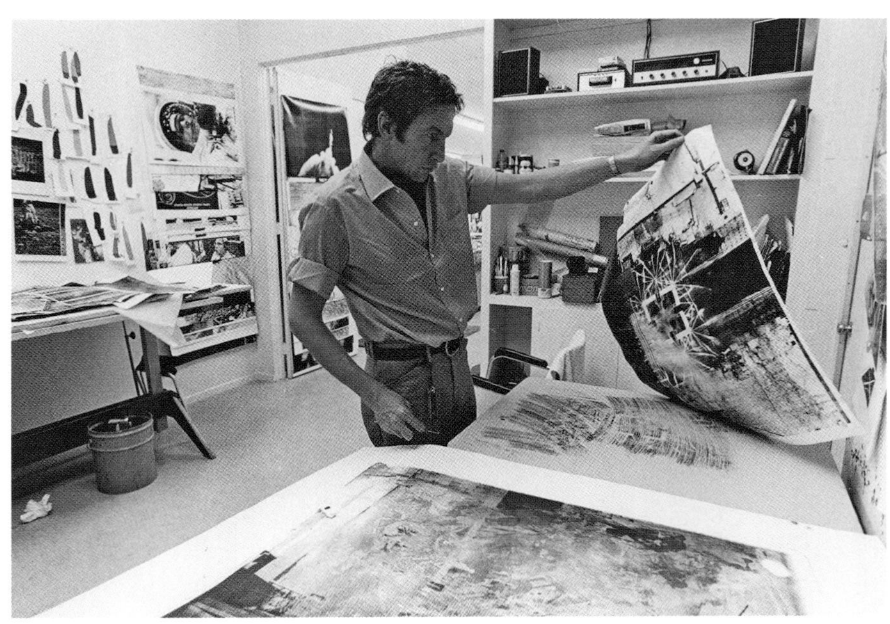

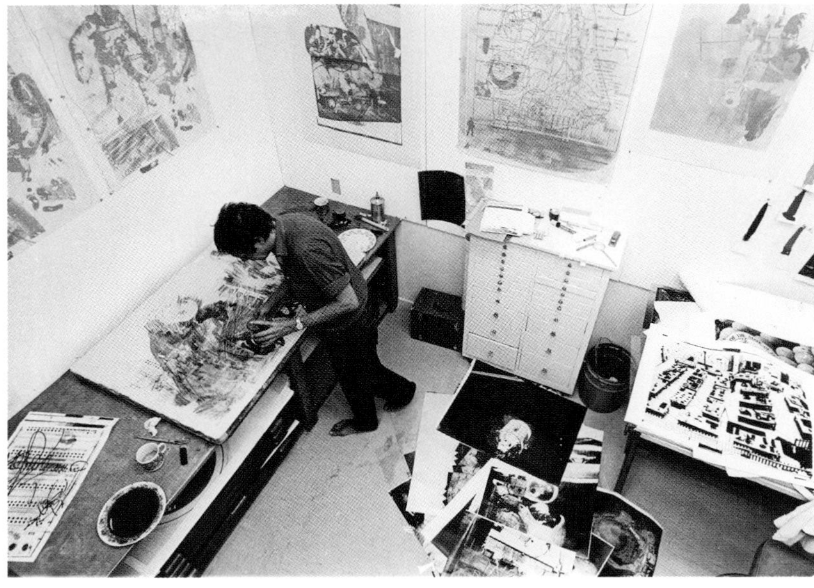

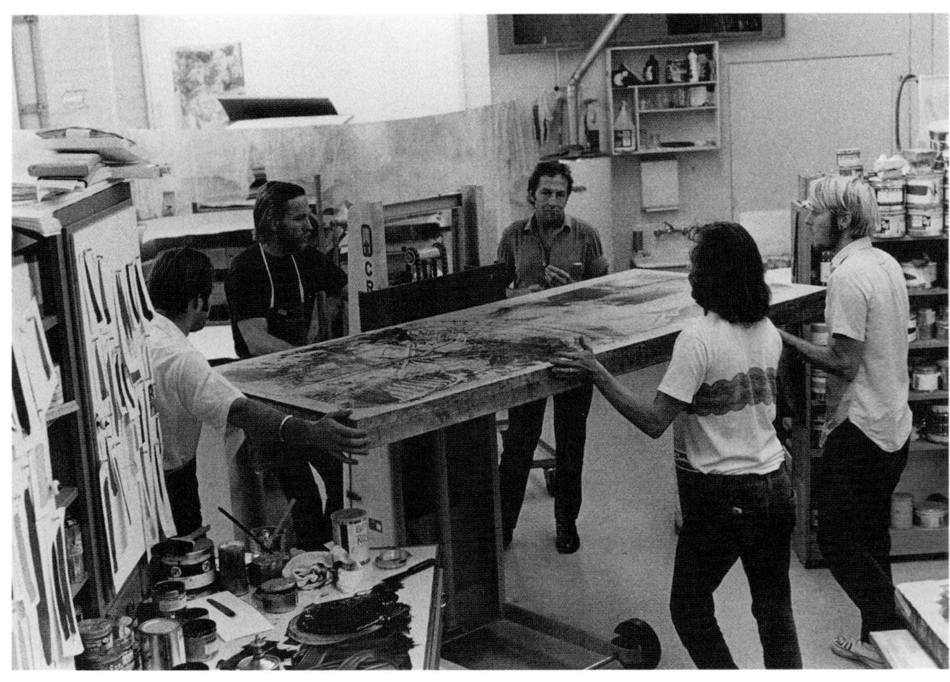

Rauschenberg working on the *Stoned Moon* series (1969–70) at Gemini G.E.L., Los Angeles, 1969.

Overhead view of Rauschenberg drawing with tusche on a lithography stone for *Air Pocket (Stoned Moon)* (1969) at Gemini G.E.L., Los Angeles, 1969.

Rauschenberg and Gemini G.E.L. printers, including Robert Petersen, moving the lithography stone for *Waves (Stoned Moon)* (1969) at Gemini G.E.L., Los Angeles, 1969.

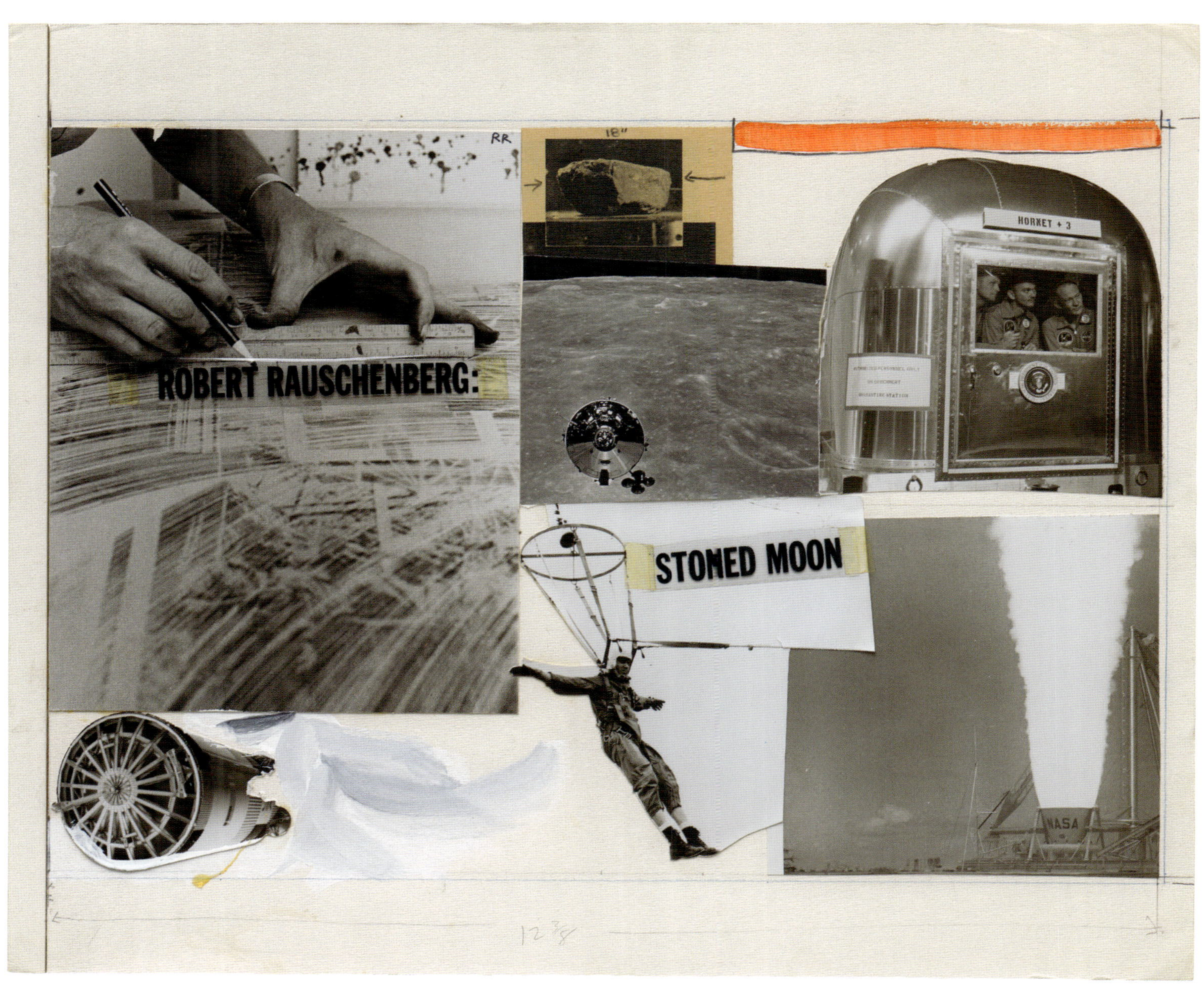

Cover Page, Stoned Moon Book, 1970
Photographs, press type, acetate, printed reproduction,
watercolor, colored pencil, graphite on illustration board
16 × 20⅛ inches (40.6 × 51.1 cm)
Robert Rauschenberg Foundation

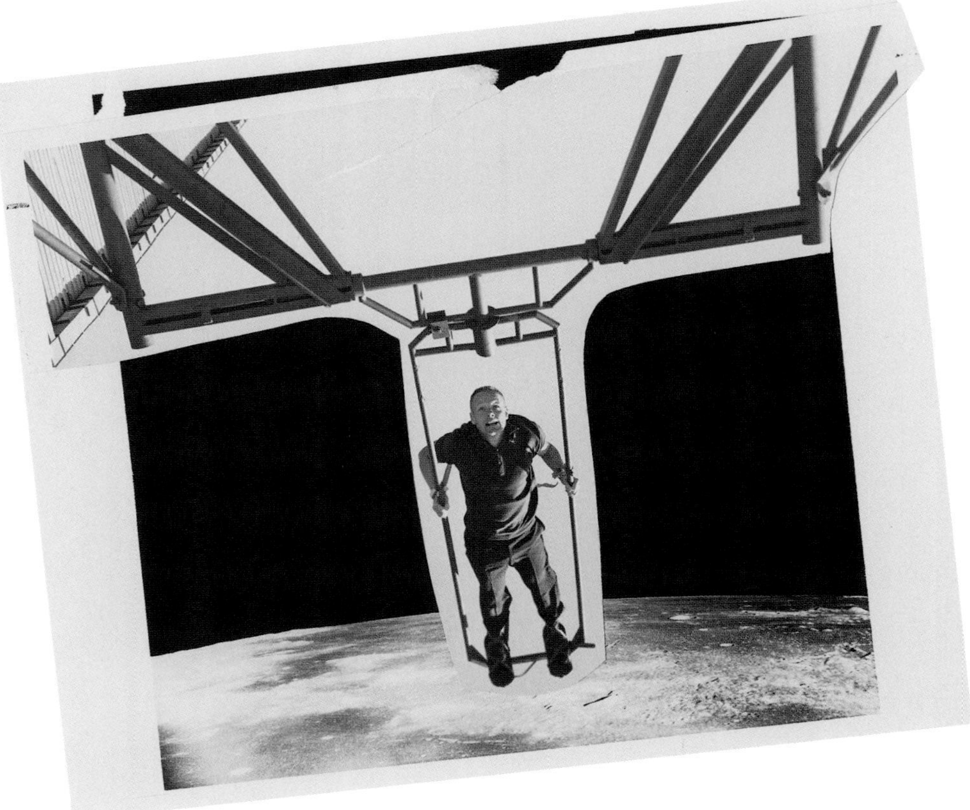

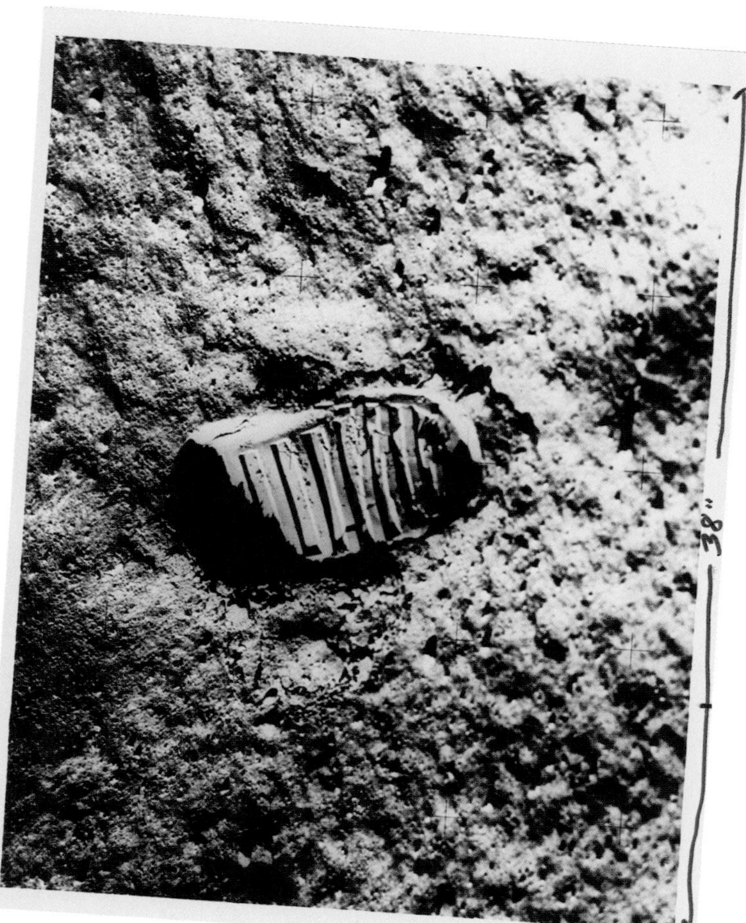

Photograph provided to Rauschenberg as source material for the *Stoned Moon* series (1969–70) depicting the lunar surface with an overlay of Apollo 11 astronaut Neil Armstrong in training.

Photograph of an astronaut's footprint in lunar soil taken during the Apollo 11 mission provided to Rauschenberg as source material during his participation in the NASA Art Program. Rauschenberg used it for the *Stoned Moon* series (1969–70), including *Sky Garden (Stoned Moon)* (1969).

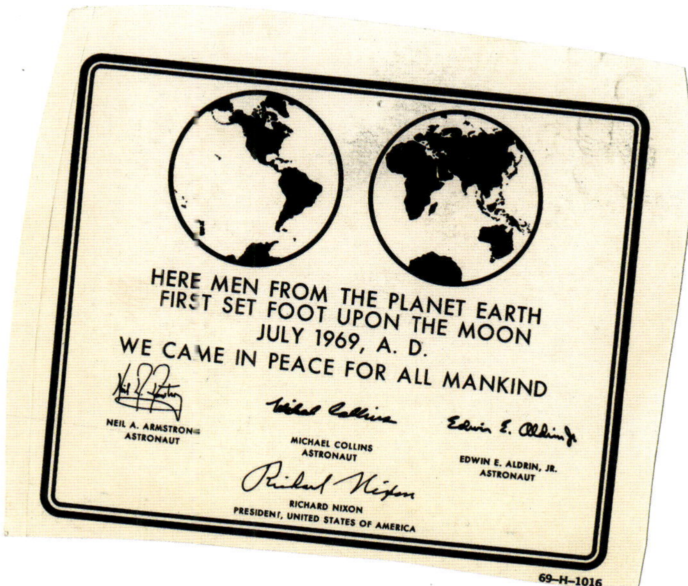

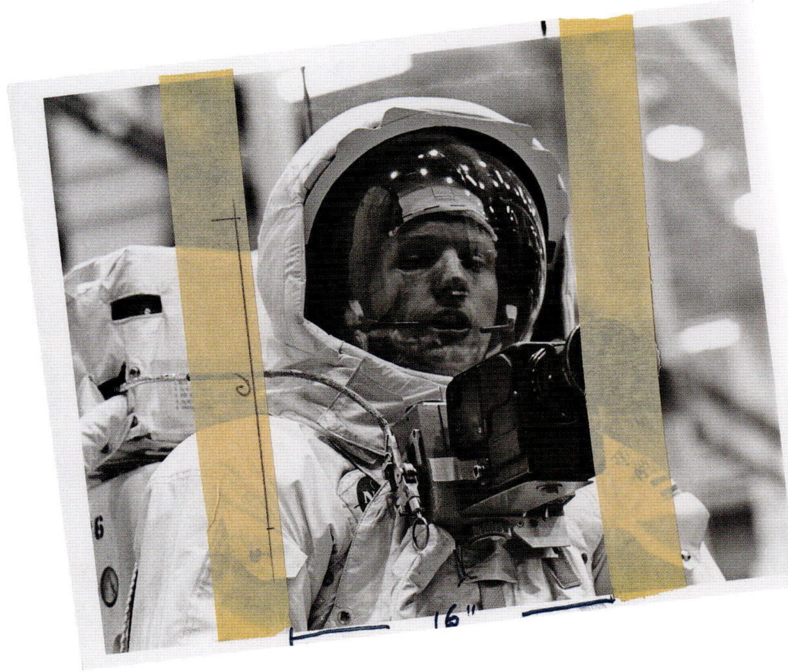

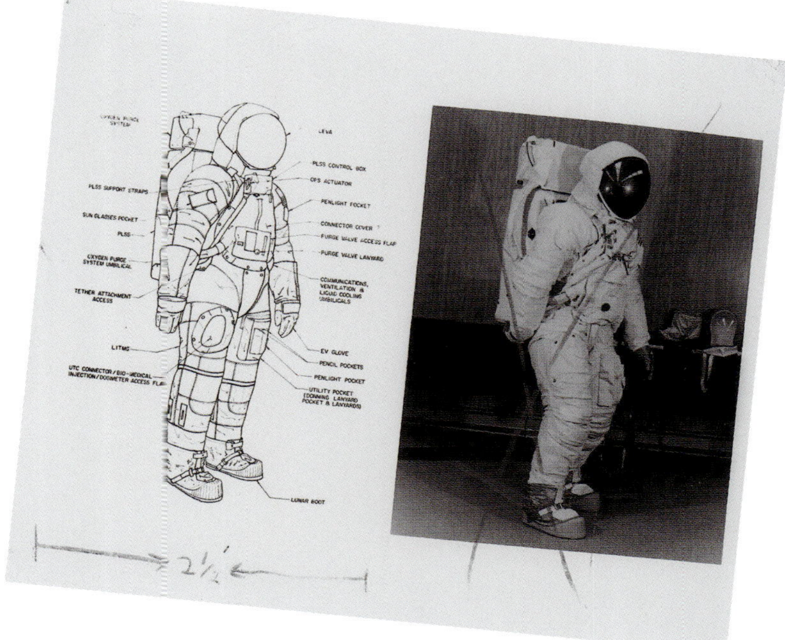

Reproduction of the plaque attached to the Apollo 11 lunar module *Eagle* and left on the Moon during the Apollo 11 mission, 1969. Rauschenberg used this image as source material for the *Stoned Moon* series (1969–70).

Photograph of astronaut Neil Armstrong in training before the Apollo 11 mission provided to Rauschenberg as source material for the *Stoned Moon* series (1969–70).

Source material related to space suits provided to Rauschenberg for the *Stoned Moon* series (1969–70).

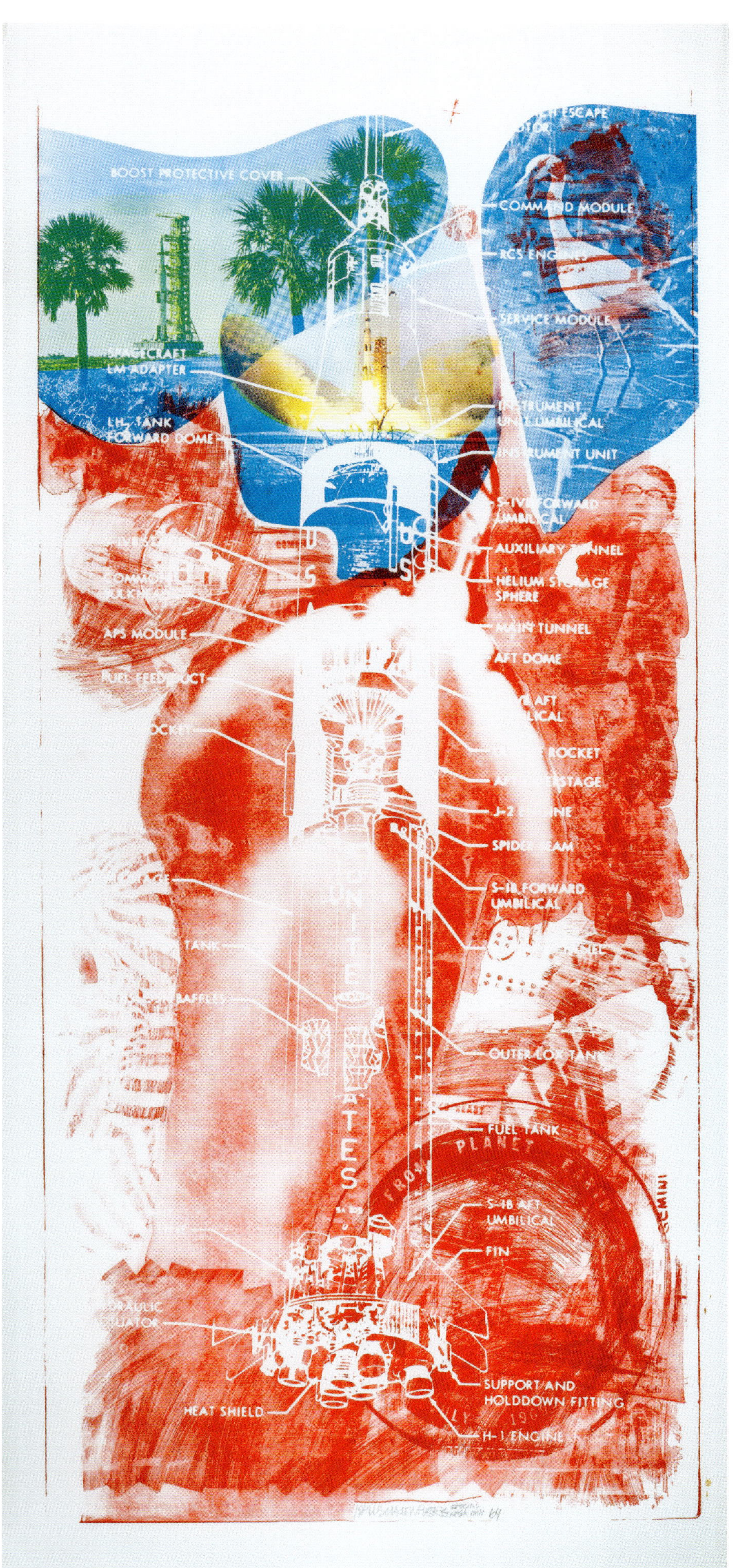

Sky Garden (Stoned Moon), 1969
Lithograph and screenprint
88 11/16 × 42 inches (225.2 × 106.7 cm)
Smithsonian National Air and Space Museum

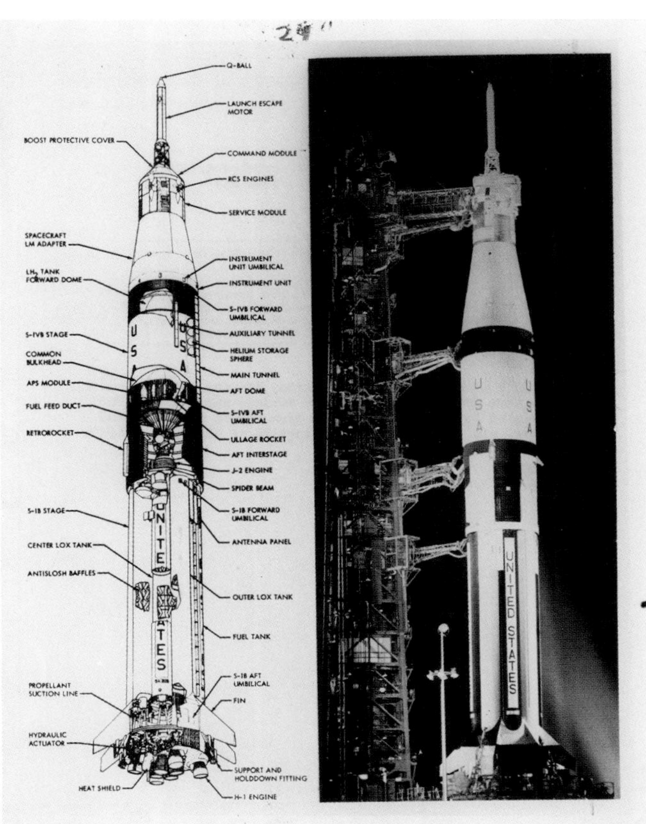

Photograph of Apollo 7 space vehicle on Launch Pad 34 at the Kennedy Space Center and cutaway drawing of the vehicle, 1968. This photograph was provided to Rauschenberg during his participation in the NASA Art Program and was used as source material for the *Stoned Moon* series (1969–70), including *Sky Garden (Stoned Moon)* (1969).

interior cockpit panel, and signs from nearby Cocoa Beach |leading to the launch site announcing "Come on *Columbia* Do it Again!" and "Shuttlemania." Two Space Shuttles appear in the work, placed vertically on each side; both have a solarized effect reminiscent of Rauschenberg's full-body X-ray in *Booster* (1967) and *Autobiography* (1968).[16] Rauschenberg also inserted a photograph of himself sitting near the ocean with a friend. In a statement about the work published in *Discover* magazine, he said, "*Hot Shot* was created to share and express my belief in the spiritual and physical improvement of life and mind through curiosity."[17] His handwritten draft is more pointed: "This involvement with the realization of abstracts directed toward the future, is not only the most important exesize [exercise] for mankind, but could bypass us into peace."[18] In 1984 Rauschenberg created the Rauschenberg Overseas Culture Interchange (ROCI) to promote world peace and cultural collaborations through art.

In the early 1980s NASA announced a search for the first citizen to fly on the Space Shuttle, and it's not surprising that Rauschenberg applied to the program.[19] An article titled "All Aboard the Shuttle" in *Life* magazine's October 1984 issue features Rauschenberg and names former CBS news anchor Walter Cronkite, singer John Denver, comedian Bob Hope, and film director Steven Spielberg as having expressed interest in the program.[20] The article included a photo of Rauschenberg painting at the Kennedy Space Center with the Space Shuttle *Discovery* framed behind him; the caption reads: "One of 70 artists chosen by NASA to portray the shuttle. Robert Rauschenberg, 58, wants a free ride as a 'purely aesthetic indulgence.'"[21] The first three civilians to fly onboard the Space Shuttle were: Senator Edwin Jacob "Jake" Garn on flight mission STS-51D in April 1985, Prince Sultan bin Salman Al Saud (STS-51-G) in June 1985, and Senator Clarence William "Bill" Nelson (STS-61C) in January 1986. Christa McAuliffe was the fourth civilian and the first teacher to fly aboard the Space Shuttle on January 28, 1986; tragically, just over a minute into the flight, the Space Shuttle *Challenger* broke apart, resulting in the loss of all seven crew members.

Even though he was not selected for the Space Shuttle program, Rauschenberg continued to think about reaching space someday. In a 1991 interview, he remarked, "I even feel restricted with the world as small as it is already. I'm trying to take advantage of as much of it as possible. I'm old enough that I probably won't run out of land, but I would like to go to the Moon.'"[22]

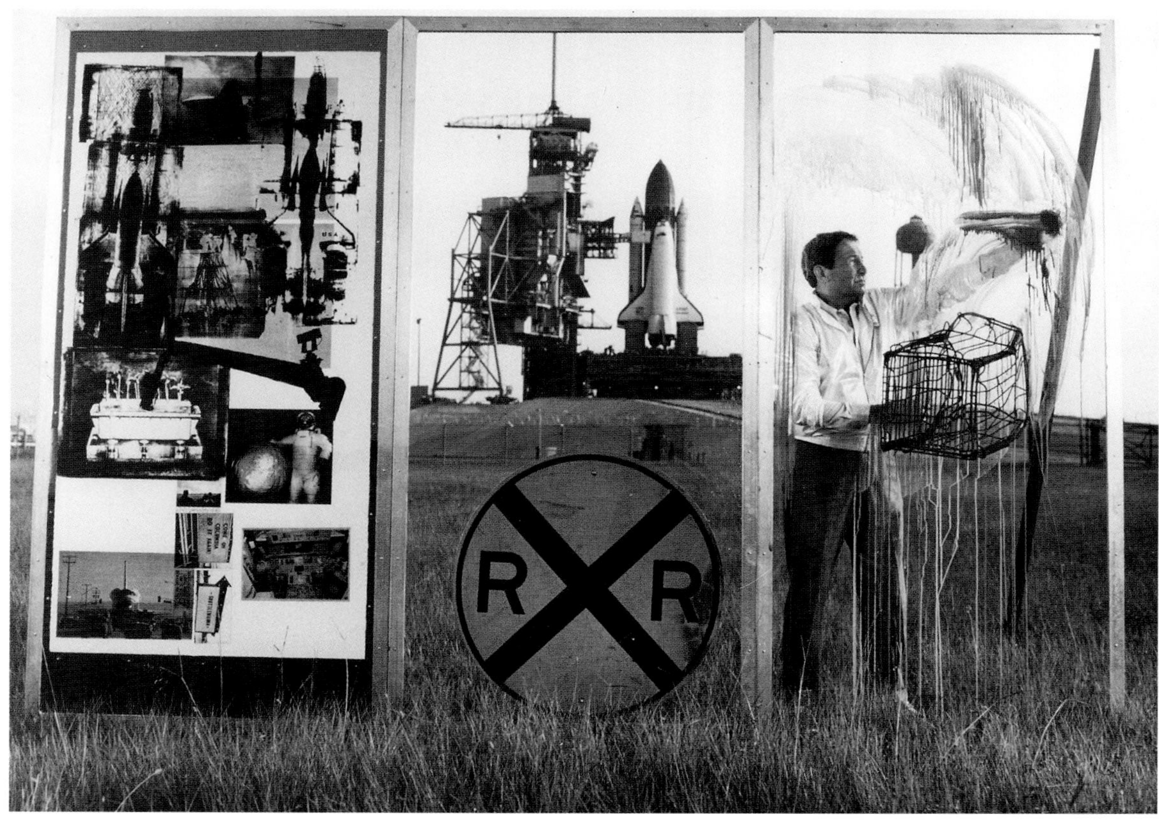

Rauschenberg at the Kennedy Space Center working on his portrayal of the Space Shuttle *Discovery* launch, 1984. This photograph was featured in *Life* magazine's October 1984 issue.

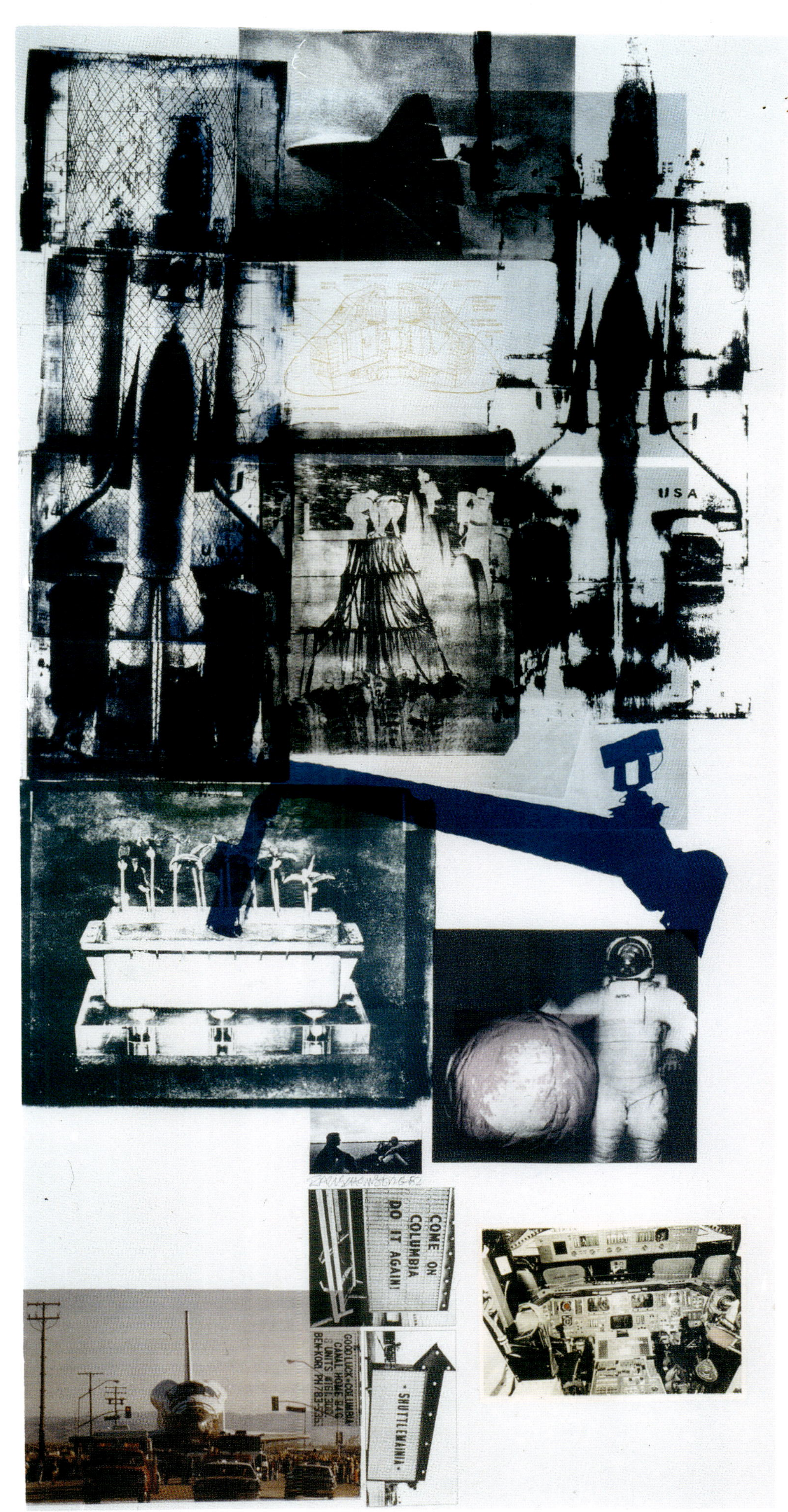

Hot Shot, 1983
Lithograph
81 × 42 inches (205.7 × 106.6 cm)
National Aeronautics and Space Administration

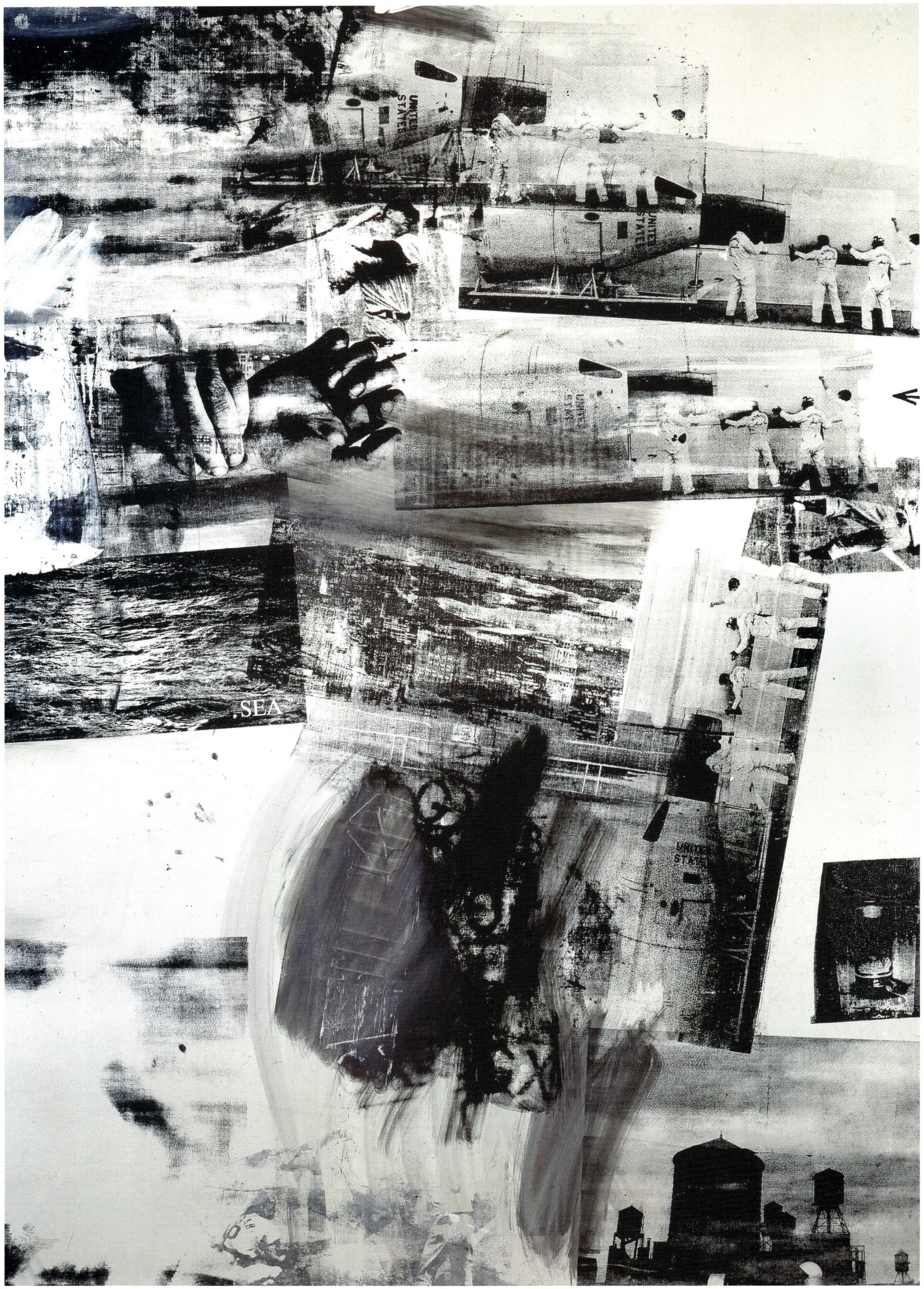

UNITED STATES
UNITED STATES
UNITED STATES
.SEA

5

Constructing Space

Apollo 11 was airborne, lifting pulling everyone's spirits with it. Nothing will already be the same.

—Robert Rauschenberg[1]

Prior to Rauschenberg's involvement with the NASA Art Program, imagery related to spaceflight appeared in several of his early works, particularly the *Silkscreen Paintings* he created between 1962 and 1964. His frequent incorporation of rockets, parachuting astronauts, the Moon, radar dishes, and satellites reveals his keen interest in the trajectory of the space race and the US space program. The primary sources for these images included newspaper and magazine clippings from the *New York Times*, the *New York Herald Tribune, Life*, *National Geographic*, *Newsweek*, and *Time*.[2] A notable aspect of these early space-themed paintings is Rauschenberg's application of painterly smears and overt brushstrokes over certain imagery, a technique that serves to obscure or erase explicit references, thereby concealing his intended meanings.

Overcast I and *Glider* (both 1962) are black-and-white *Silkscreen Paintings* that both feature an image of workers placing a cover on the tip of an Atlas rocket. The same image appears in *Barge* (1963), where it is "an obvious sexual allusion," according to Roni Feinstein, and thus serves as a phallic symbol.[3] *Overcast I* also includes various representations of water: a glass of water, water towers in Texas, the ocean, and the word "SEA." On September 12, 1962, President John F. Kennedy gave a nationally televised speech announcing his administration's plans to go to the Moon that included the iconic line, "We set sail on this new sea." At that point, the space race had intensified between the United States and the Soviet Union, especially after the cosmonaut Yuri Gagarin became the first person in space the previous year. The pressure was on America to send astronauts across the final frontier.

A month later, Rauschenberg began his *Silkscreen Paintings*.[4] It's plausible that the aquatic elements and the word "SEA" in *Overcast I* were inspired by Kennedy's speech, reflecting the spirit of exploration and innovation at a pivotal moment in history. The repetition of the image of the men working on the rocket underlines the urgency of Kennedy's goal of putting a man on the Moon by the end of the decade. Other details evoke a range of associations: Aside from being all-American symbols, the baseball players may reference the performative nature of the space race and its place as a new American pastime.[5] A disembodied hand checking a pulse, symbolizing the idiom of having a finger on the pulse, indicates Rauschenberg's acute awareness of the events of the space race. The Atlas rocket in *Glider* connects it to *Overcast I*, yet surrounding imagery, such as a satellite dish, distances it from phallic connotations and highlights the culture of technology that grew along with the space program.[6] In *Scanning* (1963) references to space and aviation include a rocket launch, a caged bird, mosquitoes, umbrellas, a white object representing the Moon, a splash of blue paint signifying sky, and the Mariner 2 satellite, which was launched earlier that year.[7] Additionally, a photograph of Merce Cunningham's dancers once more illustrates the "finger on the pulse" concept as well as reflecting the performative aspects of spaceflight.

Again and again in these works, Rauschenberg demonstrates his ability to integrate current events into his practice just as a newspaper reporter would. *Stop Gap* (1963) and *Whale* (1964) feature the Navy frogmen recovery team in the water with Walter Schirra's *Sigma* 7 space capsule after it splashed down in the Pacific Ocean in 1962.[8] *Retroactive II* (1963) and *Skyway* (1964) employ imagery of John F. Kennedy, who served as a significant advocate for advancing the United States' endeavors in space exploration and was regarded as a personal hero by the artist.[9] In *Retroactive II*, Kennedy, positioned next to an astronaut figure equipped with a parachute, points to a graphic that proclaims "Tomorrow's Weather" as an indicator to the future. In *Skyway*, produced the year following his assassination,

Kennedy's portrait appears twice accompanied by images of eagles, a parachuting spaceman, the *Sigma 7* capsule, a lunar trajectory chart, and volumetric cubes suspended within the composition. The title *Skyway* serves as a succinct reference to Rauschenberg's enduring fascination with the diverse happenings in the sky.

Rauschenberg's introduction to the NASA Art Program in 1969, along with his exploration of lithography, prompted a dynamic shift in the style and messaging of his space-related works. By incorporating imagery sourced directly from NASA, Rauschenberg infused these works with a distinctive literalness that established a new, more potent visual lexicon.[10] The series of *Stoned Moon* editions (1969–70), for example, provides a comprehensive overview of the space program while simultaneously submitting it to a subtle critique (despite Rauschenberg's positive experience at NASA). Individually and collectively, the series encapsulates a distilled narrative of the program.

Flight Trajectory

In *Trust Zone (Stoned Moon)* (1969) Rauschenberg merged two milestones in human history: the beginning of flight and its anticipated evolution through the space program. The artwork in sky blue features a reversed sepia-tone image of the Wright brothers' inaugural flight at Kitty Hawk in 1903, showing Orville piloting the Wright Flyer while Wilbur runs alongside, stopwatch in hand. This historic moment is contrasted with a graphic outline of a NASA space suit and a map highlighting the Kennedy Space Center launch facility and nearby coastline. Together, these elements form a compelling timeline of the history of human ingenuity and innovation in the domain of flight. Nevertheless, certain details also suggest a growing concern regarding the effect of technology on Florida's wetlands and wildlife. Rauschenberg emphasized his concerns for the environment by highlighting various sections with brown ink, including the "Burn Pond" associated with the 39 Pad A Launch Complex, the inscription "Oxygen Purge," and the "Occupational Health Facility."

Morals of Science

Ape (Stoned Moon) (1970) features the three astronauts—Ed White, Jim McDivitt, and Neil Armstrong—goofing around in zero-gravity training and posing as the "three wise monkeys," with their hands over their eyes, ears, and mouth ("See no evil, hear no evil, speak no evil"). Other elements include an astrolabe (an instrument used for charting stars and other celestial objects), a map of the Kennedy Space Center, an astronaut in parachute practice, and technicians at work on a life-support system. Robert Mattison highlights this moment of playfulness for the astronauts in a "fun house" carnival setting, and his brief mention of the astronauts as "human guinea pigs" is also important.[11] The title *Ape* could refer to the early phases of space exploration, when NASA launched primates into space as part of its research. The primary aim of these missions was to improve the scientific understanding of the effects of space travel on living organisms before human flights commenced. While the contributions of animals were instrumental in the advancement of protocols to protect astronauts, it's important to address questions concerning the ethical, humane treatment of these animals. Rauschenberg would likely have shared such concerns, as his decision to name his dog Laika suggests. The allusion to the three wise monkeys reveals a shrewd awareness of the secretive aspects of NASA's operations. This nuanced commentary encapsulates both the spirit of exploration in the realm of space and the moral implications inherent in the pursuit of scientific progress.

Walking a Fine Line

White Walk (Stoned Moon) (1970) portrays a floating astronaut alongside a circuit-breaker panel and an annunciator panel (the warning system inside the spacecraft), highlighting the dual nature of space exploration—remarkable achievements alongside serious risks. Rauschenberg paid tribute to Ed White, the first American astronaut to conduct a spacewalk on June 3, 1965. His historic twenty-minute extravehicular activity represents a major milestone for humanity in the realm of space travel. The portrayal of the spaceman juxtaposes the optimistic aspects of this achievement with a more solemn reflection on the dangers involved. The contrast between the astronaut's adventurous spirit and the cautionary presence of safety equipment serves as a reminder of the challenges astronauts face when venturing into the cosmos.

A Heartbreaking Pause

Brake (Stoned Moon) (1969) features heavy scrape marks across its predominantly black surface. In certain areas, faded photographic images beneath the surface emerge, showing impressions of a gantry from a rocket launch pad, various perspectives of the mission control room, and a barely discernible destroyed command module. The most distinct images are of three smiling men in space suits positioned at the bottom right corner of the print.[12] These three astronauts—Gus Grissom, Ed White, and Roger Chaffee—were on track to become the first Apollo astronauts to fly on the Saturn V rocket on February 21, 1967. Tragically, in January 1967, during a training exercise in the command module atop the launch pad, a spark from a loose wire ignited a fire within the capsule. The escape hatch failed to operate, and the capsule effectively turned into a coffin, resulting in the death of all three astronauts. The title *Brake* poignantly encapsulates the failures in safety protocols within the space program, highlighting the interruption caused by the Apollo 1 disaster. Notably, the stone used for the lithograph broke during the print run, yet Rauschenberg continued to utilize it since it reflected his emotions when working on the stone.[13] This work functions as a memorial to the astronauts, one striving for abstraction while remaining grounded in the literal. The aggressive scraping and scribbles in the black areas might represent the "scratching out" of the space program, and the title could be interpreted as a call to halt the program at a time when national attention might have been better directed toward ending the Vietnam War.

Anchored in Apollo

Score (Stoned Moon) (1970) presents the juxtaposition of several powerful symbols, including the ancient deity Apollo, shown soaring in the sky; graphics of rockets detailing the sophisticated technologies associated with the space program; a distinct lunar footprint; and an American flag. This combination of elements serves not only to highlight the dramatic transformation in humanity's understanding and interpretation of the heavens since ancient times but also to establish a connection between the god Apollo and the Apollo space program. By positioning the god of music, poetry, and knowledge alongside symbols of space exploration, the artwork engages the aspirations of modern society in relation to its historical roots. Moreover, examining the artwork against the backdrop of contemporary events reveals themes associated with the Vietnam War—the details of Apollo's arrows and the predominant use of red ink, for example—that extend the approach taken in *Brake*.

Harnessing Technology

Strawboss (Stoned Moon) (1970) includes a space capsule, the silhouette of a worker, and an astrolabe. The term "straw boss" describes a worker who holds supervisory authority and suggests themes of oversight and control. By including the distribution patch panel (used to relay data from the launch vehicle back to the flight controllers) from the Kennedy Space Center, Rauschenberg emphasized the essential role of technology in managing NASA operations, prompting us to reflect on how these intricate systems guided humanity toward significant milestones in space exploration. The superimposed image of the astrolabe invites further consideration of technological evolution, opening a dialogue about its transformative impact on human endeavors in space.

Ethics of Exploration

Sky Rite (Stoned Moon) (1969) prominently displays Wernher von Braun—the architect of the Saturn V rocket and director of NASA's Marshall Space Flight Center in Alabama—pointing toward the sky with his right hand. He is positioned amidst NASA personnel who are monitoring a launch. Von Braun was a controversial figure. A pioneer of rocket technology in Nazi Germany, he was recruited by the United States under Operation Paperclip, which involved enlisting more than one hundred scientists from Germany following World War II to contribute to US military efforts and the space program. Was Rauschenberg's choice to highlight von Braun's raised right hand intended to evoke associations with the Nazi salute? Could the brush marks covering von Braun and, indeed, the entire image (and, by implication, the entire space program) suggest the murky ethical ramifications of the US government engaging former Nazi officials in some of the most sensitive roles within national defense and space exploration? Such considerations prompt reflection on the balance between scientific advancement and the ethical implications of employing individuals with a morally complex history in the pursuit of national objectives.

National Products

A box of oranges adorned with the Florida state seal and the phrase "In God We Trust" dominates *Banner (Stoned Moon)* (1969). Around it we see symbols of space exploration, including a rocket, a space capsule, and the presidential seal. At the bottom, almost as an afterthought, we see the Apollo 11 crew—

Neil Armstrong, Edwin "Buzz" Aldrin, and Michael Collins—peering out from a Mobile Quarantine Facility after their splashdown on July 20, 1969. (President Nixon is not depicted in the artwork, but he was indeed present in the original photograph next to the Mobile Quarantine Facility, delivering a welcome address to the nation and the world). Upon returning from the Moon, the astronauts were placed in isolation to safeguard against any potential harmful lunar pathogens that could threaten Earth's environment. With this combination of elements, Rauschenberg established parallels between the astronauts; Florida, the point of departure to the Moon; and oranges, a major crop of the state. Further, it suggests that the astronauts themselves are a kind of national "product." In another context, the title might refer to the public celebration of the Apollo 11 crew and their remarkable achievement, but exactly what Rauschenberg intended is open to further interpretations.[14]

Signs of the Time

The Moon landing was achieved amidst great turmoil in the United States. *Signs* (1970), a screenprint featuring imagery pulled from various 1969 *Newsweek* covers, vividly showcases the stark contrast between national achievement and tragedy through powerful imagery. Next to a photo of the Apollo 11 astronaut Buzz Aldrin lies the civil rights leader Martin Luther King Jr. in his casket and a blood-splattered African American man—a brief encapsulation of the era's racial struggles. Other subjects reflect the tumultuous nature of the time, featuring imagery relating to the Vietnam War, the counterculture movement (with the depiction of Rauschenberg's friend Janis Joplin), and the assassinations of key national figures. Indeed, the print is a catalogue of losses, charting the assassinations of King, President John F. Kennedy, and Senator Robert F. Kennedy and the sacrifice of service members who perished in the Vietnam War.[15] Despite this tumult, the Moon landing is a testament to the resilience and determination of the US space program in the face of adversity. *Signs* is not abstracted in any way and stands as an invitation to consider the duality of triumph and tragedy in a direct, yet evocative manner.

Art on the Moon

Following the Apollo 11 Moon landing, the American sculptor Forrest Myers conceived the novel idea of placing the first intentional artwork on the Moon through the Apollo 12 mission. This work, known as *Moon Museum* (1969), features miniature drawings by Myers and five of his artist friends, including Rauschenberg, and was created in collaboration with Bell Labs engineers Fred Waldhauer and Robert Merkle.[16] Meticulous consideration was given to the size, weight, and materiality of the artwork to ensure it would withstand the arduous journey to the Moon—238,855 miles (384,400 km) with temperatures ranging from 250° F (121° C) to -208° F (-133° C). In the end, *Moon Museum* took the form of a tantalum-nitride-film lithograph on a ceramic wafer about the size of a thumbnail that contained the six miniscule drawings. At the top left, Andy Warhol made a play on his initials in the shape of a rocket or more likely a penis.[17] Next to it is a line by Rauschenberg; that single simple line might represent a horizon line, a kind of graphic representation of art from here to eternity—although, as the art historian Susan Davidson notes, Rauschenberg often began his paintings by drawing a pencil line across a blank canvas.[18] To the right of Rauschenberg's line is a geometric representation by David Novros. The bottom row consists of a sculptural design by Myers based on his early computer art, a sketch of Mickey Mouse by Claus Oldenburg representing his mouse sculptures, and a drawing of a circuitry diagram by John Chamberlain.

Myers's official request to NASA to transport the artwork to the Moon was not granted. It is alleged that an engineer who was working on the Apollo 12 mission covertly affixed *Moon Museum* to a hatch port on the leg of the lunar lander *Intrepid*, concealing it beneath the gold-colored Kapton film.[19] As it constituted a breach of NASA protocol, the project was carried out in secrecy, with a notable absence of official documentation or acknowledgement from the individuals involved. Consequently, the claim that this represents the first artwork on the Moon can't be verified. However, Myers discussed the initiative with the *New York Times* shortly after the mission's completion, presenting as evidence a cryptic telegram received a few days prior to the launch that stated, "Your On. A.O.K. All Systems Go!" It is enigmatically signed, "John F."[20] Rauschenberg appeared to provide confirmation in an interview with a student: "The smallest piece I have ever made is also the furthest away. I made a piece that is approximately 1 inch by ½ inch. It was flown to the Moon by NASA and stored there for future discovery."[21] The Canadian artist Philip Pocock called *Moon Museum* "the first colonial claim to cultural territory in outer space."[22] It is likely that Rauschenberg would have found the term "colonial claim" disconcerting and would have preferred the work to be perceived as an innovative collaboration between the realms of art and science.

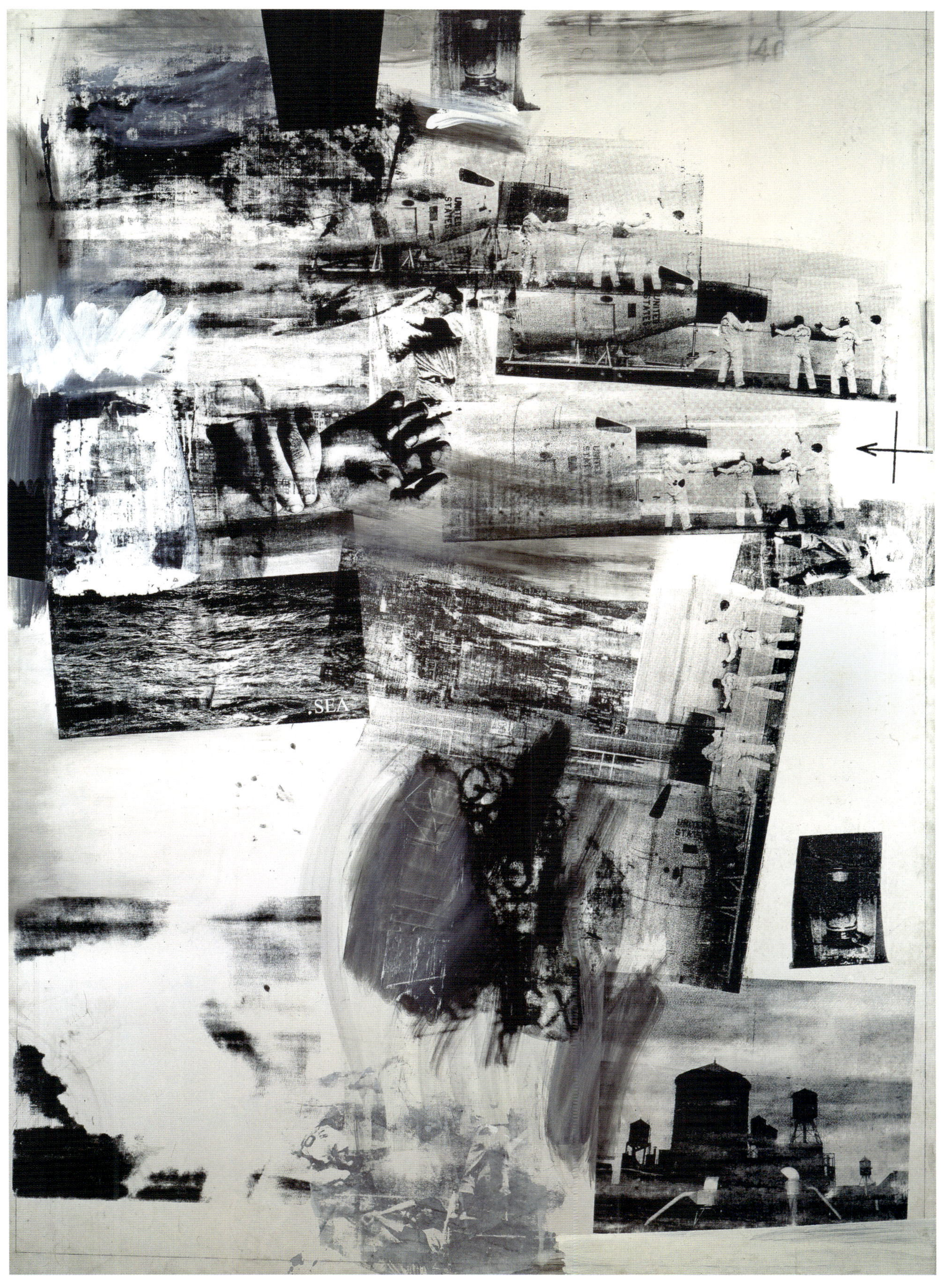

Overcast I, 1962
Oil and silkscreen ink on canvas
97½ × 72 inches (247.7 × 182.9 cm)
Tokyo Metropolitan Museum

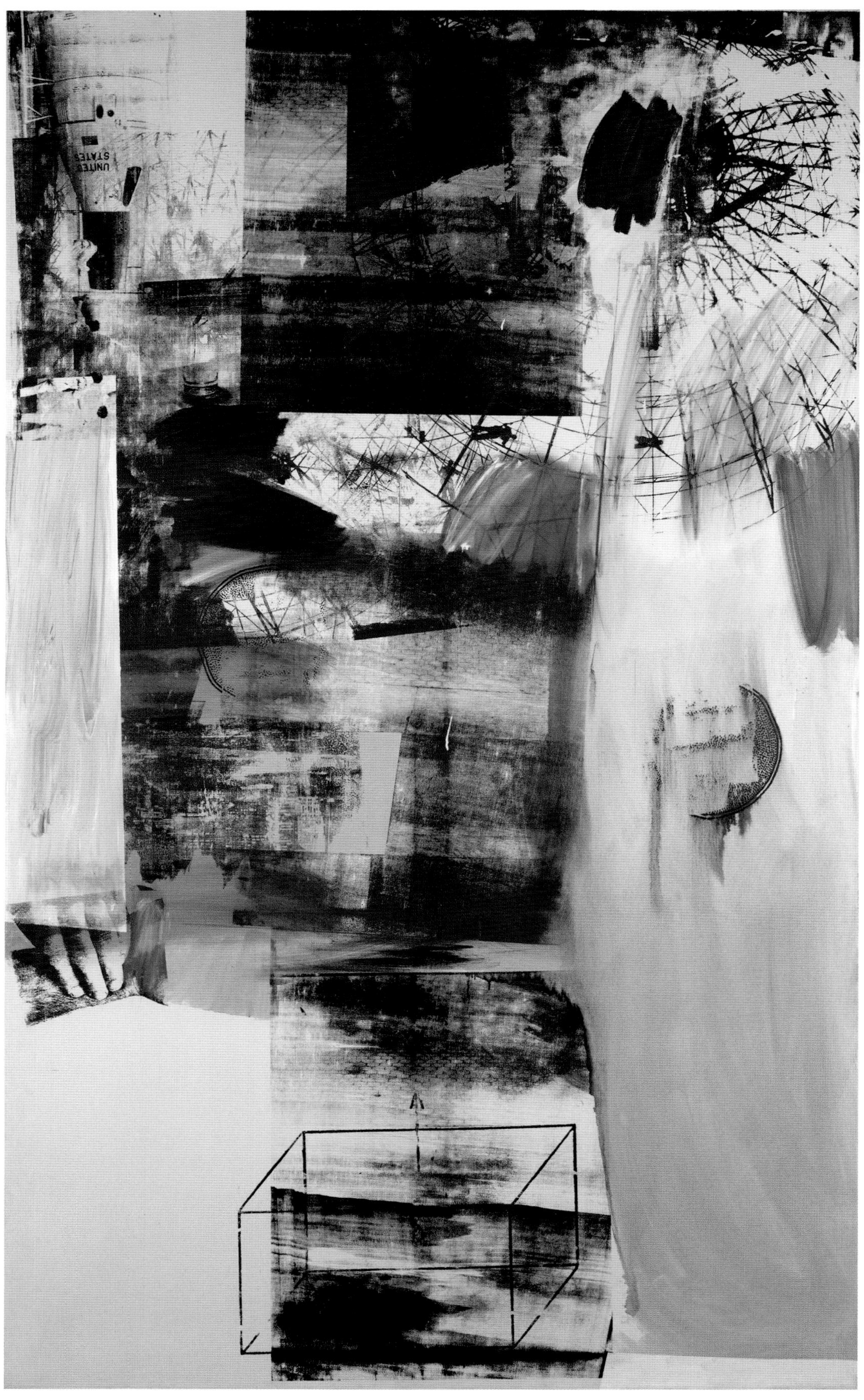

Glider, 1962
Oil and silkscreen ink on canvas
96 × 60 inches (244.2 × 152.4 cm)
The Menil Collection

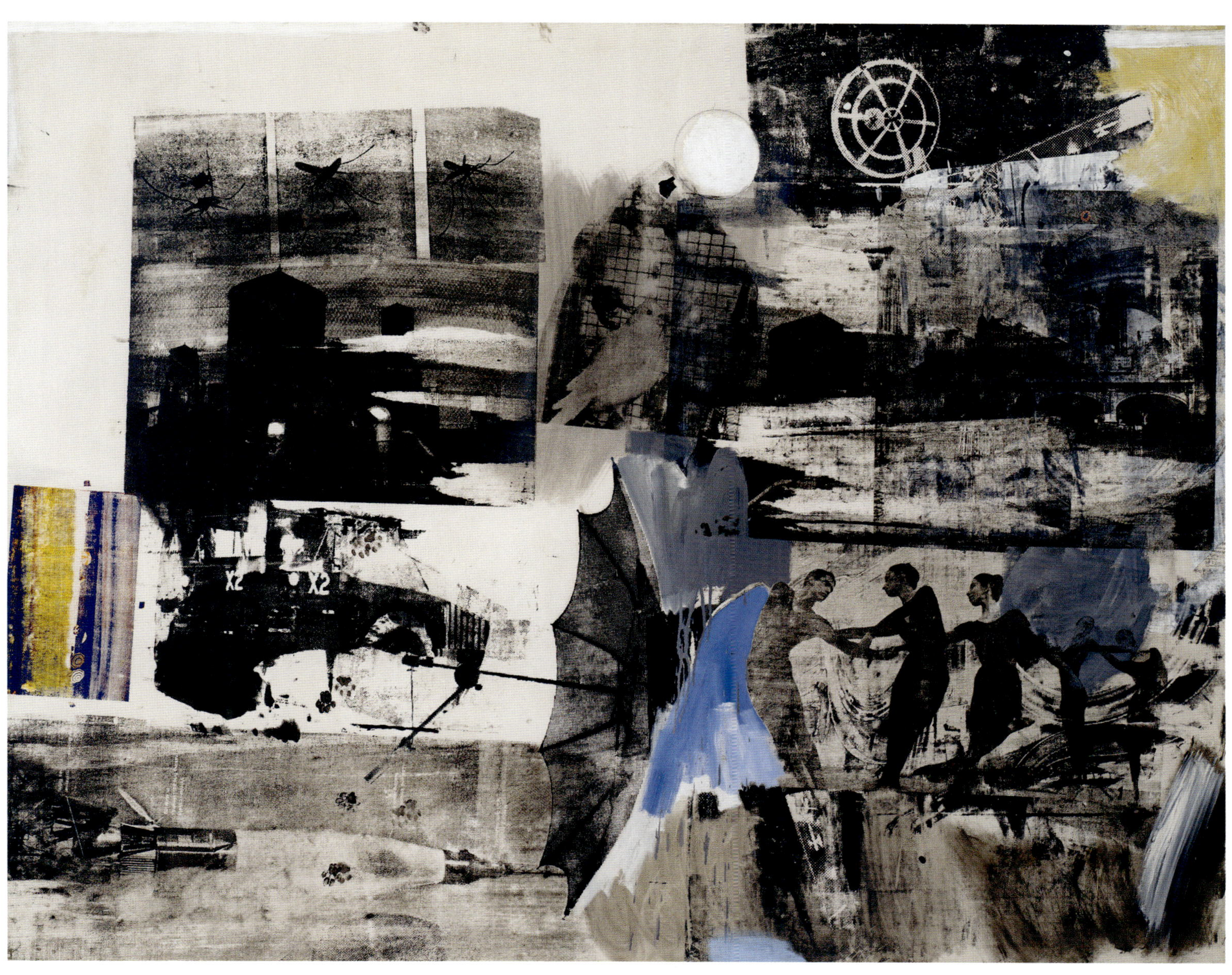

Scanning, 1963
Oil and silkscreen ink on canvas
55¾ × 73 inches (141.6 × 185.4 cm)
San Francisco Museum of Modern Art

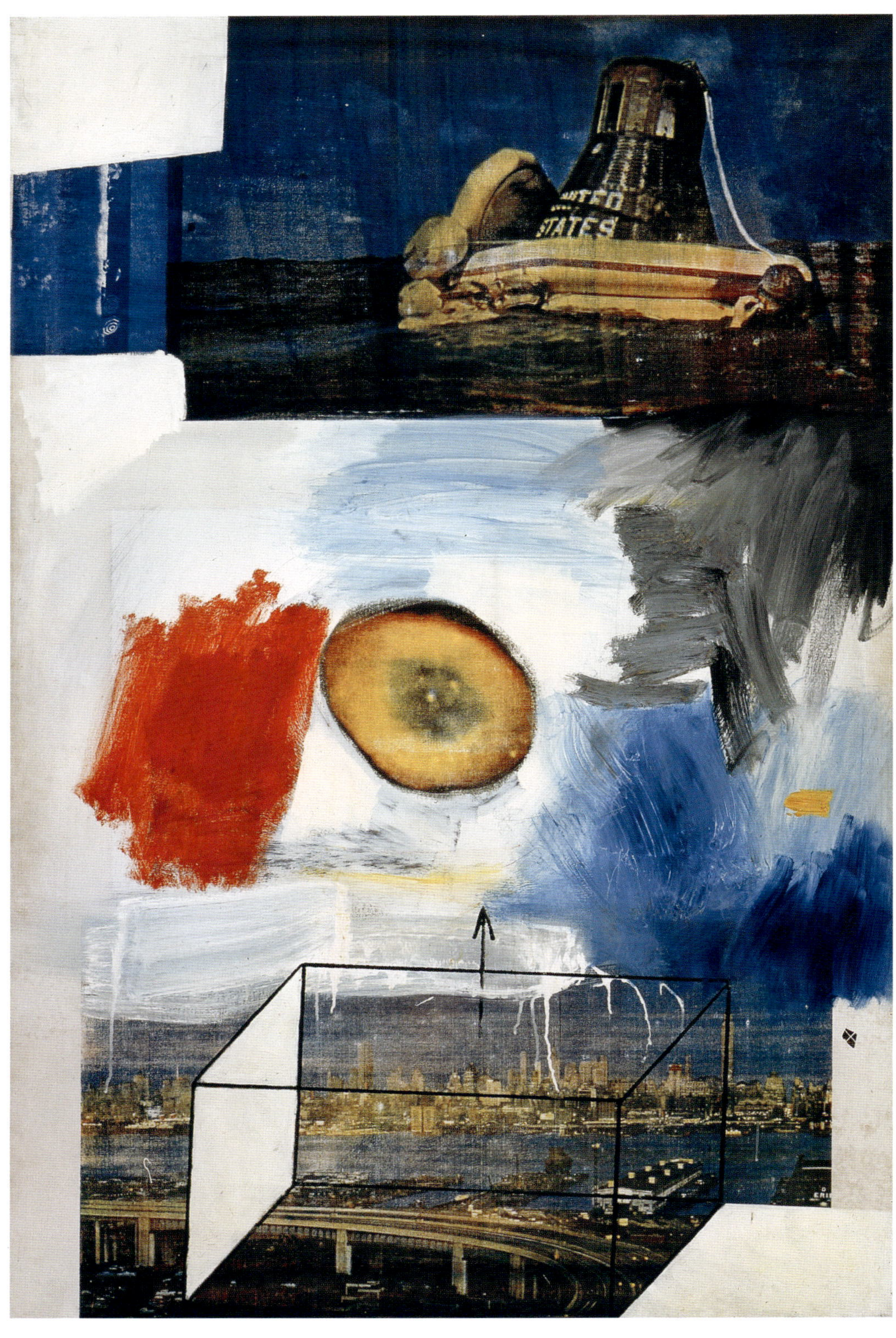

Stop Gap, 1963
Oil and silkscreen ink on canvas
58 × 40 inches (147.3 × 101.6 cm)
Foundation Arc-en-Ciel/Hara Museum Collection

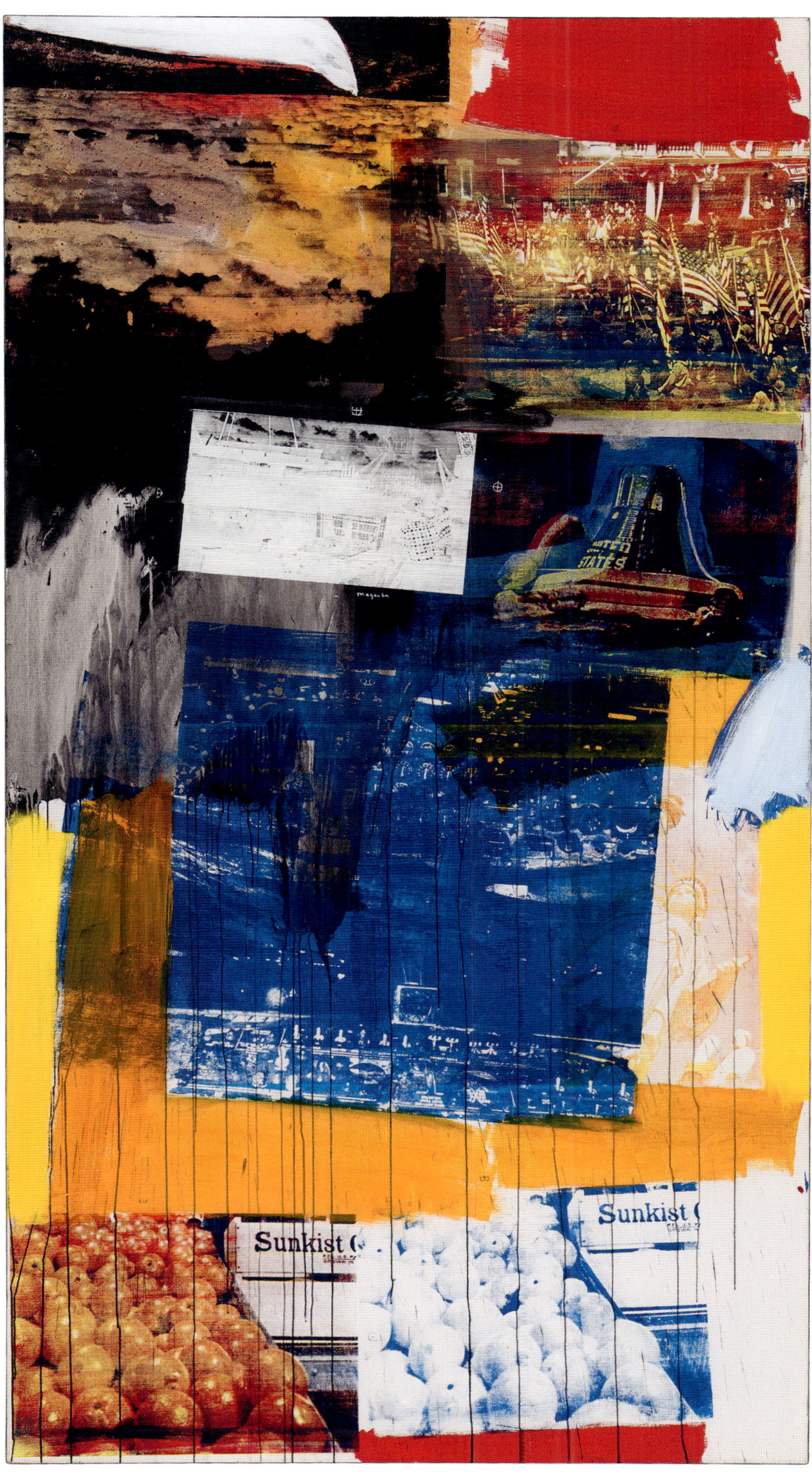

Whale, 1964
Oil and silkscreen ink on canvas
108 × 60 inches (274.3 × 152.4 cm)
Hirshhorn Museum and Sculpture Garden

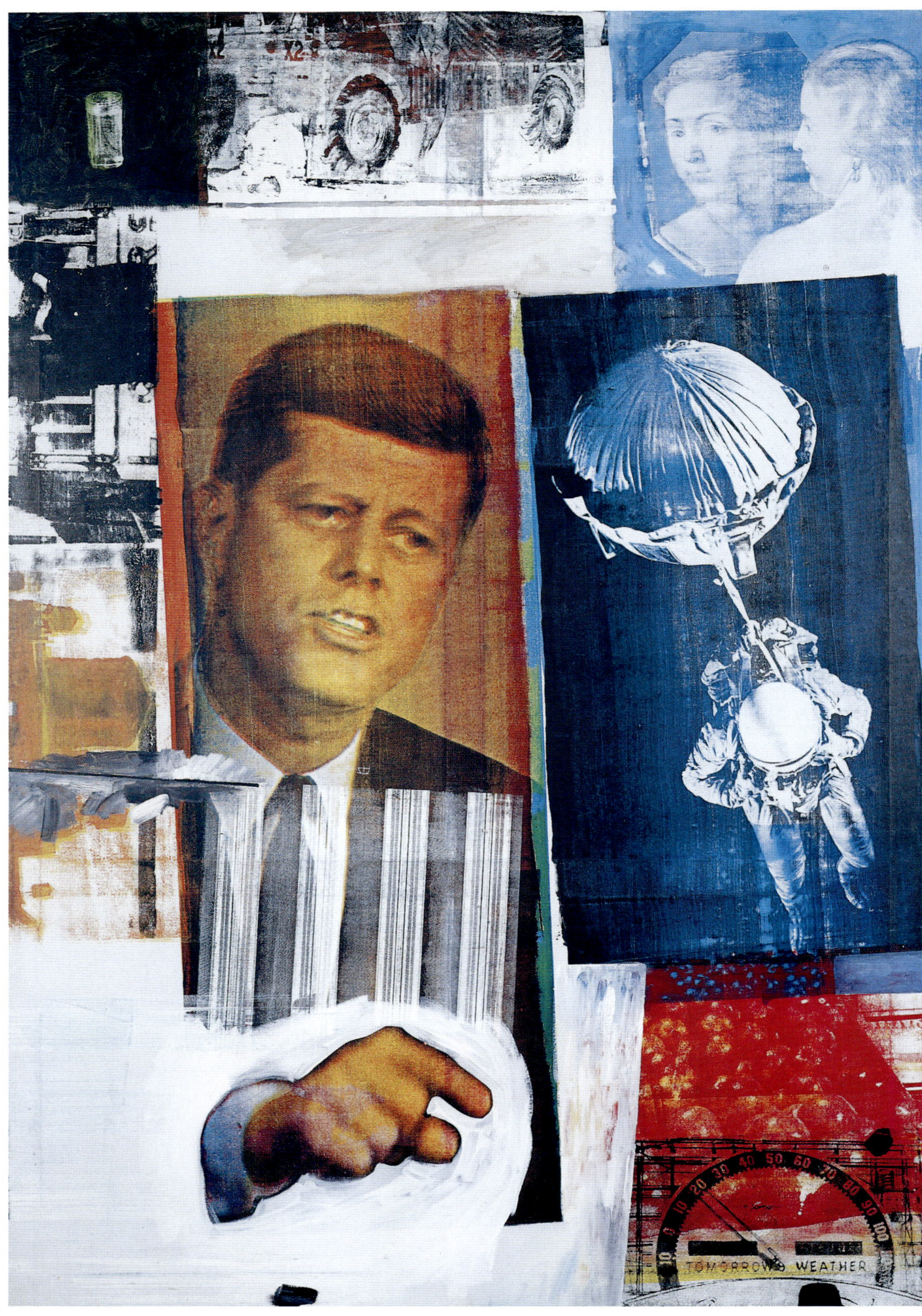

Retroactive II, 1963
Oil and silkscreen ink on canvas
84 × 60 inches (213.2 × 152.4 cm)
Museum of Contemporary Art Chicago

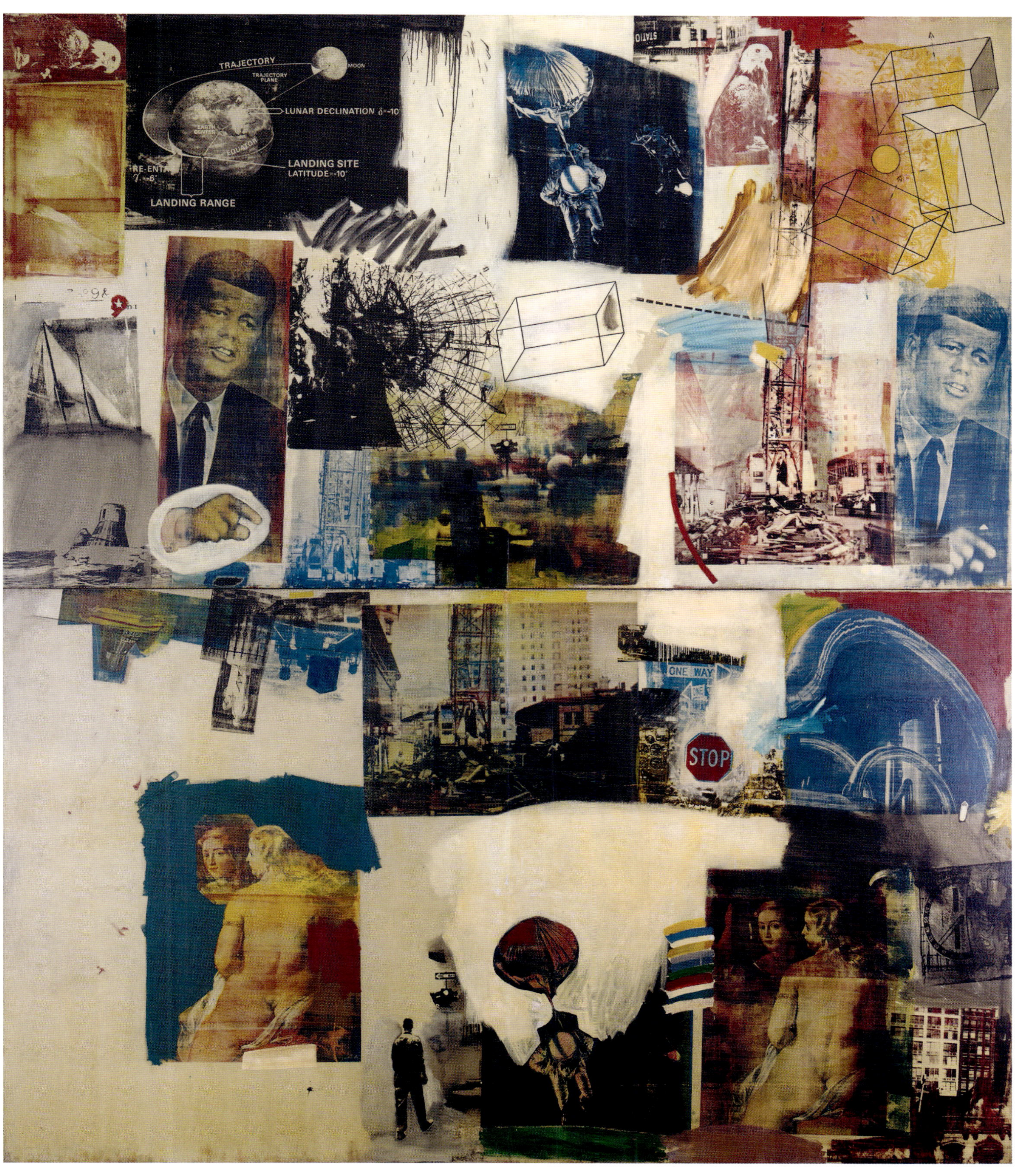

Skyway, 1964
Oil and silkscreen on canvas
216 × 192 inches (548.6 × 487.7 cm)
Dallas Museum of Art

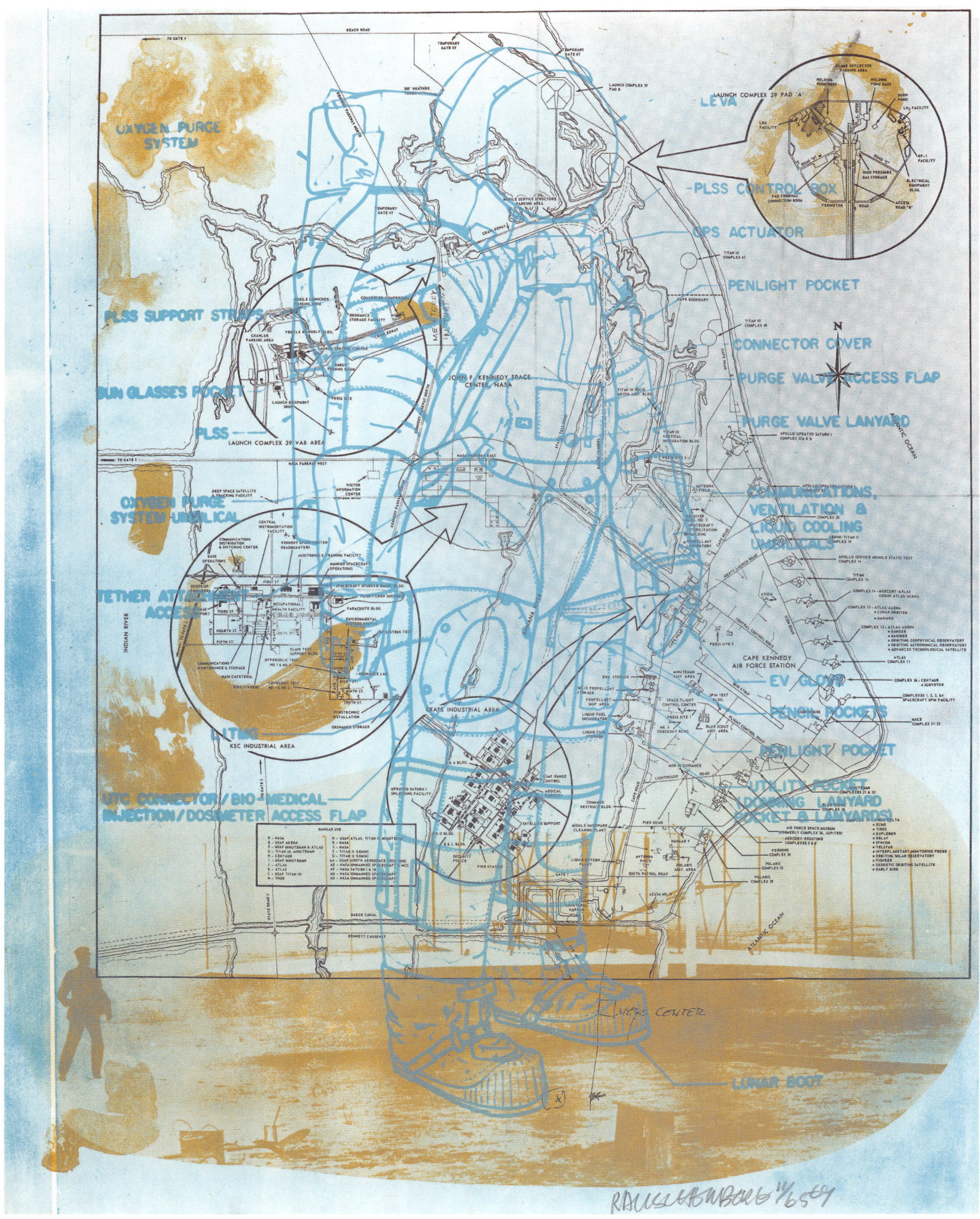

Trust Zone (Stoned Moon), 1969
Lithograph
40 × 33 inches (101.5 × 83.8 cm)
Hirshhorn Museum and Sculpture Garden

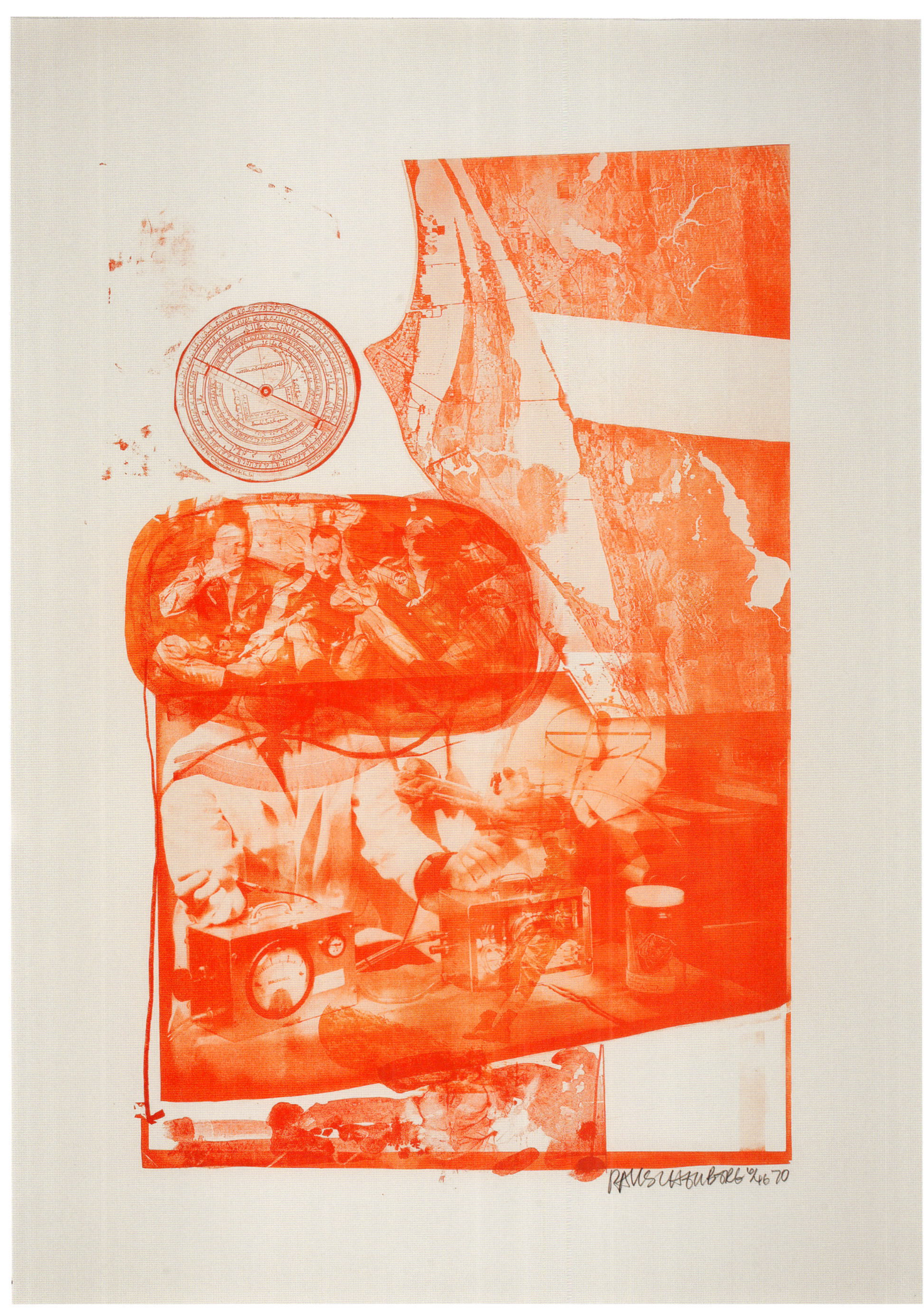

Ape (Stoned Moon), 1970
Lithograph
46 × 33 inches (116.8 × 83.9 cm)
Hirshhorn Museum and Sculpture Garden

White Walk (Stoned Moon), 1970
Lithograph
42¼ × 29½ inches (107.4 × 74.9 cm)
Hirshhorn Museum and Sculpture Garden

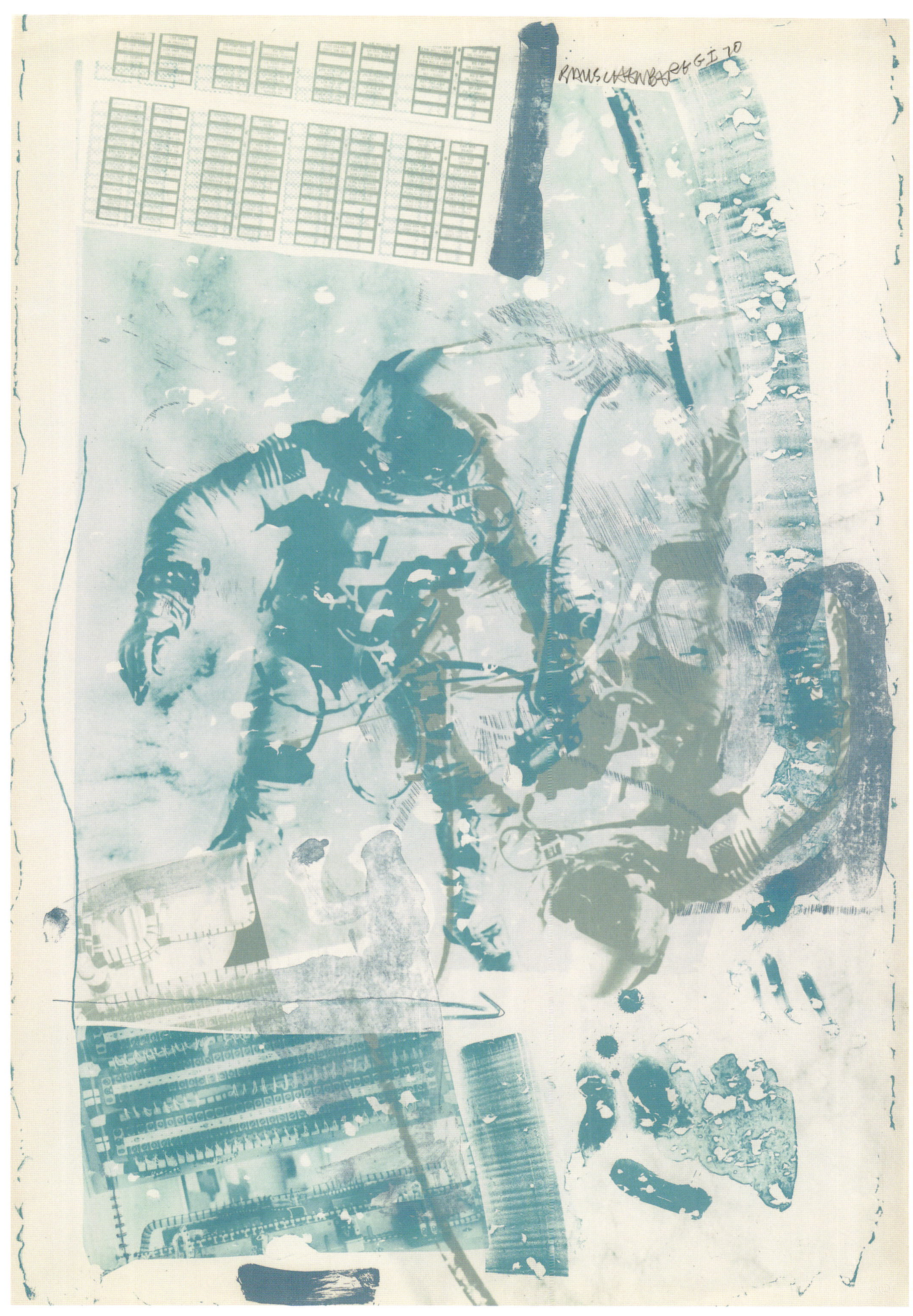

RAUSCHENBERG I 70

Brake (Stoned Moon), 1969
Lithograph
42 × 29 inches (106.7 × 73.6 cm)
Hirshhorn Museum and Sculpture Garden

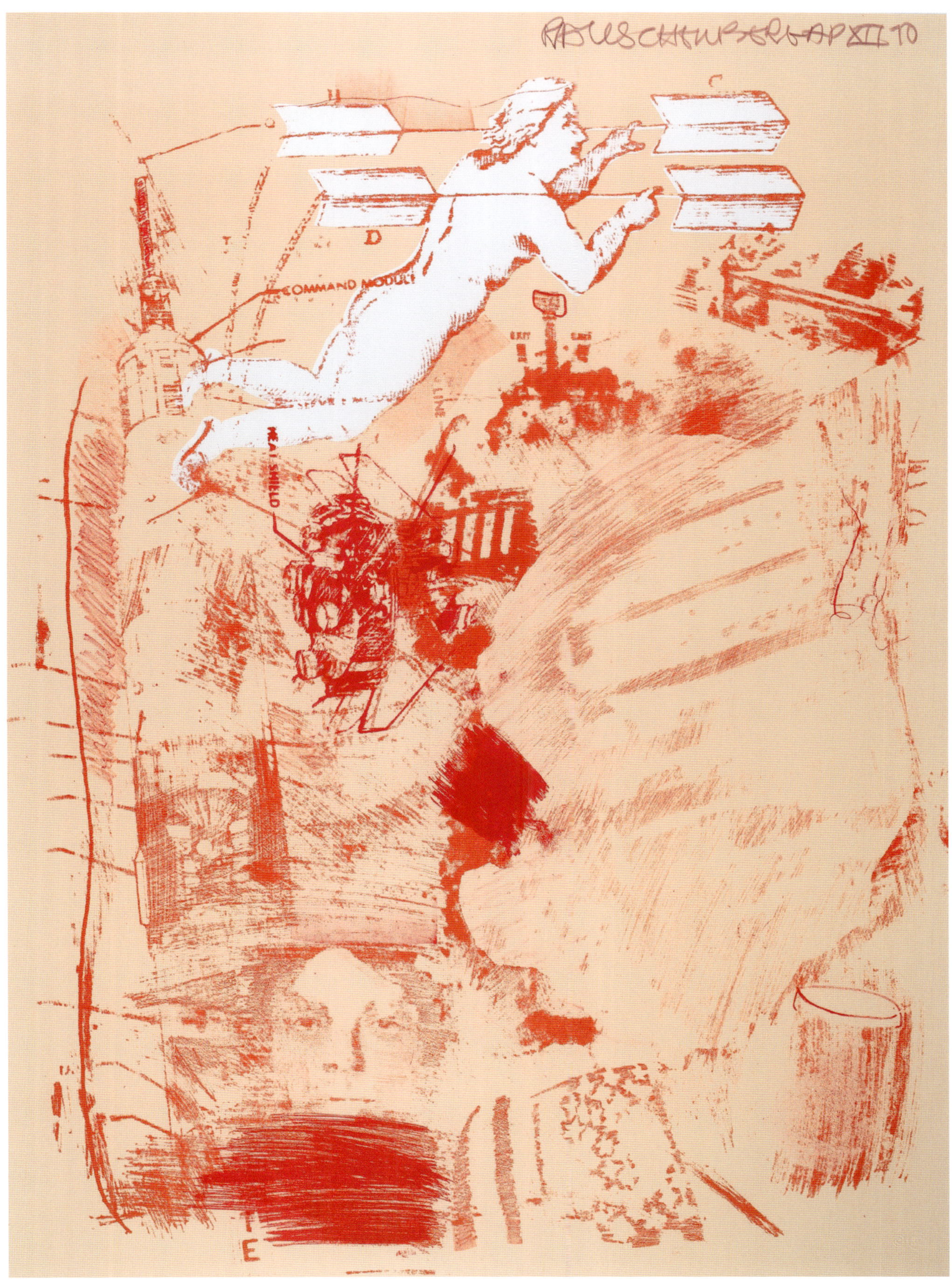

Score (Stoned Moon), 1970
Lithograph
26 × 19½ inches (66 × 49.5 cm)
National Gallery of Art, Washington, DC

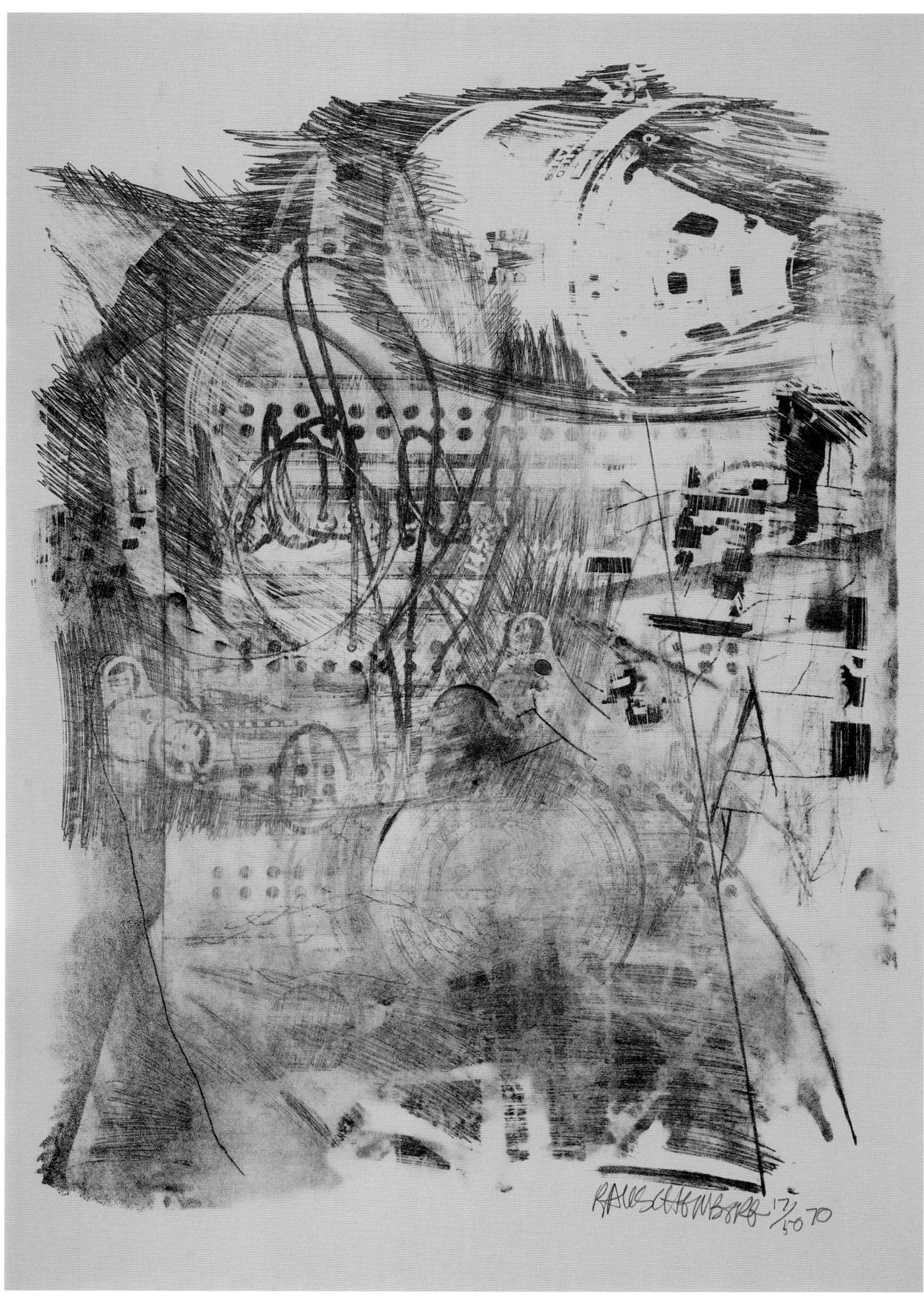

Strawboss (Stoned Moon), 1970
Lithograph
30 × 22 inches (76.1 × 55.9 cm)
Hirshhorn Museum and Sculpture Garden

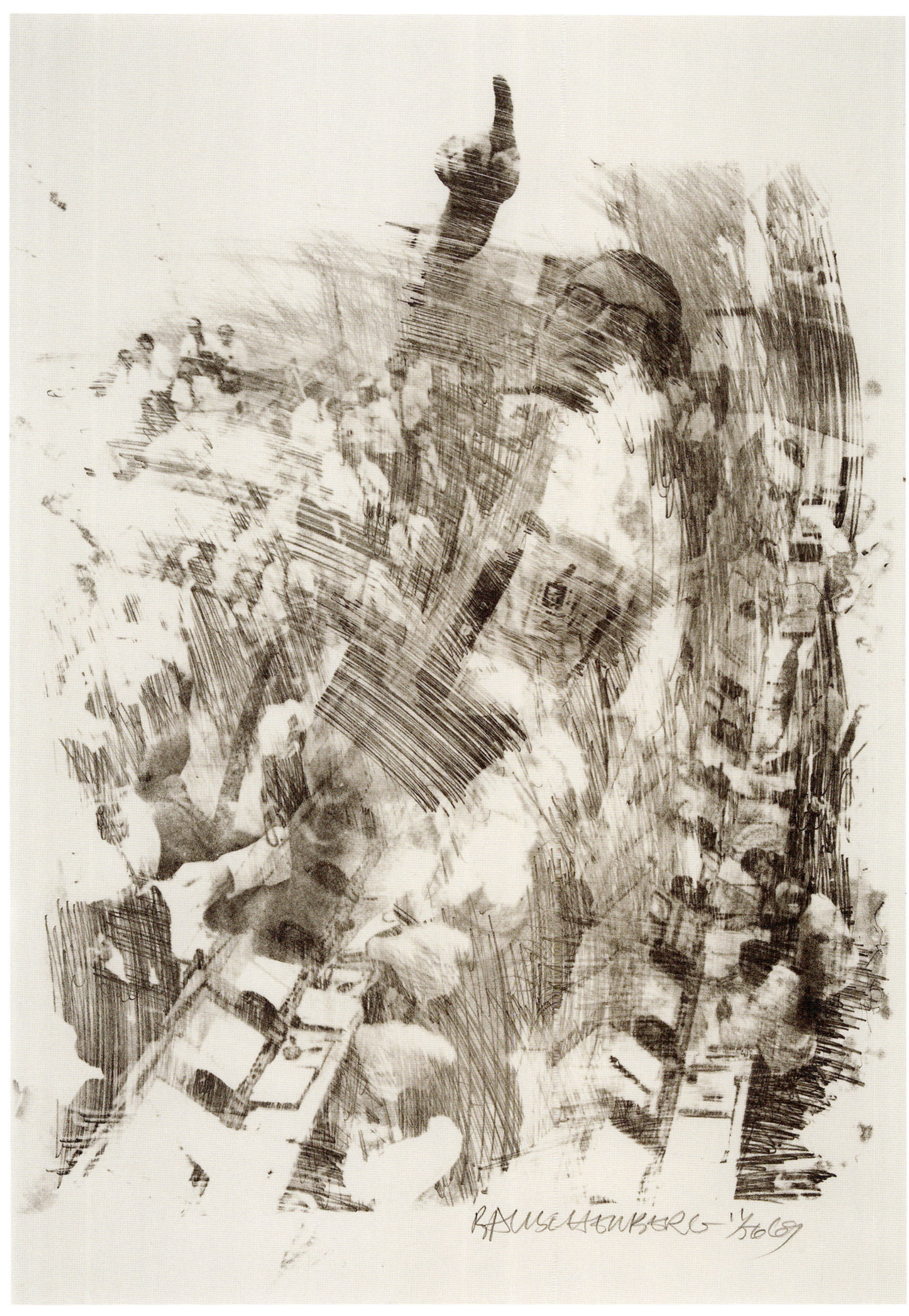

Sky Rite (Stoned Moon), 1969
Lithograph
33 × 23 inches (83.8 × 58.4 cm)
Hirshhorn Museum and Sculpture Garden

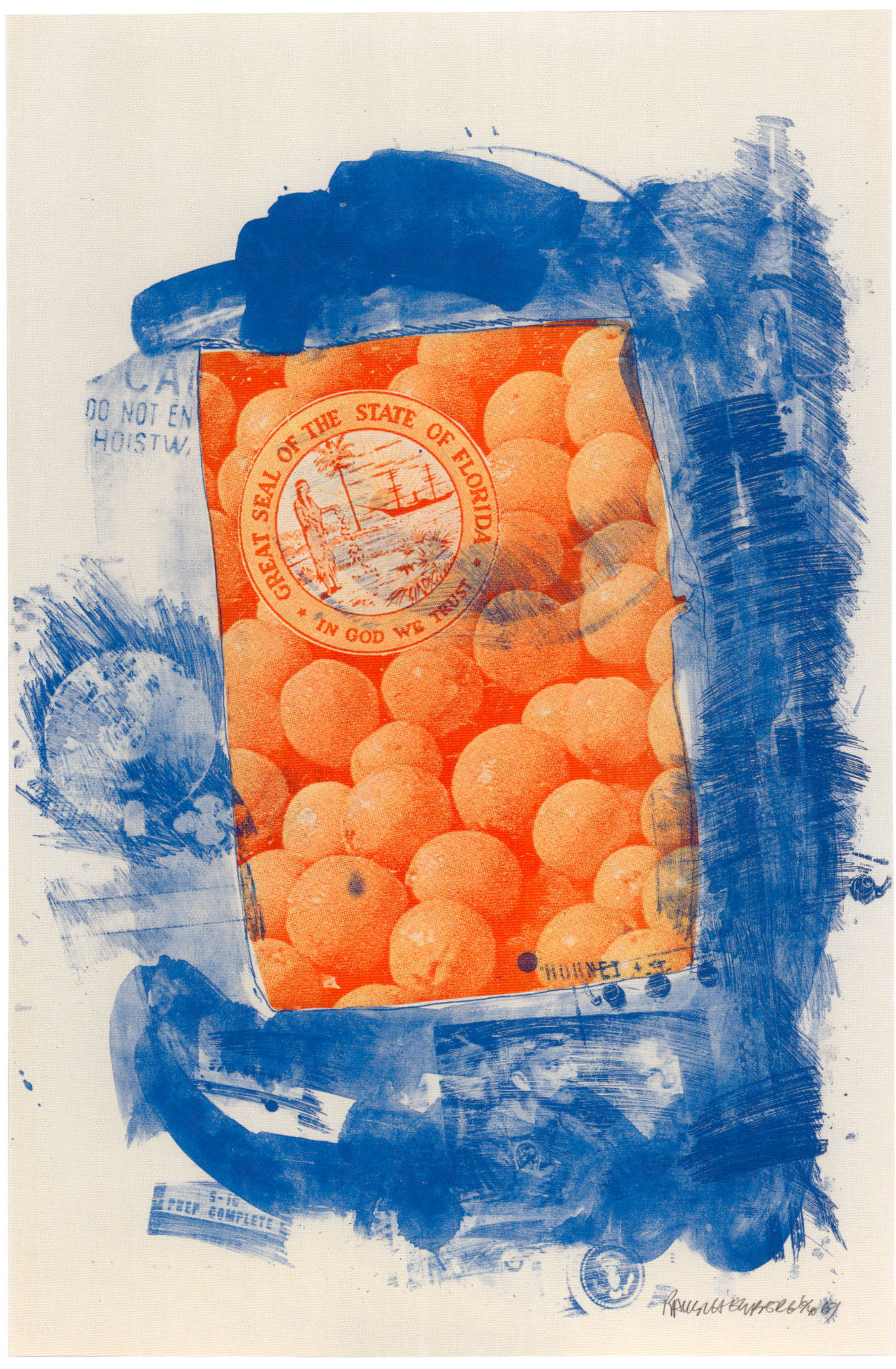

Banner (Stoned Moon), 1969
Lithograph
54½ × 36 inches (138.4 × 91.4 cm)
San Francisco Museum of Modern Art

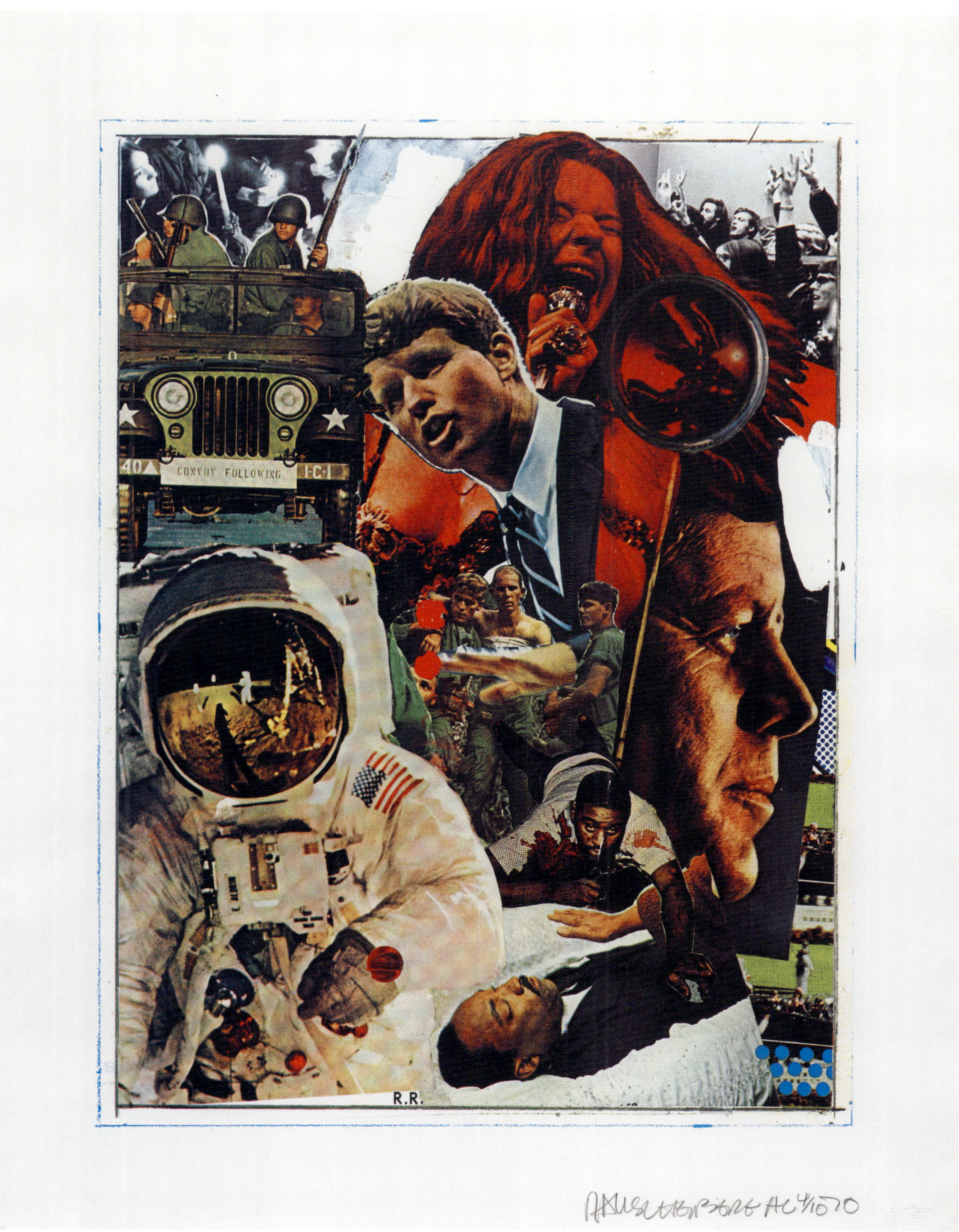

Signs, 1970
Screenprint
43 × 34 inches (109.2 × 86.4 cm)
Robert Rauschenberg Foundation

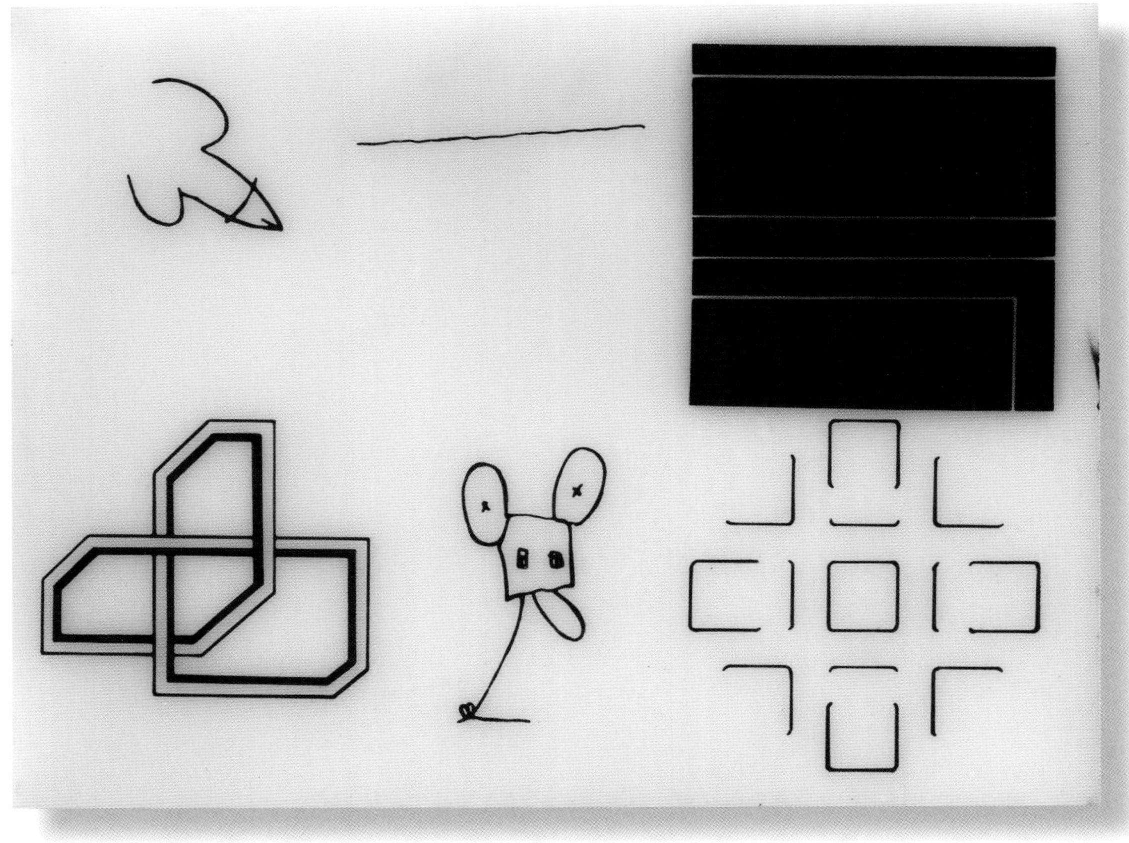

Forrest Myers (b. 1941), in collaboration with John Chamberlain (1927–2011), David Novros (b. 1941), Claes Oldenburg (b. 1929–22), Robert Rauschenberg (1925–2008), and Andy Warhol (1928–87)
Moon Museum, 1969
Lithograph of tantalum-nitride film on ceramic wafer
½ × ¾ inch (1.4 × 1.9 cm)
Robert Rauschenberg Foundation

1. I FEEL LIKE I AM VERY LUCKY TO BE THE FIRST PERSON TO SEE SOMETHING I HAVE NEVER SEEN BEFORE.

2. THE SMALLEST PIECE I HAVE EVER MADE IS ALSO THE FUTHER IST AWAY. I MADE A PIECE THAT IS APROX. 1"×½". IT WAS FLOWN TO THE MOON BY NASA AND STORED THERE FOR FUTURE DISCOVERY.

3. I DON'T RECALL I ALWAYS DREW AND PAINTED AND STILL DO. I HAVE DYSLEXIA, DIFFICULT TO READ, SO I DREW IN ALL MY SCHOOL BOOKS.

Rauschenberg's responses to questions sent from Alexa Voytek for a school report, 2001. The topics discussed included *Moon Museum* (1969) and Rauschenberg's experiences with dyslexia.

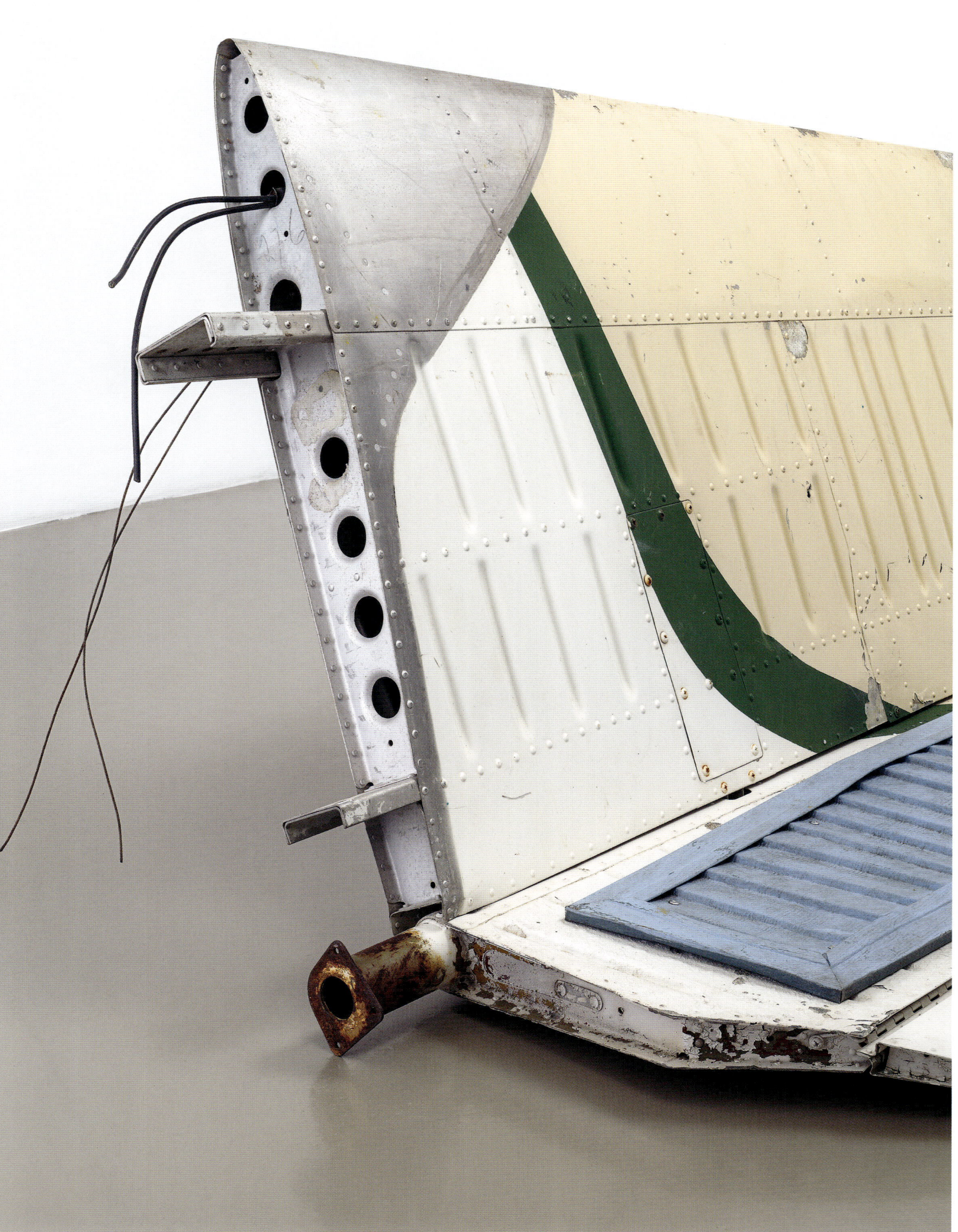

6

Reinventing Flight

**The reason I find material in junkyards is because each piece
of material already has its history and I rediscover it.**

—Robert Rauschenberg[1]

Robert Rauschenberg's innovative approach to art making, particularly his use of found objects from junkyards, can be traced back to his experiences as a student at Black Mountain College in North Carolina from fall 1948 through spring 1949, as well as in 1951 and 1952. During that time, he collaborated with the artist Susan Weil, to whom he would be married from 1950 to 1952. Their work as campus trash collectors not only provided valuable materials for their artistic endeavors but also fostered a spirit of resourcefulness and creativity that significantly shaped Rauschenberg's artistic vision.

The couple explored the campus in a truck, collecting trash and discarded items from various locations. Occasionally, Weil's French teacher would leave surprise gifts in the refuse, adding an element of delight to their adventures. Weil said, "We'd go to the dump, and it was like playtime! … Bob was that way in the rest of his life, you know, having so much happiness in the dump!"[2] In a 2003 interview, Rauschenberg expounded on his passion for common and abandoned objects: "My aesthetics have a lot to do with the availability of materials. I believe that art always starts from zero."[3]

Such a stance underscores the impact of Rauschenberg's artistic influences, particularly Marcel Duchamp. The groundbreaking Dada artist is celebrated for incorporating everyday objects into his work and challenging conventional notions of art. In 1912 Duchamp, along with fellow artists Fernand Léger and Constantin Brâncuși, attended a Paris air show that would have a lasting impact on the art world. Léger recalled: "Marcel was a rather reserved individual, but there was an intriguing quality about him. As we walked among the motors and propellers in silence, he suddenly turned to Brancusi and proclaimed, 'It's all over for painting. Who could better that propeller? Tell me, can you do that?'"[4] Duchamp's "readymade" *Bicycle Wheel*, created in 1913 by attaching a bicycle wheel to a kitchen stool, served as

a pivotal influence for Rauschenberg, who fondly recalled his first encounter with the work: "I saw Marcel Duchamp's stool with the bicycle wheel and thought that's the most fantastic piece of sculpture I've ever seen."[5]

Duchamp's example is evident in Rauschenberg's *Prehistoric Rose Spore (Kabal American Zephyr)* (1981). Featuring a faux wooden propeller mounted on a wooden stool, the sculpture pays tribute to Duchamp and acknowledges the importance of aviation to both artists, who recognized how it reflected the changing societal landscape and encouraged fresh, unconventional perspectives in their work.

Resurrected Tail Feathers

The integration of found objects, such as parts from flying machines, played a significant role in the sculptures of Rauschenberg's *Glut* series (1986–89/1991–94). This series emerged in the wake of an oil glut in Texas that sparked an economic crisis in the artist's hometown of Port Arthur and surrounding areas. (The supply of oil outpaced demand, drastically lowering prices and causing a financial downturn.) As a result, the landscape became littered with a wealth of abandoned materials, including signage from closed gas stations, discarded vehicles, and various industrial components, reflecting both the challenges and the creative opportunities of that time.[6] Susan Davidson explains that some of the *Glut* works were presented "simply as found"; for others, Rauschenberg "combined or assembled two or three or four elements into a whole."[7] In a few of the works, he adeptly incorporated components from the tail sections of aircraft—colloquially referred to among aviators as the "tail feathers."

Nagshead Summer Glut Sketch (1987) incorporates a horizontal stabilizer, a component that plays a critical role in controlling the aircraft's pitch (the vertical movement of the

Detail of **Wing Swing Glut**, 1988

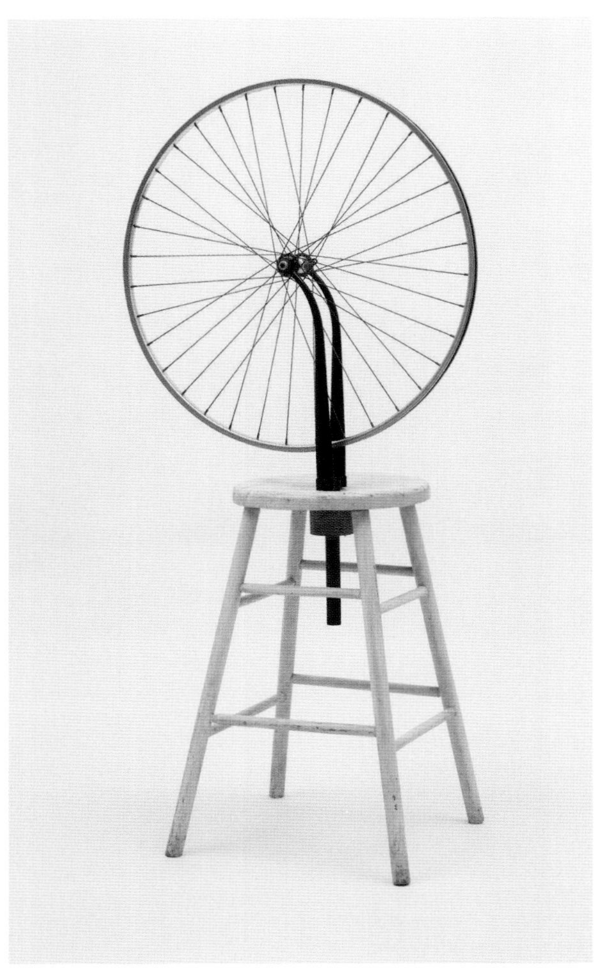

Marcel Duchamp (1887–1968), *Bicycle Wheel,* 1951 (third version, after lost original of 1913). Metal wheel mounted on painted wood stool, 51 × 25 × 16½ inches (129.5 × 63.5 × 41.9 cm). The Museum of Modern Art, New York.

nose of the plane) and is essential for maintaining stability during flight. The work also includes a wooden two-person seat from a swing set and a bicycle frame—always a powerful symbol of flight and innovation throughout Rauschenberg's oeuvre. The title nods to Nags Head, a town about ten miles south of Kitty Hawk, the site where the Wright brothers achieved their first flight. This connection enriches the artwork's narrative of exploration and technological progress.

One of the two metal parts of *Finn Early Winter Glut* (1987) is a triangular component resembling part of a plane's fixed vertical stabilizer, which helps maintain an aircraft's steady flight path. As the title makes clear, it also resembles the fin of a fish or a boat, highlighting the intersection of nature and technology in the artwork.

Wing Swing Glut (1988) is constructed from a horizontal elevator, stabilizer, and a trim tab sourced from the tail section of an aircraft. When positioned on a flat surface, it recalls the seat of a swing, the first taste of flight for many children, as the title of the work suggests. It may also reference the Swing Wing, a toy

introduced in 1965 in the aftermath of the hula-hoop craze. It consisted of a plastic helmet to which were attached plastic streamers that wearers could twirl by spinning their head. A television commercial for the toy featured a memorable jingle with the phrases, "It is a new thing, it is a fun thing, it is a Swing Wing."[8] It's possible that Rauschenberg, who had a television constantly playing in the background in his home and studio, would have heard the commercial.[9] Certainly, the goofy commercial with dizzy kids would have resonated with Rauschenberg's sense of humor. A "swing wing" is also a type of airplane wing that can be swept back during flight and then restored to its original position, allowing for mid-flight modifications to the aircraft's shape and enhancing its speed performance. The sculpture is a multilayered work that invites viewers to consider the interplay of aviation, wordplay, and human-powered propulsion.

The relationship between the titles of Rauschenberg's sculptures and their underlying concepts enhances the interpretation of his artwork, providing clues to his perspectives on flight and aerodynamics. Rauschenberg said, "Usually, I think I try to relate titles to imagery that is already there. Titles are normally related puns…. Giving titles to my paintings is the last thing I do. It is almost dessert for me…. They are not necessary for the understanding of the work; rather, they serve as an extension—like an additional color—that broadens the work's scope. Titles should not impose limitations or persuade; instead, they should encourage viewers to explore further."[10] Rauschenberg's personal collection contains a wealth of books on the history of aviation, highlighting his knowledge of the field and illustrating how these publications informed his titling of artworks.[11]

Flight Exchange

Twin Bloom / ROCI TIBET (1985) is an interactive sculpture that captures the essence of a flying insect. The design incorporates bicycle pedals that spin fan blades, evoking a sense of flight. Its dual or "twin" fan system is reminiscent of twin-engine aircraft or perhaps the wings of a butterfly. This sculpture stands out among Rauschenberg's flight-inspired sculptures for its petite size, vibrant colors, and capacity for motion. It was made for the 1985 exhibition in Tibet mounted as part of the Rauschenberg Overseas Culture Interchange (ROCI) project, an initiative the artist conceived and funded to promote global peace and

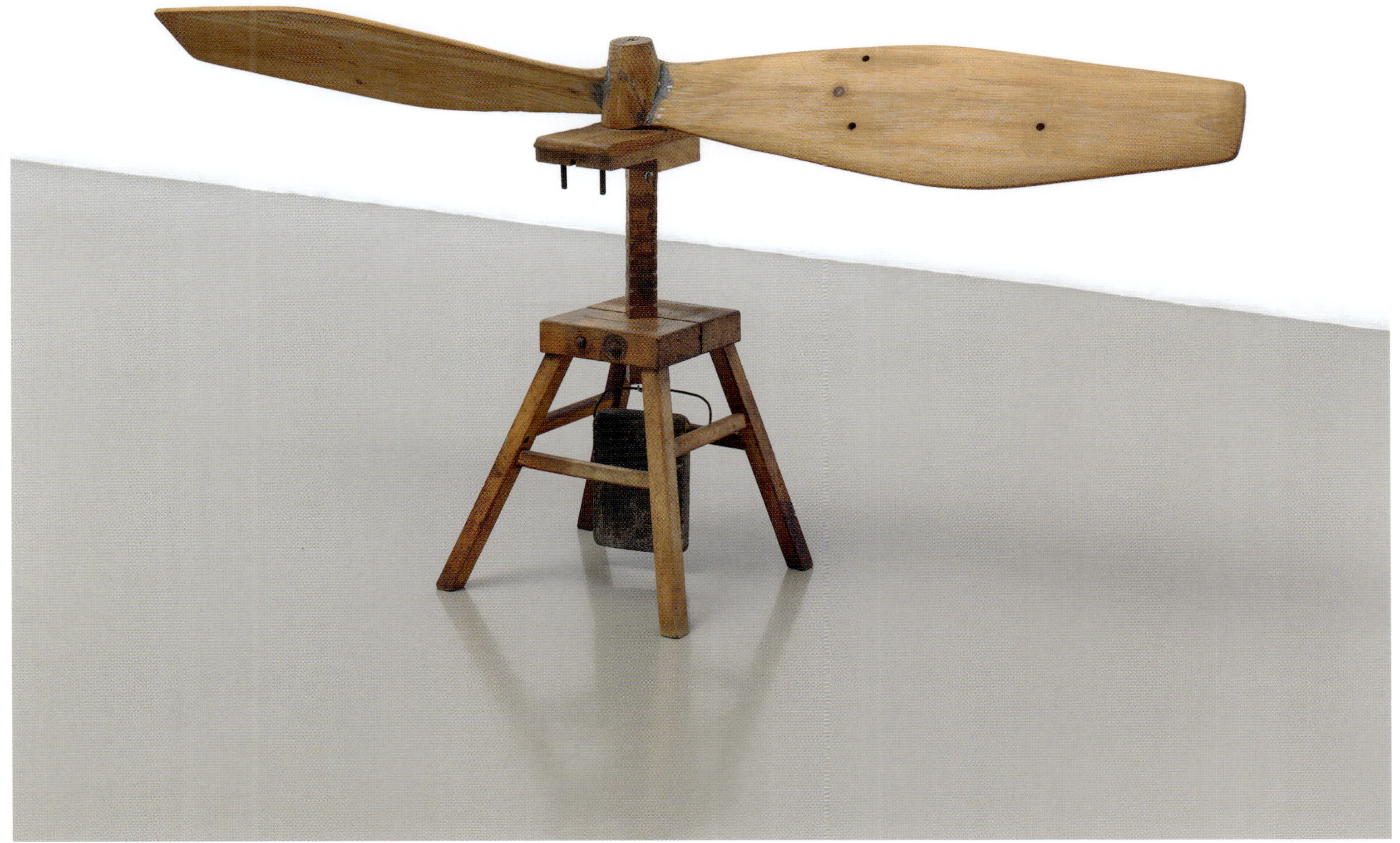

Prehistoric Rose Spore (Kabal American Zephyr), 1981
Assembled wood, stone, and metal
34½ × 76½ × 15¼ inches (87.6 × 194.3 × 38.7 cm)
Robert Rauschenberg Foundation

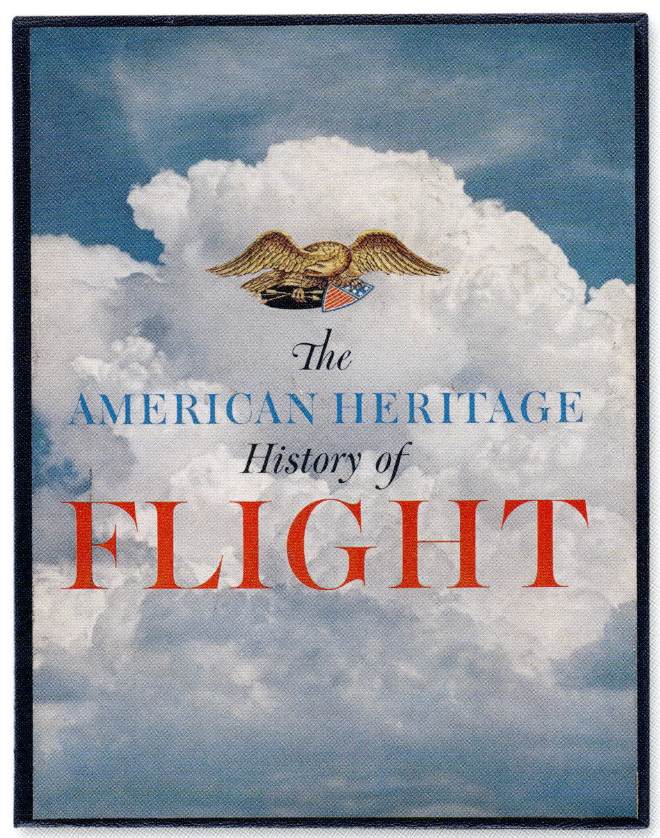

mutual comprehension through artistic expression from 1984 to 1991. ROCI (named for Rauschenberg's pet turtle Rocky) involved travel to ten countries—Mexico, Chile, Venezuela, China, Tibet, Japan, Cuba, the USSR, Germany, and Malaysia, followed by a final exhibition held in 1991 at the National Gallery of Art, Washington, DC—where he collected ideas and materials for paintings and sculptures and mounted exhibitions.[12] In Tibet, he was intrigued by the local practice of blessing or anointing quotidian items with yak butter. Rauschenberg said, "I made [*Twin Bloom / ROCI TIBET*] so it could be touched. I loved the Tibetans . . . . I thought they were so close to my sensibilities."[13] Turning the pedals in *Twin Bloom* causes the fan blades to spin, recalling the Tibetan prayer wheels seen throughout the Himalayas.

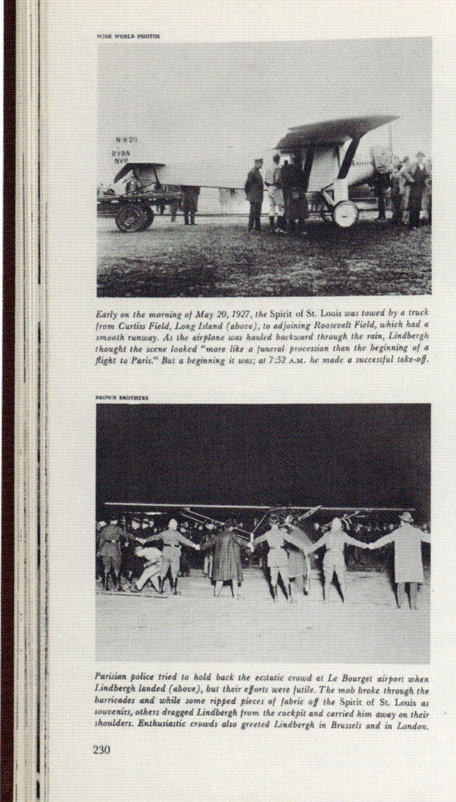

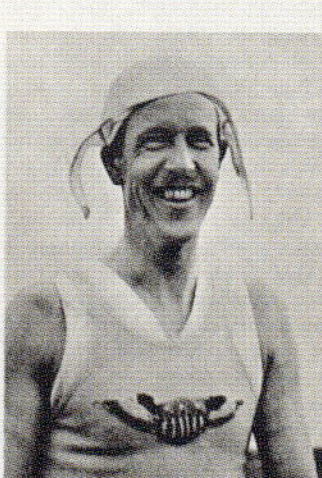

Rauschenberg's personal collection contains books on flight highlighting his interest in and knowledge of the field. Some of the pages of the books served as source materials in his artworks. For example, a full-page portrait of Charles Lindbergh was removed from *The American Heritage History of Flight*.

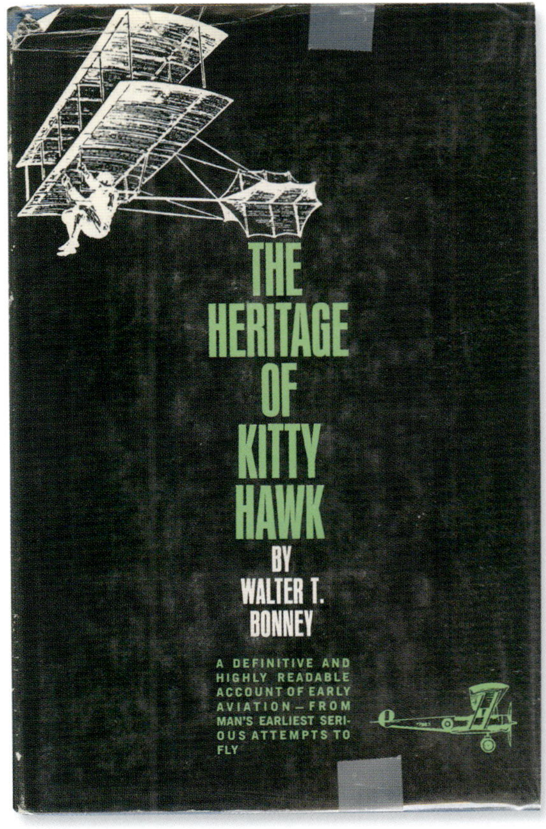

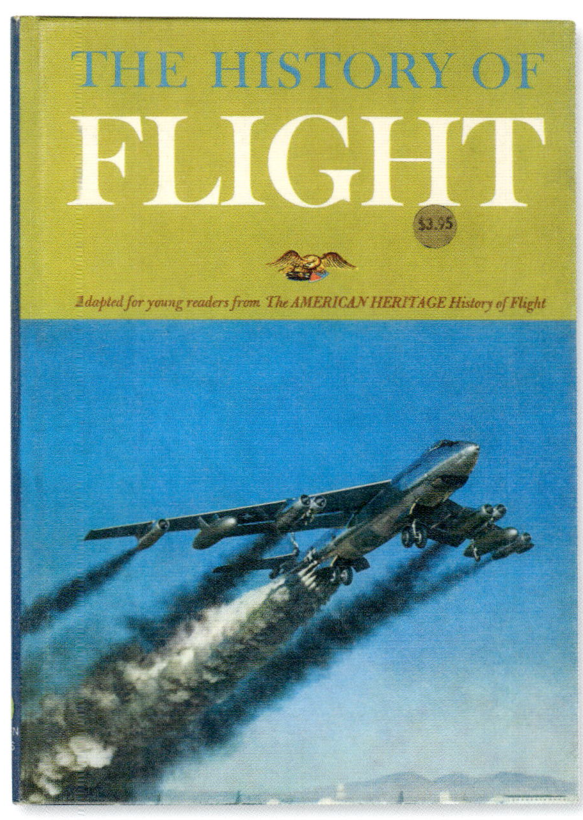

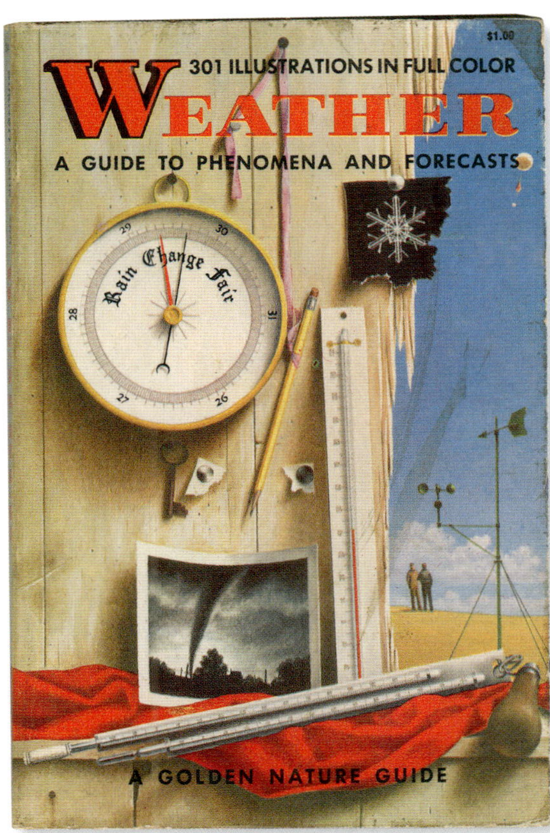

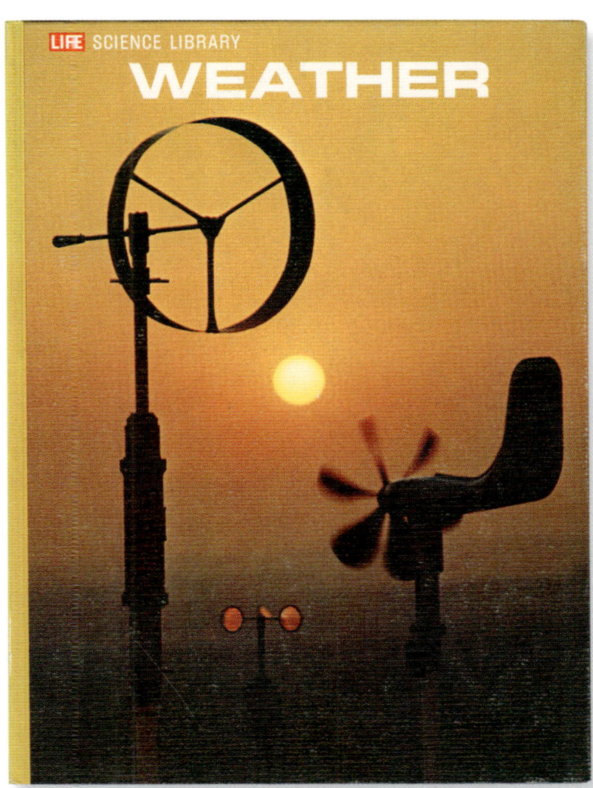

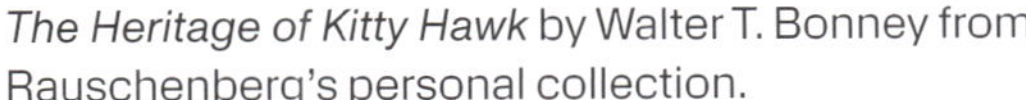

The Heritage of Kitty Hawk by Walter T. Bonney from Rauschenberg's personal collection.

Weather: A Guide to Phenomena and Forecasts by Paul E. Lehr, R. Will Burnett, and Herbert S. Zim, and illustrated by Harry McNaught from Rauschenberg's personal collection.

An image of the Montgolfier hot-air balloon and a photograph of John Stringfellow's steam engine were removed from Rauschenberg's copy of *The History of Flight* and used as source materials.

Weather by Philip Duncan Thompson and Robert O'Brien from Rauschenberg's personal collection.

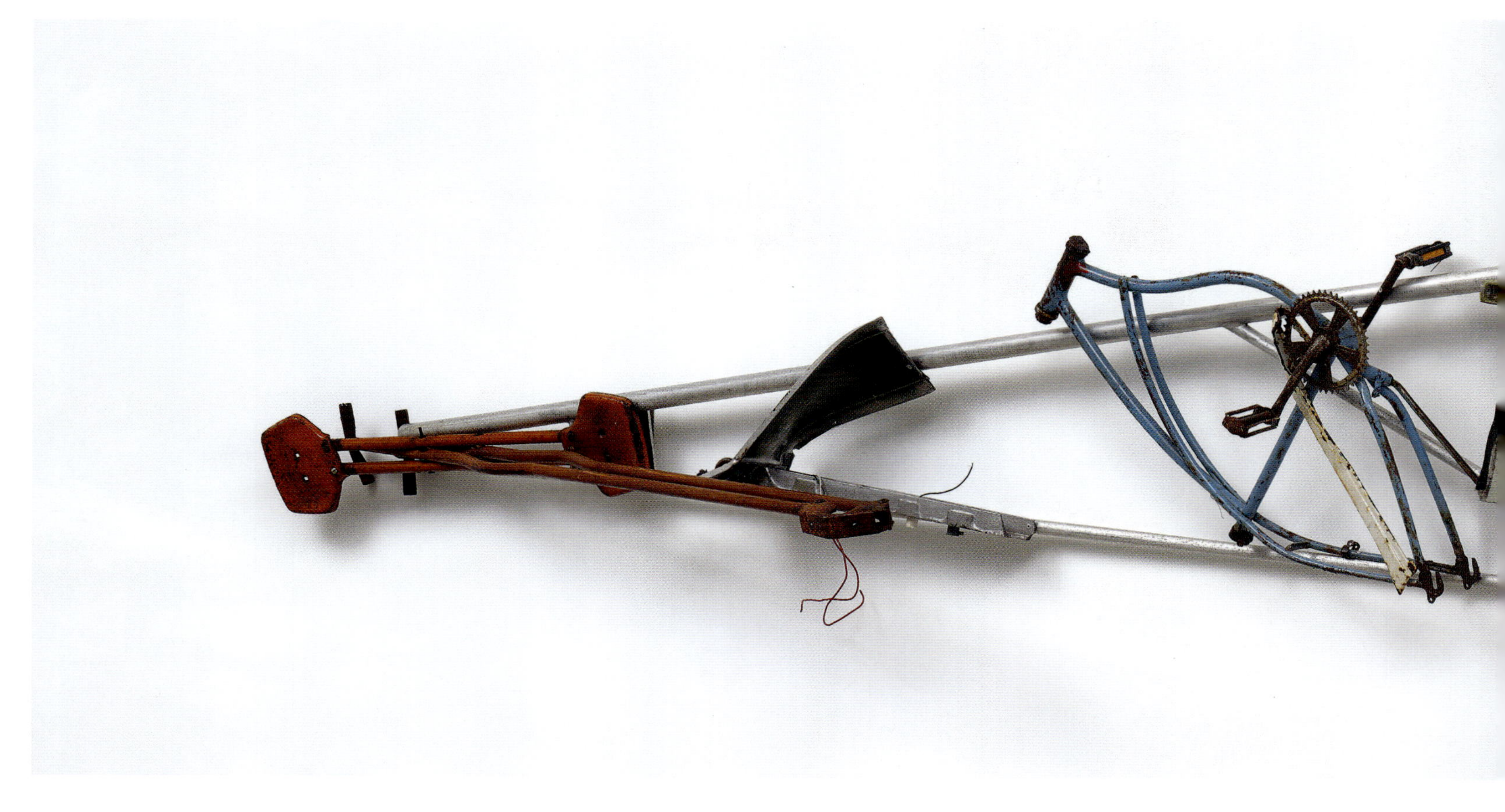

Nagshead Summer Glut Sketch, 1987
Assembled metal
33 × 184 × 19 inches (83.8 × 467.4 × 48.3 cm)
Robert Rauschenberg Foundation

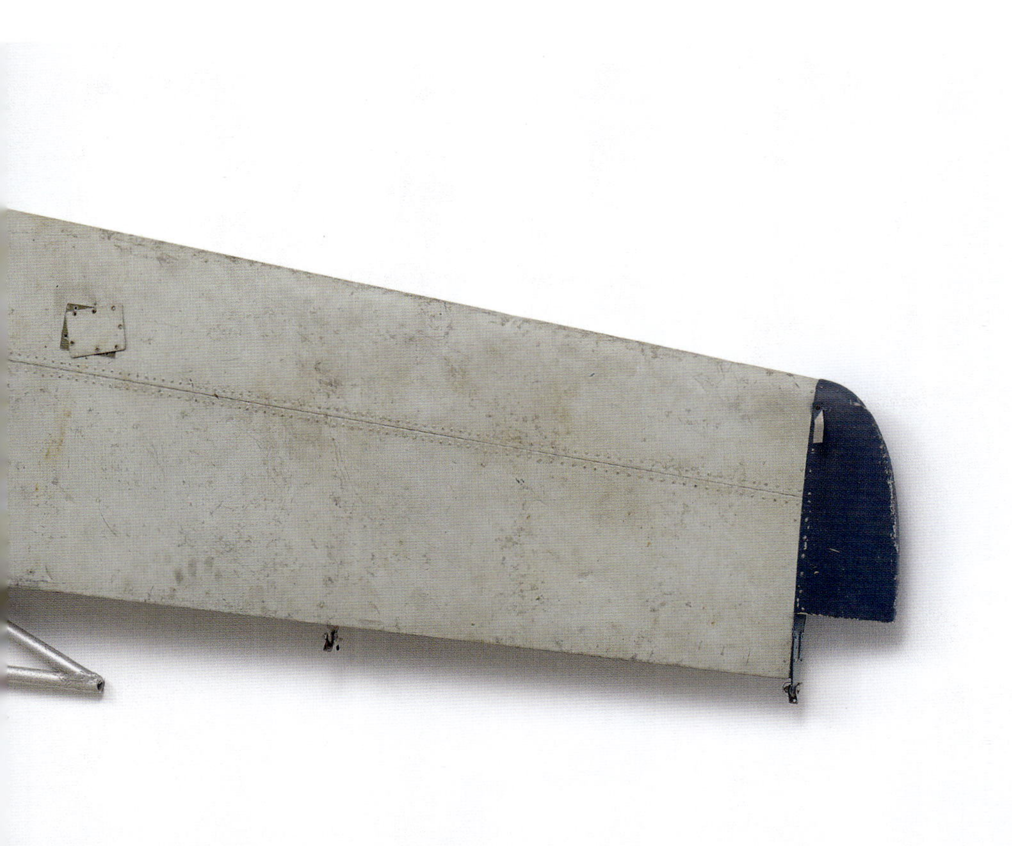

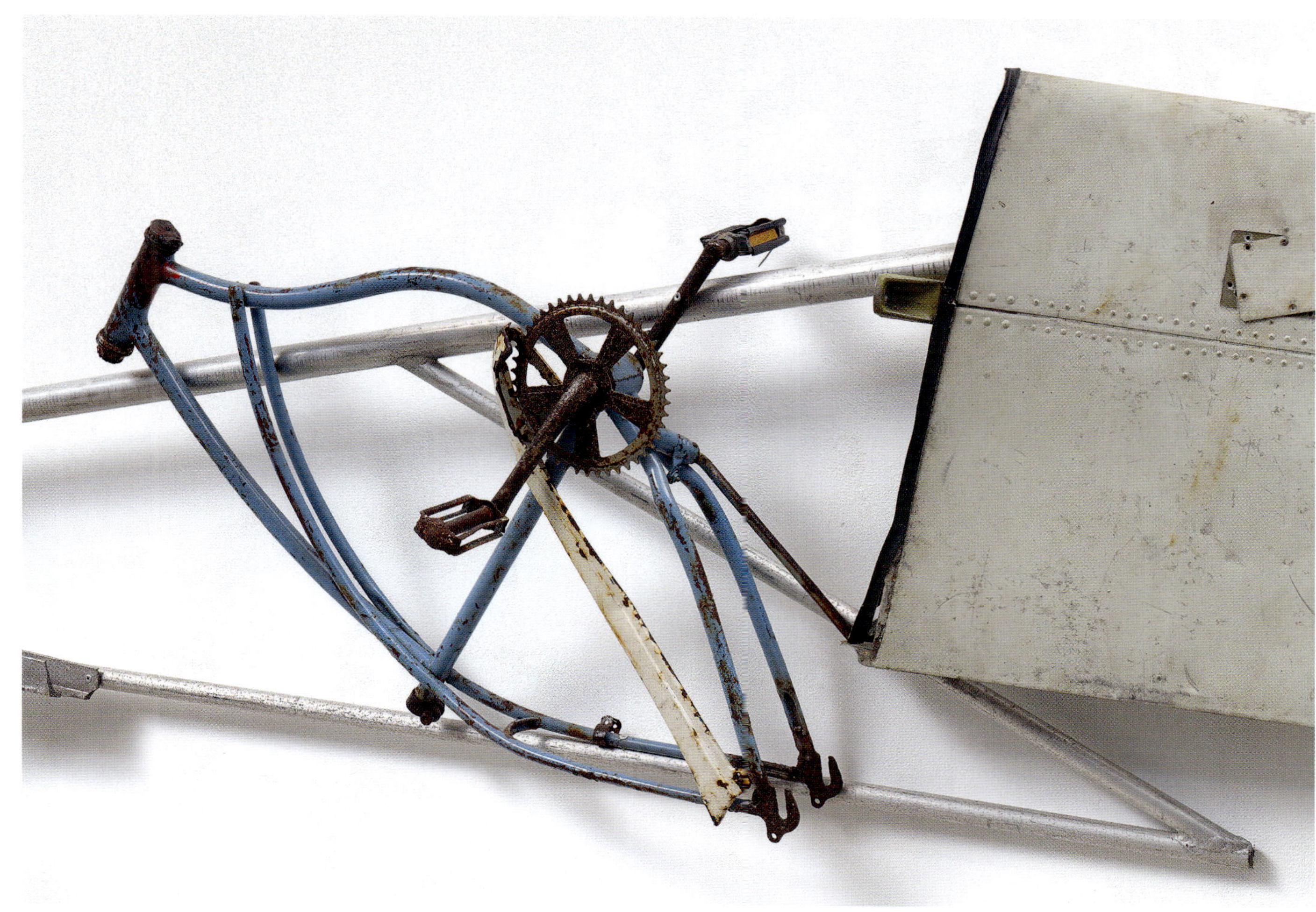

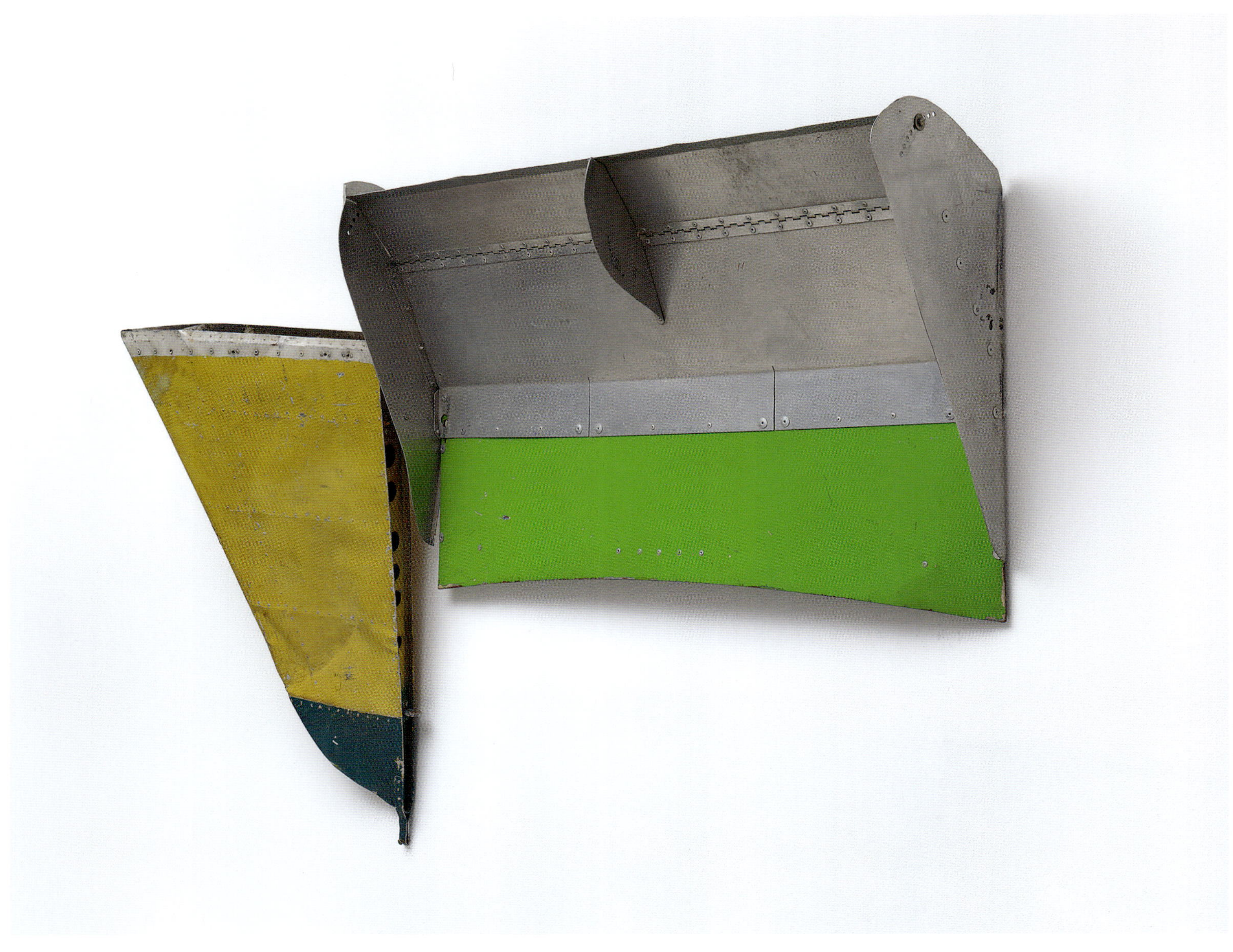

Finn Early Winter Glut, 1987
Assembled metal
46¾ × 68½ ×11½ inches (118.7 × 174 × 29.2 cm)
Robert Rauschenberg Foundation

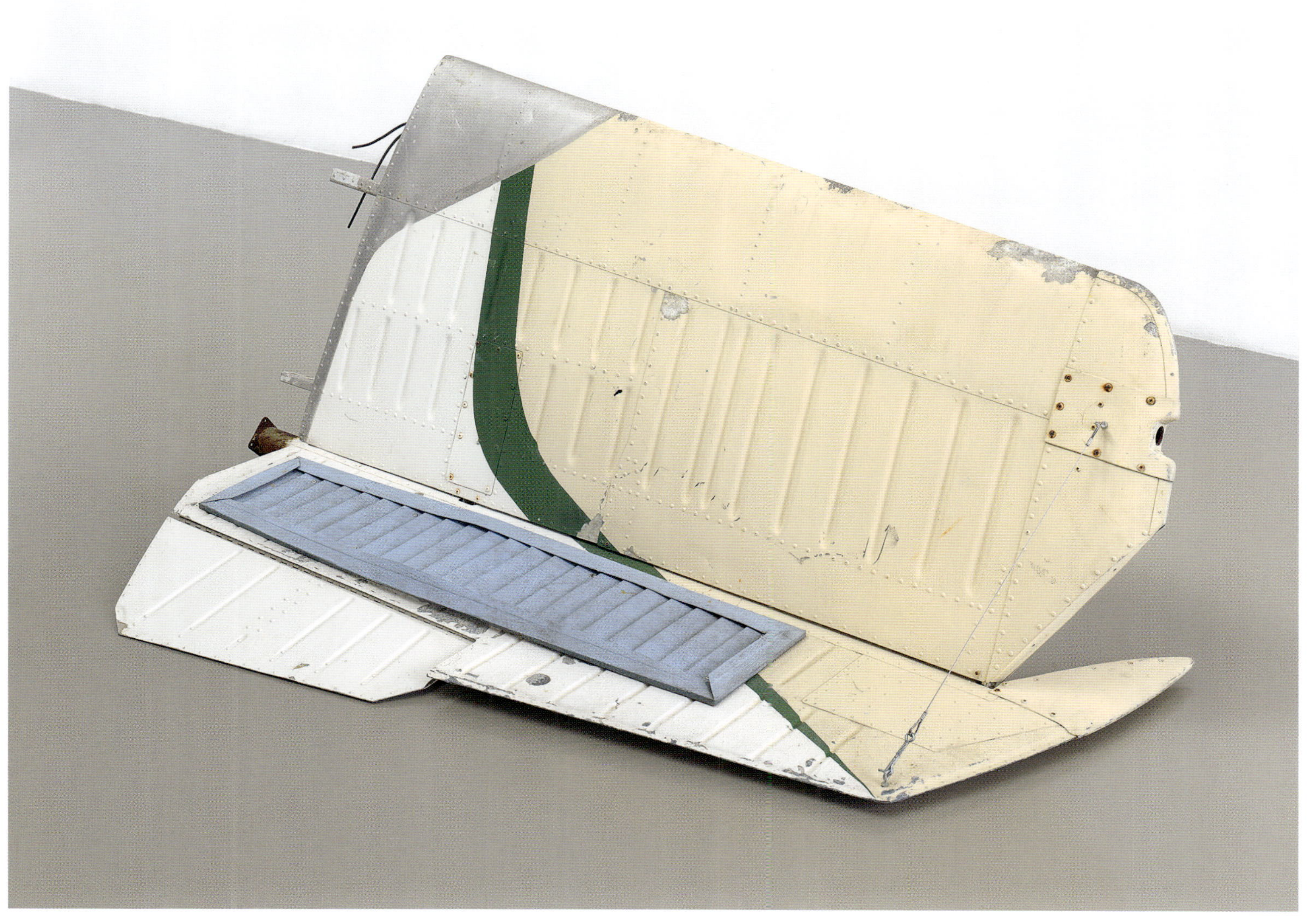

Wing Swing Glut, 1988
Assembled metal
27¾ × 64⅞ × 35¾ inches (70.4 × 164.7 × 90.8 cm)
Robert Rauschenberg Foundation

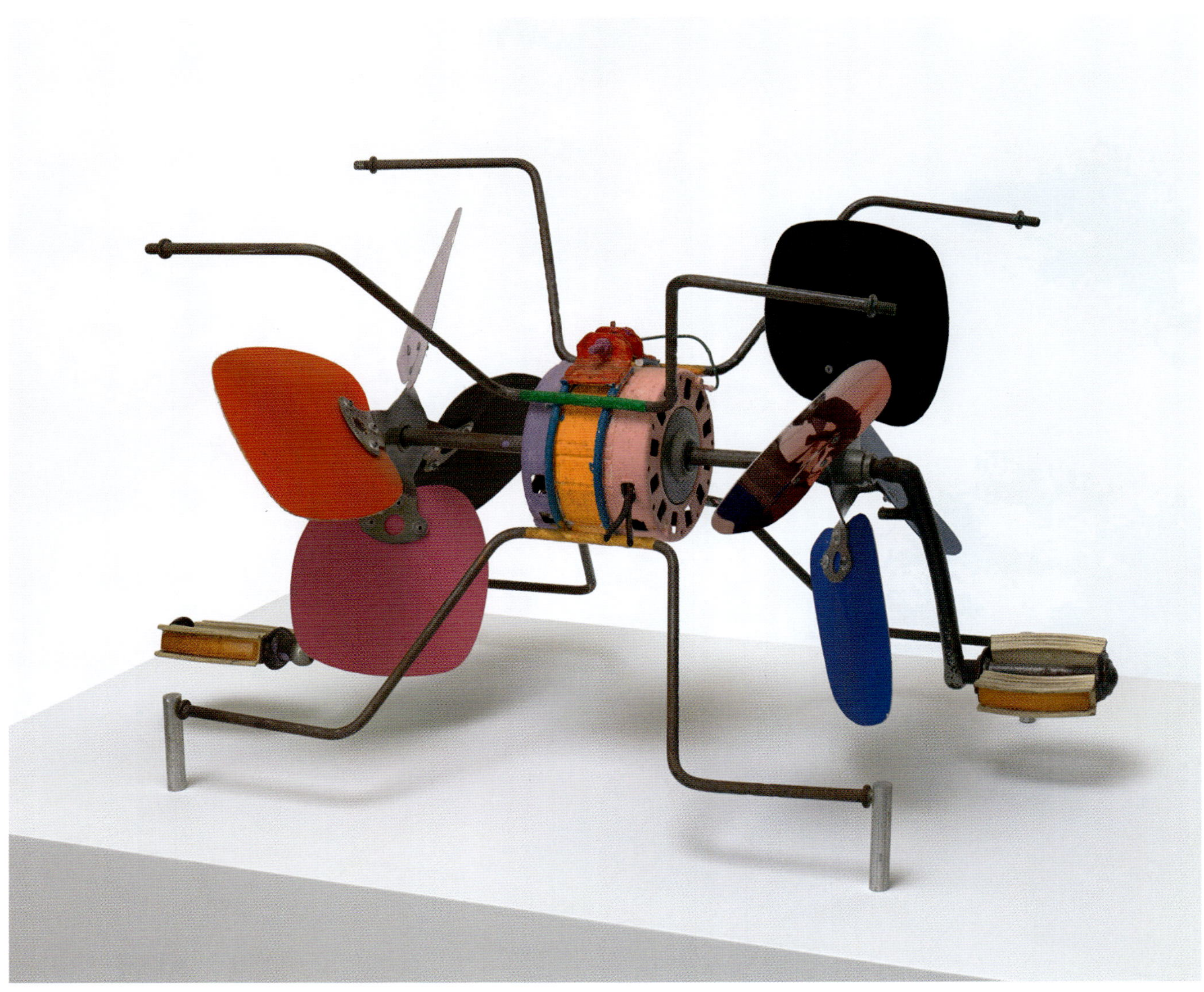

Twin Bloom / ROCI TIBET, 1985
Construction with metal, bicycle parts, acrylic, and fabric
17 × 28½ × 14 inches (43.2 × 72.4 × 35.6 cm)
Robert Rauschenberg Foundation

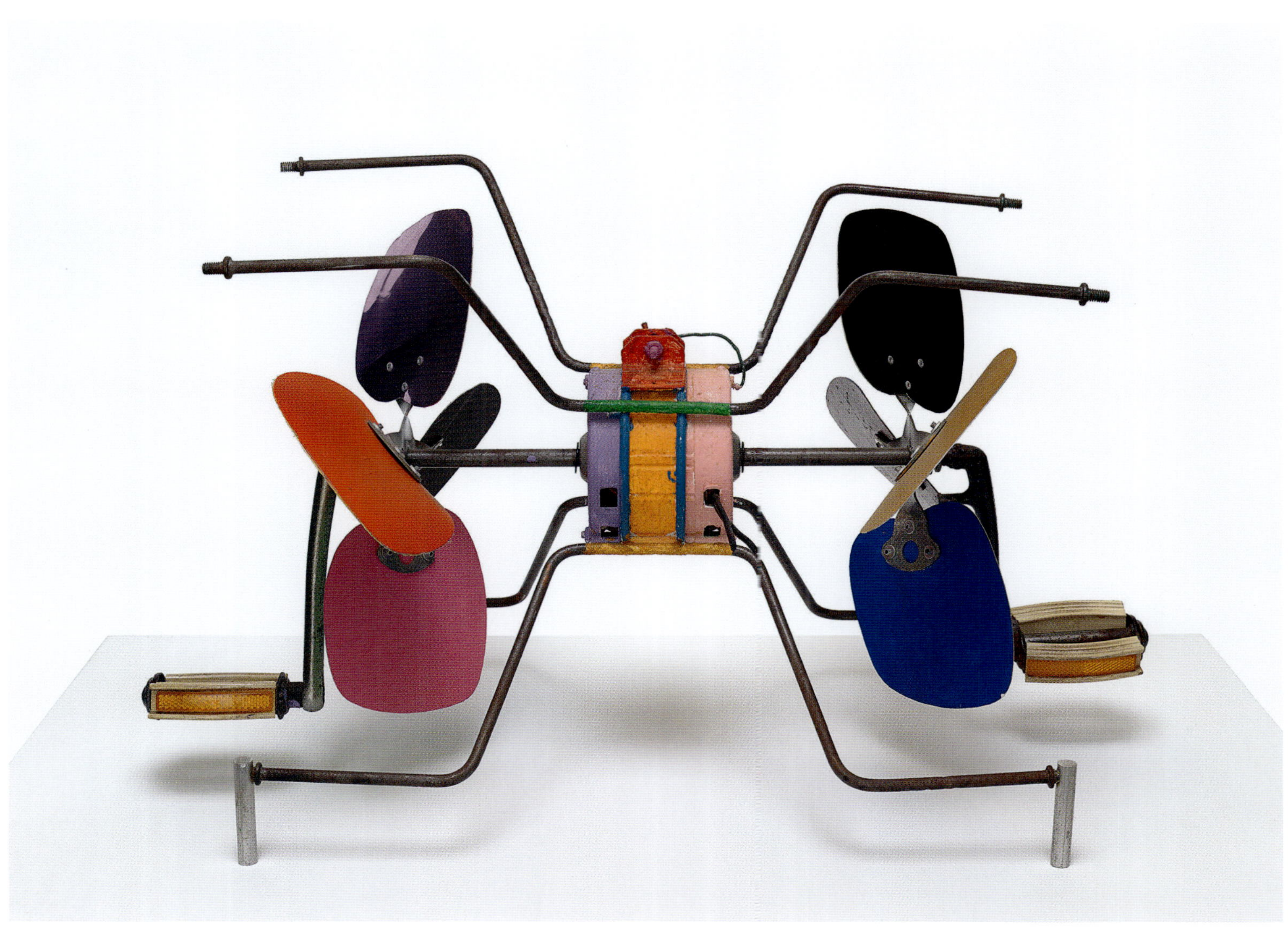

Alternate view of **Twin Bloom / ROCI TIBET**, 1985

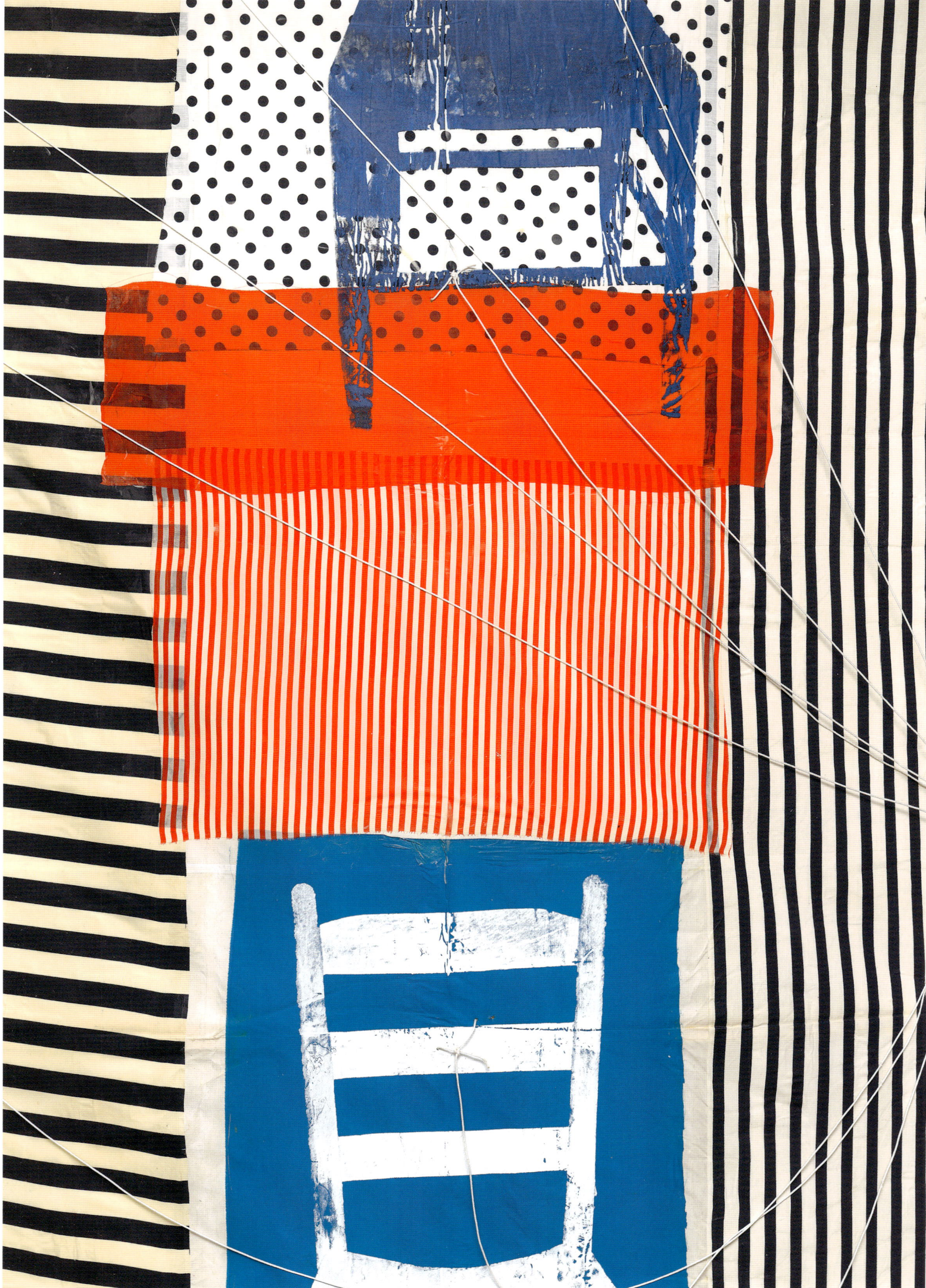

7

Seated in the Sky

We (the Kite and I) were vulnerable to the wind of that moment, as was the existence and proof of the art. We were put into a mutual contact with immediate consequence of place, conditions and time.

—Robert Rauschenberg[1]

In early April 1989 Rauschenberg brought his artistic vision to life in the skies above Himeji, Japan, during the international Art Kite Festival. He was one of more than a hundred artists from twenty countries invited by the Goethe Institute to contribute designs for kites. His collaged artworks for two kites were created on silk at his studio in Florida and then meticulously transformed into traditional Japanese *kaku dako* kites.[2] The rich tradition of Japanese kitemaking was first documented in the Nara period (645–794) and has been refined over centuries.[3]

The aptly named Vernissage in the Sky event was held against the backdrop of Himeji Castle, a UNESCO site and prominent symbol of Japan's rich cultural heritage. Perched high on a hilltop, the castle (built in 1581) resembles a bird in flight, with its white facade and outstretched architectural wings contrasting with the landscape. Locally, it is called the "White Egret Castle."[4] Augmenting the visual spectacle of the kites was a musical composition, "Voyage absolu des Unaris vers l'Andromède" (Voyage of the *unari* toward Andromeda), created by the composer Iannis Xenakis; it is based on the sound made by the *unari*, a device attached to kite strings that hums in the wind.[5] Reflecting on the experience, Rauschenberg said, "My indulgence in the kites was excited by my appetite for making art that entered into my own sense of thrill, threat and adventure. To create a painting that would not be art if nature would not accept it."[6] These remarks underscore Rauschenberg's embrace of the Japanese understanding that a kite should not only be beautiful but also "must fly well."[7]

Go Fly a Kite, Rauschenberg!
Rauschenberg's kites *Sky House I* and *Sky House II* (both 1988) share as a central motif chairs—a recurring theme in his artistic journey that encourages a deeper exploration of notions of comfort, space, and the human experience. When asked about these "heavenly" pieces, he remarked, "Well, there is no furniture up there, no place to sit."[8] This choice symbolizes the absence of material comfort in the celestial realm, inviting viewers to contemplate the relationship between everyday objects and their significance in a more abstract context.

Sky House I features horizontal and vertical stripes in black, red, white and blue. The arrangement of these stripes is reminiscent of venetian window blinds, with the white spaces allowing glimpses into the outside world. Centrally featured are two chairs separated by red stripes. The upper chair is rendered in blue and is positioned over a white field adorned with blue polka dots, which imparts a sense of domesticity. The lower chair appears as a white "ghost" version, set against a blue background. The chair, blinds, and domestic patterns denote the "house" in the title. The kite's patriotic color scheme and striped design evoke imagery associated with an American flag fluttering in the wind, thereby instilling a sense of national identity.

The empty chairs suggest absence and raise questions about who is invited to occupy a position within this heavenly realm. The phrase "seated at the right hand of power" from the Bible resonates with Rauschenberg's early upbringing, as he was raised in the Church of Christ and memorized Bible verses on a weekly basis. Mary Lynn Kotz notes that he had ambitions to become a minister but changed his mind when he understood dancing was not allowed. (Rauschenberg loved to dance.) She notes that he "took to heart the teachings of Jesus … especially blessed are the meek … blessed are the poor … a value system that would inform his life and art."[9] Therefore, the chairs on Rauschenberg's kites reveal a connection to spirituality, just

Detail of **Sky House I**, 1988

Sky House I, 1988
Silkscreen ink, fabric, Japanese rice paper, bamboo, and string mounted on fabric
161⅜ × 119¾ inches (409.9 × 304.2 cm)
Robert Rauschenberg Foundation

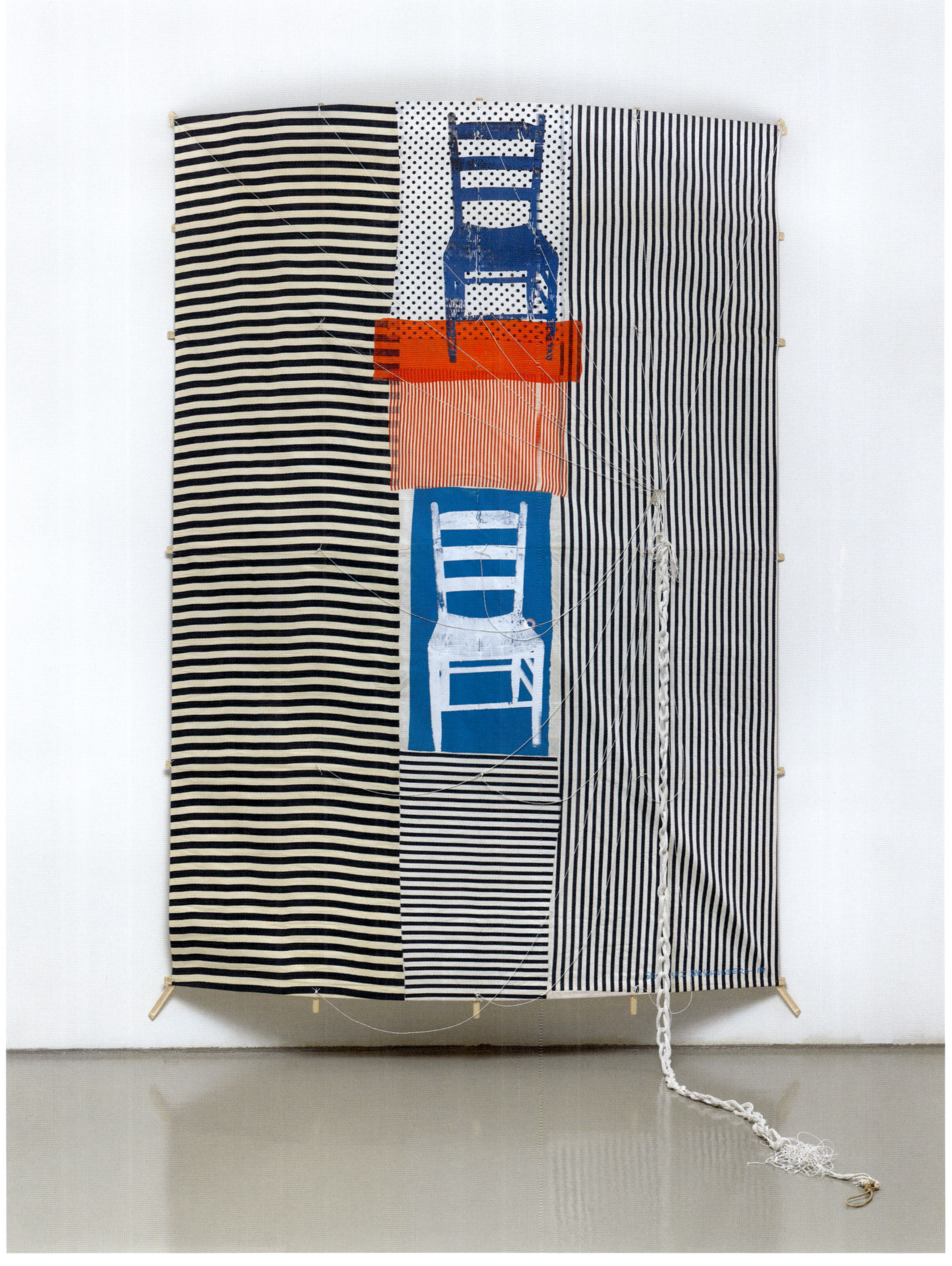

Sky House II, 1988
Silkscreen ink, fabric, Japanese rice paper, bamboo, and string mounted on fabric
140²⁹⁄₃₂ × 90¹³⁄₆₄ inches (358 × 229 cm)
Private collection

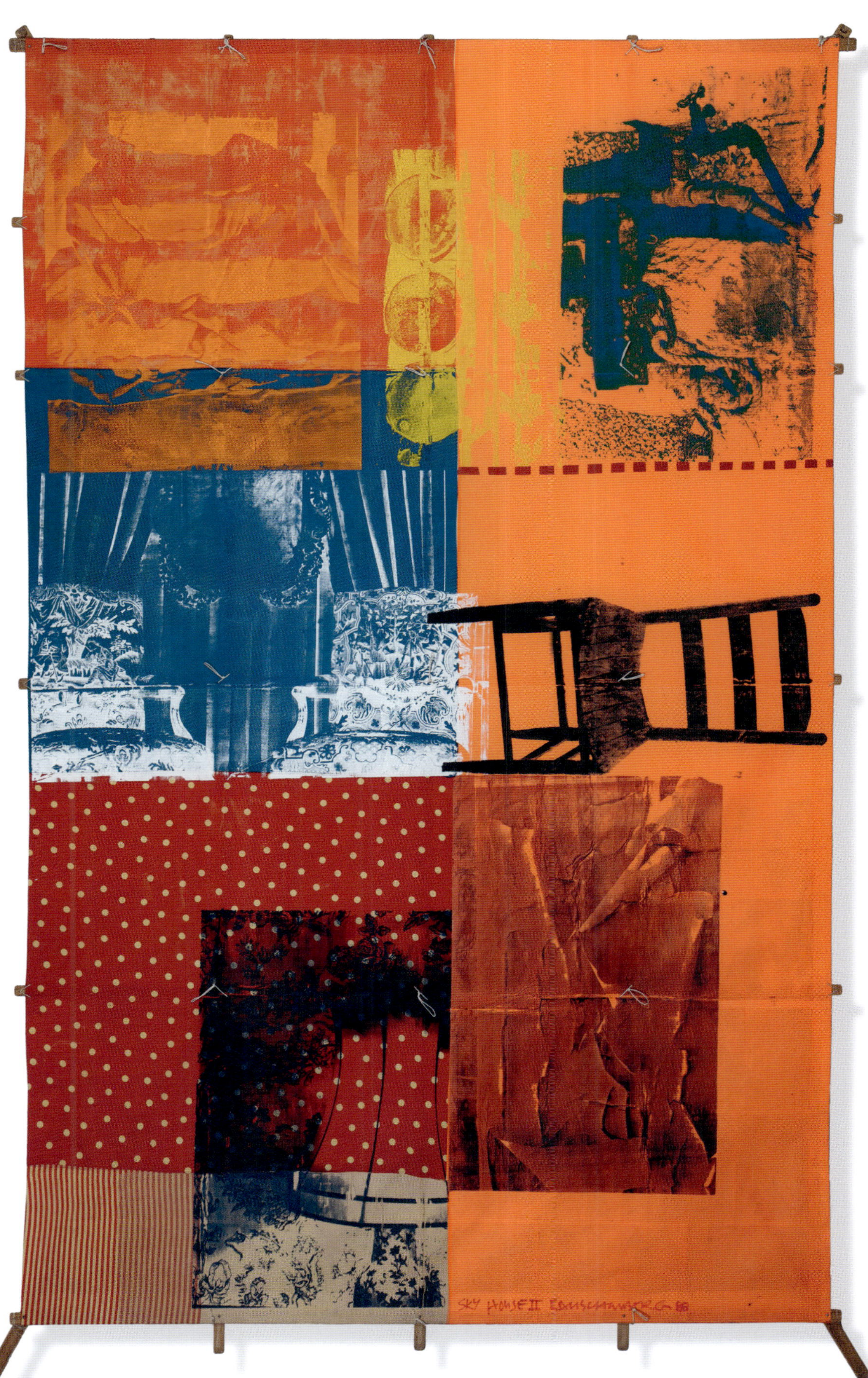
SKY HOUSE II RAUSCHENBERG 88

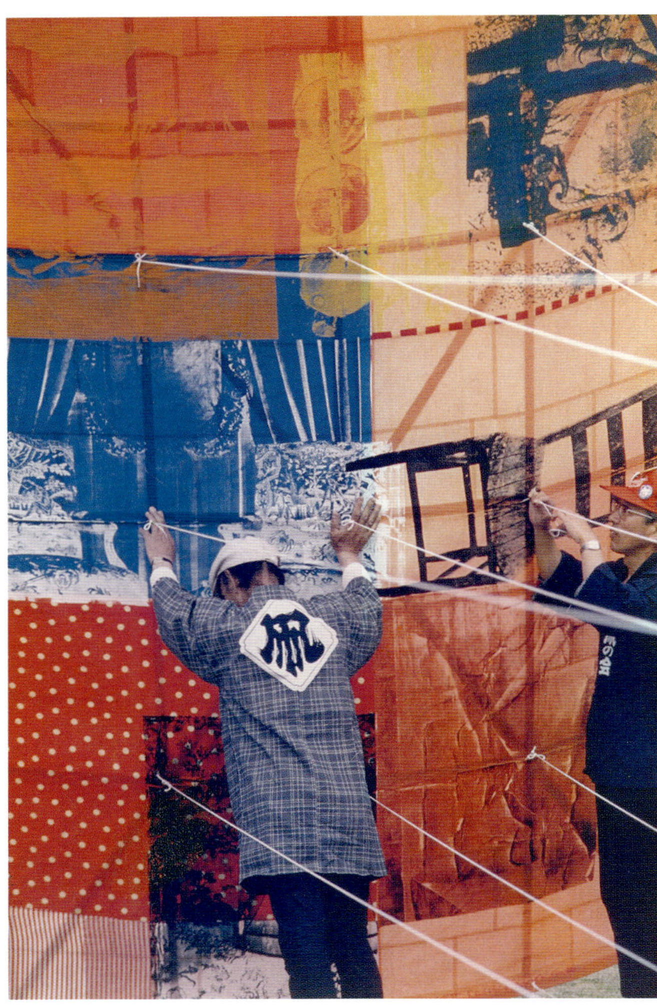

Kite handlers holding *Sky House II* (1988) at the Art Kite Festival in Himeji, Japan, 1989.

Flying Fish

Rauschenberg's ROCI trip to Japan in November 1986 inspired works such as *Wall-Eyed Carp / ROCI JAPAN* (1987) and *Doubleluck* (1995). This connection highlights the impact of his cultural experiences on artistic expression. These paintings incorporate traditional Japanese *koinobori* windsocks shaped like carp, a fish known for its ability to swim against strong currents, thus embodying resilience. These vibrant windsocks are flown throughout Japan in the early spring. Initially used during the Edo period (1603–1868) to represent military units, today *koinobori* are flown during Children's Day, a national holiday, to invoke good fortune and ensure the strength and health of children.[12] *Wall-Eyed Carp* integrates Japanese kanji characters, a photograph of geishas, and an aerial map of Japan with a windsock. The splattering of a radioactive green serves as a powerful reminder of the devasting impact of the atomic bombs on Japan at the conclusion of World War II. *Doubleluck* features familiar signifiers of flight such as a flattened umbrella and a photograph of bicycle-powered rickshaws along with two *koinobori*. Other pairs of images include two piles of rocks at the right of the composition and two-color blocks beneath the umbrella. Rauschenberg, with his fondness for punning titles, demonstrates an awareness of the Japanese significance of the *koinobori*—as good fortune or luck. His pairing or doubling of imagery celebrates the symbolism as "double" luck and prosperity in this culturally thoughtful composition.

Hoarfrost and Hang Gliders

The *Hoarfrost* series (1974–76) and related *Hoarfrost Edition* (1974) were a significant development in Rauschenberg's oeuvre. His selection of lightweight fabrics, specifically silk and

as the earliest manifestations of Asian kites were utilized in religious ceremonies, based on the belief that the kite could journey to the remote abode of deities and facilitate blessings.[10] As such, *Sky House I* transcends conventional air-space boundaries into a higher realm.

Sky House II offers a more domestic aesthetic, featuring imagery of a wooden chair, two upholstered chairs, and swatches of decorative fabrics like those used to upholster chairs. The inclusion of French toile wallpaper, a lamp, and a lampshade in the photographic image effectively position the upholstered chairs within a cozy "house" setting. Polka dot, striped, and color-block fabrics recall Rauschenberg's groundbreaking *Bed* (1955), where he painted directly on a quilt and incorporated a pillow into the composition; when hung on the wall, the work challenged conventional notions of how both paintings and beds are perceived. Similarly, Rauschenberg's kites break away from traditional museum and gallery conventions, utilizing the sky itself as a dynamic backdrop for artistic expression.[11]

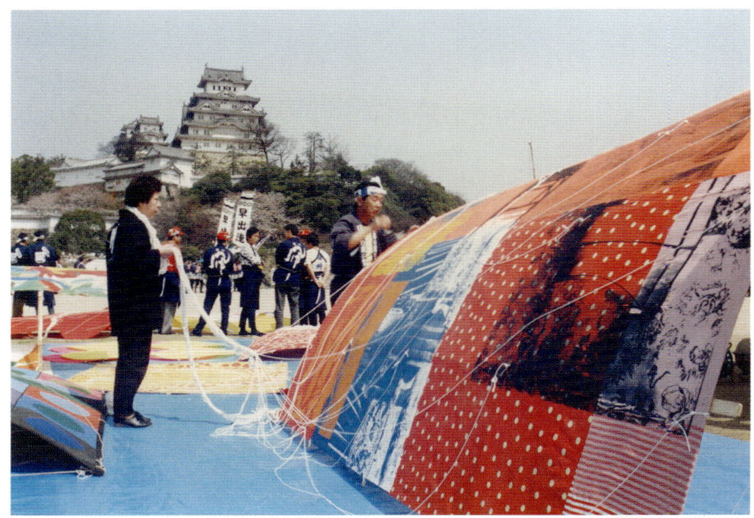

Kite handlers with Rauschenberg's *Sky House II* (1988) at the Art Kite Festival near Himeji Castle in Himeji, 1989.

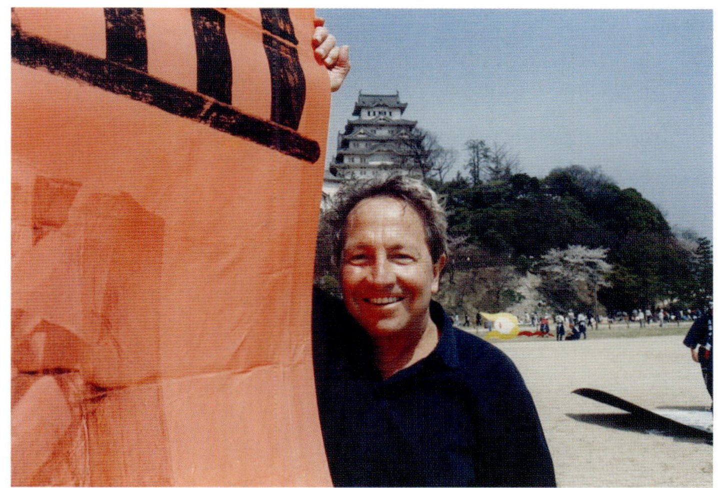

Rauschenberg Folding *Sky House II* (1988) at the Art Kite Festival near Himeji Castle in Himeji, Japan, 1989.

chiffon, for these works emphasizes not only their texture but also their potential for movement. The unframed works are pinned directly to the wall, allowing the slightest breeze or draft to animate the fabric. These works draw on Rauschenberg's background as a costume designer for Merce Cunningham, Trisha Brown, and others, where he developed a familiarity with the properties of lightweight textiles.[13] Indeed, the *Hoarfrosts* echo the interplay between fabric and a dancers' movements. The title of the series references the frost that forms when water vapor condenses into delicate feather-like ice crystals—an apt characterization of the works. This nod to natural phenomena enriches the viewer's understanding of the themes and materials inherent in the series.

Scrape (Hoarfrost Edition) (1974) is divided into three sections, with the top third dedicated to a sunset scene with clouds in the sky. The middle section shows a Cessna aircraft; below it, a landscape unfolds, offering a bird's-eye view of farm fields. The bottom section depicts elements associated with the ocean, including a surfer and a variety of marine life. Additionally, the cover of a publication displays the title "The Wing," with flocks of birds in the same space. The interplay of aerial and marine elements invites us to consider the contrasts and connections between these two realms.

The predominant theme in Untitled *(Hoarfrost)* and *Plus Fours (Hoarfrost Edition)* (both 1974) is the imagery of hang gliders. Modern hang gliders are constructed from plastic and composite materials mounted on a tubular frame, in contrast to earlier models that were made from fabric, wood, and string. Otto Lilienthal, a pioneer in the field, designed and successfully flew gliders in the late nineteenth century, and his aerodynamic research informed the work of the Wright brothers.[14] Like parachutes, which fascinated Rauschenberg, hang gliders are also maneuvered by shifting one's body weight during flight. In

Untitled *(Hoarfrost)*, rotated images of hang gliders illustrate the various orientations that aircraft can adopt while navigating the wind. These gliders are suspended over the depiction of a tree canopy, underscoring their intended altitude above the treetops.

Hang gliders are positioned at the top of two identical silk banners in *Plus Fours (Hoarfrost Edition)*. Beneath each glider are two empty buckets, which recall several of Rauschenberg's earlier works, notably *Gift for Apollo* (1959) and *Pail for Ganymede* (1959), which are replete with references to flight and the exhilaration and fear it can provoke. A third banner divides and connects the outer two, bearing images of a skyscraper, a newspaper page that includes the headline "Divers Hunt for Flood Victims," a weather report featuring the lunar phases, and panels from Mort Walker's *Beetle Bailey* comic strip showing Sergeant Snorkel struggling with an old chair and remarking, "I have greased this spring, lubricated the swivel, and oiled all the wheels." Is this, perhaps, another of Rauschenberg's chairs in the sky?

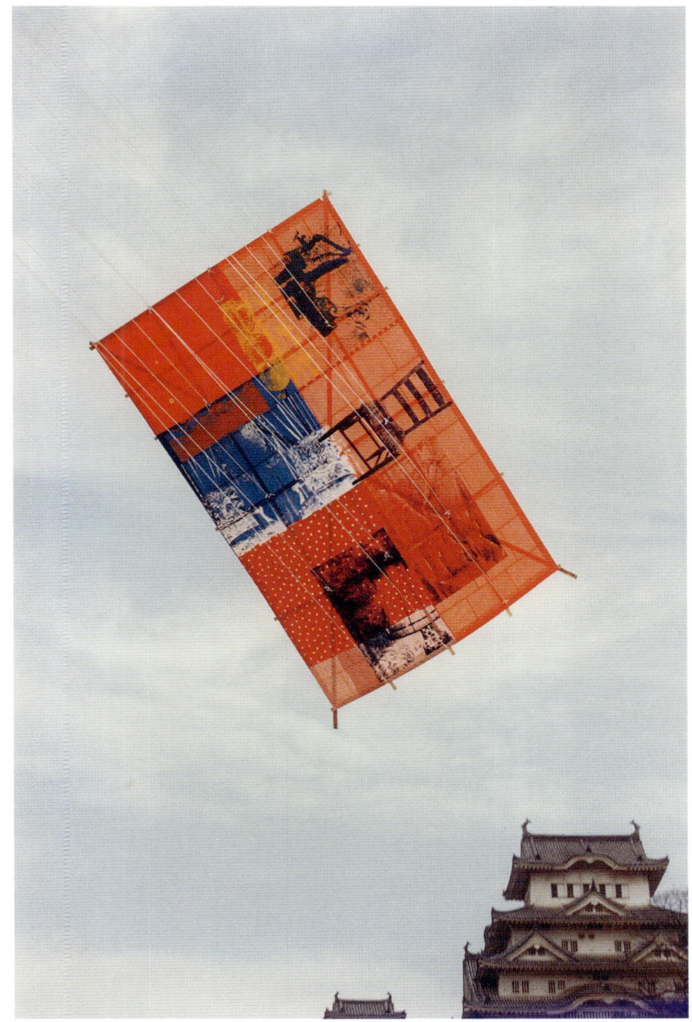

Rauschenberg's *Sky House II* (1988) in flight at the Art Kite Festival in Himeji, with Himeji Castle in background, 1989.

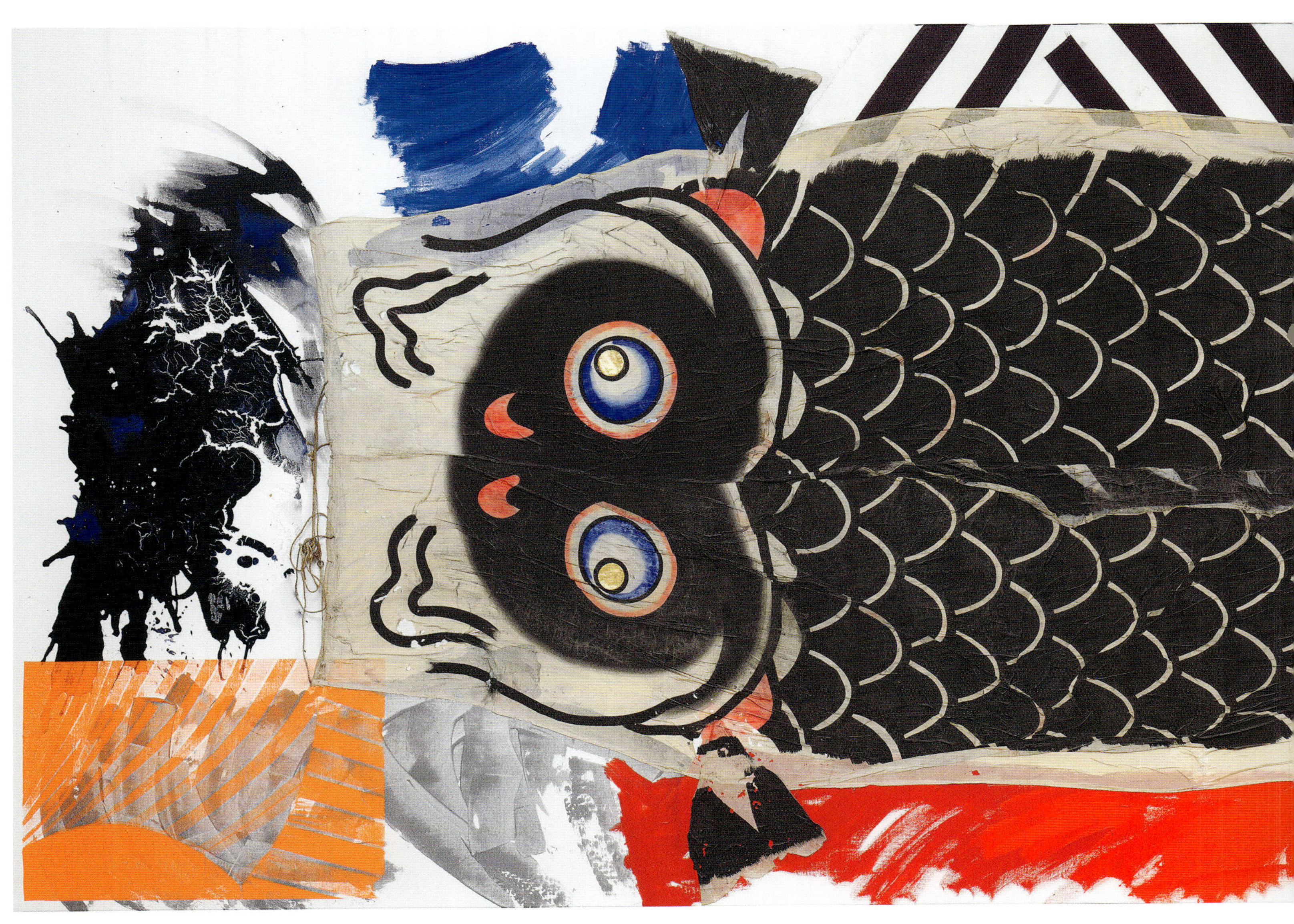

Wall-Eyed Carp / ROCI JAPAN, 1987
Silkscreen ink, acrylic, and fabric on canvas
80 × 243 inches (203.2 × 617.2 cm)
National Gallery of Art, Washington, DC

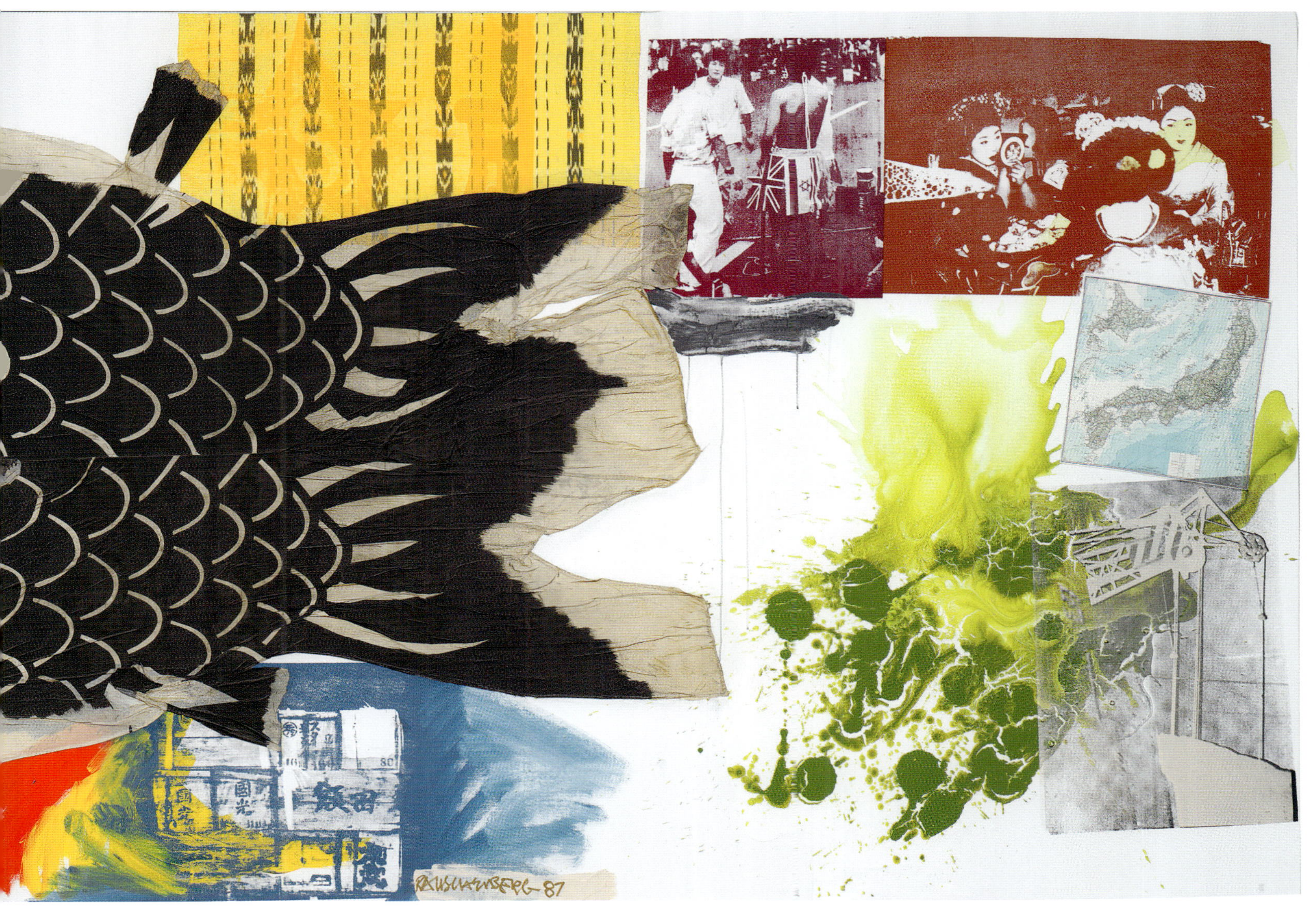

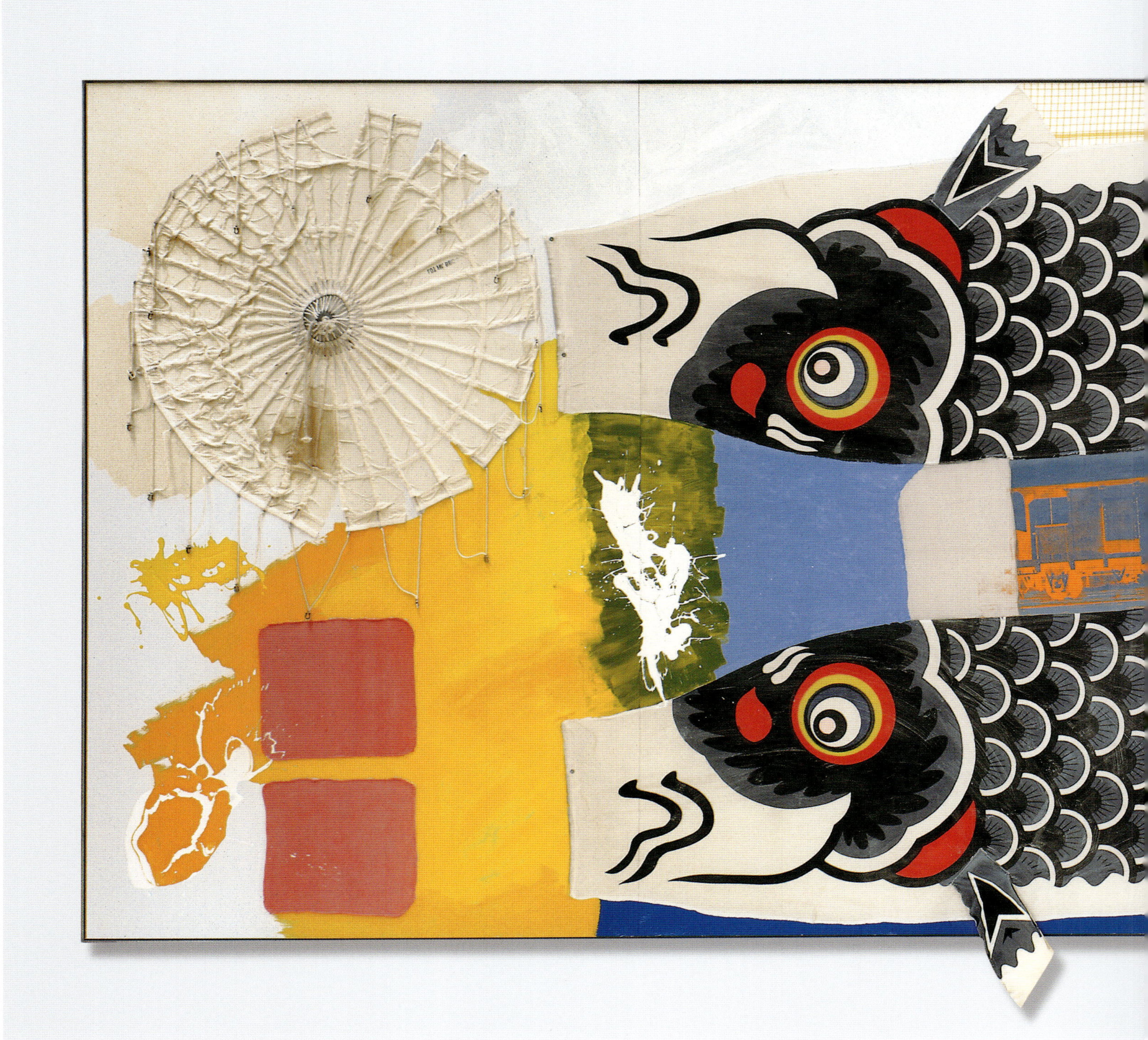

Doubleluck, 1995
Silkscreen ink, acrylic, Japanese kite, parachute, and fabric on bonded aluminum
97 × 249 inches (246.4 × 632.5 cm)
Private collection

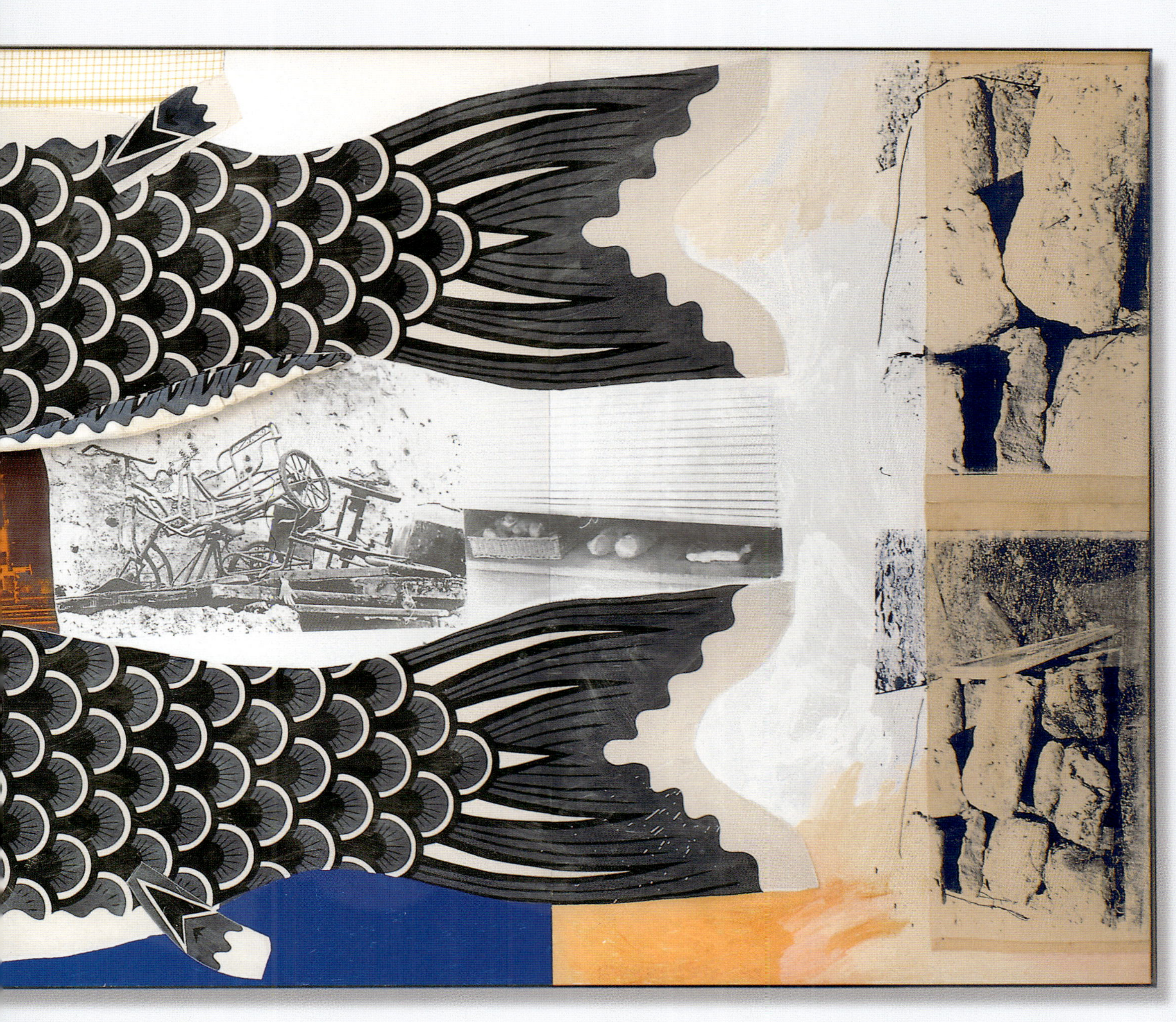

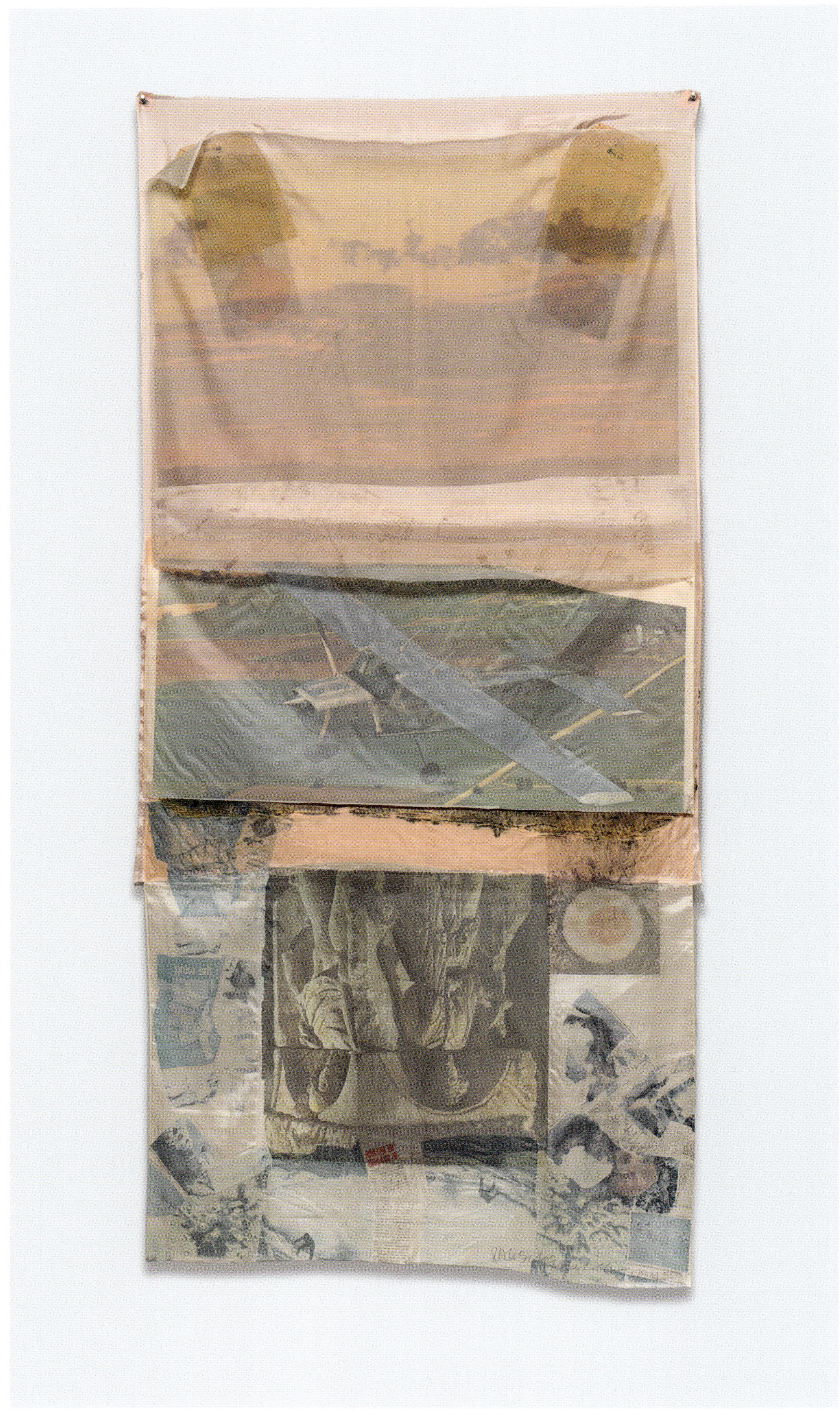

Scrape (Hoarfrost Edition), 1974
Solvent transfer and offset lithograph on fabric with paper bags
76 × 36 inches (193 × 91.4 cm)
National Gallery of Art, Washington, DC

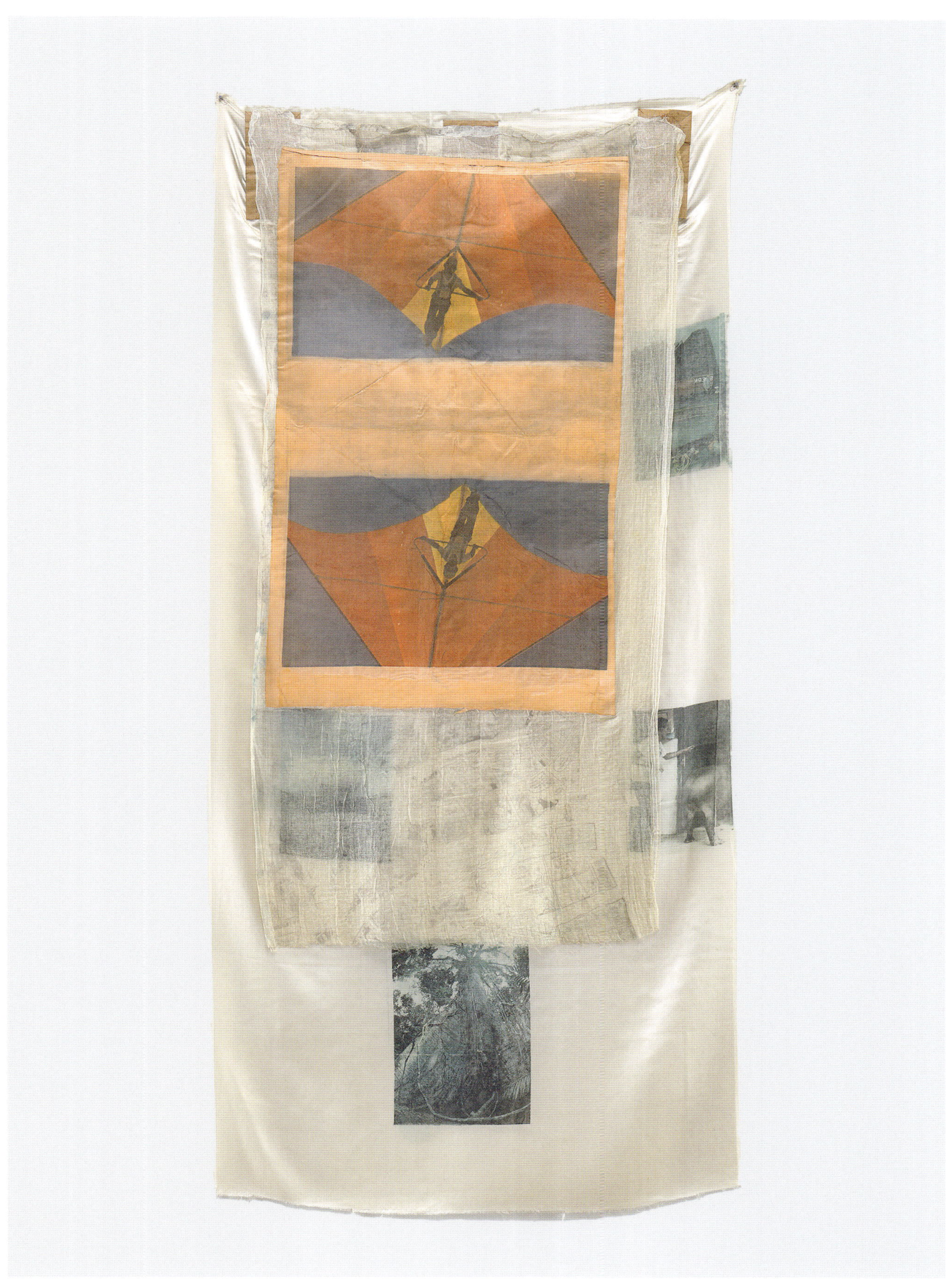

Untitled (Hoarfrost), 1974
Solvent transfer on fabric with paper bags
84⅝ × 40¼ inches (214.8 × 102.2 cm)
Robert Rauschenberg Foundation

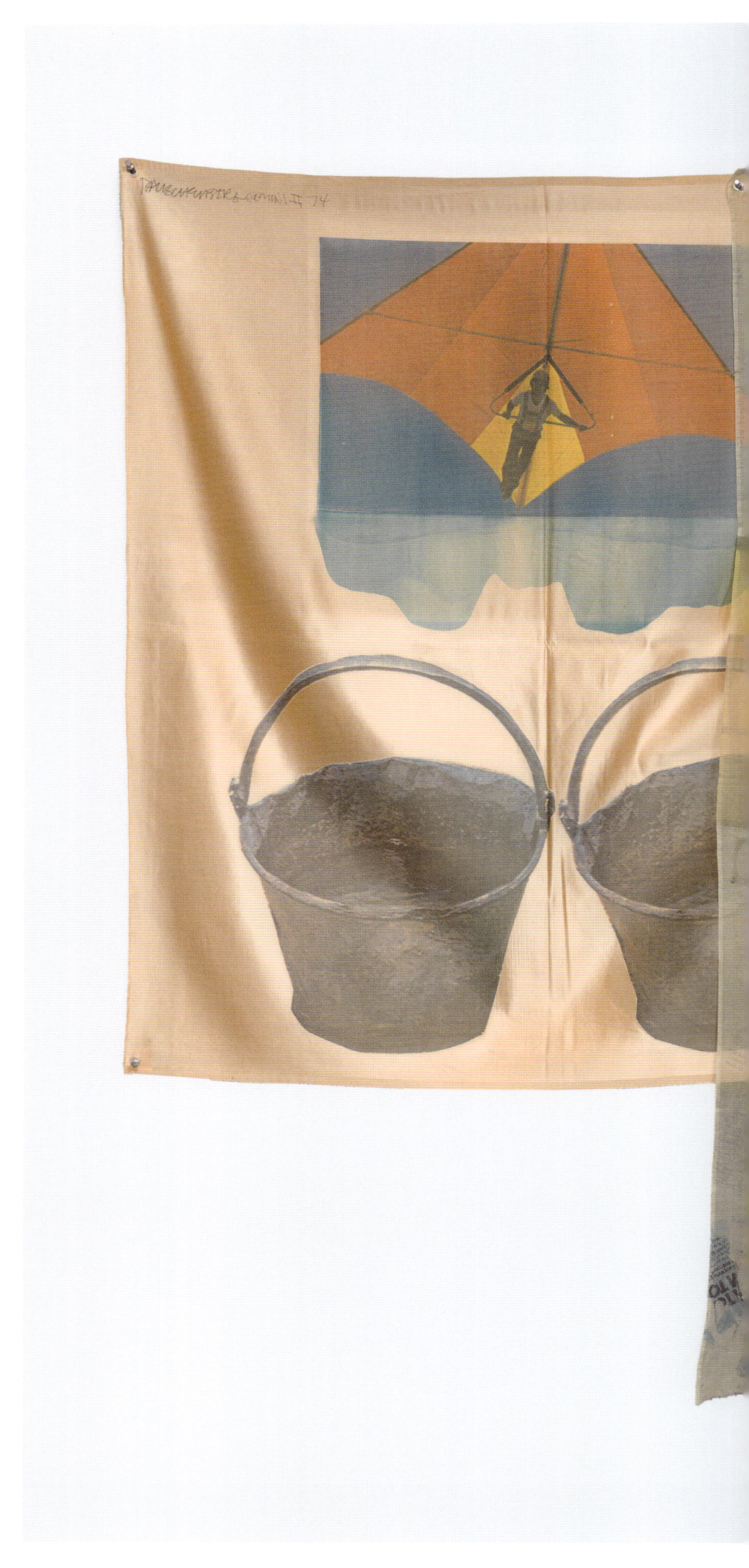

Plus Fours (Hoarfrost Edition), 1974
Solvent transfer, offset lithograph, and screenprint on fabric
67 × 95 inches (170.2 × 241.3 cm)
National Gallery of Art, Washington, DC

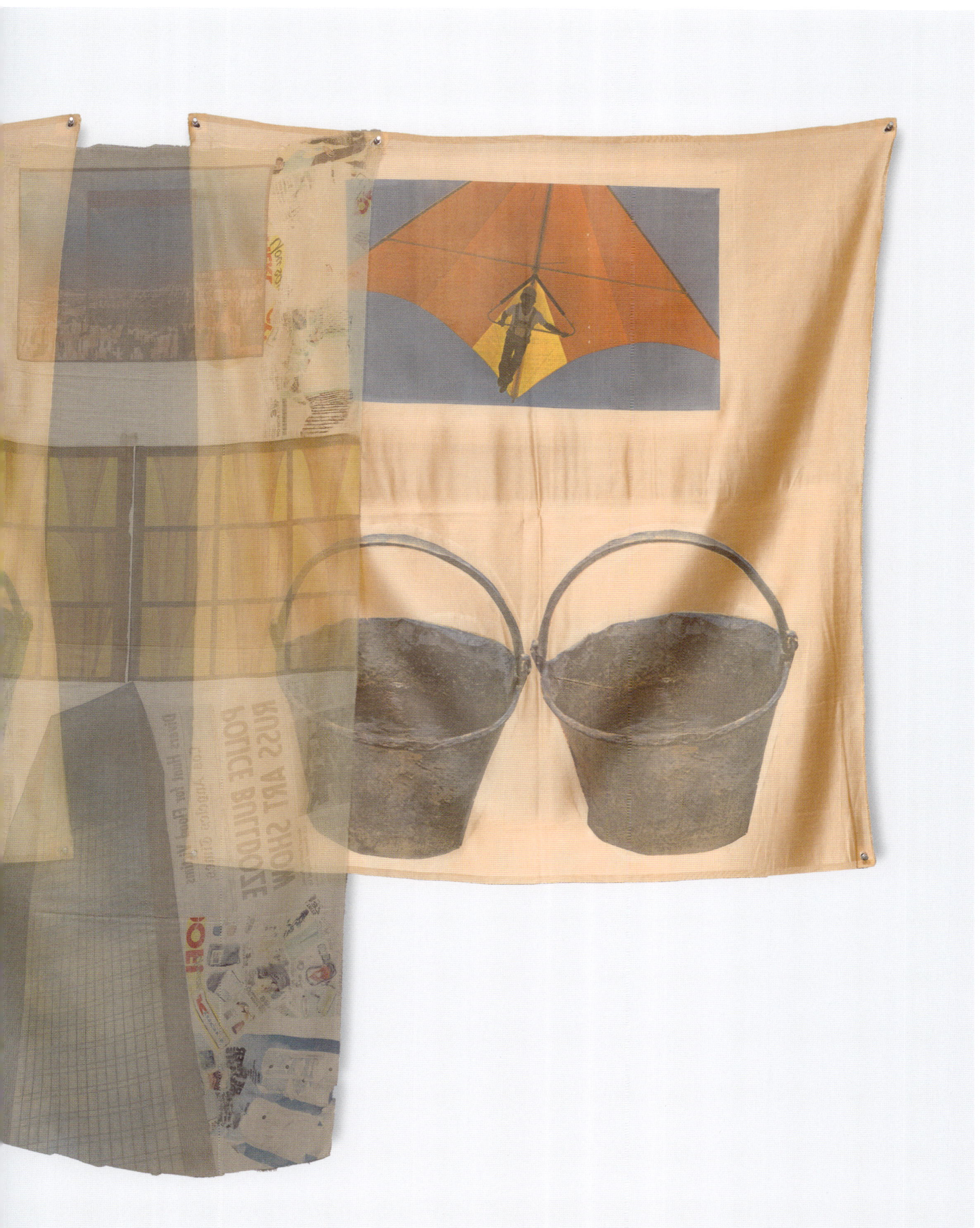
POLICE BUILDING
RUSS ART SHOW

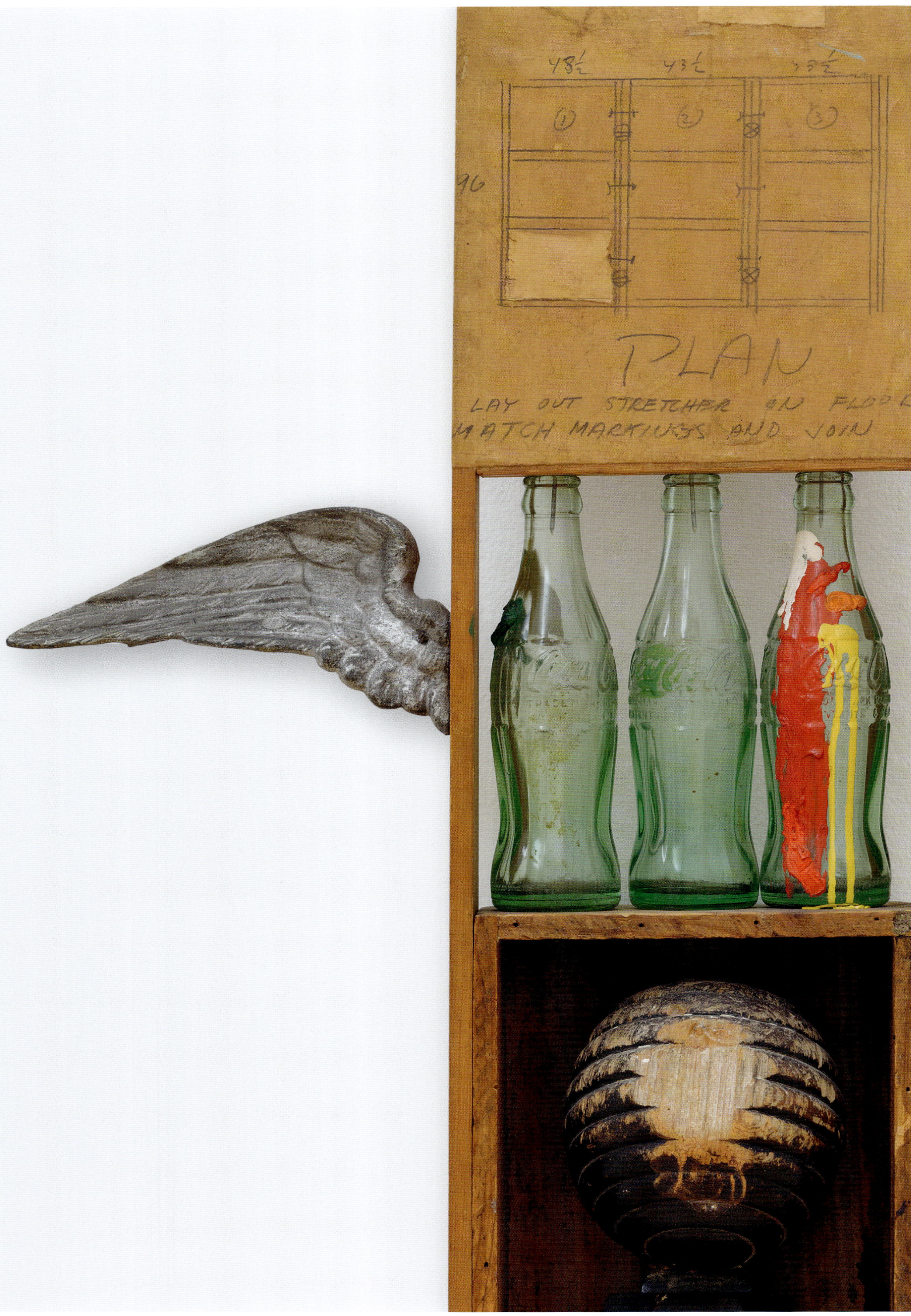
48½   43½   38½
96
①   ②   ③
PLAN
LAY OUT STRETCHER ON FLOOR
MATCH MARKINGS AND JOIN

8

Down to Earth

I think all important artists are politicians. So their poetics stand for what's right and what's wrong. They chose the world they wanted to live in. This applies to every aspect [of an artist's life].

—Robert Rauschenberg[1]

Rauschenberg addressed nature and environmental issues through his art, often utilizing aerial perspectives and references to air and space. These choices provide an insightful view of the natural world, revealing both its beauty and vulnerability. His commitment to raising awareness of and encouraging dialogue on these topics extends beyond his personal artistic endeavors. He actively supported environmental initiatives, contributing artwork for events such as the United Nations conferences. Notably, his print for the Earth Summit of 1992, *Last Turn—Your Turn* (1991), states, "I pledge to make the Earth a secure and hospitable home for present and future generations," reflecting his vision for a sustainable planet.[2]

A Winged World

Coca-Cola Plan (1958) is a landmark early Combine that consists of a rectangular box with metal wings attached to either side. The upper portion of the box displays a grid—defined by Rauschenberg as a "sketch for a [canvas] stretcher"—above the word "PLAN."[3] In the central section, three Coke bottles are presented, one of which is adorned with paint drippings, creating a provocative element through their unexpected presence. The lower section presents a spherical object that represents a globe. This celebrated artwork has sparked a myriad of interpretations. The curator Walter Hopps highlighted the contrast between the wings and the Coke bottles, viewing them as symbols of high and low culture, respectively, with the "humble bottles" of a soft drink juxtaposed with symbolism that can be traced back to the Greek sculpture the *Winged Victory of Samothrace*.[4] Marjorie Welish aptly characterizes the glass bottles as potent embodiments of Neo-Dadaism, calling them as "surrealist in their heterogeneity" as assemblages and "at

odds with those of Dadaist predecessors."[5] Lisa Wainwright describes the bottles as "America's bounty" and relates the wings to transcendence and spirituality.[6] It's also possible to discern in *Coca-Cola Plan* a reference to the role aviation has played in the process of globalization.

In May 1950, the cover of *Time* magazine featured an illustration of an anthropomorphized planet Earth consuming a bottle of Coke while being embraced by a Coca-Cola logo.[7] The related article described Coca-Cola's global reach, from "the dusty Mexican hills" to "the unastonished eyes of the great Sphinx." It depicts the gentle burps produced by the beverage resonating in the lively atmosphere of Parisian sidewalk cafés alongside the melodic sounds of Siamese temple bells. Furthermore, the same issue of *Time* contains an advertisement for the United Aircraft Corporation that asserts, "The air is yours, use it—to reach your markets at their peak," and encourages businesses to use air freight to capitalize on market opportunities.[8] *Coca-Cola Plan* anticipates a globalized, commercialized future driven by advances in aviation, the proliferation of satellites for communication and information dissemination, and the growing interconnectedness of lives and goods facilitated by developments in aviation and space exploration.

Earth Day

Aerial perspectives serve as a powerful tool in Rauschenberg's advocacy efforts, effectively highlighting his dedication to environmental causes. This found its most potent expression in his print and related poster for the inaugural Earth Day on April 22, 1970. This initiative was inspired by a significant oil spill off the Southern California coast in 1969, underscoring the need for urgent action. Wisconsin Senator Gaylord Nelson proposed an

Detail of **Coca-Cola Plan**, 1958

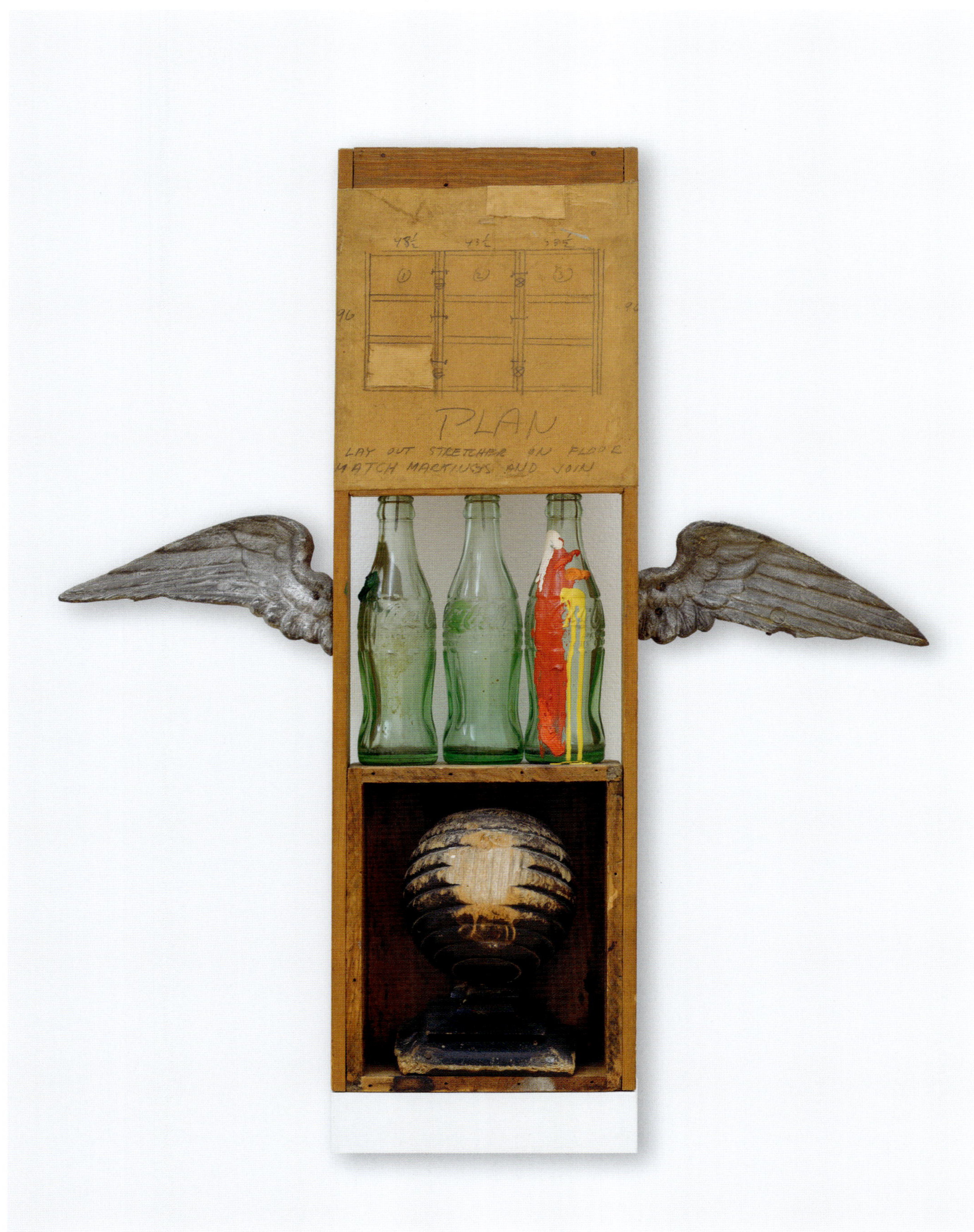

Coca-Cola Plan, 1958
Combine: graphite on paper, oil on three Coca-Cola bottles, wood newel cap, and cast-metal wings on wood structure
26¾ × 25¼ × 4¾ inches (67.9 × 64.1 × 12.1 cm).
The Museum of Contemporary Art, Los Angeles

Earth Day to foster greater public awareness of the pressing challenges posed by air and water pollution, encouraging collective responsibility and proactive engagement in environmental stewardship. What began as a grassroots movement is now commemorated as a designated observance in nearly 200 countries worldwide.[9] Rauschenberg's print *Earth Day* (1970) employs a monochromatic collage of black-and-white photographs that surround a bald eagle depicted in tones reminiscent of a paper bag. Aerial imagery documents various disturbing scenes of environmental degradation, including industrial smokestacks belching smoke, rooftops of housing developments that signify urban sprawl, landscapes devastated by mining, and overcrowded beach scenes where the sand is obscured by throngs of people. Additional images include litter, deforested land, a gorilla clutching its stomach, and a sign reading "Danger, Keep Out, Water Contaminated" strategically placed over the crowded beach. This combination of imagery reinforces Rauschenberg's objective of enhancing awareness about the environmental challenges confronting the world.[10]

Ozone Layer

It's not hard to discern an environmental message in *American Pewter with Burroughs I* (1981), where the ghostly words of the Beat author William S. Burroughs "THE SKY IS THIN AS PAPER HERE" are embossed alongside imagery of foreboding clouds and fabric hanging from an awning and blowing in the wind. Taken together these elements comment on the harmful changes taking place in the atmosphere. A decade later, Rauschenberg collaborated with Transportation Displays Inc. to produce billboards that were prominently featured on buses nationwide. Among them was *Ozone Bus Billboard* (1991), which sought to raise awareness about the health of the planet's protective atmospheric shield.[11]

In the 1950s Burroughs popularized the cut-up, whereby a finished text is cut up and rearranged to create a new work.[12] This verbal collage technique parallels the mastery of juxtaposing found imagery Rauschenberg demonstrated throughout his career and may have influenced his approach in *Dream of William Burroughs* (1972). The work was created at the behest of Rauschenberg's attorney Theodore W. Kheel, who invited several artists—including Romare Bearden and Christo—to explore the implications of the Highway Trust Fund, established in 1954 to finance the Interstate Highway System, which has

had a profound impact on a range of issues from air pollution to the decline in public transportation.[13] The print presents an analysis of various modes of transportation through a collage of images: a tire, an armored truck, a rider on horseback, and an astronaut on the Moon. Burroughs's sobering statement—"They did not fully understand the technique in a very short time they nearly wrecked the planet"—originated in a dream Burroughs shared with the artist.[14] Rauschenberg crafted the design with precision, layering each hand-cut letter over the underlying collage. The words serve as an urgent call to action before irreparable damage occurs.

Blue Marble

The term "Blue Marble" is a reference to the profound color depiction of our entire planet as captured from space. The first human-made "Blue Marble" image was recorded during the Apollo 17 mission in 1972 from a distance of 28,000 miles away, highlighting the stunning beauty and delicate nature of Earth. This theme resonates powerfully in Rauschenberg's work commissioned for the United Nations International Conference on Population and Development held in Cairo, Egypt, in 1994. It features as a focal point a Robinson-projection map of the Earth that simulates the "blue marble" effect, presenting the entire planet in a single glance. Rauschenberg also included an image of his pet turtle Rocky superimposed over a crowded beach scene. The contrast between the map of the world and the crowded beach effectively illustrates the concept of population concentration.[15] The presence of Rocky further underscores how human density can interfere with marine life on coastlines. For the original artwork for the poster, Rauschenberg opted to use biodegradable and soy-based dyes and pigments alongside a water-based transfer technique, which he termed "vegetable dye transfer." This practice reflects his dedication to environmental stewardship, as he was among the early adopters of water-soluble digital printing technologies that emerged in the late 1980s.[16]

One impression of the variable edition *Horsefeathers Thirteen I* (1972) presents an image of a hand holding the planet Earth along with a graph delineating trends in the gross national product in relation to energy expenditures from 1947 to 2000, a crate with the emblem of First National City Bank, and the image of a ram's head. The ram may reference the zodiac sign Aries, which normally connotes power and strength but is here depicted in a weakened or sickly state, with its head bowed to the ground. In this work, Rauschenberg underscored the intricate relationship between humanity and the Earth, emphasizing the responsibility we collectively bear to steward our planet, encapsulated in the notion that our fate lies in the palm of our hand.

In 1994 Rauschenberg participated in a humanitarian aid initiative called Tribute 21, which sought to generate funding for various charitable organizations. For the project he created twenty-one prints, each representing a humanitarian theme and honoring cultural figures whose contributions made a significant positive impact. *Space (Tribute 21)* (1994) illustrates the iconic spacewalk of Ed White floating above the Earth during the Gemini IV mission. This historic milestone took place in June 1965, making White the first American to conduct an extravehicular activity, spending twenty-three minutes outside the spacecraft while secured by a tether. The composition depicts clouds over the Pacific Ocean into which Rauschenberg incorporated a color-enhanced visualization of Saturn's rings that had been released by NASA's Jet Propulsion Laboratory as part of the Voyager program in 1981. The lithograph conveys the fragility of human existence and the ecological health of the planet within the vast expanse of space and serves as an homage to Carl Sagan (1934–96), capturing the sense of wonder and awe the astronomer and planetary scientist experienced while contemplating the cosmos. To create the original artworks for the *Tribute 21* prints, Rauschenberg utilized an environmentally conscious approach by employing a water-transfer process in lieu of chemical solvents. This technique imparts a distressed quality to the imagery, enhancing its aesthetic appeal while aligning it with sustainable practices.

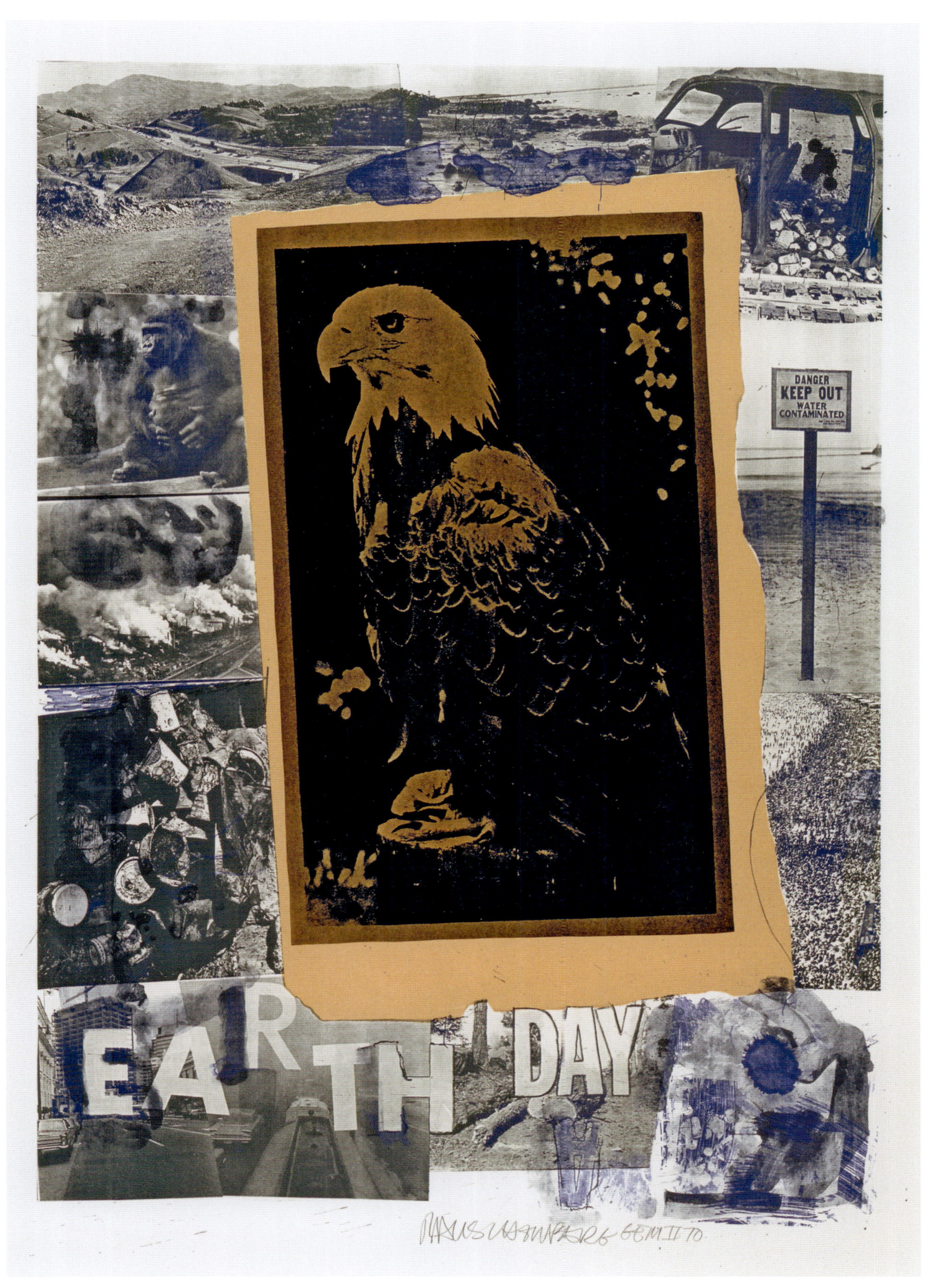

Earth Day, 1970
Lithograph with chine collé
52½ × 37½ inches (133.4 × 95.3 cm)
Walker Art Center, Minneapolis

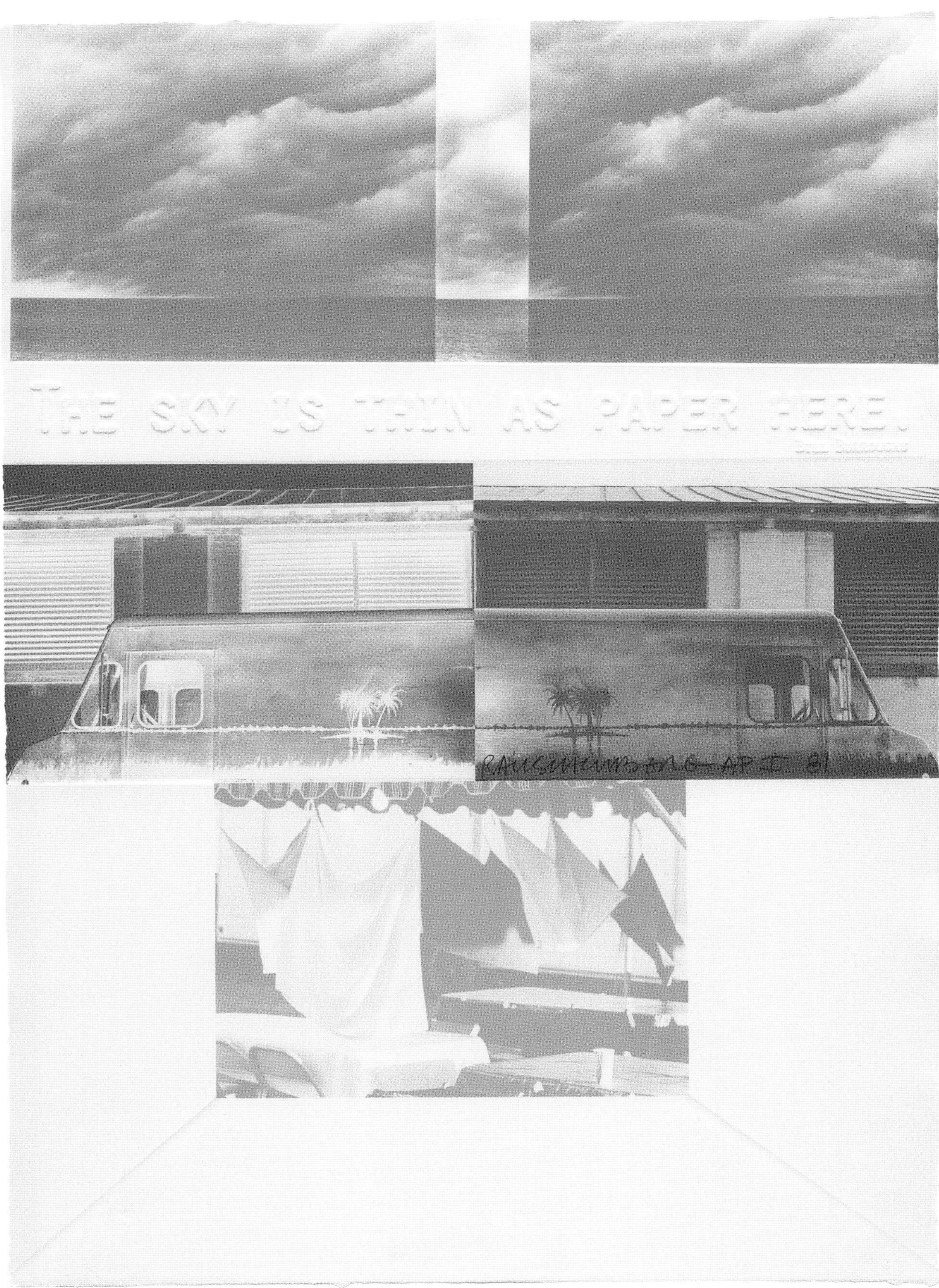

American Pewter with Burroughs I, 1981
Lithograph with embossing
31½ × 23½ inches (80 × 59.7 cm)
Robert Rauschenberg Foundation

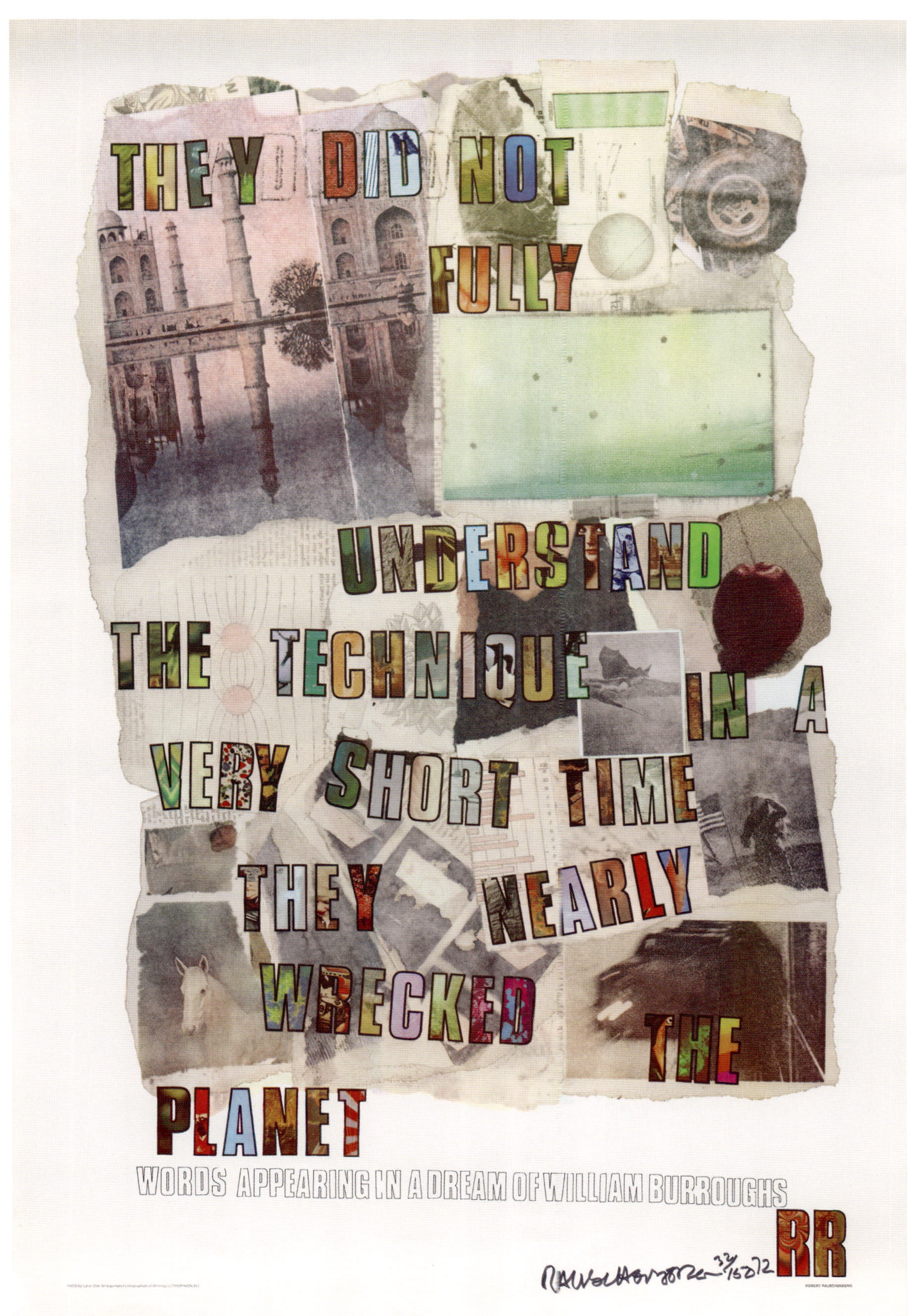

Dream of William Burroughs, 1972
Offset lithograph
34½ × 24 inches (87.6 × 61 cm)
Robert Rauschenberg Foundation

Print for United Nations International Conference on Population and Development, 1993
Offset lithograph
40¾ × 29 inches (103.5 × 73.7 cm)
Robert Rauschenberg Foundation

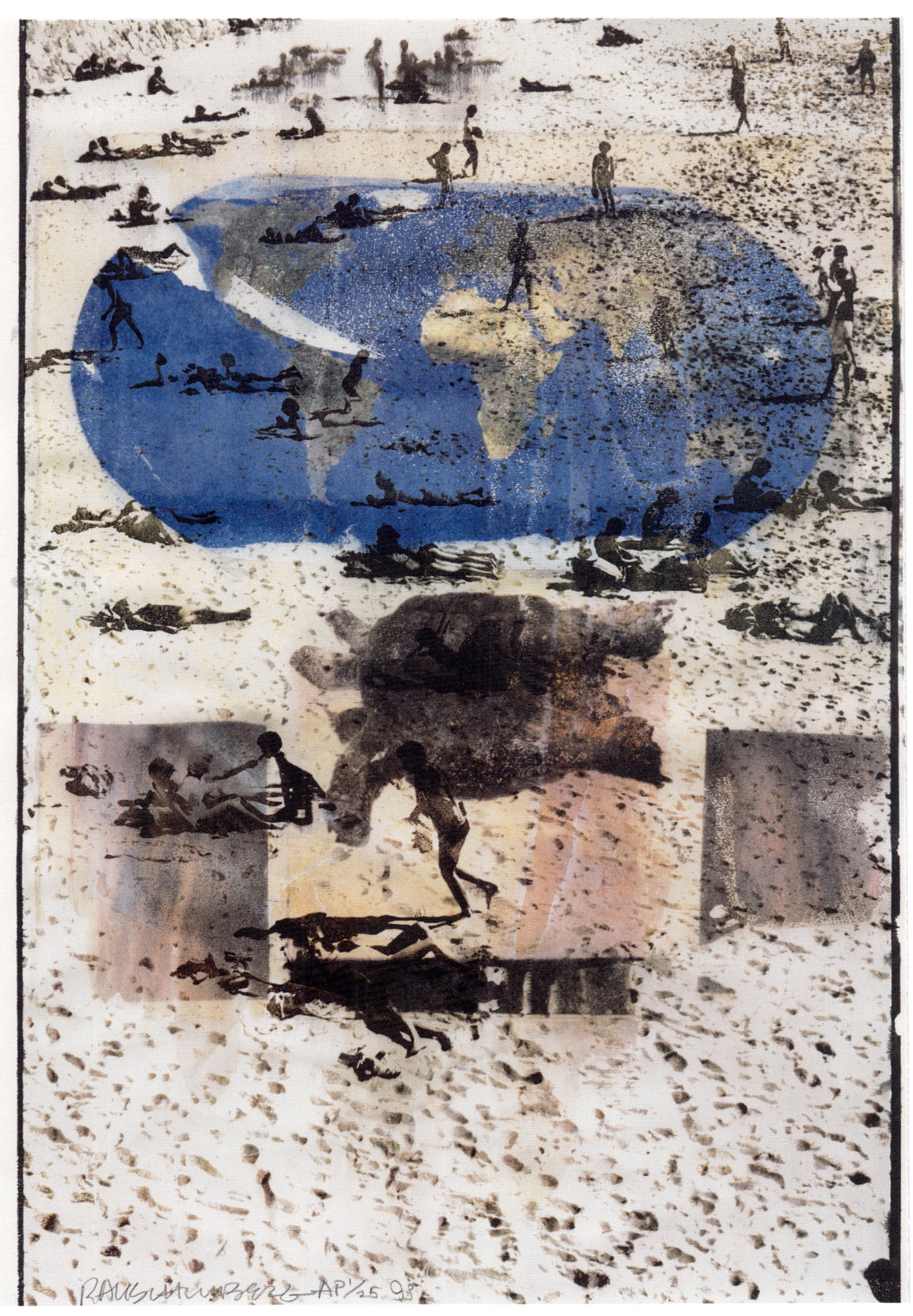

RAUSCHENBERG AP 1/25 98

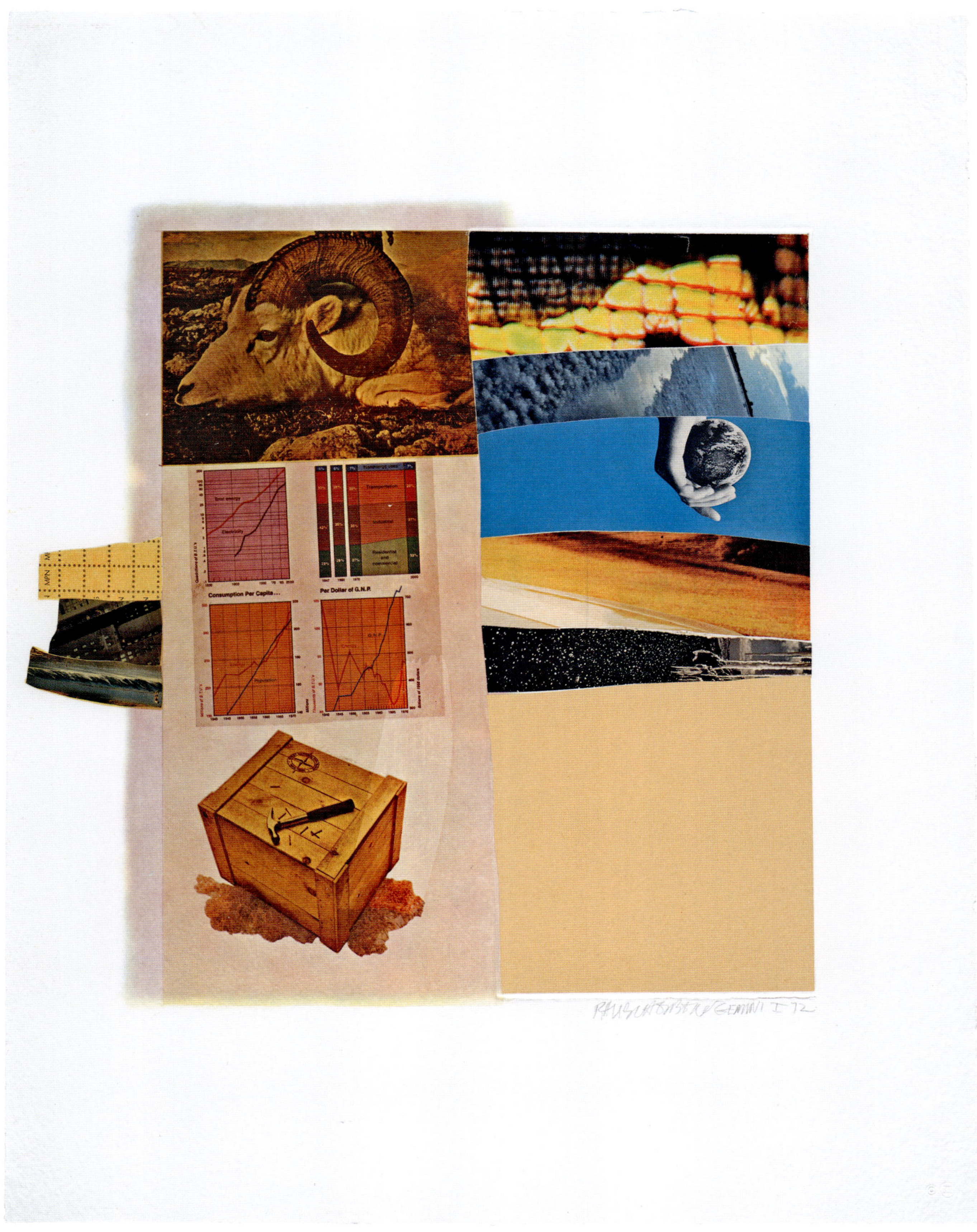

Horsefeathers Thirteen I, 1972
Lithograph, screenprint, pochoir, printed reproductions, and embossing on paper
28 × 22½ inches (71.1 × 57.2 cm)
Walker Art Center, Minneapolis

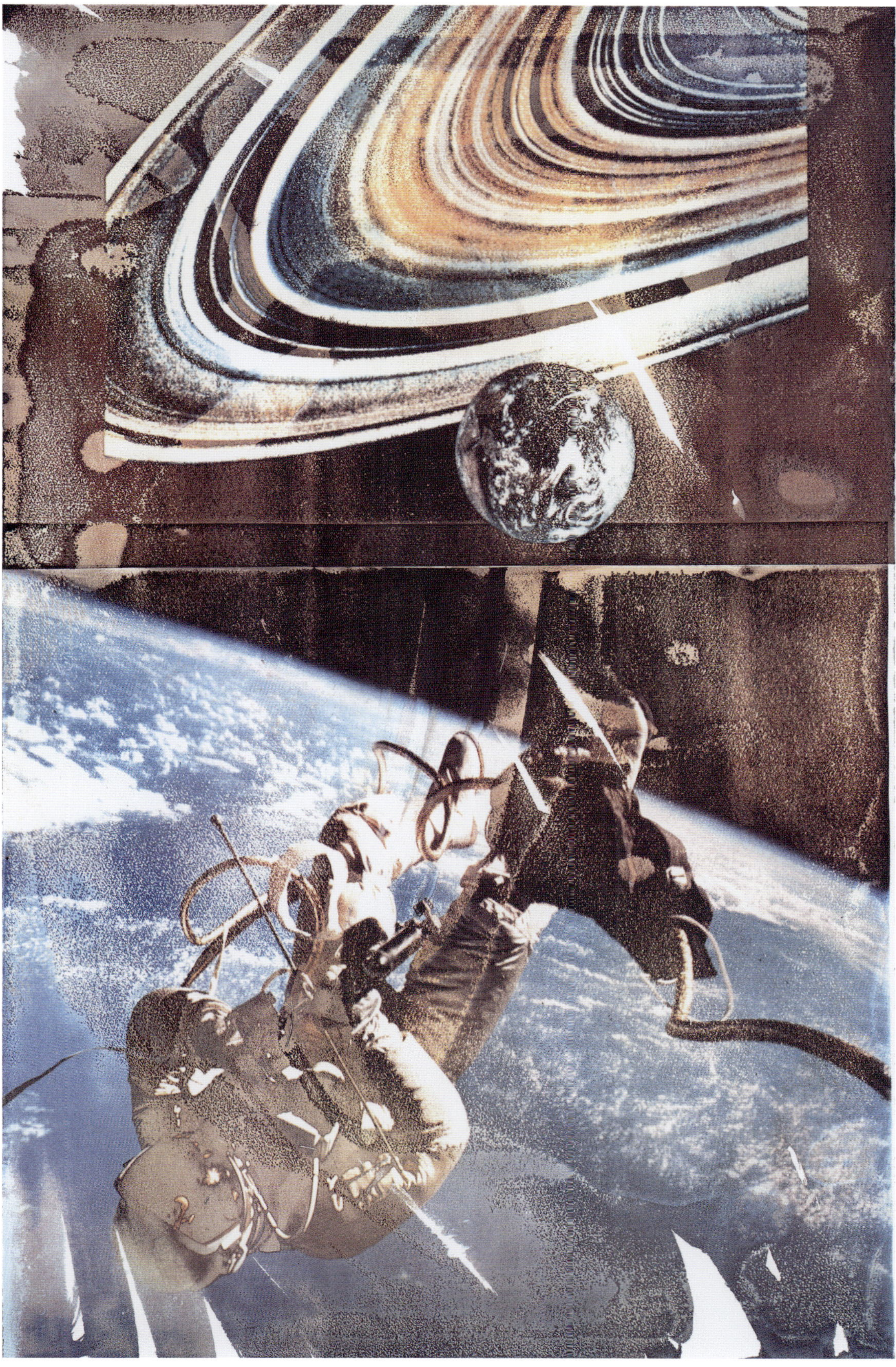

Space (Tribute 21), 1994
Offset lithograph
41 × 27 inches (104.14 × 68.58 cm)
San Francisco Museum of Modern Art

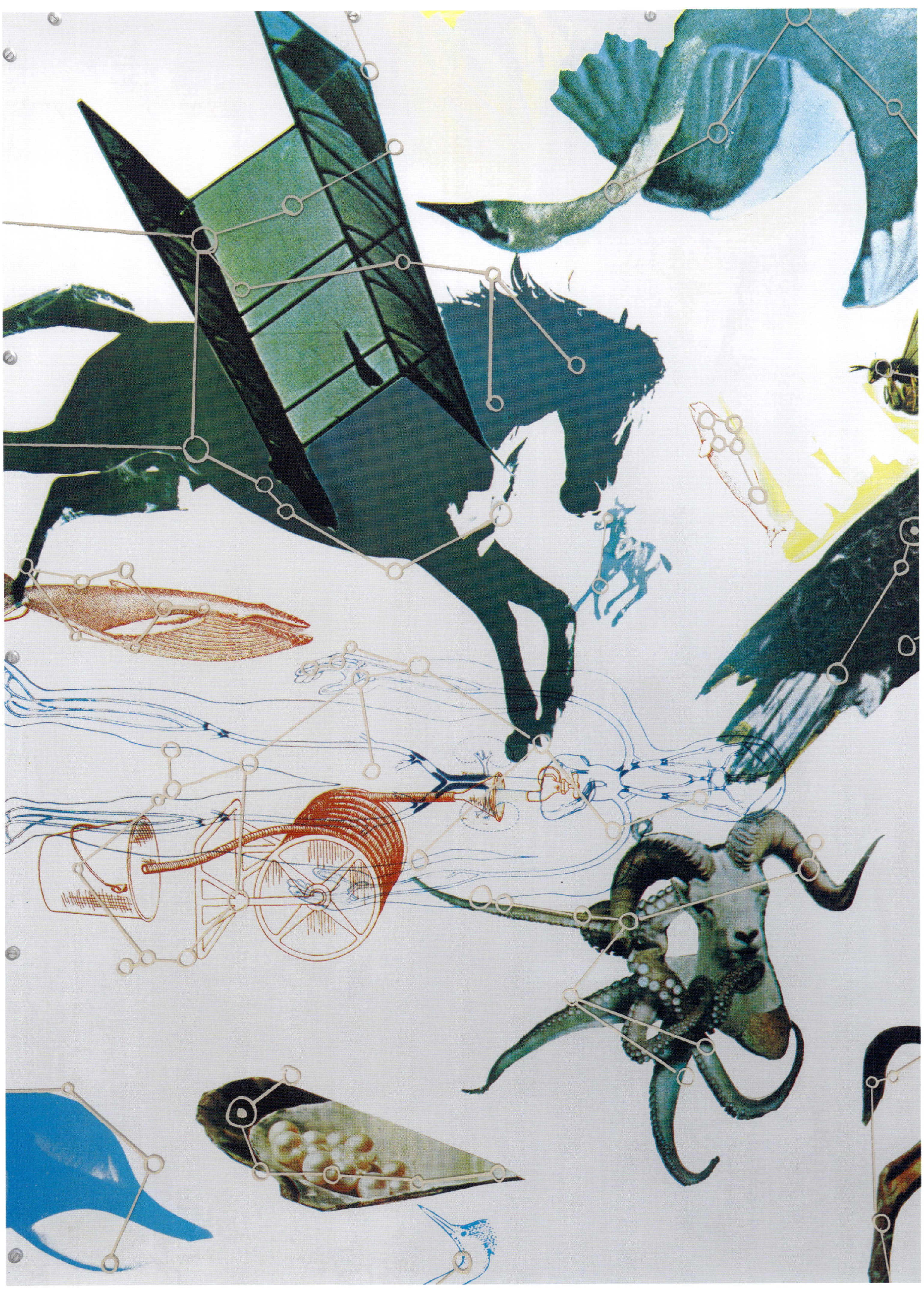

9

Interpreting the Night Sky

A subject foreign to no one; the sky. The common curiosity, mystery and reasoning that the heavens have excited endlessly, encourages my artistic invasion.

—Robert Rauschenberg[1]

Rauschenberg's interest in celestial phenomena and the night sky prompted an extensive reimagining of constellations, planetary entities, and mythological deities in his art. His adaptations of astral elements give a twist to traditional narratives and are a testament to the artist's unflagging ability to find inspiration in a range of sources and create bridges between past and present.

Contemporary Constellations

Star Quarters I–IV (1971) consists of four panels that present a contemporary reinterpretation of the constellations. In his notebook, Rauschenberg described the work (entirely in capital letters):

> STAR QUARTERS ARE A SENSUAL VISUAL ENCOUNTER. A FOURSOME CONSTRUCTED TO MERGE INTO A SINGLE WORK OR SEASONAL SEPARATE. EACH UNIT IS SELF SUPPORTING. MYTH, MATH, AND SYMBOLISM ARE RESEARCHED AND SCREENED ONTO PLASTIC PANELS THAT ARE THEN VACU[U]M CHAMBER COATED, MIRRORIZING THE SURFACE TO ENABLE EACH PIECE [TO] REFLECT AND RESPOND TO EACH UNIQUE LOCATION AND TIME. HERE BY ADDING YOUR EVERCHANGING LIFE TO ITS.[2]

Benjamin Genocchio's critique of the work in the *New York Times* called it a hodgepodge: "It is like an astrological charting of everything that popped into the artist's mind."[3] Quite to the contrary, Rauschenberg thought through the imagery in *Star Quarters I–IV* very carefully. Reference materials found in the Robert Rauschenberg Foundation Archives make clear his

efforts to accurately depict the constellations—down to their proper placement in the night sky. To make the connection obvious, Rauschenberg overlaid his interpretations of the constellations with their star charts.

In the first panel, *Star Quarters I*, Rauschenberg reimagined Pegasus, known in Greco-Roman mythology as a winged horse-god, with biplane wings reminiscent of those cloth-covered wings on the Wright Flyer and other early aircraft. Aquila, the eagle that carried the thunderbolts of Zeus, is placed alongside Cygnus, represented by a swan. In addition to these representational figures, the series incorporates symbols and icons from pop culture, including a space suit and spacecraft. In *Star Quarters I*, the boxer and civil rights activist Muhammad Ali stands for the constellation Hercules, known in Roman mythology for his unwavering strength.

Rauschenberg's sky map includes all twelve zodiac constellations (unsurprising in a devotee of astrology who based life decisions on the counsel of a professional astrologer).[4] Some of his depictions stick to traditional imagery—a ram for Aries, a lion for Leo, a crab for Cancer, and so on—while others are more novel. In *Star Quarters III*, Diane Arbus's photograph *Identical Twins, Roselle, N.J.* (1966) represents Gemini and perhaps serves as a tribute to Arbus, who passed away in 1971.[5]

Likewise, many of Rauschenberg's constellations have apparent connections to their sources—Lepus the hare, Cetus the whale—others, less so. Telescopium was, appropriately enough, named in the eighteenth century for a telescope, but here it is shown as a telescope snail. Horologium, known as "the Clock," is represented by an aviation instrument showing an artificial horizon and automatic direction finder. And Orion, the hunter, is a diver or gymnast in Rauschenberg's hands. His

Detail of **Star Quarters I**, 1971

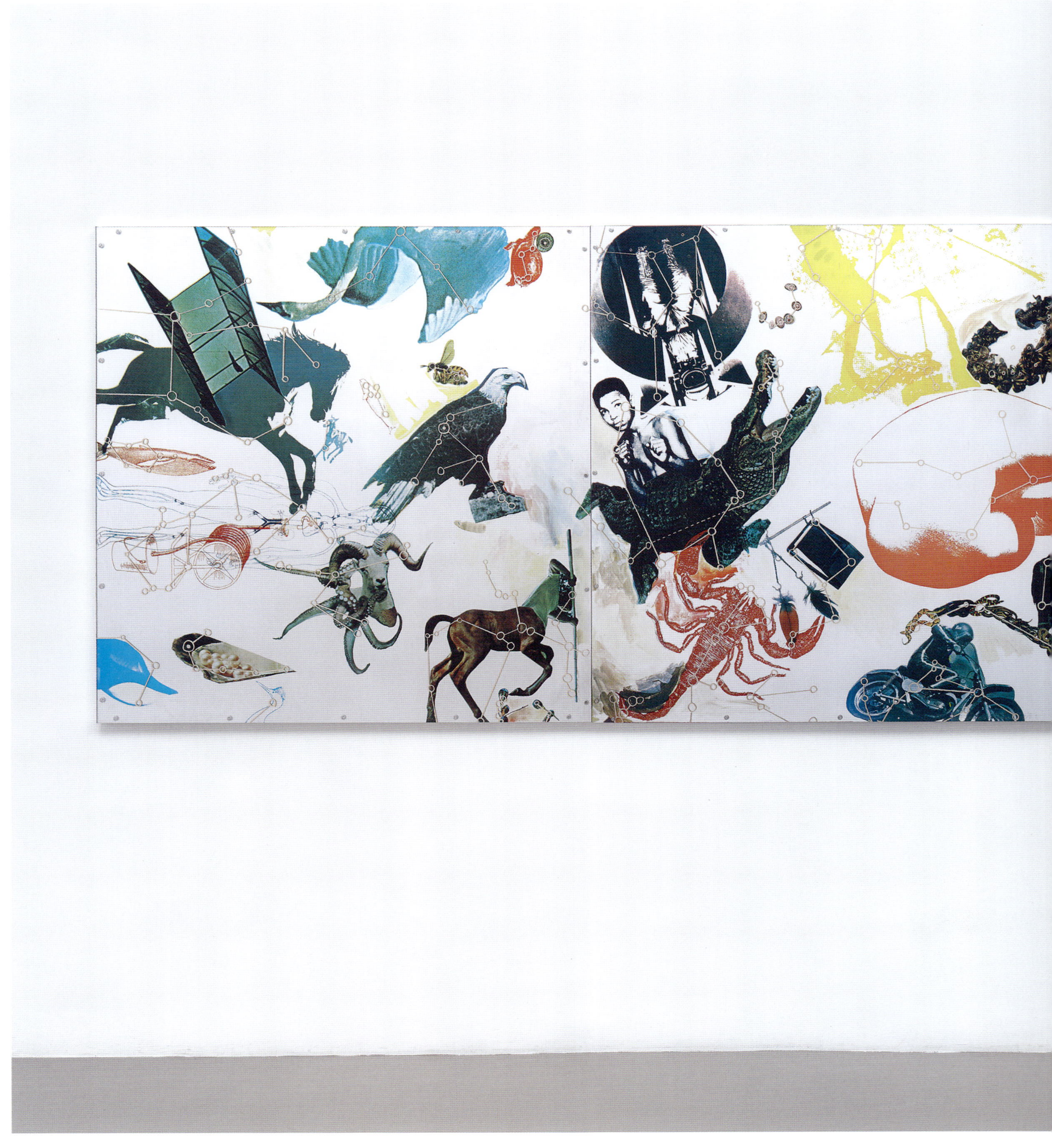

Star Quarters I–IV, 1971
Screenprint on mirrored Plexiglas, four panels
48 × 192 inches (121.9 × 487.7 cm) overall
Robert Rauschenberg Foundation

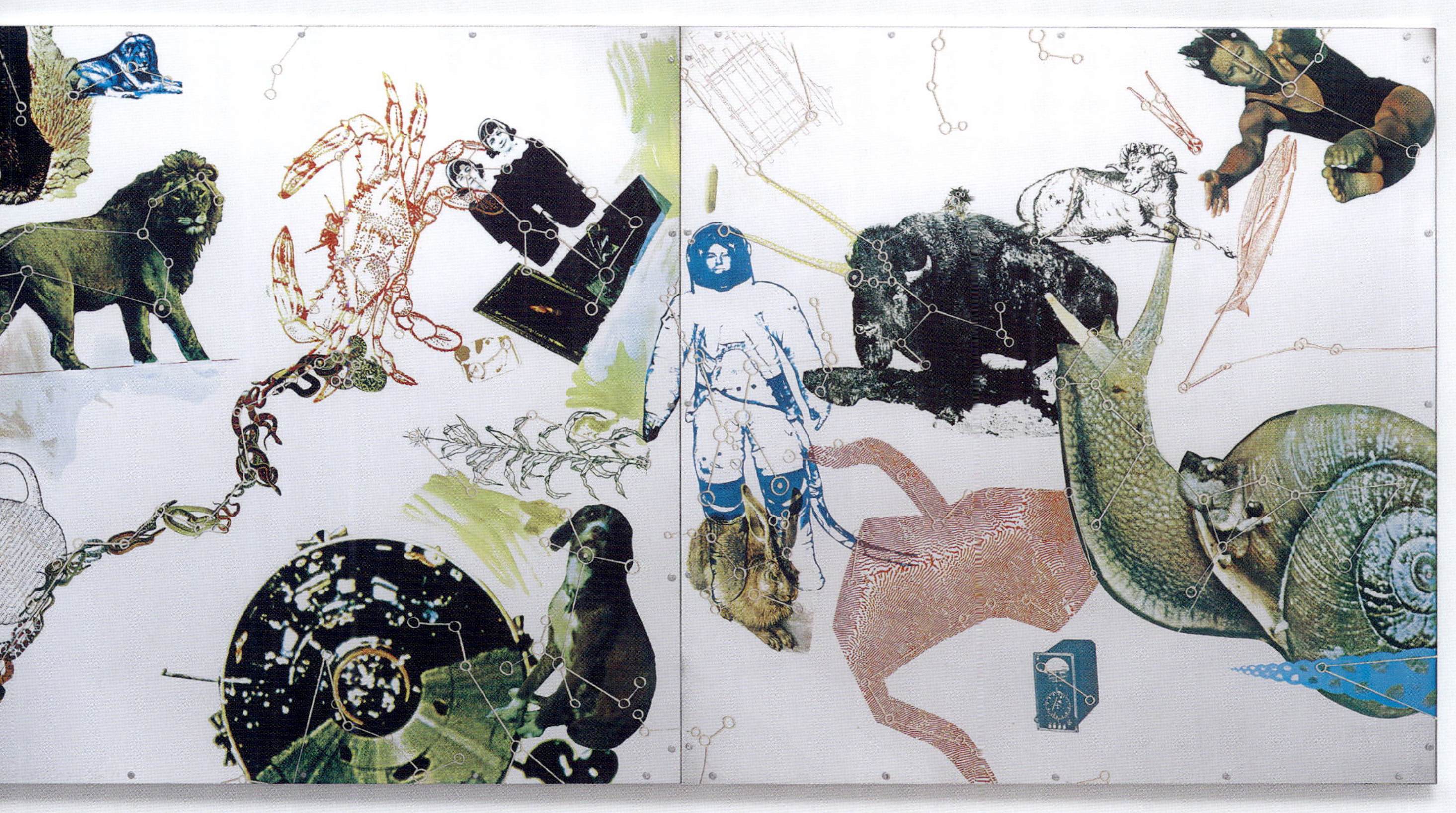

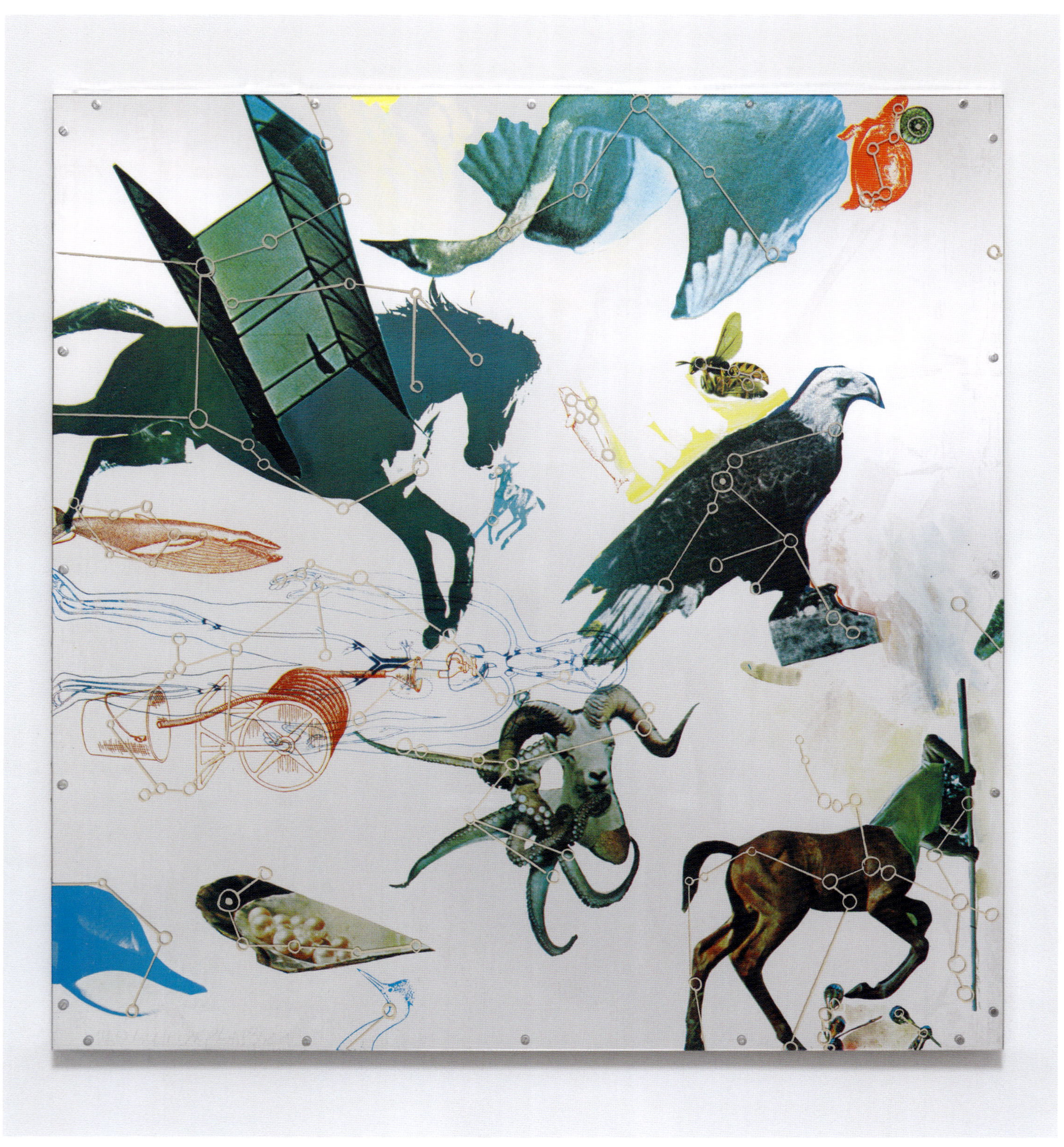

Star Quarters I, 1971
Silkscreen on mirrored Plexiglas
48 × 48 inches (121.9 × 121.9 cm)
Robert Rauschenberg Foundation

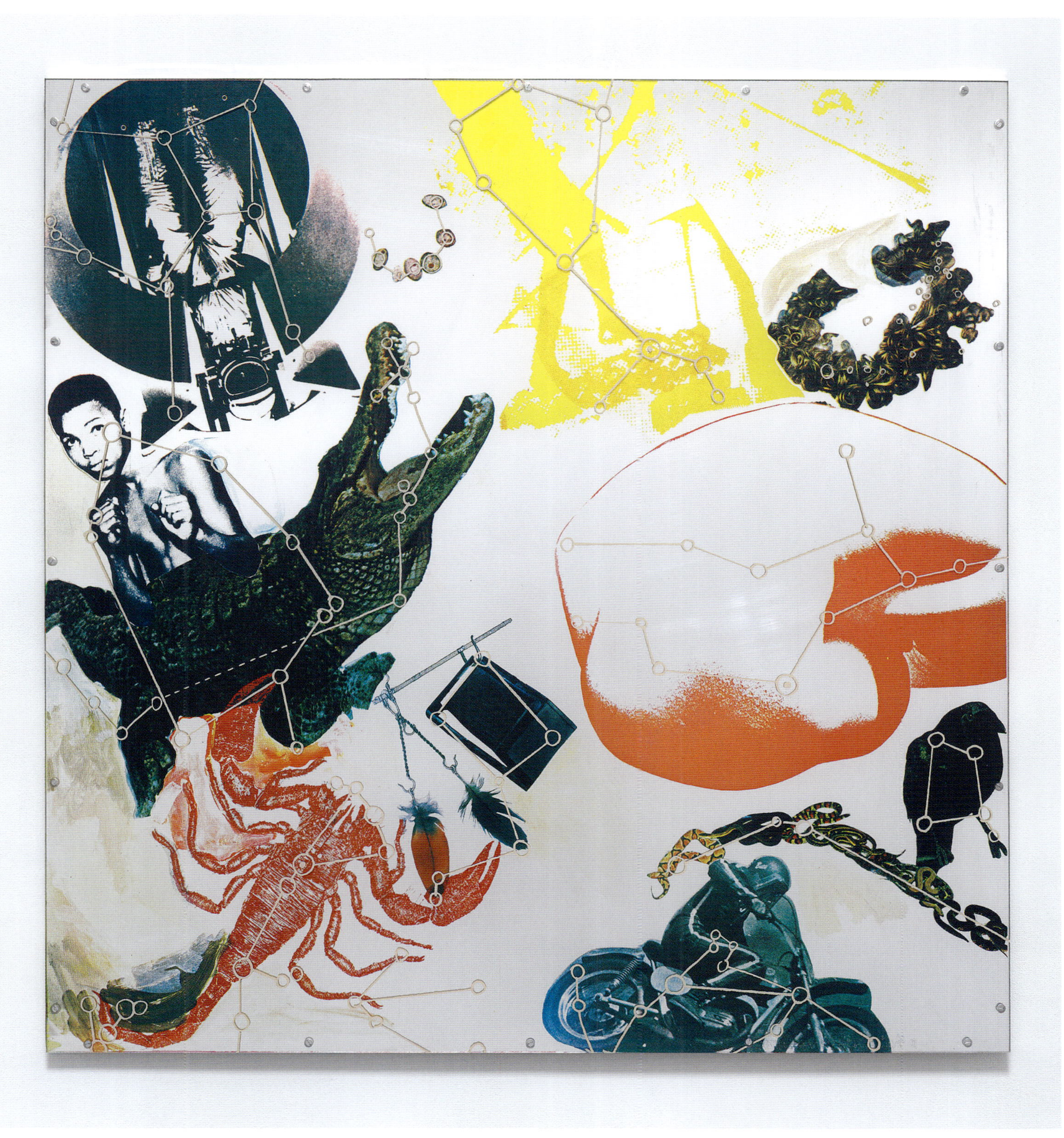

Star Quarters II, 1971
Silkscreen on mirrored Plexiglas
48 × 48 inches (121.9 × 121.9 cm)
Robert Rauschenberg Foundation

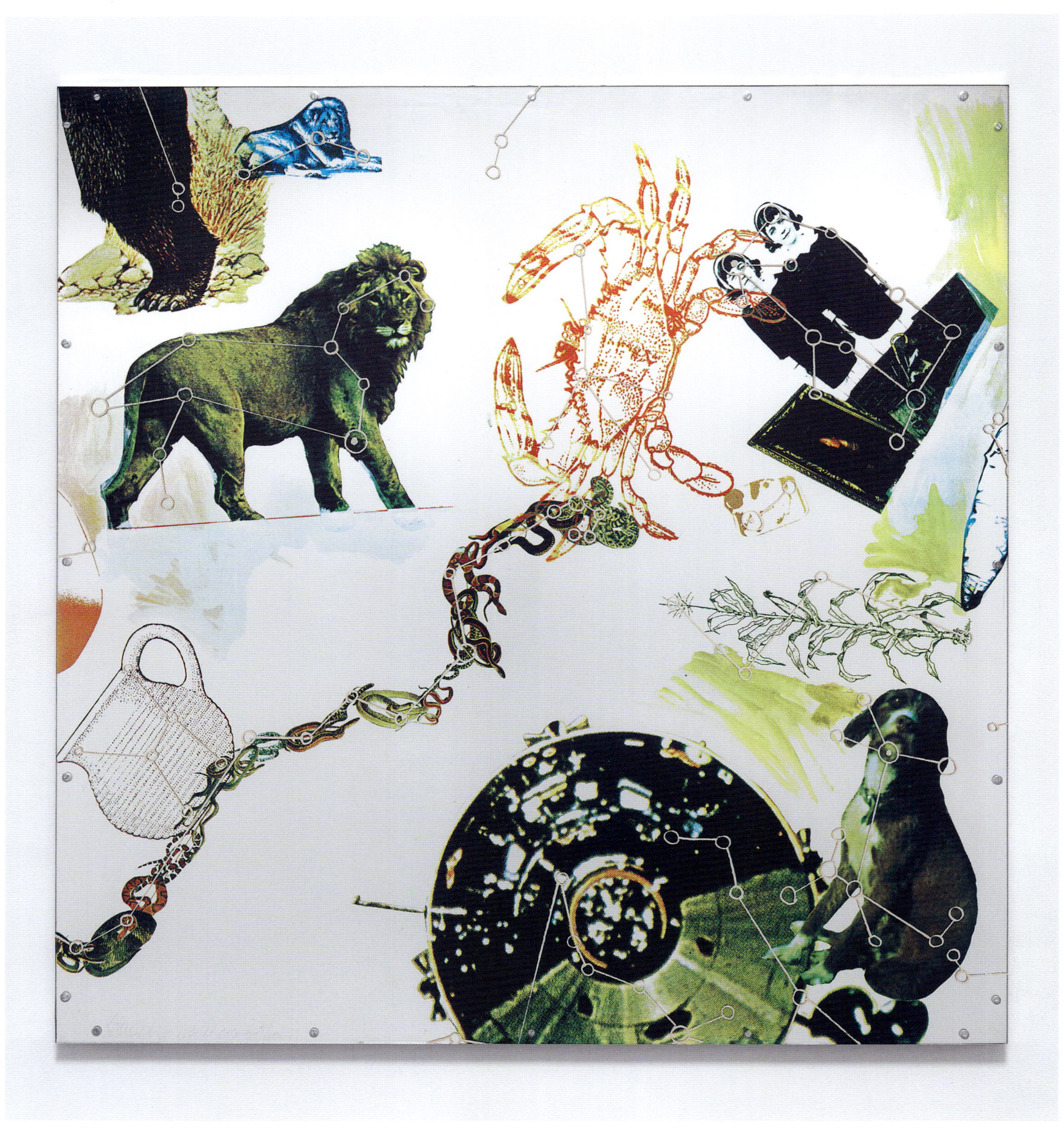

Star Quarters III, 1971
Silkscreen on mirrored Plexiglas
48 × 48 inches (121.9 × 121.9 cm)
Robert Rauschenberg Foundation

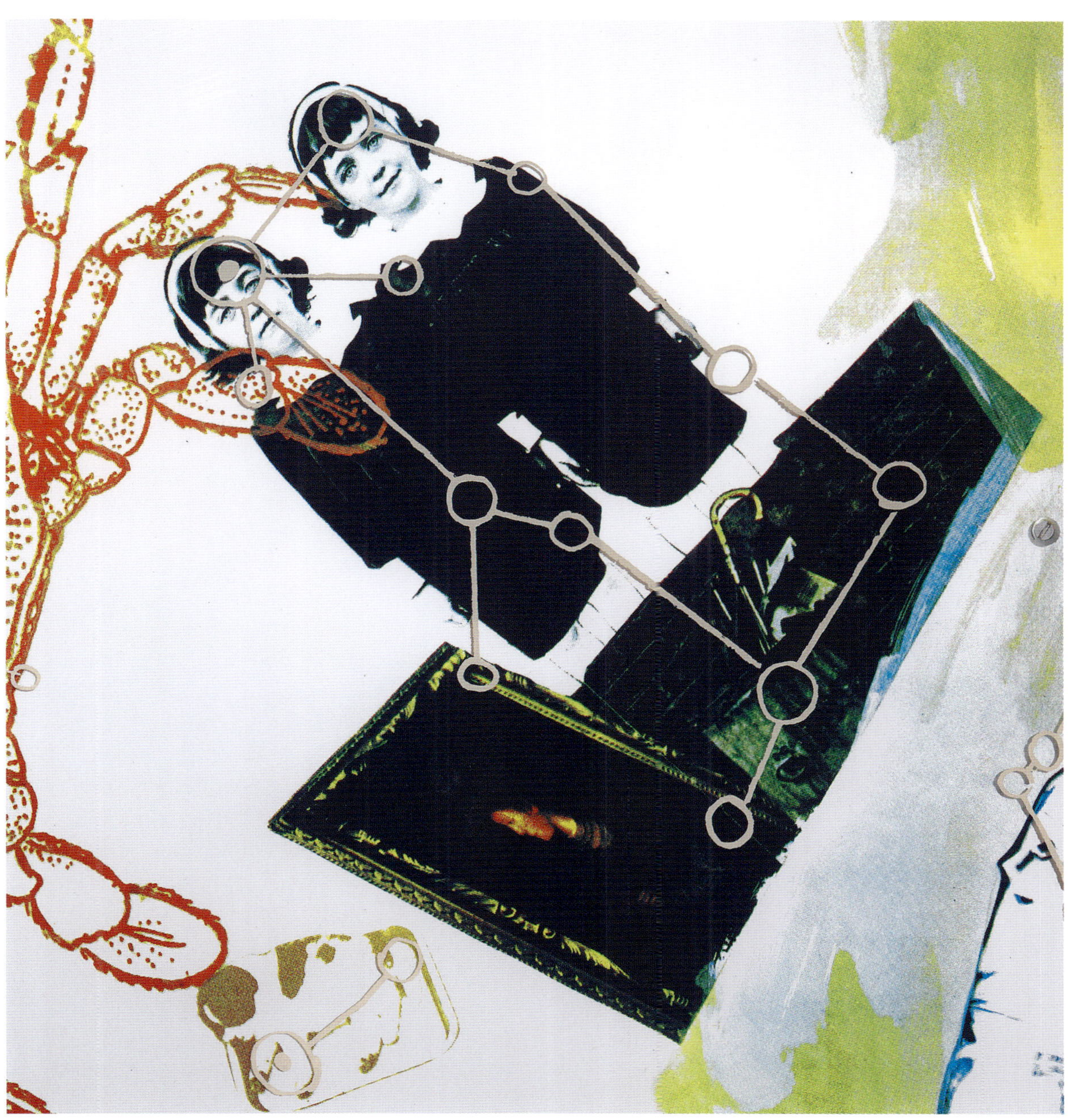

Detail of **Star Quarters III**, 1971

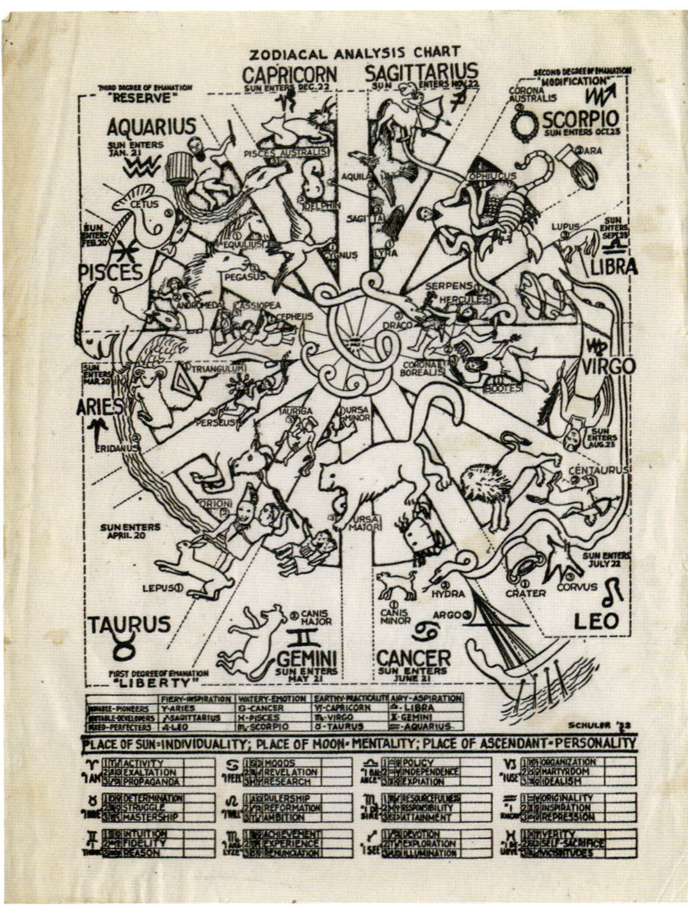

Zodiac chart published by Schuler in 1932 and used by Rauschenberg as research material for *Star Quarters I–IV* (1971).

utilization of myth, math, and symbolism as articulated in his description of *Star Quarters I–IV* is substantiated by the proper placement of the constellations and reference materials found in the Robert Rauschenberg Foundation Archives. The project involved the use of star and zodiac charts, as well as books on stars, constellations, and astrology, to delineate and contemporize the night sky.

Flying Deities

Pegasus reemerges in *Rodeo Olympics Glut* (1988), where two of the winged horse-gods face each other and flank imagery from two screenprinted photographs. One was taken by Rauschenberg during a 1984 trip to Chile and was silhouetted to focus on bicycle handles (as always, in Rauschenberg's lexicon, a reference to the Wright brothers and the invention of flight).[6] The other photographic image features an ancient sculpture believed to represent Hermes, the divine messenger of Greek myth whose winged sandals and helmet enabled his speedy travel.[7] The piece is part of the *Glut* series (1986–89/1991–94), which was inspired by the 1980s oil glut in Texas; fittingly, the

bright red Pegasus Rauschenberg selected here serves as a corporate logo for the Mobile petroleum company.

Mercury Zero Summer Glut (1987) combines parts of an electric fan with a metal cut-out wing. The title namechecks Mercury—the Roman god of commerce, travel, and luck (among other attributes) and, like his Greek counterpart, Hermes, the messenger of the gods—and underscores the sculpture's focus on the essential atmospheric and physical elements of flight, specifically air and wings.

Celestial Aura

Avian creatures and celestial bodies are integrated in *7–UP (Shales)* (1994) and *Interscape Mirage* (2000), two works created for distinct purposes. The *Shales* series (1994–95) saw Rauschenberg experimenting with ancient encaustic techniques, which he dubbed "fire-wax." Donald Saff, founder of Saff Tech Arts, developed the "fire-wax" transfer technique and collaborated with Rauschenberg on this project. The planet Saturn, a bald eagle, and an arrow pointing up surround a paintbrush positioned vertically, akin to a rocket ship. The inclusion of the number seven, along with the emphasis on ascending elements, alludes to the soft drink 7UP®. The fire-wax process involves transferring photographs onto a wax coated canvas, with additional images embedded between layers of wax. It produces a three-dimensional effect where the images appear to hover over the canvas.[8]

Rauschenberg collaborated with many artists throughout his career, and his work as a designer of sets, costumes, and lighting for dance and theater productions was both formative and a source of ongoing inspiration. *Interscape Mirage* was printed on fabric and used as the backdrop for the performance of *Interscape* in the same year at the Kennedy Center Performing Arts Center in Washington, DC, by the Merce Cunningham Dance Company that featured music by John Cage. At the center of the composition is a depiction of the Moon that appears partially eroded, suggesting a history of meteorite impacts. Below the Moon, a goose is shown alongside a figurine of an Asian woman gazing skyward. Adjacent to the Moon are a leaping carousel horse and the Parthenon, suggesting a link to the mythological Pegasus. On the far right, a vibrant red skyscape contrasts with more subdued, nebulous imagery rendered in greens and blues below. Beneath this is a blend of smeared colors representing an intergalactic explosion. Next

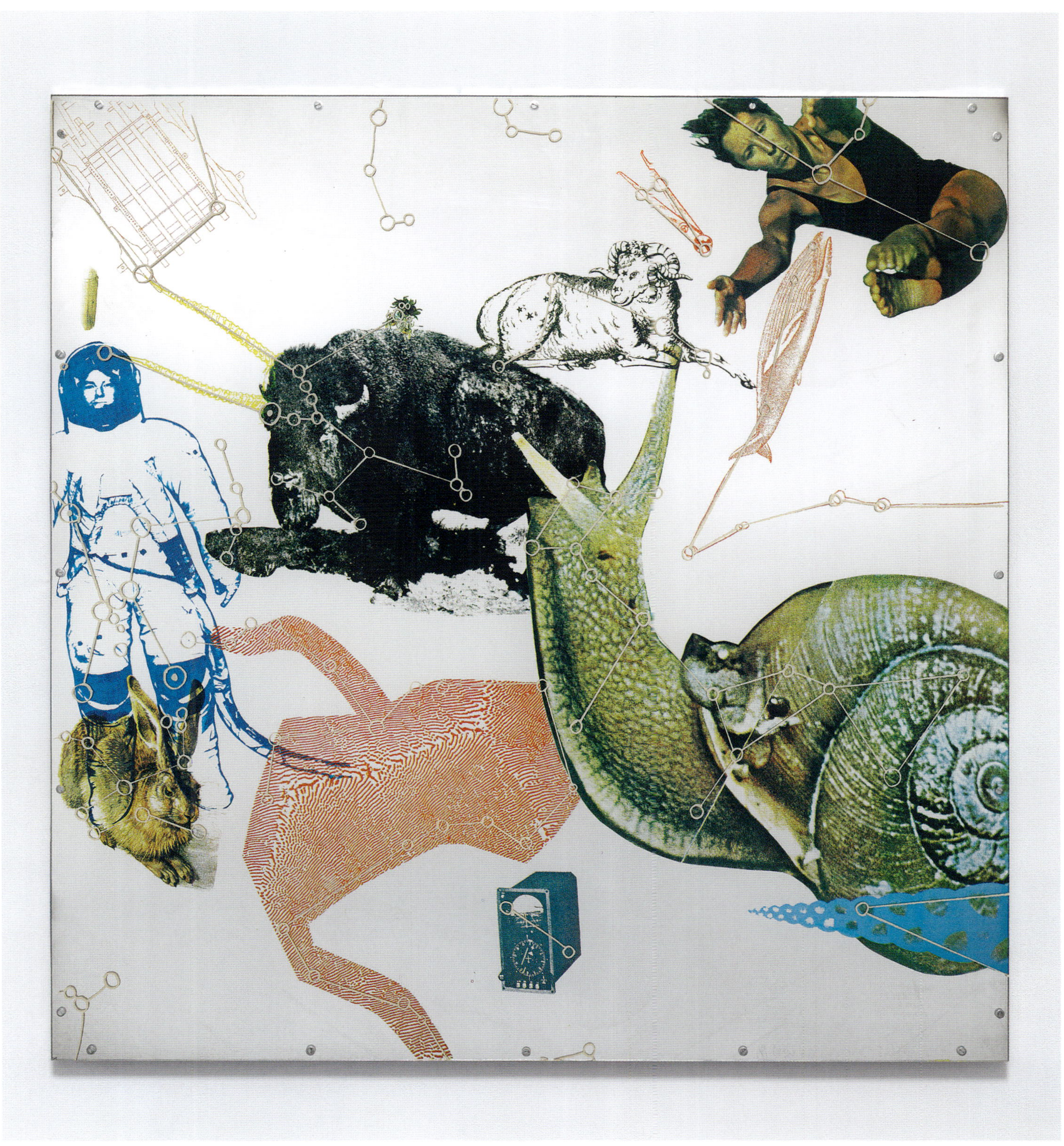

Star Quarters IV, 1971
Silkscreen on mirrored Plexiglas
48 × 48 inches (121.9 × 121.9 cm)
Robert Rauschenberg Foundation

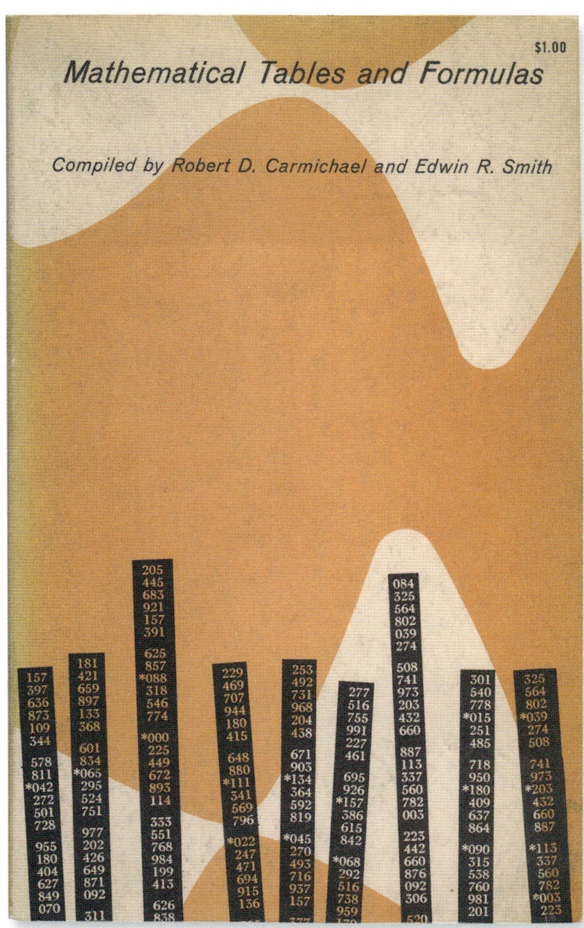

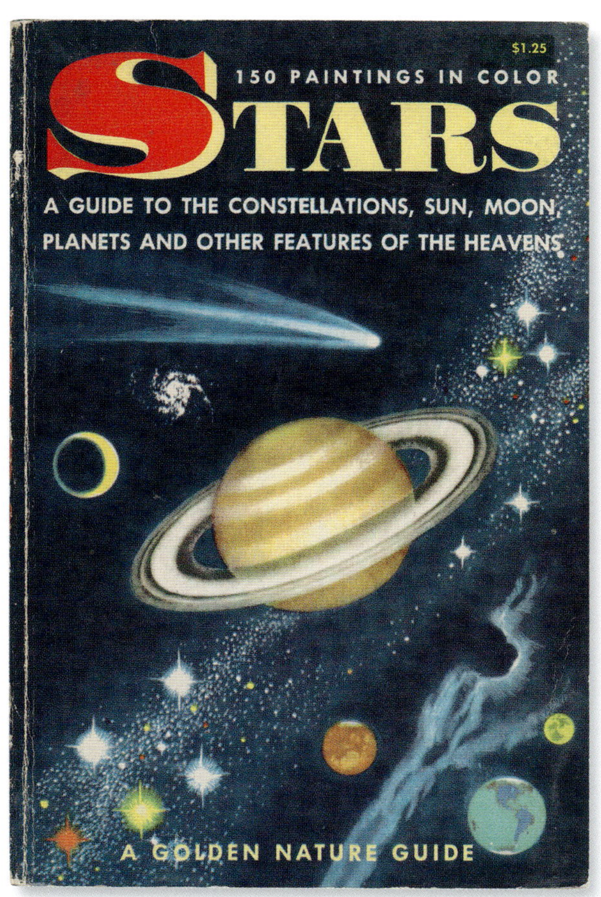

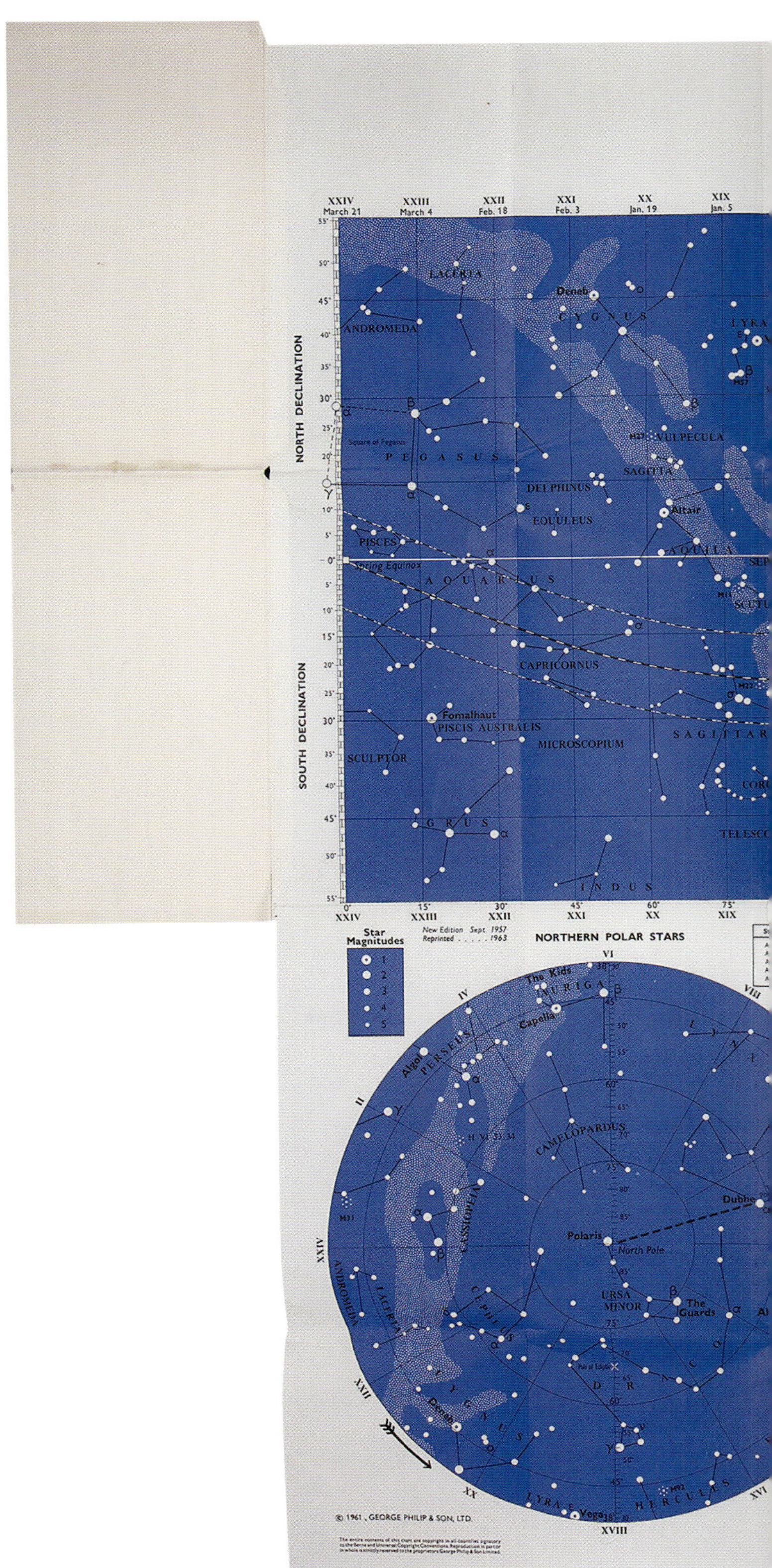

Mathematical Tables and Formulas by R. D. Carmichael and Edwin R. Smith from Rauschenberg's personal collection.

Stars: A Guide to the Constellations, Sun, Moon, Planets, and Other Features of the Heavens by Herbert S. Zim and Robert H. Baker, and illustrated by James Gordon Irving from Rauschenberg's personal collection.

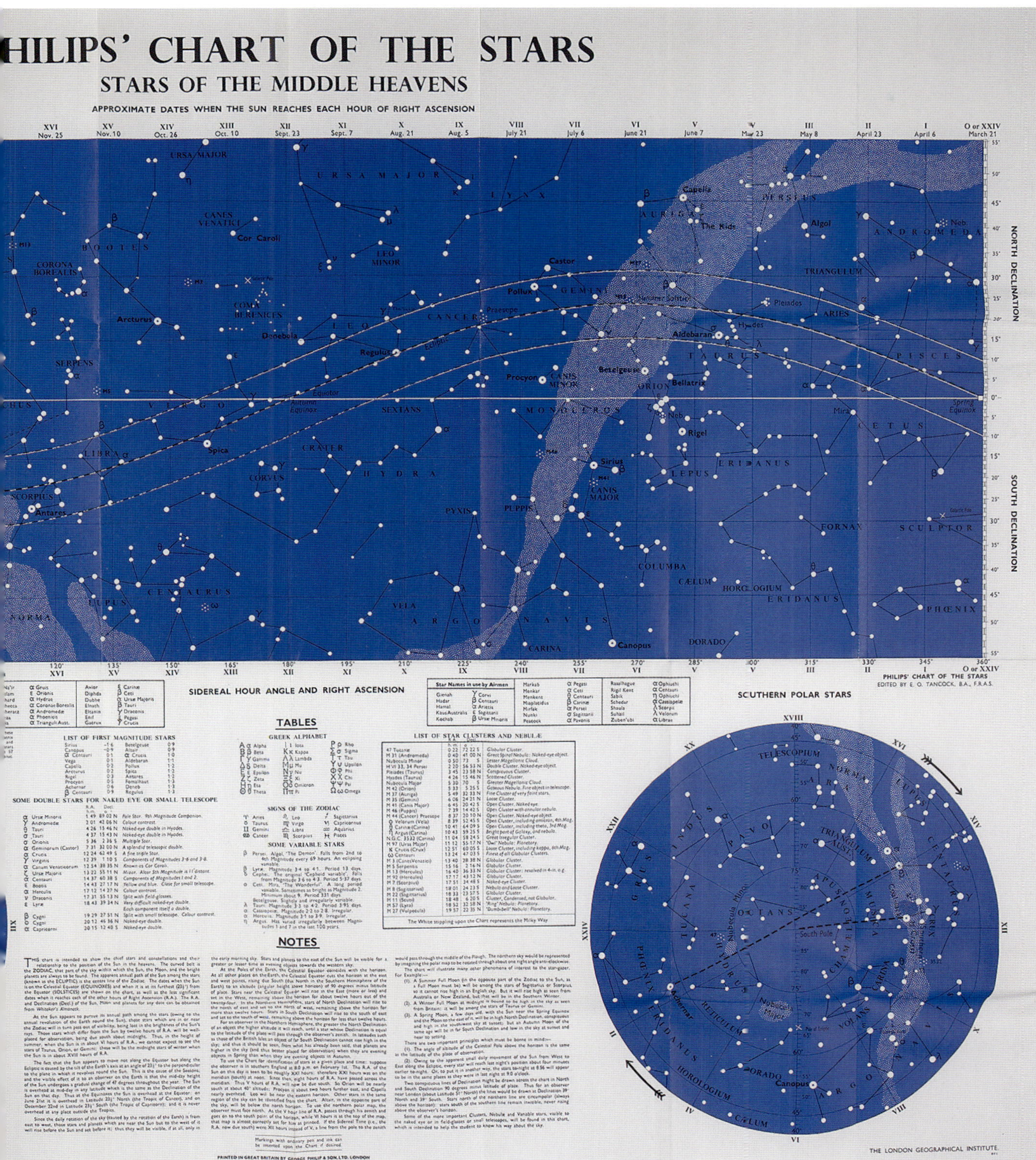

Phillips' Chart of the Stars, edited by E. O. Tancock, used by Rauschenberg as source material for *Star Quarters I–IV* (1971).

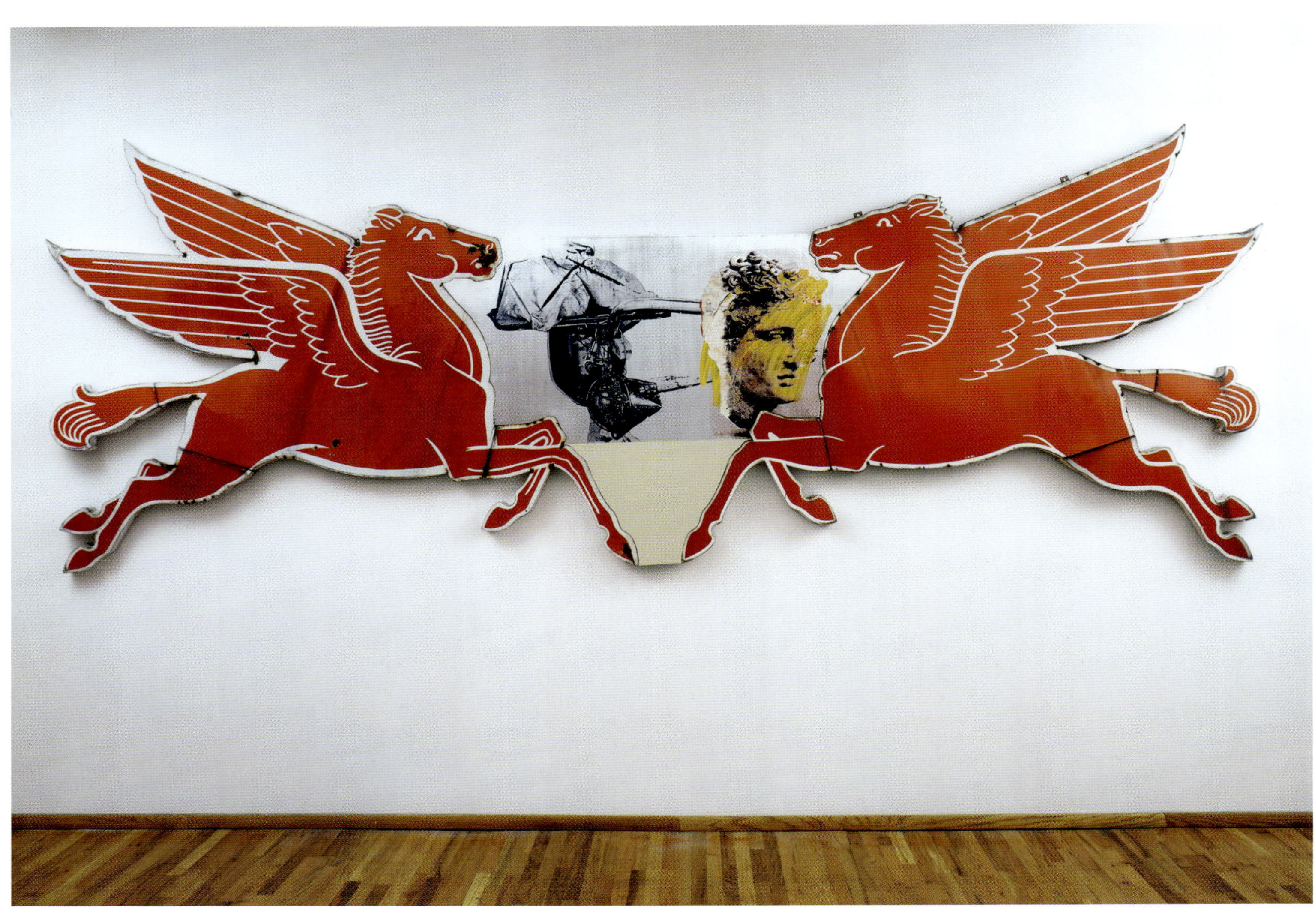

Rodeo Olympics Glut, 1988
Assembled metal and silkscreen ink on aluminum
69½ × 196⅛ × 5½ inches (176.5 × 498.2 × 14 cm)
Robert Rauschenberg Foundation

to this, an arrow points up toward a star cluster composed of cut-out human figures. For the dance performance, a sheer black-and-white version of this composition was used as a scrim that revealed dancers warming up on stage, with the color version behind them as the backdrop; the resulting combination created a "mirage" effect. When the scrim was raised, performers wearing costumes created by Rauschenberg danced. Repetitive movements in the choreography included "head thrown back, arms linked, back-to-back dancing, and shifts of weight, sometimes in the pelvis alone."[9] By activating these celestial elements, *Interscape Mirage* prompts viewers to contemplate space—as well as the space between the dancers, the music, the Earth, and the Moon.

Solar Elephant (Kabal American Zephyr) (1982) features imagery that includes a blank paint-by-number board of an owl, a person standing inside a hot-air balloon during inflation, and planets of the solar system, notably Jupiter and Saturn, along with the Sun and an image of the Milky Way galaxy. At the lower left and again at the upper right, the (reversed) outstretched finger of God from Michelangelo's Sistine Chapel frescoes reaches out not for Adam's hand but a foot—an image likely drawn from an advertisement. On either side of the hand-and-foot image at the upper right are slices of an orange, which may represent Florida (Rauschenberg's home and location of NASA space activities). The middle of the piece is dominated by an embedded wooden storm door, which, with its surround of celestial bodies, seems to ask us what lies beyond the portal the artist has fashioned.

Angelic Musings

Rauschenberg's celestial obsessions seem unavoidably intertwined with his Christian upbringing. The art historian Lisa Wainwright has explored the correlation between Rauschenberg's Christian background and his use of flight as a "metaphor for his passion for ideals of transcendence."[10] *Easter Angel Flap Winter Glut* (1989) is animated by angelic connotations. It's two wings, made from pale corrugated metal, resemble feathers and harp strings. The midsection features a window frame with space for six symmetrical panes, though here only glass shards remain at some of the edges. Absent glass, the window frame resembles a ladder, signifying the journey to heaven; in this reading, the shards of glass represent sins or tribulations to overcome. The title *Easter Angel Flap Winter Glut* references the observance of Christ's resurrection along with the movement of angels' wings.[11]

In 1998 Rauschenberg received a commission from the Vatican to create art for a modern basilica in San Giovanni Rotondo, Italy, designed by the architect Renzo Piano. The church is the pilgrimage site for Saint Padre Pio (1887–1968), who is venerated by Catholics for his supernatural visions of Christ and his lifelong manifestation of stigmata.[12] Piano worked with the Vatican to consider contemporary art for the shrine, and Rauschenberg was tasked with coming up with a concept for a huge stained-glass window.

From a distance, *The Happy Apocalypse* (1999) appears to be a colorful collaged mosaic in mostly blues and oranges, with a bright gold satellite dish bearing images of the Earth at the center. Swarming around it are scenes of human culture (the Great Sphinx of Giza, a gargoyle from Notre-Dame in Paris, the Parthenon, the Statue of Liberty, a mosque) and natural disasters (hurricanes, crashing waves, fires, a biohazard suit). To the right of the dish, however, this intense crush of images softens and brightens with scenes of nature (birds, seals, swans, sea creatures, landscapes, and skyscapes), spherical objects that suggest planets or molecules, enigmatic pastel washes, and, finally, the Moon. Speculative religious connotations abound: sheep or lambs (the Lamb of God?), a mountain (Moses on Mount Sinai?), arrows pointing to the Parthenon (false gods?), and so on. When Rauschenberg was asked how God was represented in the work, he replied, "As a satellite dish, as he sees and hears everything. But they did not accept it."[13]

It wasn't the first time the Holy See rejected an artwork. The Catholic Church has sometimes struggled to accept contemporary expression, and artists including Roy Lichtenstein and Gerhard Richter have likewise been rebuffed.[14] Yet, twenty-five years later *The Happy Apocalypse* feels ever more prophetic. Rauschenberg anticipated a world riven by turmoil, climate crises, and the false god of technology, while maintaining a vision of the future that is bright—even celestial.

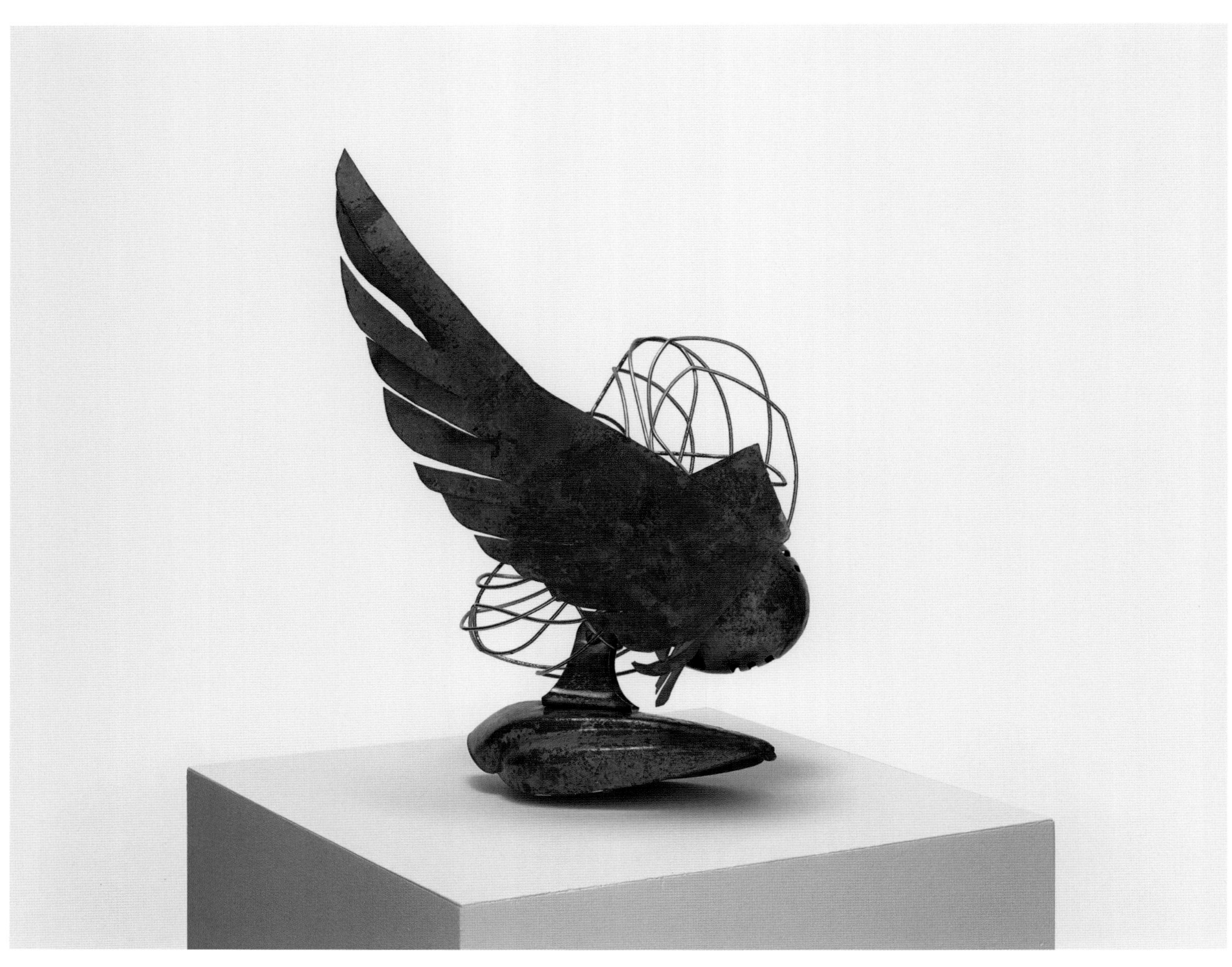

Mercury Zero Summer Glut, 1987
Assembled metal
10⅝ × 17½ × 8½ inches (27 × 44.5 × 21.6 cm)
Robert Rauschenberg Foundation

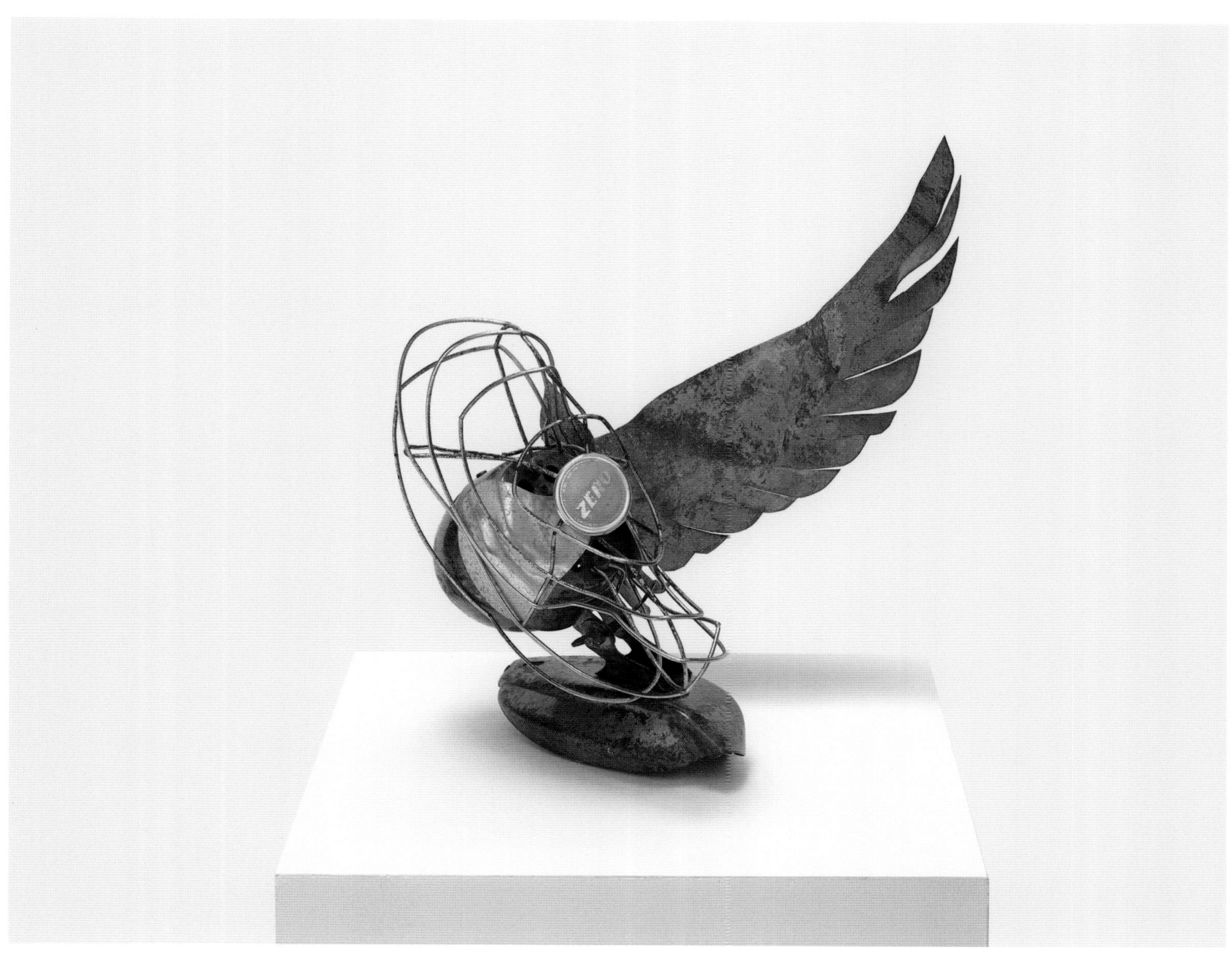

Alternate view of **Mercury Zero Summer Glut**, 1987

7–UP (Shales), 1994
Fire wax and transfer on canvas mounted on board with painted aluminum frame
48 × 36 inches (121.9 × 91.4 cm)
Collection, Ruth and Don Saff

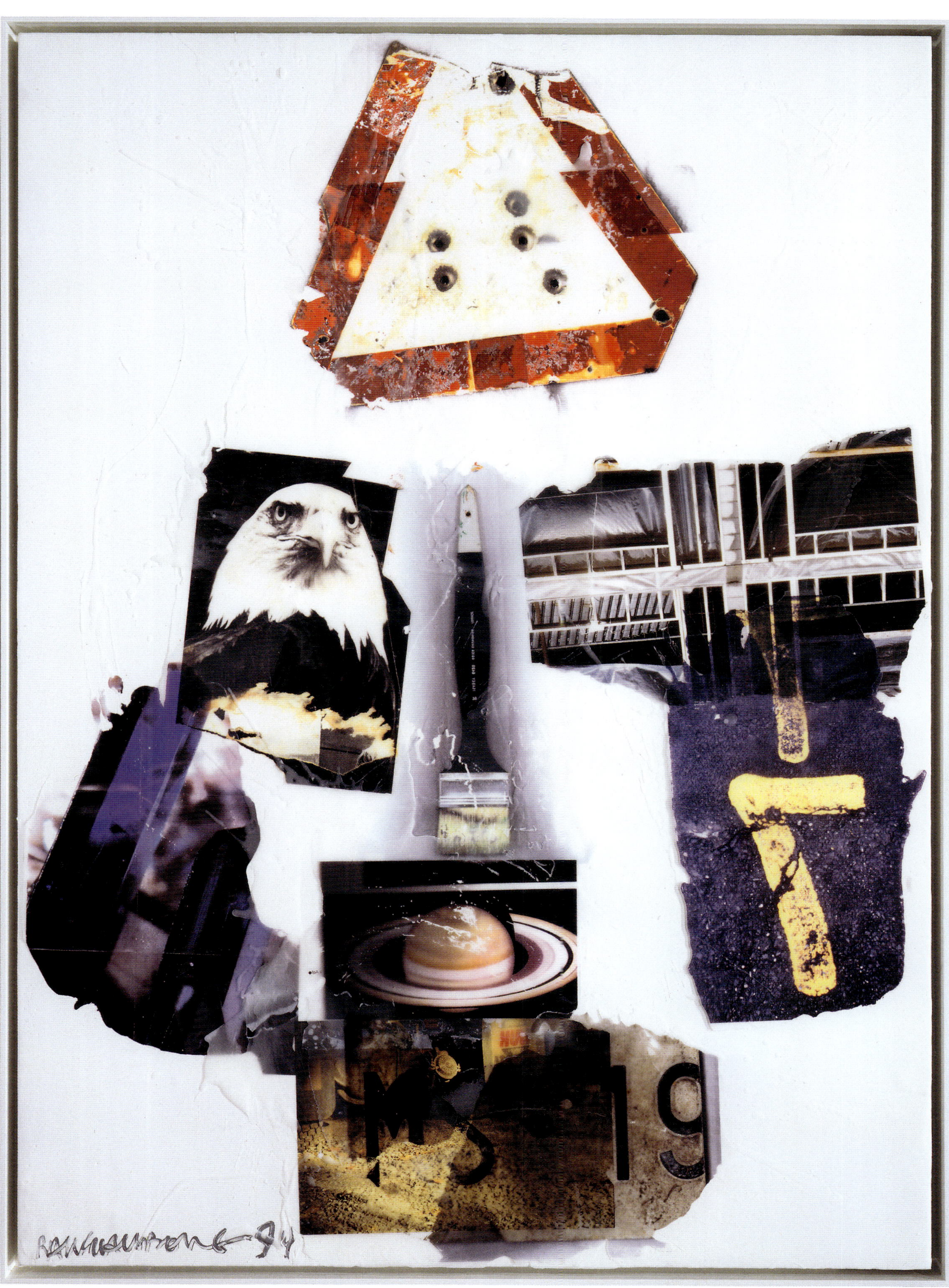
Rauschenberg 94

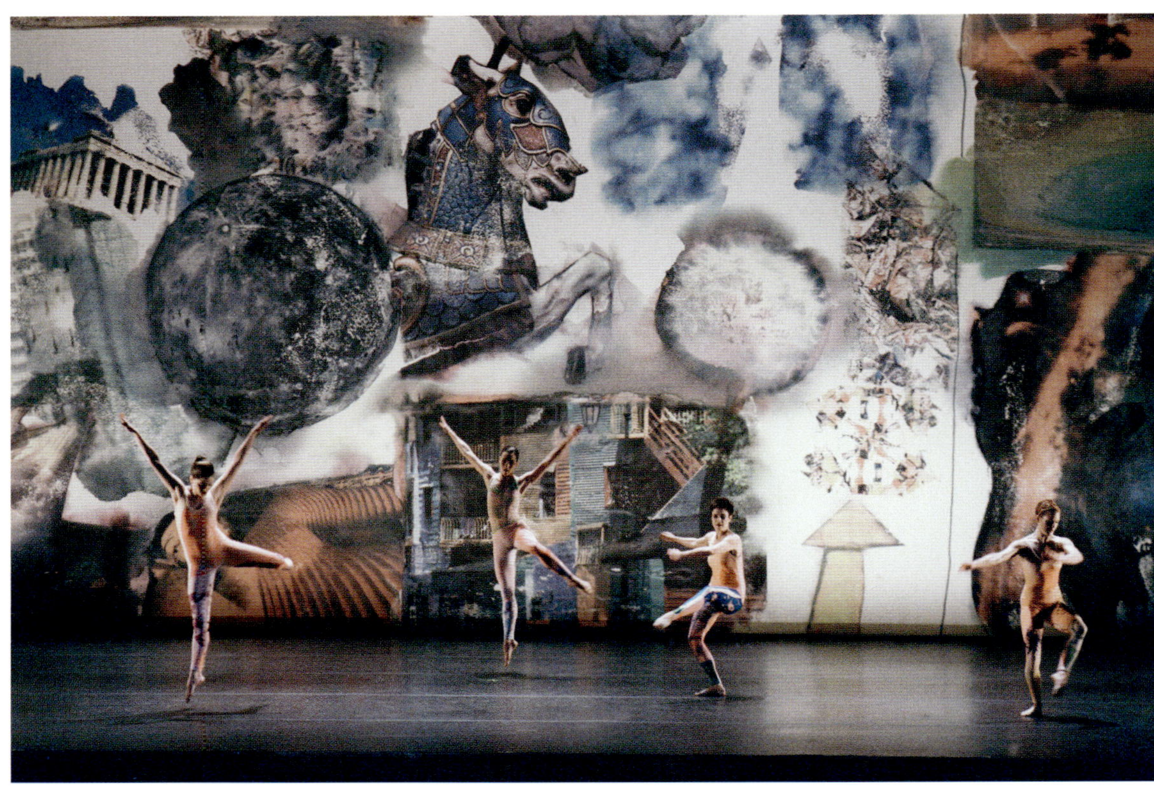

Jeannie Steele, Derry Swan, Maydelle Fason, and Holley Farmer performing in
Merce Cunningham Dance Company's *Interscape* (2000), with set and costume
design by Robert Rauschenberg.

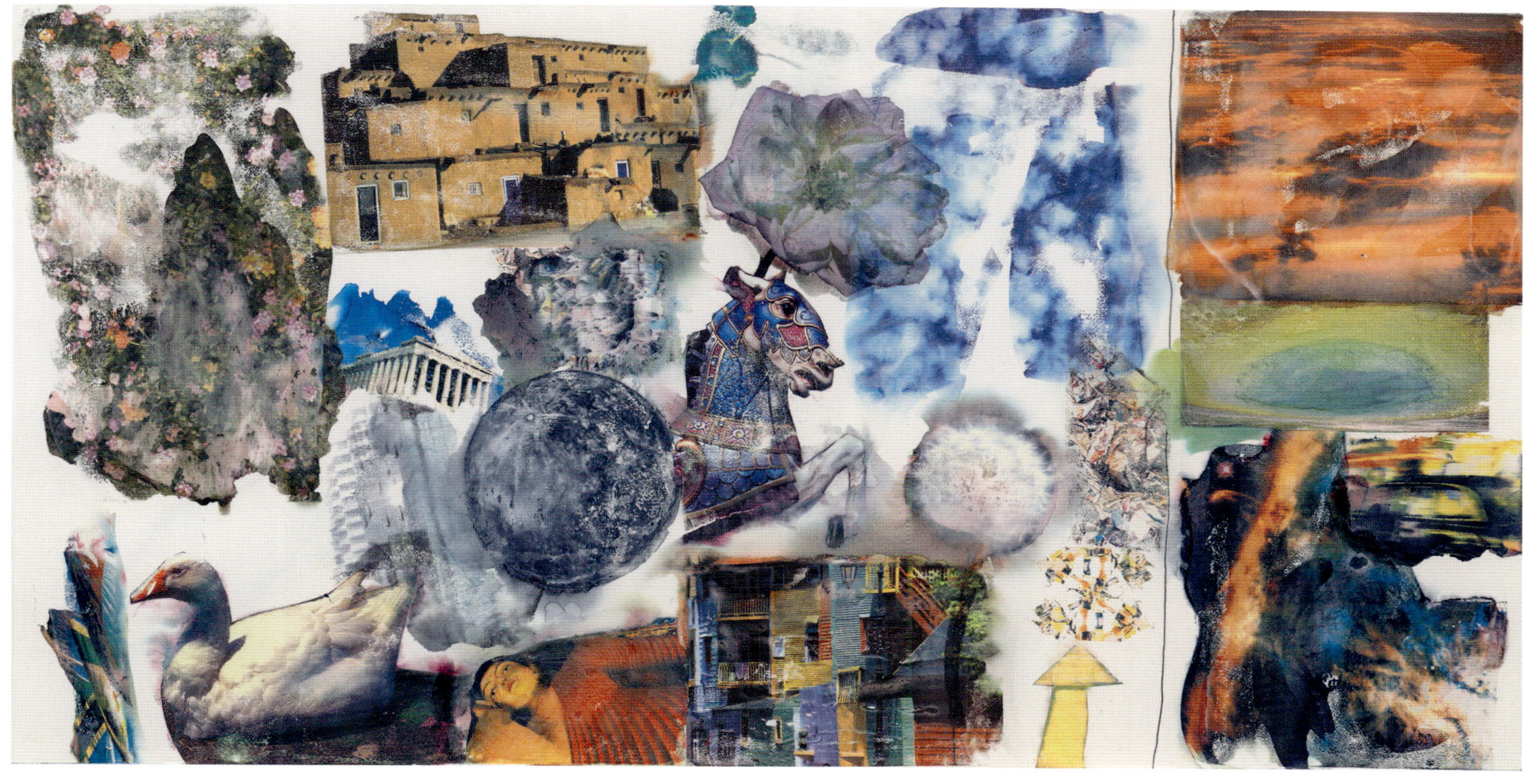

Interscape Mirage, 2000
Inkjet pigment transfer and graphite on polylaminate
36 × 72 inches (91.4 × 182.9 cm)
Robert Rauschenberg Foundation

Solar Elephant (Kabal American Zephyr), 1982
Solvent transfer, fabric, acrylic, wood door, wood mallet, metal spring, and string on plywood
106¾ × 83⅛ × 15⅞ inches (271 × 211 × 40.3 cm)
Robert Rauschenberg Foundation

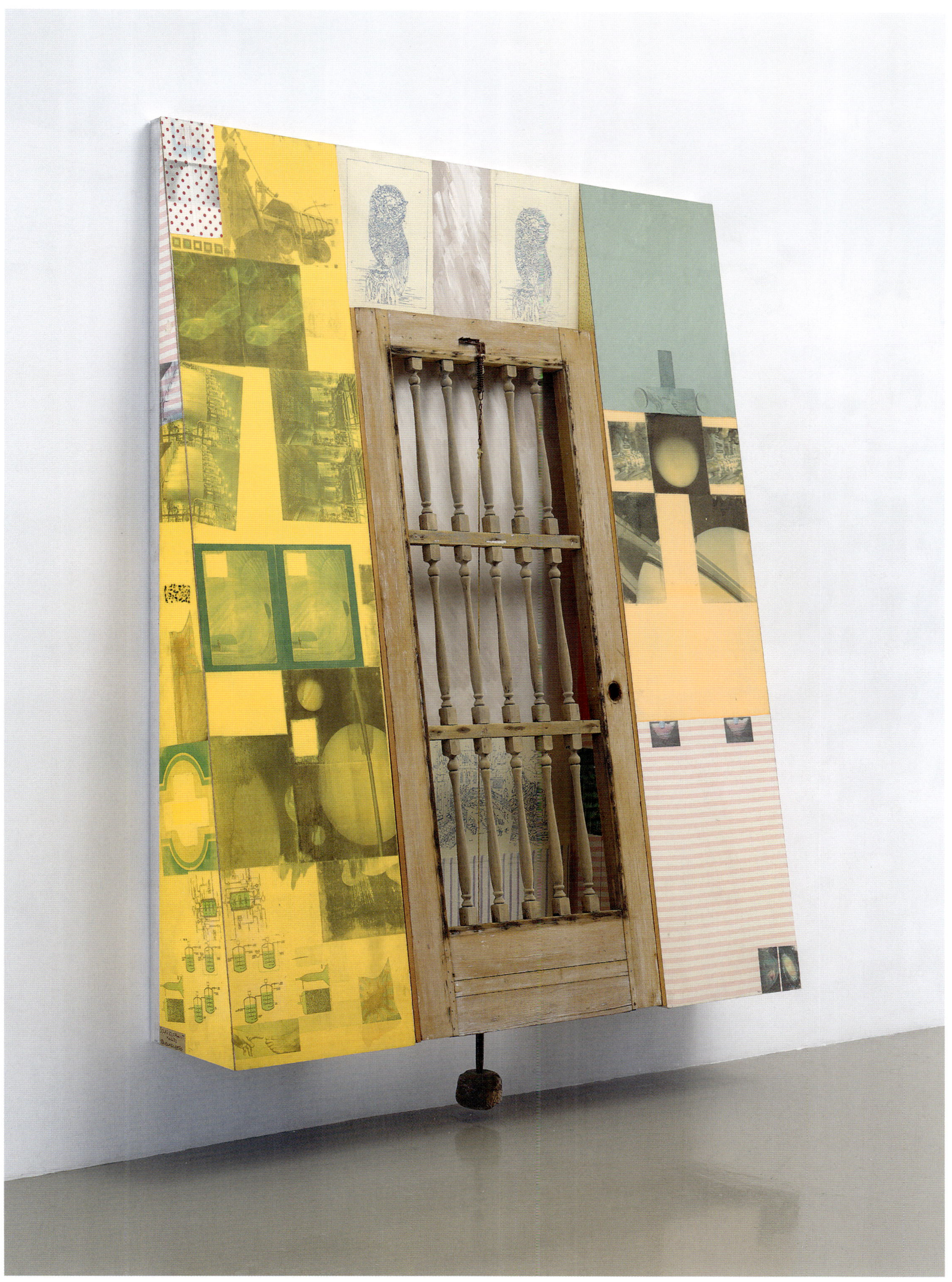

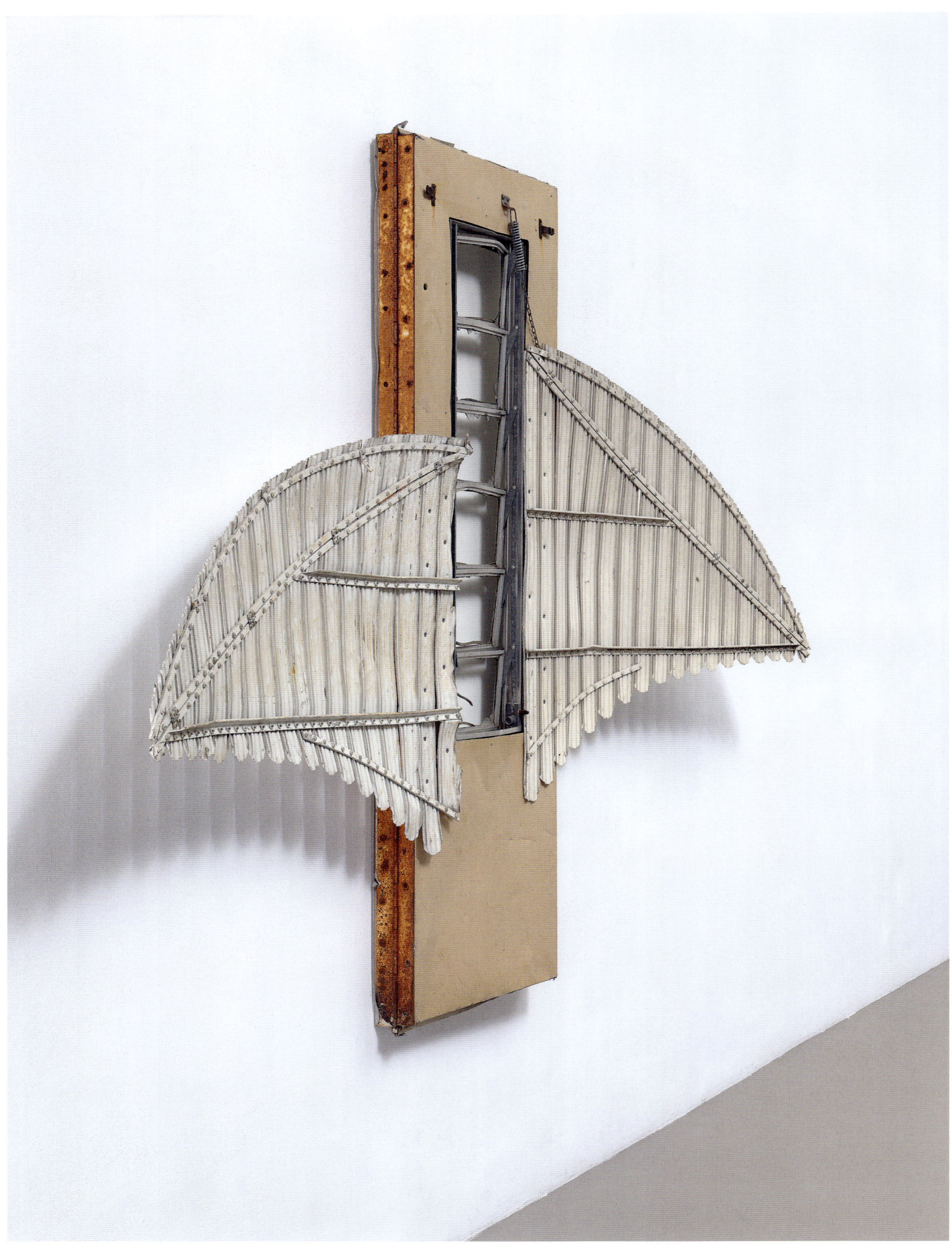

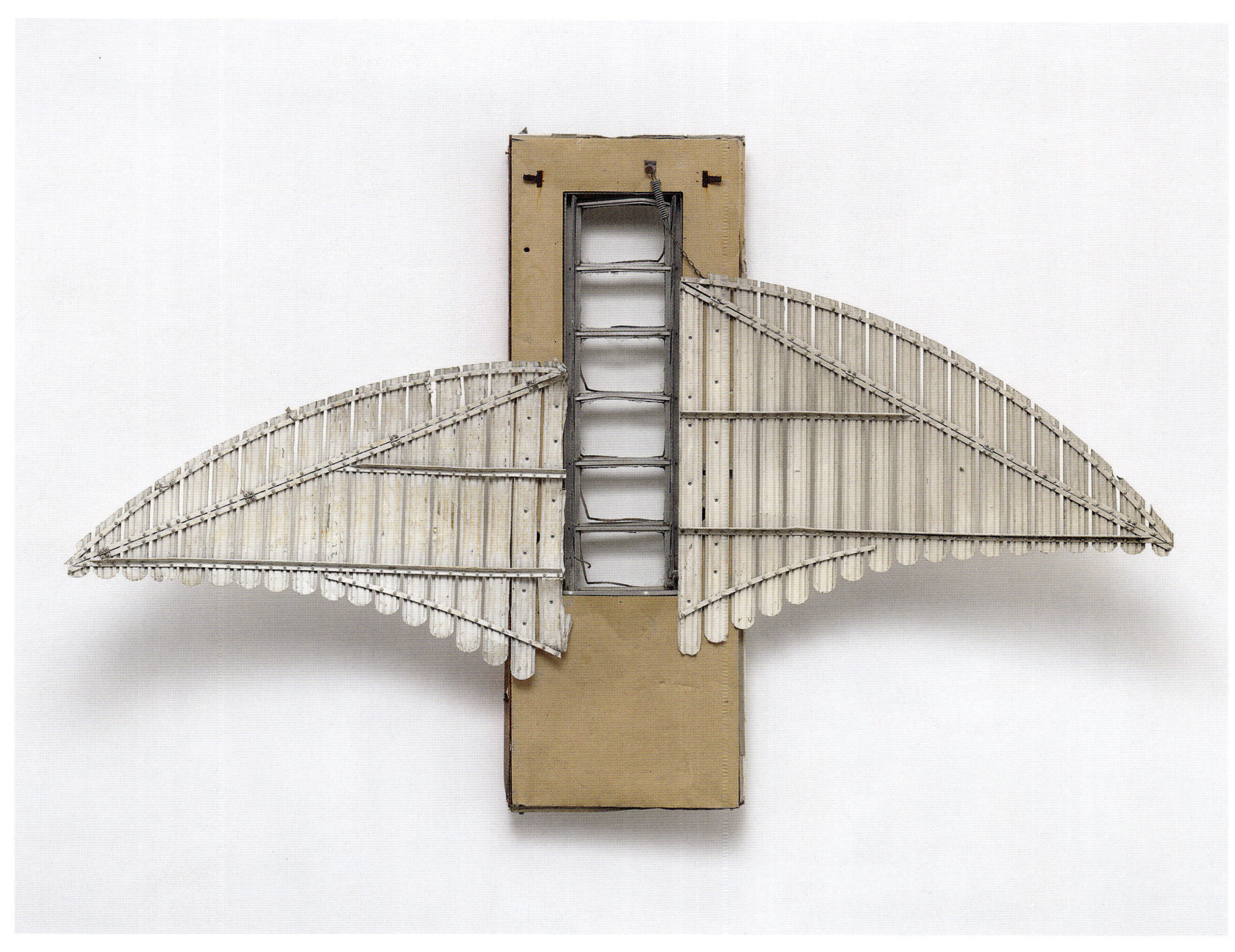

Easter Angel Flap Winter Glut, 1989
Aluminum, glass, and galvanized steel
69½ × 106½ × 18½ inches (176.5 × 270.5 × 47 cm)
Robert Rauschenberg Foundation

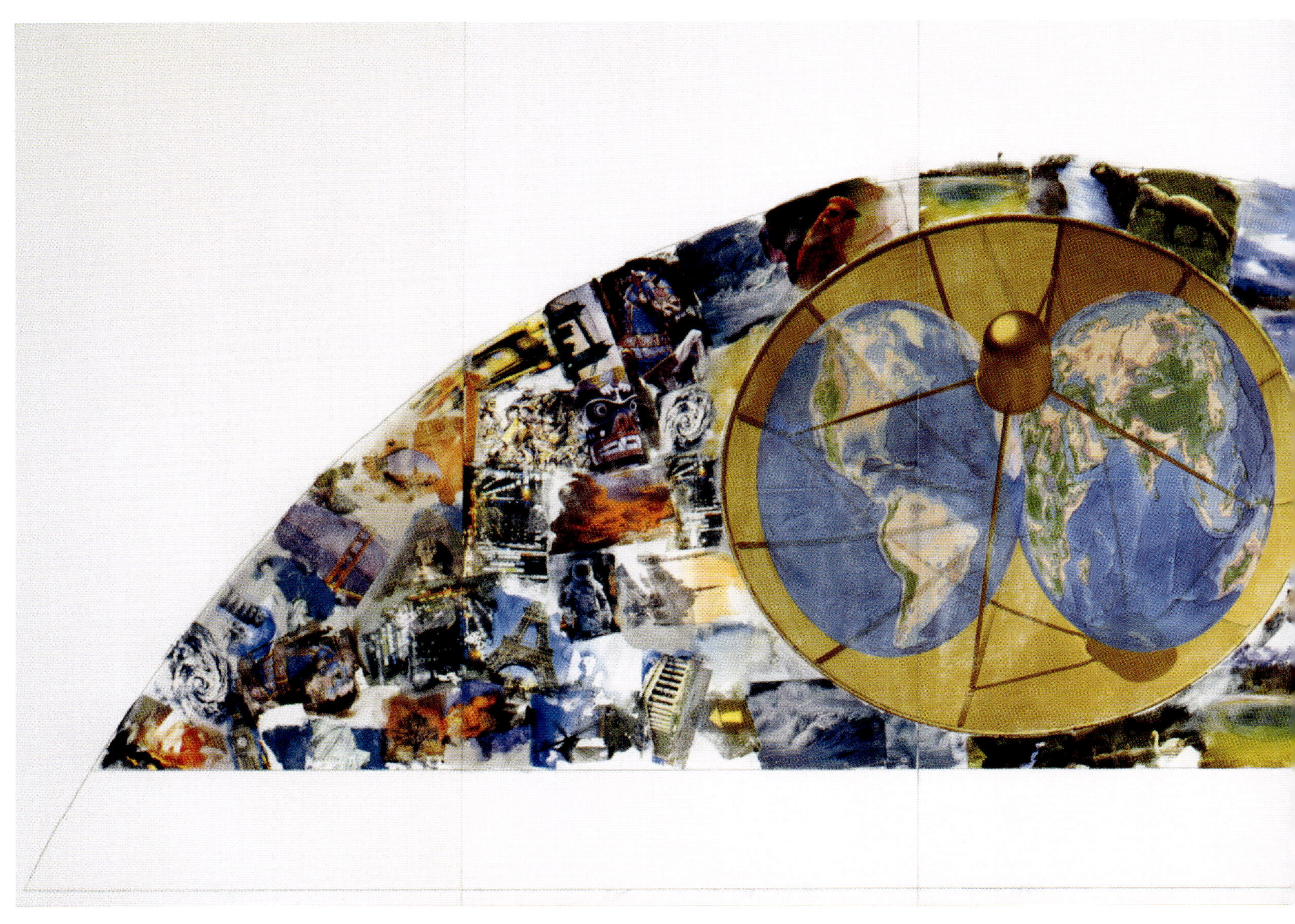

The Happy Apocalypse [Original artwork for Padre Pio Liturgical Hall], 1999
Inkjet pigment transfer, acrylic, and graphite on polylaminate
96 × 250⅛ × 2 inches (243.8 × 635.2 × 5.1 cm)
The Menil Collection

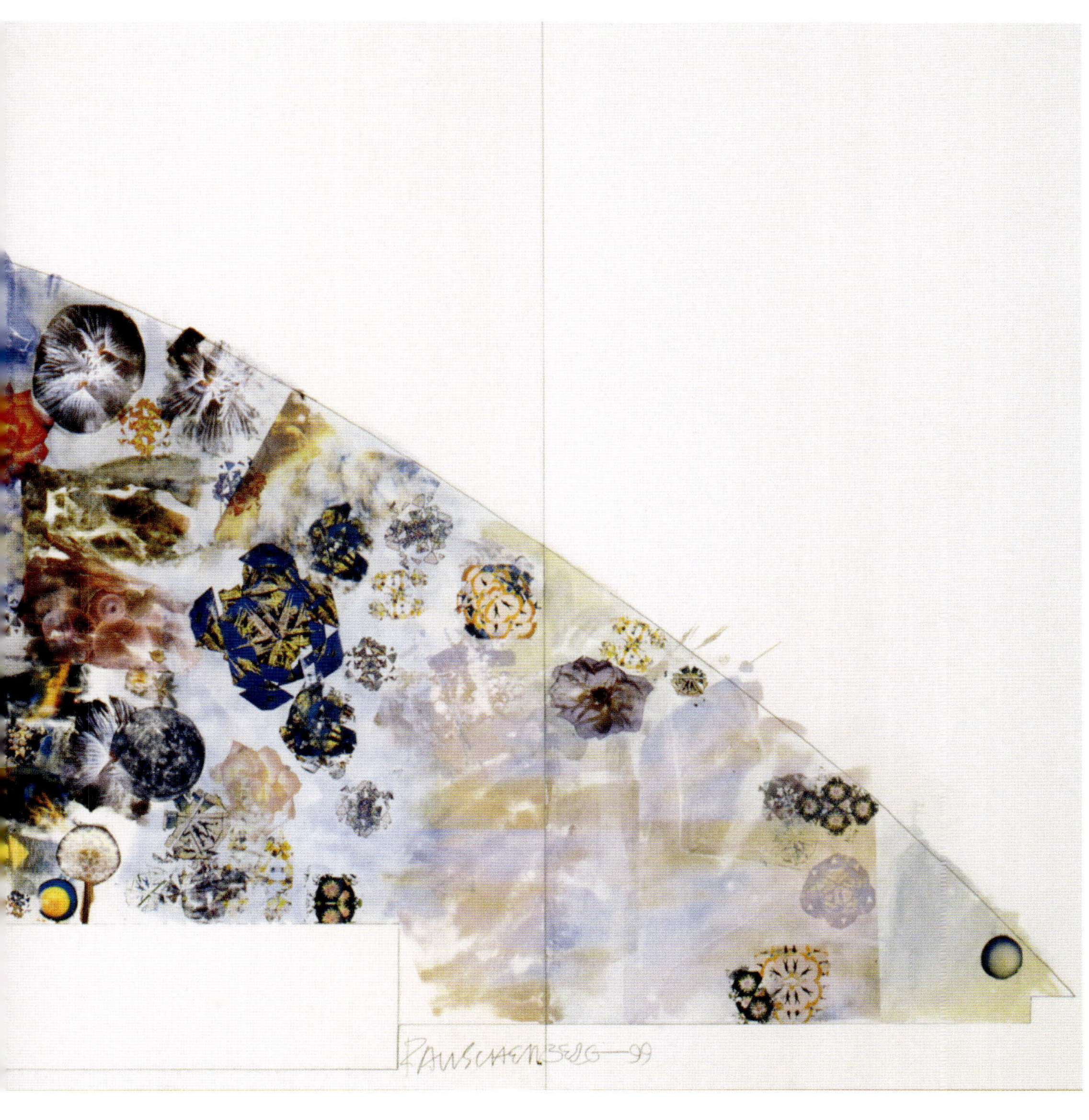

Notes

Introduction

1. Robert Rauschenberg and Julia Brown Turrell, "Talking to Robert Rauschenberg," in *Rauschenberg Sculpture,* ed. Julia Brown Turrell (Fort Worth, TX: Modern Art Museum of Fort Worth, 1995), 58.

2. Thyrza Nichols Goodeve, "Genius Envy" *Artforum* 35, no. 3. (November 1996): 10.

3. Robert Rauschenberg, interview by Cathy McClintock, Captiva Island, Florida, March 25, 1987, transcript. Robert Rauschenberg papers. Robert Rauschenberg Foundation Archives, New York.

4. Erika Doss, *American Art of the 20th–21st Centuries* (New York: Oxford University Press, 2017), 148.

5. Mary Lynn Kotz, *Rauschenberg: Art and Life*, 3rd ed. (New York: Abrams, 2018), 322.

6. Roni Feinstein, *Robert Rauschenberg: The Silkscreen Paintings, 1962–64* (New York: Whitney Museum of American Art, 1990), 75.

7. Robert S. Mattison, *Robert Rauschenberg: Breaking Boundaries* (New Haven, CT: Yale University Press, 2003), 109–10.

8. Feinstein, *Silkscreen Paintings*, 75.

9. Noah Randolph, Temple University, Philadelphia, telephone conversation with author, February 18, 2021.

10. Doss, *American Art*, 58.

11. "The reason I find material in junkyards is because each piece of material already has its history and I rediscover it." Robert Rauschenberg, quoted in Turrell, "Talking to Robert Rauschenberg," 51.

12. Rauschenberg quote on kite project for *Abitare*, December 18, 1991, Robert Rauschenberg papers, Robert Rauschenberg Foundation, New York.

13. "Students May Fly with Both Feet on the Ground," *Los Angeles Herald Examiner*, May 21, 1973, Robert Rauschenberg papers, Robert Rauschenberg Foundation Archives, New York.

14. Letter from Walter Hopps to James Dean, August 12, 1976, Art Curatorial Files, National Air and Space Museum, Washington, DC. Although the performance did not materialize due to Rauschenberg's busy calendar, Dean arranged for an exhibition featuring twenty-two lithographs from the *Stoned Moon* series, on loan from the Hirshhorn to be displayed in the museum's Space Hall from November 8, 1976, to January 3, 1977.

15. Douglas Davis, "Artist of Everything," *Newsweek*, October 25, 1976, 94.

16. Kotz, *Rauschenberg: Art and Life*, 210.

17. Smithsonian Institution press release from the Office of Public Affairs, June 22, 1976, Art Curatorial Files, National Air and Space Museum, Washington, DC.

1 Embodying Flight

1. Robert Rauschenberg's handwritten notes about and quotations from Chippewa songs, n.d., Robert Rauschenberg papers, Robert Rauschenberg Foundation Archives, New York. See also Margot Astrov, ed., *American Indian Prose and Poetry, An Anthology* (New York: Capricorn, 1962), 76.

2. Barbara Rose, *Rauschenberg* (New York: Vintage, 1987), 86.

3. Robert S. Mattison, *Robert Rauschenberg: Breaking Boundaries* (New Haven, CT: Yale University Press, 2003), 110.

4. Erica Abeel, "Daedalus at the Rollerdrome," *Saturday Review*, August 28, 1965, 51–53. See also Kotz, *Art and Life*, 123.

5. Mattison, *Breaking Boundaries*, 107.

6. Mattison, *Breaking Boundaries*, 109.

7. Stephen Petronio, interview by David White, Robert Rauschenberg Foundation, July 14, 2022, for Stories Project: ACC54, Robert Rauschenberg Archives, New York.

8. Rauschenberg's answers to questions from Robert Tracy for "Designing for Dance," in *Vogue Paris*, December 4, 1991, Robert Rauschenberg papers, Robert Rauschenberg Foundation Archives, New York.

9. Rauschenberg was not officially registered as a tribal member. He said his paternal grandmother was Cherokee and passed away before he was born.

10. Rose, *Rauschenberg*, 108.

11. Rauschenberg's handwritten notes on and quotations from Chippewa songs, n.d., Robert Rauschenberg papers, Robert Rauschenberg Foundation Archives, New York. For a description of the spiritual nature of the dream song, see Astrov, *American Indian Prose and Poetry*, 76.

12. Another detail in Untitled (1969) is Rauschenberg's symbolic association with Norman Rockwell, who was at Cape Kennedy on commission for *Look* magazine at the same time. Rauschenberg made this connection by incorporating a graphic published with Rockwell's commemorative painting *Apollo & Beyond* (1969) in a July 1969 issue of *Look*. The painting, a group portrait highlighting the extensive workforce behind the space program, includes the Apollo astronauts, engineers, various NASA workers, the directors of the NASA facilities and programs, and the wives of the astronauts. The accompanying graphic serves to highlight the names and roles of these individuals. By integrating the graphic into the drawing, Rauschenberg envisioned himself among the individuals supporting the monumental effort of the space program.

13. The motif is echoed in Rauschenberg's *Stoned Moon Book* (1970), which features a photograph of his left foot alongside his quote: "Open curiosity supported by courage, risk, respect, and work. To look up face with the sun foot on the Moon and heart in the Earth." Robert Rauschenberg, *Stoned Moon Book, Page 9* (1970), in *Robert Rauschenberg: Stoned Moon* (New York: Craig Starr Gallery, 2019), 39.

14. Blake Gopnik, "Robert Rauschenberg: Big Feet, Big … Talent," *Artnet*, May 9, 2017, https://news.artnet.com/art-world-archives/robert-rauschenberg-drawing-foundation-953195.

15. "How the Navy Talks [1942]," Naval History and Heritage Command, https://www.history.navy.mil/research/library/online-reading-room/title-list-alphabetically/h/how-the-navy-talks.html.

16. Julie Martin, Notes on Airplane in 381 Lafeyette, Documentation note (P2866), Robert Rauschenberg Foundation Archives Collections Management System, n.d., Robert Rauschenberg Foundation, New York.

17. The auction, a benefit for E.A.T., was organized by Christie's of London. The exhibition took place June 6–8, 1967, in Rauschenberg's studio at 381 Lafayette Street, New York, with the auction held on the final day. Four giant model aircraft were auctioned. They included Lot 1: Fokker DR-1 Triplane; Lot 2: S. E. 5A Scout biplane; Lot 3: S. E. 5A Scout biplane; and Lot 4: Giant Model Box, pine frame approximately four by ten feet. Giant Model Box, the plane pictured in the photograph from the auction brochure, was purchased by Rauschenberg. *Giant Model Airplanes* exhibition and auction brochure, published by Christie's of London, 1967, Robert Rauschenberg papers, Robert Rauschenberg Foundation Archives, New York.

2 Birdland

1. In this quote, Rauschenberg referred to the Plymouth Rock chicken in his Combine Untitled, ca. 1954/58 (currently in the collection of the Museum of Contemporary Art, Los Angeles). Odalisque refers to *Odalisk* (1955/58). Rose, *Rauschenberg*, 58, 60–61.
2. John D. Anderson Jr., *Inventing Flight* (Baltimore: Johns Hopkins University Press, 2004), 6–7.
3. Nicholas Cullinan, "Double Exposure: Robert Rauschenberg's and Cy Twombly's Roman Holiday," *The Burlington Magazine* 150, no. 1264 (July 2008): 462.
4. John Yau, *Robert Rauschenberg: North African Collages and Scatole Personali c. 1952* (New York: Craig Starr Gallery, 2012), 3.
5. Calvin Tomkins, *Off the Wall: Robert Rauschenberg and the Art World of Our Time* (Garden City, NY: Doubleday, 1980), 73.
6. *Robert Rauschenberg: National Collection of Fine Arts, 1976* (Washington, DC: Smithsonian Institution, 1977), 88.
7. Graham Smith, "Robert Rauschenberg's 'Odalisque,'" *Wallraf-Richartz-Jahrbuch* 44 (1983), 375.
8. Rose, *Rauschenberg*, 61.
9. Paul Schimmel, "Autobiography and Self-Portraiture in Rauschenberg's Combines," in *Robert Rauschenberg: Combines*, ed. Paul Schimmel (Los Angeles: Museum of Contemporary Art, 2005), 226. See also Kenneth Bediner, "Robert Rauschenberg's Canyon," *Arts Magazine* (New York) 56, no. 10 (June 1982): 57–59, for discussion of the Ganymede connection.
10. Leah Dickerman, *Rauschenberg: Canyon* (New York: Museum of Modern Art, 2013), 31.
11. Lawrence Alloway, "Rauschenberg's Development," in *Robert Rauschenberg: National Collection of Fine Arts, 1976*, 13. See also Dickerman, *Rauschenberg: Canyon*, 20–25, for details of imagery.
12. See Richard Meyer, "An Invitation, Not A Command," in *Robert Rauschenberg*, by Leah Dickerman et al. (New York: Museum of Modern Art, 2016), 190.
13. See hummingbird photograph in *Stopping Time: The Photographs of Harold Edgerton*, ed. Gus Kayafas (New York: Abrams, 1987), 156.
14. Meyer, "An Invitation, Not A Command," 196.
15. For more on *Link (Fuses)* and the printing process, see Howardena Pindell, "Robert Rauschenberg's 'Link,'" *MoMA* 1 (Autumn 1974), 7.
16. Richard Bach, *Jonathan Livingston Seagull* (1970; New York: Scribner, 2014), 3.
17. Robert Rauschenberg, interview by Mark Rosenthal, Los Angeles, September 22, 1991, transcript, Robert Rauschenberg papers, Robert Rauschenberg Foundation Archives, New York.

3 Aerial Meditations

1. Robert Rauschenberg, interview by Carol Friedman, unedited quotes, 1995, Robert Rauschenberg papers, Robert Rauschenberg Foundation Archives, New York.
2. Typed list of old working titles and new titles of Rauschenberg's drawings, ca. September 1986, Robert Rauschenberg papers, Robert Rauschenberg Foundation Archives, New York.
3. Thomas Crow, "Rise and Fall: Theme and Idea in the Combines of Robert Rauschenberg," in Schimmel, *Robert Rauschenberg: Combines*, 235–37.
4. Crow, "Rise and Fall," 234.
5. Robert Rauschenberg, interview by Esther Sparks, Sheraton Grand Hotel, Washington, DC, October 25, 1985, transcript, Robert Rauschenberg papers, Robert Rauschenberg Foundation Archives, New York.
6. Anderson, *Inventing Flight*, 152.
7. Feinstein, *Silkscreen Paintings,* 82, 98.
8. Milton Orshefsky, "We Wade Deeper into Jungle War: Stark Color of the Vicious Struggle in Vietnam," *Life*, January 25, 1963, 22–33.
9. Feinstein, *Silkscreen Paintings,* 82.
10. Feinstein, *Silkscreen Paintings,* 82.
11. Feinstein, *Silkscreen Paintings,* 82.
12. Mattison, *Breaking Boundaries,* 110, 264.
13. Walter Hopps, et al. *Robert Rauschenberg, a Retrospective* (New York: Guggenheim Museum, 1999), 294.
14. Feinstein, *Silkscreen Paintings,* 46.
15. Mattison, *Breaking Boundaries*, 119.
16. Rosalind E. Krauss, "Perpetual Inventory," in *October Files: Robert Rauschenberg,* ed. Branden W. Joseph (Cambridge, MA: MIT Press, 2002), 99.
17. For the description of an aerobatic box, see Geza Szurovy and Mike Goulin, *Basic Aerobatics* (Blue Ridge Summit, PA: TAB Books, 1994), 188.
18. Barry Rubin and Judith Colp Rubin, *Chronologies of Modern Terrorism* (London: Routledge, 2015), 186.
19. Randolph, telephone conversation with author, February 18, 2021.
20. Tomkins, *Off the Wall,* 244.
21. The song "Yellow Bird" was popularized by the Mills Brothers and the Brothers Four during the 1950s and 1960s. Rauschenberg also included an image of Janis Joplin's band, Big Brother and the Holding Company, from San Francisco's Haight Ashbury district, another subtle reference to "Yellow Bird."
22. Rauschenberg's handwritten note on an airline ticket sleeve, 1988, Robert Rauschenberg papers, Robert Rauschenberg Foundation Archives, New York.
23. Helen Hsu, Robert Rauschenberg Foundation, New York, message to author, January 31, 2025.
24. Lisa Wainwright refers to ladders in Rauschenberg's work as a means to ascend, with allusions to Christian religious iconography. Lisa Wainwright, "Reading Junk: Thematic Imagery in the Art of Robert Rauschenberg from 1954 to 1964" (PhD diss., University of Illinois, 1993), 78.
25. Pontus Hultén interprets *Sor Aqua (Venetian)* (1973) as a cloud, "I always thought about this piece as a cloud, kind of a thunderstorm. Then it's attached to a floating anchor, so it is suddenly reversed." On defying

gravity, Hultén says: "I think in Rauschenberg's sculptures the rejection of gravity is often present. They are levitated, that are clearly above the ground, somehow. They are in relation to earth, but in the sense that they are off the ground. It's interesting to see how many of them have associations to wings or clouds or in general to be very light and levitated." See Pontus Hultén and Julia Brown Turrell, "A Conversation about the Sculpture of Robert Rauschenberg," in Turrell, *Rauschenberg Sculpture,* 42, 36.

26. The image is from an Otis Elevator Company advertisement, ca. 1965–66, illustrating the company's level in the atmosphere with "Otisphere." Robert Rauschenberg papers, Robert Rauschenberg Foundation Archives, New York.

4 NASA Inception

1. Robert Rauschenberg, *Stoned Moon Book, Page 7* (1970), in *Rauschenberg: Stoned Moon*, 35.

2. Letter from Lane Slate, National Educational Television, to Robert Rauschenberg, February 1969, regarding Rauschenberg's participation in the NASA Art Program, Robert Rauschenberg papers, Robert Rauschenberg Foundation Archives, New York.

3. Hereward Lester Cooke and James D. Dean, *Eyewitness to Space: Paintings and Drawings Related to the Apollo Mission to the Moon, Selected, with a Few Exceptions, from the Art Program of the National Aeronautics and Space Administration (1963 to 1969)* (New York: Abrams, 1971), 12.

4. NASA Art Program documents, Art Curatorial Files, Smithsonian National Air and Space Museum, Washington, DC.

5. James Dean, telephone interview with author, December 29, 2021.

6. Letter from James Dean, NASA, to Robert Rauschenberg, April 11, 1969, regarding Rauschenberg's participation in the NASA Art Program, Robert Rauschenberg papers, Robert Rauschenberg Foundation Archives, New York.

7. Cooke and Dean, *Eyewitness to Space*, 12.

8. James Dean, telephone interview with author, June 3, and December 29, 2021. Dean also shared the following with the author in an email of August 1, 2019, regarding photographs he took of Rauschenberg at NASA: "I took the photo of Bob and the Saturn 5 on the launchpad with the Apollo 11 spacecraft at the ready. He sat there on that mound of grass for a long time. Then he said to me, 'See that fin on the bottom of the Saturn rocket?' I said, 'Yes.' Then he said, 'My taxes paid for that.' I could tell he was starting to feel a part of what was going on preparing for the Moon visit. . . . I did a second photo of Bob and the Saturn. This time he is stretched out looking at the Apollo 11 launch vehicle chewing on a blade of grass, looking very thoughtful. But he is more identifiable in the first photo."

9. In an interview with Tim Marlow, Rauschenberg said, "I was invited as one of the artists to witness the take off of Apollo 11, and everybody was sketching or had their watercolour sets out but things were happening too fast, so I just took pictures." Robert Rauschenberg, interview by Tim Marlow for *Tate: The Art Magazine*, transcript July 1998, Robert Rauschenberg papers, Robert Rauschenberg Foundation Archives, New York.

10. Randolph, telephone conversation with author, February 18, 2021.

11. Letter from James Dean, NASA, to Robert Rauschenberg, July 26, 1973, regarding NASA's equipment junkyard, Robert Rauschenberg papers, Robert Rauschenberg Foundation Archives, New York.

12. Letter from James Dean, NASA, to Robert Rauschenberg, July 2, 1970, regarding Rauschenberg's $800 payment for participation in the "Sky Garden" project and follow-up, Robert Rauschenberg papers, Robert Rauschenberg Foundation Archives, New York.

13. Mattison, *Breaking Boundaries*, 153.

14. Letter from Terry Van Brunt to James Dean via Robert Rauschenberg, Captiva, Florida, Labor Day 1981, Art Curatorial Files, Smithsonian National Air and Space Museum, Washington, DC.

15. Mattison, *Breaking Boundaries*, 159.

16. Mattison, *Breaking Boundaries*, 160.

17. "The Artist and the Space Shuttle," *Discover*, December 1982, 74–81.

18. Rauschenberg's handwritten draft of a statement about his print *Hot Shot* (1983), October 1982, Robert Rauschenberg papers, Robert Rauschenberg Foundation Archives, New York.

19. Mattison, *Breaking Boundaries*, 163.

20. David Friend, "Space: All Aboard the Shuttle!" *Life*, October 1984, 72–73.

21. Friend, "All Aboard," 72–73.

22. Robert Rauschenberg and Donald Saff, "A Conversation about Art and ROCI," in *Rauschenberg: Overseas Culture Interchange*, ed. Mary Yakush (Washington, DC: National Gallery of Art, 1991), 179.

5 Constructing Space

1. Robert Rauschenberg, *Stoned Moon Book, Page 10* (1970), in *Rauschenberg: Stoned Moon*, 43.

2. Feinstein, *Silkscreen Paintings*, 75.

3. Feinstein, *Silkscreen Paintings,* 86.

4. Helen Hsu, Robert Rauschenberg Foundation, New York, email to author, November 6, 2024, on silkscreen dates.

5. Mattison, *Breaking Boundaries*, 118.

6. Mattison, *Breaking Boundaries*, 120.

7. Feinstein, *Silkscreen Paintings*, 99.

8. Feinstein, *Silkscreen Paintings*, 79.

9. Feinstein, *Silkscreen Paintings*, 83.

10. Randolph, telephone conversation with author, January 28, 2021.

11. Mattison, *Breaking Boundaries*, 144.

12. Mattison, *Breaking Boundaries*, 150–51.

13. Mattison, *Breaking Boundaries*, 151.

14. For further interpretations, see Mattison, *Breaking Boundaries*, 146.

15. Tomkins, *Off the Wall*, 244.

16. Grace Glueck, "New York Sculptor Says Intrepid Put Art on the Moon," *New York Times*, November 22, 1969, 19.

17. Philip Pocock, "Look Up! Art in the Age of Orbitization," in *Imagining Outer Space: European Astroculture in the Twentieth Century*, ed. Alexander C. T. Geppert (Basingstoke, UK: Palgrave Macmillan, 2018), 370–71.

18. Susan Davidson, "Ideas Have Elbows," in *Robert Rauschenberg: Gluts*, ed. Susan Davidson and David White (New York: Solomon R. Guggen-

heim Foundation, 2009), 17. Davidson references Rauschenberg's use of the straight line and his practice of often beginning a painting by drawing a pencil line across a blank canvas.
19. Pocock, "Look Up!" 370.
20. Glueck, "New York Sculptor." Also learned more about the telegram and the *New York Times* article from Beau R. Ott (art collector and writer on Forrest Myers), January 1, 2022. The original telegram is held in the Forrest Myers Archives in Damascus, Pennsylvania.
21. Robert Rauschenberg, interview by Alexa Voytek, 2001, Handwritten letter and questions submitted to Rauschenberg by Alexa Voytek for a school report, with Rauschenberg's handwritten responses on a scrap of notepad paper, Robert Rauschenberg papers, Robert Rauschenberg Foundation, New York.
22. Pocock, "Look Up!" 371.

6 Reinventing Flight

1. Rauschenberg and Turrell, "Talking to Robert Rauschenberg," 51.
2. Susan Weil, "Robert Rauschenberg Oral History Project: The Reminiscences of Susan Weil," interview by Mary Marshall Clark, Columbia Center for Oral History Research, Columbia University, New York, January 27, June 6, and September 10, 2014, 146.
3. Mario Codognato and Mirta d'Argenzio, "Interview with Robert Rauschenberg," in *Rauschenberg*, ed. Susan Davidson and David White (Ferrara: Ferrara Arte, 2004), 100.
4. Natalia Dumitresco and Alexandre Istrati, "Brancusi: 1876–1957," in *Brancusi*, ed. Pontus Hultén (New York: Abrams, 1987), 92.
5. Rose, *Rauschenberg*, 57.
6. Davidson, "Ideas Have Elbows," 20.
7. Susan Davidson, "Robert Rauschenberg Oral History Project: The Reminiscences of Susan Davidson," interview by Sara Sinclair, Columbia Center for Oral History Research, Columbia University, New York, March 3, March 31, and May 5, 2015, 140.
8. See "Swing Wing Toy Commercial," Internet Archive, https://archive.org/details/swing_wing.
9. Mattison, *Breaking Boundaries*, 10.
10. Codognato and d'Argenzio, "Interview with Robert Rauschenberg," 94.
11. My research in the Robert Rauschenberg Foundation Archives in 2019 shows that many of the pages and images in Rauschenberg's books were also used as source materials. For example, in *The American Heritage History of Flight*, a full-page portrait of Charles Lindbergh on page 231 was removed from the book; and an image of the Montgolfier brothers' hot-air balloon on page 12 and a photograph of John Stringfellow's steam engine on page 25 were cut from the pages of *The History of Flight*. Alvin M. Josephy, ed., *The American Heritage History of Flight* (New York: American Heritage, 1962); Alvin M. Josephy, ed., *The History of Flight* (New York: Golden Press, 1962).
12. Tomkins, *Off the Wall*, 287.
13. Rauschenberg and Saff, "Art and ROCI," 170.

7 Seated in the Sky

1. Typed copy of Rauschenberg's statement on the kite project for *Abitare*, December 18, 1991, Robert Rauschenberg papers, Robert Rauschenberg Foundation Archives, New York.
2. Rauschenberg was also assisted by the kite maker Tatsuro Kashima. Paul Eubel, ed., *Pictures for the Sky: Art Kites* (Osaka: Goethe-Institut; Munich: Prestel, 1992), 300.
3. Tal Streeter, "High Art: Keeping Ancient Asian Kitemaking Traditions Alive in Modern Japan," in *Kites: Paper Wings over Japan*, eds. Scott Skinner and Alison Fujino (New York: Thames and Hudson, 1997), 16.
4. Nicholas Bornoff, *The National Geographic Traveler: Japan* (Washington, DC: National Geographic Society, 2000), 256.
5. Eubel, *Pictures for the Sky*, 346.
6. Rauschenberg's statement on the kite project for *Abitare Magazine*, December 18, 1991.
7. Streeter, "High Art," 26.
8. Eubel, *Pictures for the Sky*, 300. Other artists included Ay-O, Jean Tinguely, Arman, David Nash, Gerhard Richter, and Frank Stella. A world tour of the art kites was sponsored by Lufthansa Airlines.
9. "Then Jesus answered, 'I am; and "you will see the Son of Man seated at the right hand of the Power and coming with the clouds of heaven."'" Mark 14:62, New American Bible, Revised Edition. See also Kotz, *Art and Life*, 52, for a discussion of how Rauschenberg grew up in a deeply religious household and memorized Bible verses every week.
10. Streeter, "High Art," 15.
11. But about chairs—they do, in fact, have a place in the sky. They come in a variety of designs and are integral to numerous types of aircraft, including helicopters, blimps, and sport aviation ultralights. An extraordinary journey of a "sky chair" occurred on July 2, 1982, when Larry Walters of San Pedro, California, attached forty-two helium-filled weather balloons to his aluminum lawn chair and ascended to an impressive altitude of 16,000 feet (4,880 meters). While he enjoyed the breathtaking views, he soon encountered the challenges of low oxygen levels and freezing temperatures. To safely descend, he cleverly used a BB gun to pop the balloons one by one. This unauthorized flight took place near Los Angeles International Airport, prompting commercial pilots to report the unusual sighting to air traffic control. (As a result, Walters was cited by the Federal Aviation Administration for several air safety violations.) See Larry Walter's lawn chair on display in the Thomas W. Haas We All Fly general aviation gallery curated by Dorothy Cochrane at the Smithsonian National Air and Space Museum, Washington, DC. Nevertheless, there are, indeed, unique places to sit among the clouds, and Rauschenberg, a global frequent flyer, was fully knowledgeable about the different types, despite his quip, "There is no furniture up there, no place to sit."
12. Skinner and Fujino, *Kites: Paper Wings over Japan*, 93. See also Michiyo Kagawa, "Kodomo no hi: Children's Day Celebration," in Japan Society, About Japan, A Teacher's Resource, https://aboutjapan.japansociety.org/kodomo_no_hi_childrens_day_celebration#sthash.3opnOFMJ.dpbs and "Koinobori," Koinobori-Japan, https://koinobori-japan.jp/koinobori.html.
13. Codognato and d'Argenzio, "Interview with Robert Rauschenberg," 99.
14. Anderson, *Inventing Flight*, 66–69.

8 Down to Earth

1. Codognato and d'Argenzio, "Interview with Robert Rauschenberg," 97.

2. Robert S. Mattison, *Last Turn, Your Turn: Robert Rauschenberg and the Environmental Crisis* (New York: Jacobson Howard Gallery, 2008), 3.

3. Marjorie Welish, "Pail for Ganymede," in Turrell, *Rauschenberg Sculpture*, 100.

4. Wainwright, "Reading Junk," 95.

5. Welish, "Pail for Ganymede," 100.

6. Wainwright, "Reading Junk," 210–11.

7. "The Sun Never Sets on Cacoola," *Time*, May 15, 1950, cover. See also Lisa Wainwright, "Robert Rauschenberg," virtual lecture, posted on March 26, 2018, by Kadenze, YouTube, 24 min., 40 sec., https://www.youtube.com/watch?v=-zHf22mON9w.

8. "The Sun Never Sets on Cacoola," 28–32, 99.

9. Mattison, *Last Turn, Your Turn*, 10.

10. The representation of the eagle is significant within Native American culture, symbolizing the purity of the American landscape. It is plausible that Rauschenberg's poster influenced the idea for the popular 1970s public service announcement "Keep America Beautiful," which featured a Native American man standing in a polluted landscape, a tear streaming down his cheek. Italian American actor Iron Eyes Cody portrayed the Native American.

11. Mattison, *Last Turn, Your Turn*, 14.

12. For Burroughs's cut-word technique, see Daniel Punday, "Word Dust: William Burroughs's Multimedia Aesthetic," *Mosaic: An Interdisciplinary Critical Journal* 40, no. 3 (2007): 33–49.

13. "Dream of William Burroughs, 1972," Robert Rauschenberg Foundation, accessed January 15, 2025, https://www.rauschenbergfoundation.org/art/art-context/earth-day and Mattison, *Last Turn, Your Turn*, 10.

14. Mattison, *Last Turn, Your Turn*, 11–12.

15. Kotz references the beach as Ipanema in Rio de Janeiro in *Art and Life*, 283.

16. *Waterworks* (1992–95), Robert Rauschenberg Foundation, accessed January 15, 2025, https://www.rauschenbergfoundation.org/art/galleries/series/waterworks-1992-95.

9 Interpreting the Night Sky

1. Rauschenberg's handwritten draft of a statement about *Star Quarters I–IV* (1971), n.d., Robert Rauschenberg papers, Robert Rauschenberg Foundation Archives, New York.

2. Rauschenberg's draft statement about *Star Quarters I–IV* (1971).

3. Benjamin Genocchio, "Art Review; Master of Mixed, And Stirred, Media," *New York Times*, March 8, 2017, https://www.nytimes.com/2005/02/13/nyregion/art-review-master-of-mixed-and-stirred-media.html.

4. Rose, *Rauschenberg*, 86.

5. It's plausible the addition of the Diane Arbus photograph is also a tribute to the photographer, who passed away July 26, 1971. Rauschenberg began the *Star Quarters* series (referred to as "Astrology") in August 1971. Timeline confirmed with Helen Hsu, Robert Rauschenberg Foundation, New York, in email to author, January 2, 2024.

6. Helen Hsu, Robert Rauschenberg Foundation, New York, email message to author on photograph identifying bicycle, October 1, 2024.

7. Hsu, Robert Rauschenberg Foundation, New York, email to author on photograph identifying Hermes, October 1, 2024.

8. *Shales* (1994–95), Robert Rauschenberg Foundation, accessed January 15, 2025, https://www.rauschenbergfoundation.org/art/galleries/series/shales-1994-95.

9. Alastair Macaulay, "Rauschenberg and Dance, Partners for Life," *New York Times*, May 14, 2008, https://www.nytimes.com/2008/05/14/arts/dance/14coll.html.

10. Wainwright, "Reading Junk," 79.

11. The reference to winter in the title, both as season and the pale whitish color of the sculpture, evokes the idea of children playing in the snow, envisioning themselves as flying angels, extending their arms and flapping to leave an impression of "wings" behind in the snow.

12. Michael A. Di Giovine, "Re-Presenting a Contemporary Saint: Padre Pio of Pietrelcina" *Critical Inquiry* 35, no. 3 (Spring 2009): 481.

13. Codognato and d'Argenzio, "Interview with Robert Rauschenberg," 97.

14. Barbie Nadeau, "The Vatican Breaks Its Davinci Code," *Newsweek*, September 22, 2008, 70–72.

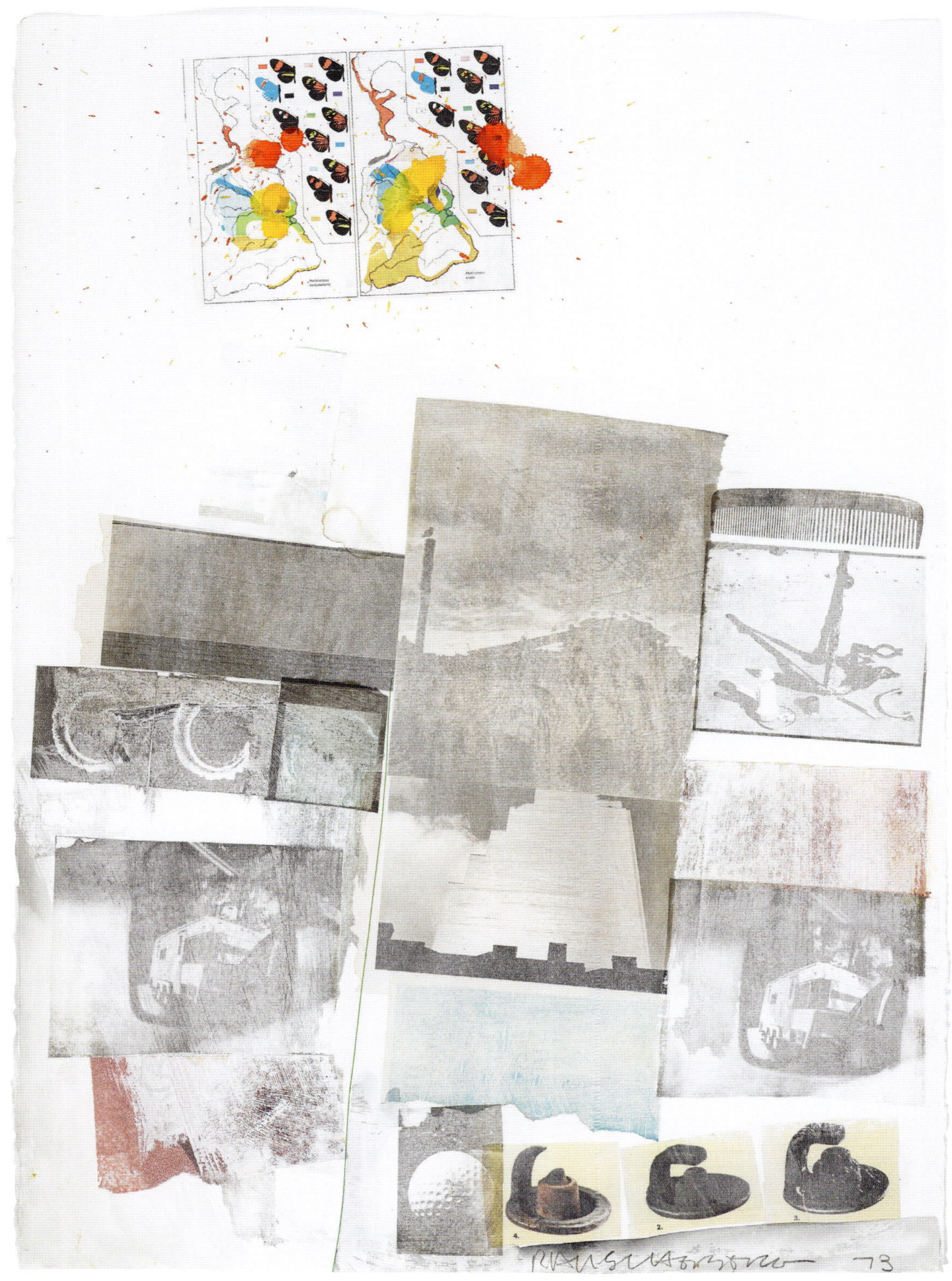

Untitled, 1973
Solvent transfer, gouache, printed reproduction, and paint marker or paper
29⅞ × 22½ inches (75.9 × 57.1 cm)
Walker Art Center, Minneapolis

Acknowledgments

Coram Deo

The realization of any project comes to fruition through the guidance, support, generosity, and encouragement of many individuals. First and foremost, I express my sincere gratitude to the Robert Rauschenberg Foundation for its vital collaboration on this endeavor. This book and exhibition were conceived during my time in the Robert Rauschenberg Archives Research Residency Program, which provided me with the opportunity to delve into the artist's profound relationship with the concept of flight. I am especially grateful for the Foundation's generous permission to utilize archival materials, images for the book, and artworks on loan for the exhibition. A special acknowledgment to Francine Snyder for her instrumental support and guidance as my primary liaison throughout the project and for offering insightful advice and essential resources. I would like to express my appreciation to the entire team at the Robert Rauschenberg Foundation—Courtney J. Martin, Ron Amstutz, Julia Blaut, Anne Boissonnault, Kristen Clevenson, Gina Guy, Erika Hendrix, Helen Hsu, Esperanza Mayobre, Sarah Moskowitz, Thomas Roach, Berenice Sarafzadeh, and David White—for their consistent assistance, enthusiasm, and support in bringing this project to life.

I am truly honored to have Alexander Nemerov contribute the foreword to this work and for his eloquent and poetic reflections on Rauschenberg's art and the theme of flight. Thank you, Alexander, for your insightful words, which beautifully frame the project.

My heartfelt thanks go to Noah Randolph of Temple University, whose support during the early stages of research was crucial to the development of this project. Your generous gifts of time, insight, and enthusiasm have significantly shaped this work.

I am immensely grateful to professors at American University—Nika Elder, Juliet Bellow, Andrea Pearson, and Joanne Allen—for their mentorship, encouragement, and belief in my potential. An assignment in Juliet Bellow's Approaches in Art History seminar was a pivotal moment that sparked my curiosity about the intersection of Rauschenberg and flight, ultimately leading to this project.

At Smithsonian Books, I thank Director Carolyn Gleason for believing in this book and supporting its development. A sincere thank you to Senior Editor Jaime Schwender for her guidance and tireless efforts in shaping this book; your attention to detail and expertise have been invaluable. Thanks also to Paige Elliott, Sarah Fannon, Matt Litts, Hadley Robbins, Steve Schwacke, and Bill Whitcher for their contributions. I extend my gratitude to Tom Fredrickson and Sharon Silva for their editing and thoughtful feedback, which helped refine the manuscript. A special thank you to Anjali Pala for her book design; your creative vision reflects the themes and spirit of the project.

This book would not have been possible without the critical assistance of numerous institutions and individuals who graciously provided images of Robert Rauschenberg's art and supporting photographs. I extend special thanks to Sophie Jones and Jennifer Belt (Art Resource Inc.); Laura Horne (Craig Starr Gallery, New York); Paul Molinari (Dallas Museum of Art); Hannah Green (Hirshhorn Museum and Sculpture Garden); Margaret McKee, Philip Karjeker, and Krista Hollis (The Menil Collection); Dan Dennehy (Minneapolis Institute of Art); Luis Velasquez (Museum of Contemporary Art, Los Angeles); Marty Stein (Museum of Fine Arts, Houston); Fabio Straub and Gerda Lenßen-Wahl (Nagel Auktionen); Lauren Katz (NASA); Mark Avino, Kate Igoe, Melissa Keiser, Patrick Leonini, and Brian Nicklas (National Air and Space Museum Archives); Zak Meek (Nelson-Atkins Museum of Art); Peter Huestis (National Gallery of Art, Washington, DC); Lexy Hartford (Portland Art Museum); Rebecca Conrad (San Diego Air & Space Museum); David Rozelle (San Francisco Museum of Modern Art); Richard Sorensen (Smithsonian American Art Museum); Queenie Wong (Sonnabend Collection Foundation); Kova Walker-Lečić and Joseph King (Walker Art Center); and Ruth and Don Saff, Zach Bruder, and Shana Miller from private collections.

To the Smithsonian National Air and Space Museum staff, I extend my deepest gratitude for their steadfast support of this project. I am grateful to Russell Lee and the leadership team—Ellen Stofan, Chris Browne, Megan Caulk, Jeremy Kinney, Beth Crownover, Francisco Torres, and Elizabeth Garcia. My sincere appreciation also extends to other staff members and curators, including Beatrice Mowry, Bob van der Linden, Mike Hankins, Roger Connor, Dorothy Cochrane, Amy Stamm, Alison Wood, former Katzenberger Fellow Claire Rasmussen, and volunteer Ramsey Gorchev, for their integral assistance throughout this endeavor.

I wish to honor former National Air and Space Museum art curators Tom Crouch and James Dean (1931–2024) for their encouragement and support. I am especially grateful to Jim Dean for sharing countless hours about his experiences with the NASA Art Program and reflections on Robert Rauschenberg.

I sincerely thank the Flight and the Arts Center exhibition team—Liz Wissner, Leslie McMillan, Beth Wilson, Diane Kidd, Madeline Chinnici, Judy Tasse, Sarah Bartlett, Marcy Borger, Erik Satrum, Jessica Bulger, Emily Smithberger, Deborah Parr, Lauren Horelick, Lisa Young, Malcolm Collum, Elizabeth Beesley, Dave Cremer, Tenzin Phuntsok, the Exhibits Production Team, Kelly Bloom, and Jessica McNally—for their boundless energy, dedication, and creativity in bringing this exhibition to life. It has been a true honor to collaborate with each of you.

A special thanks to the curators and staff members who facilitated the loan of artworks for this project including Evelyn C. Hankins and Lizzie Baikie (Hirshhorn Museum and Sculpture Garden); Melissa Ho, Jennifer Schneider, and Trisha Brockmeyer (Smithsonian American Art Museum); Shelly Langdale, Amy Hughes, Lisa MacDougall, and Shannon Schuler (National Gallery of Art, Washington, DC); and Francine Snyder, Gina Guy, and Thomas Roach (Robert Rauschenberg Foundation).

Thank you, Allan and Shelley Holt, for your support and generosity in making the exhibition possible.

To my dear friends—Ana Schwar, Michelle Rathje, Holly Reichert, Anna Potts, David Kressler, Lissa Masters, Reena Jehle, Mangai Balasegaram, Thanh Dang, Dagery Grant, Elizabeth Pleeter, Peggy Raisovich, Diane Tedeschi, Hugh and Alice Talman, and others—thank you for your constant encouragement and support. To Nicholas Pyenson, thank you for your mentorship. I want to express my heartfelt gratitude to the choir at St. Clare of Assisi in Clifton, Virginia—especially Mary Dash, Audrey Short, and Chris DeBenedictis—for their prayers and care.

Finally, I want to express my deepest gratitude to my family—Maxwell Craddock and Rei Abe; Jack Craddock; Joan Russo; John Russo and Kate Russo; Eva, Fred, and Cora Eberhard; Vincent Russo and Aimee Hwang Russo; Bob Craddock and Sarah Dawson-Craddock; and my beloved companions Major, Eartha, and Eros—for your unconditional love and support. And to Mother Mary and her son, thank you for your continuous guidance and strength throughout this journey.

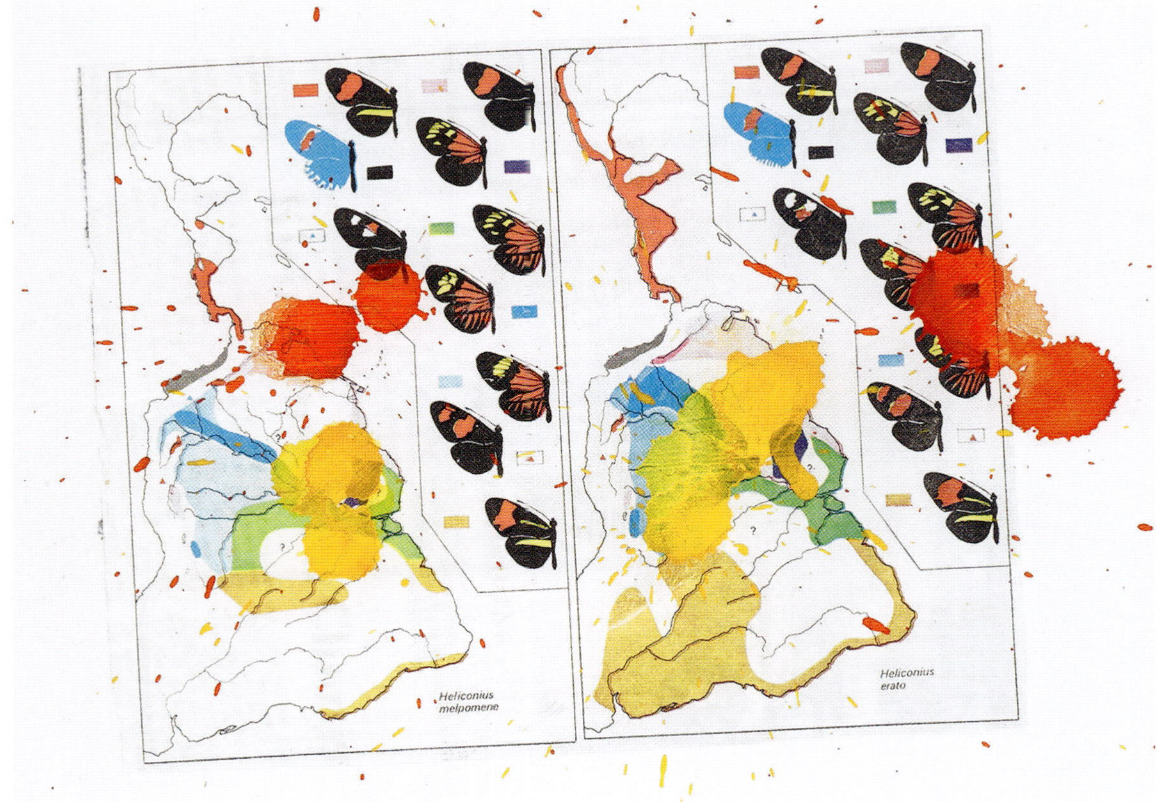

Detail of **Untitled**, 1973

Index to Works

Image credits

2: From an edition of 29 unique variants, published by Gemini G.E.L, Los Angeles. Gift of Gemini G.E.L., Los Angeles, and the Artist. National Gallery of Art, Washington, DC, 1981.5.78. © Robert Rauschenberg Foundation and Gemini G.E.L., Los Angeles. **6:** Smithsonian National Air and Space Museum, Washington, DC (NASM 2006-10277). **7t:** Library of Congress Prints and Photographs Division, Washington, DC. **7m:** Library of Congress Prints and Photographs Division, Washington, DC. **7b:** Photo: San Diego Air & Space Museum. **8:** Photo: Seymour Rosen. Photograph Collection. Robert Rauschenberg Foundation Archives, New York. **10t:** Photo: Malcolm Lubliner. Photograph Collection. Robert Rauschenberg Foundation Archives, New York. **10b:** Photo: Peter Moore. © Barbara Moore, courtesy of Paula Cooper Gallery, New York. Photograph Collection. Robert Rauschenberg Foundation Archives, New York. **11:** Photo: Shunk-Kender. © J. Paul Getty Trust. Photograph Collection. Robert Rauschenberg Foundation Archives, New York. **12t:** Photo: James Dean. Art Curatorial Files, Smithsonian National Air and Space Museum, Washington, DC. **12b, 13:** Photo: Malcolm Lubliner. Photograph Collection. Robert Rauschenberg Foundation Archives, New York. **14, 15:** Robert Rauschenberg Foundation. Photo: Ron Amstutz. © Robert Rauschenberg Foundation. **16:** From an edition of 2000, published by Broadside Art, Inc., New York. Gift of Robert Rauschenberg, Milton Glaser, and Marian B. Javits. National Gallery of Art, Washington, DC, 1992.63.1. © Robert Rauschenberg Foundation. **18:** Photo: Seymour Rosen. Photograph Collection. Robert Rauschenberg Foundation Archives, New York. **19t:** Photo: Walker's San Diego. Photograph Collection. Robert Rauschenberg Foundation Archives, New York. **19b:** From an edition of 50, published by Gemini G.E.L., Los Angeles. Gift of the Joseph H. Hirshhorn Foundation, 1974. Hirshhorn Museum and Sculpture Garden, Washington, DC. Photo: Rick Coulby. © Robert Rauschenberg Foundation. **20, 21:** From an edition of 2000, published by Broadside Art, Inc., New York. Gift of Robert Rauschenberg, Milton Glaser, and Marian B. Javits. National Gallery of Art, Washington, DC, 1992.63.1. © Robert Rauschenberg Foundation. **22:** From an edition of 200, published by Racolin Inc., produced by Styria Studio, New York. Minneapolis Institute of Art, The Martha T. Wallace Fund, P.76.2. Photo: Minneapolis Institute of Art. © Robert Rauschenberg Foundation. **23:** Private collection. © Robert Rauschenberg Foundation. **24:** Robert Rauschenberg Foundation. © Robert Rauschenberg Foundation. **25:** From an edition of 50, published by Gemini G.E.L., Los Angeles. Gift of the Joseph H. Hirshhorn Foundation, 1974. Hirshhorn Museum and Sculpture Garden, Washington, DC. Photo: Rick Coulby. © Robert Rauschenberg Foundation. **26:** Image courtesy of Craig Starr Gallery, New York. © Robert Rauschenberg Foundation. **30l, 30r:** Robert Rauschenberg Foundation. © Robert Rauschenberg Foundation. **31, 32, 33:** Image courtesy of Craig Starr Gallery, New York. © Robert Rauschenberg Foundation. **35:** The Menil Collection, Houston; Purchased with funds provided by an anonymous donor. Photo: Paul Hester. © Robert Rauschenberg Foundation. **36:** Museum Ludwig, Cologne. Donation Ludwig Collection 1976. © Robert Rauschenberg Foundation. **37:** Gift of Claire B. Zeisler and purchase with funds from the Mrs. Percy Uris Purchase Fund, inv. n.: 91.85. Whitney Museum of American Art, New York; Digital image © Whitney Museum of American Art / Licensed by Scala / Art Resource, New York. © Robert Rauschenberg Foundation. **39:** The Museum of Modern Art, New York; Gift of the family of Ileana Sonnabend. Digital image © The Museum of Modern Art / Licensed by SCALA / Art Resource, New York. © Robert Rauschenberg Foundation. **40:** The Museum of Modern Art, New York. Promised Gift of Glenn and Eva Dubin. © Robert Rauschenberg Foundation. **41:** Private collection. © Robert Rauschenberg Foundation. **42:** Robert Rauschenberg Foundation. © Robert Rauschenberg Foundation. **43:** Published by Gemini, G.E.L., Los Angeles. Collection Walker Art Center, Minneapolis; Gift of Kenneth E. Tyler, 1985. © Robert Rauschenberg Foundation. **44–45:** From an edition of 29 unique variants, published by Gemini G.E.L, Los Angeles. Gift of Gemini G.E.L., Los Angeles, and the Artist. National Gallery of Art, Washington, DC, 1981.5.78. © Robert Rauschenberg Foundation and Gemini G.E.L., Los Angeles. **46:** Private collection. © Robert Rauschenberg Foundation. **47:** Robert Rauschenberg Foundation. © Robert Rauschenberg Foundation. **48:** The Museum of Contemporary Art, Los Angeles, The Panza Collection © Robert Rauschenberg Foundation. **49:** Smithsonian National Air and Space Museum, Washington, DC; Gift of the American Institute of Aeronautics and Astronautics. **50:** The Museum of Contemporary Art, Los Angeles, The Panza Collection. © Robert Rauschenberg Foundation. **51:** The Art Institute of Chicago; Gift of Edlis | Neeson Collection, 2015.122. Photo: The Art Institute of Chicago / Art Resource, New York © Robert Rauschenberg Foundation. **52:** Robert Rauschenberg papers. Robert Rauschenberg Foundation Archives, New York. **54l:** From an edition of 28, printed by Bill Goldston and published by Universal Limited Art Editions Ltd., West Islip, NY. The Museum of Fine Arts, Houston; Museum purchase funded by Art + Paper 2022, 2022.90; Photograph © The Museum of Fine Arts, Houston; Will Michels. © Robert Rauschenberg Foundation / Licensed by VAGA at Artists Rights Society (ARS), New York. **54–55:** From an edition of 42, published by Universal Limited Art Editions, West Islip, NY. The Museum of Fine Arts, Houston; Museum purchase funded by Grant and Elizabeth Harvey, Rob and MaryEllen Kimbrough, Susanna V. and Andrew E. Townend, Kareen P. and Frederick L. Townend, Hugh A. Armstrong, and Theodore J. Lee and Marc A. Sekula, 2021.47; Photograph © The Museum of Fine Arts, Houston; Will Michels. © Robert Rauschenberg Foundation / Licensed by VAGA at Artists Rights Society (ARS), New York. **56, 57:** From an edition of 76, published by Gemini G.E.L., Los Angeles. Smithsonian American Art Museum, Washington, DC, Museum purchase, 1969.88. © Robert Rauschenberg Foundation. **58:** The Sonnabend Collection Foundation. © Robert Rauschenberg Foundation. **59:** Collection of the Robert and Jane Meyerhoff Modern Art Foundation. © Robert Rauschenberg Foundation. **60:** The Nelson-Atkins Museum of Art, Kansas City, MO; Purchase of the Nelson Gallery Foundation, F84-70. Image courtesy of Nelson-Atkins Digital Production & Preservation. © Robert Rauschenberg Foundation. **61:** Robert Rauschenberg Foundation. Photo: Ron Amstutz. © Robert Rauschenberg Foundation. **62:** Gift of the Robert Rauschenberg Foundation, 1998. The Solomon R. Guggenheim Museum, New York. © Robert Rauschenberg Foundation / Licensed by VAGA at Artists Rights Society (ARS), New York. **64:** From an edition of 50, published by Dayton's Gallery 12, Minneapolis, and Castelli Graphics, New York; produced by Styria Studio, Glendale, CA. Robert Rauschenberg Foundation. Photo: Ron Amstutz. © Robert Rauschenberg Foundation. **65:** From an edition of 50, published by Dayton's Gallery 12, and

Castelli Graphics, New York; produced by Styria Studio, Glendale, CA. Robert Rauschenberg Foundation. Photo: Ron Amstutz. © Robert Rauschenberg Foundation. **66, 67:** Robert Rauschenberg papers. Robert Rauschenberg Foundation Archives, New York. **68, 69:** Museum Purchase: Funds provided by Carol and John Hampton. Portland Art Museum, Portland, OR. © Robert Rauschenberg Foundation, 2007.5a,b. **70:** The Museum of Fine Arts, Houston; Museum purchase funded by the Caroline Wiess Law Foundation, 2002.4.A,B. Photo: © The Museum of Fine Arts, Houston; Will Michels. © Robert Rauschenberg Foundation / Licensed by VAGA at Artists Rights Society (ARS), New York. **71:** The Museum of Fine Arts, Houston; Gift of Joan Morgenstern in honor of Isabell Smith Herzstein, 95.447. © Robert Rauschenberg Foundation / Licensed by VAGA at Artists Rights Society (ARS), New York. **72:** From an edition of 35, published by Gemini G.E.L., Los Angeles. Transferred from NASA. Smithsonian National Air and Space Museum, Washington, DC. © Robert Rauschenberg Foundation. **74*l*, 74*r*, 75:** Robert Rauschenberg papers. Robert Rauschenberg Foundation Archives, New York. **76:** Photo: James Dean. Art Curatorial Files, Smithsonian National Air and Space Museum, Washington, DC. **77*t*, 77*m*:** Robert Rauschenberg papers. Robert Rauschenberg Foundation Archives, New York. **77*b*:** Photo: Unattributed. Photograph Collection. Robert Rauschenberg Foundation Archives, New York. **78*tl*, 78*bl*, 78*mr*, 79*l*:** Robert Rauschenberg papers. Robert Rauschenberg Foundation Archives, New York. **79*tr*:** Oran W. Nicks, ed., *This Island Earth* (Washington, DC: Scientific and Technical Information Division, Office of Technology Utilization, National Aeronautics and Space Administration; United States Government Printing Office, 1970). Special Collections. Robert Rauschenberg Foundation Library, New York. **79*br*:** Special Collections. Robert Rauschenberg Foundation Library. **80*tl*, 80*tr*, 80*b*:** Robert Rauschenberg papers. Robert Rauschenberg Foundation Archives, New York. **81:** Photo: Unattributed. Art Curatorial Files, Smithsonian National Air and Space Museum, Washington, DC. **82*t*, 82*m*, 82*b*:** Photo: Malcolm Lubliner. Photograph Collection. Robert Rauschenberg Foundation Archives, New York. **83:** Robert Rauschenberg Foundation. © Robert Rauschenberg Foundation. **84*t*, 84*b*, 85*t*, 85*m*, 85*b*:** Photo: NASA. Robert Rauschenberg papers. Robert Rauschenberg Foundation Archives, New York. **86:** From an edition of 35, published by Gemini G.E.L., Los Angeles. Transferred from NASA. Smithsonian National Air and Space Museum, Washington, DC. © Robert Rauschenberg Foundation. **87:** Photo: NASA. Robert Rauschenberg papers. Robert Rauschenberg Foundation Archives, New York. **88:** Photo: Theo Westenberger. Photograph Collection. Robert Rauschenberg Foundation Archives, New York. **89:** From an edition of 29, published by Universal Limited Art Editions, West Islip, NY. National Aeronautics and Space Administration. © Robert Rauschenberg Foundation. **90, 95:** Tokyo Metropolitan Museum © Robert Rauschenberg Foundation. **96:** The Menil Collection, Houston, purchased with funds provided by The Brown Foundation, Inc., Scaler Foundation, Inc., The Search Foundation, and the following individuals: Christophe de Menil, Frances Dittmer, James A. Elkins III, Windi Grimes, Agnes Gund, Walter Hopps, Adelaide de Menil Carpenter, Janie C. Lee, Roy Nolen, Francesco Pellizzi, Harry Pinson, Louisa Stude Sarofim, George Stark, Charles B. Wright III, and Michael Zilkha. Photo: James Craven. © Robert Rauschenberg Foundation. **97:**

San Francisco Museum of Modern Art; Fractional and promised gift of Helen and Charles Schwab; Photo: Ben Blackwell. © Robert Rauschenberg Foundation. **98:** Foundation Arc-en-Ciel/Hara Museum Collection © Robert Rauschenberg Foundation. **99:** Gift of Joseph H. Hirshhorn, 1972. Hirshhorn Museum and Sculpture Garden, Washington, DC. Photo: Cathy Carver. © Robert Rauschenberg Foundation. **100:** Museum of Contemporary Art Chicago / Art Resource, New York. Artist: Rauschenberg, Robert (1925–2008). © VAGA at ARS, New York. Partial gift of Stefan T. Edlis and H. Gael Neeson, 1998.49. Location: Museum of Contemporary Art Chicago, Chicago, Illinois. © Robert Rauschenberg Foundation / Licensed by VAGA at Artists Rights Society (ARS), New York. **101:** Dallas Museum of Art; The Roberta Coke Camp Fund, The 500, Inc., Mr. and Mrs. Mark Shepherd Jr., and General Acquisitions Fund, 1986.8.A-B © Robert Rauschenberg Foundation. **102:** From an edition of 65, published by Gemini G.E.L., Los Angeles. Gift of the Joseph H. Hirshhorn Foundation, 1974. Hirshhorn Museum and Sculpture Garden, Washington, DC. Photo: Rick Coulby © Robert Rauschenberg Foundation and Gemini G.E.L. **103:** From an edition of 46, published by Gemini G.E.L., Los Angeles. Gift of the Joseph H. Hirshhorn Foundation, 1974. Hirshhorn Museum and Sculpture Garden, Washington, DC. Photo: Lee Stalsworth. © Robert Rauschenberg Foundation and Gemini G.E.L. **105:** From an edition of 53, published by Gemini G.E.L., Los Angeles. Gift of the Joseph H. Hirshhorn Foundation, 1974. Hirshhorn Museum and Sculpture Garden, Washington, DC. Photo: Lee Stalsworth. © Robert Rauschenberg Foundation and Gemini G.E.L. **106:** From an edition of 60, published by Gemini G.E.L., Los Angeles. Gift of the Joseph H. Hirshhorn Foundation, 1974. Hirshhorn Museum and Sculpture Garden, Washington, DC. Photo: Rick Coulby. © Robert Rauschenberg Foundation and Gemini G.E.L. **107:** From an edition of 75, published by Gemini G.E.L., Los Angeles. Gift of Benjamin B. Smith. National Gallery of Art, Washington, DC, 1985.47.161. © Robert Rauschenberg Foundation and Gemini G.E.L. **108:** From an edition of 50, published by Gemini G.E.L., Los Angeles. Gift of the Joseph H. Hirshhorn Foundation, 1974. Hirshhorn Museum and Sculpture Garden, Washington, DC. Photo: Lee Stalsworth. © Robert Rauschenberg Foundation and Gemini G.E.L. **109:** From an edition of 56, published by Gemini G.E.L, Los Angeles. Gift of the Joseph H. Hirshhorn Foundation, 1974. Hirshhorn Museum and Sculpture Garden, Washington, DC. Photo: Lee Stalsworth. © Robert Rauschenberg Foundation and Gemini G.E.L. **110:** From an edition of 40, published by Gemini G.E.L., Los Angeles. San Francisco Museum of Modern Art; Gift of Harry W. and Mary Margaret Anderson. Photo: Ben Blackwell. © Robert Rauschenberg Foundation and Gemini G.E.L. **111:** From an edition of 250, published by Castelli Graphics, New York; produced by Styria Studio, New York. Robert Rauschenberg Foundation. Photo: Ron Amstutz. © Robert Rauschenberg Foundation. **112:** Robert Rauschenberg Foundation. Photo: Ron Amstutz. ©Robert Rauschenberg Foundation **113:** Robert Rauschenberg papers. Robert Rauschenberg Foundation Archives, New York. **114:** Robert Rauschenberg Foundation. Photo: Ron Amstutz. © Robert Rauschenberg Foundation. **116:** The Sidney and Harriet Janis Collection, The Museum of Modern Art, New York. Digital Image © The Museum of Modern Art / Licensed by SCALA / Art Resource, New York © Association Marcel Duchamp / ADAGP, Paris / Artists Rights Society (ARS), New York 2024. **117:** Robert Rauschenberg

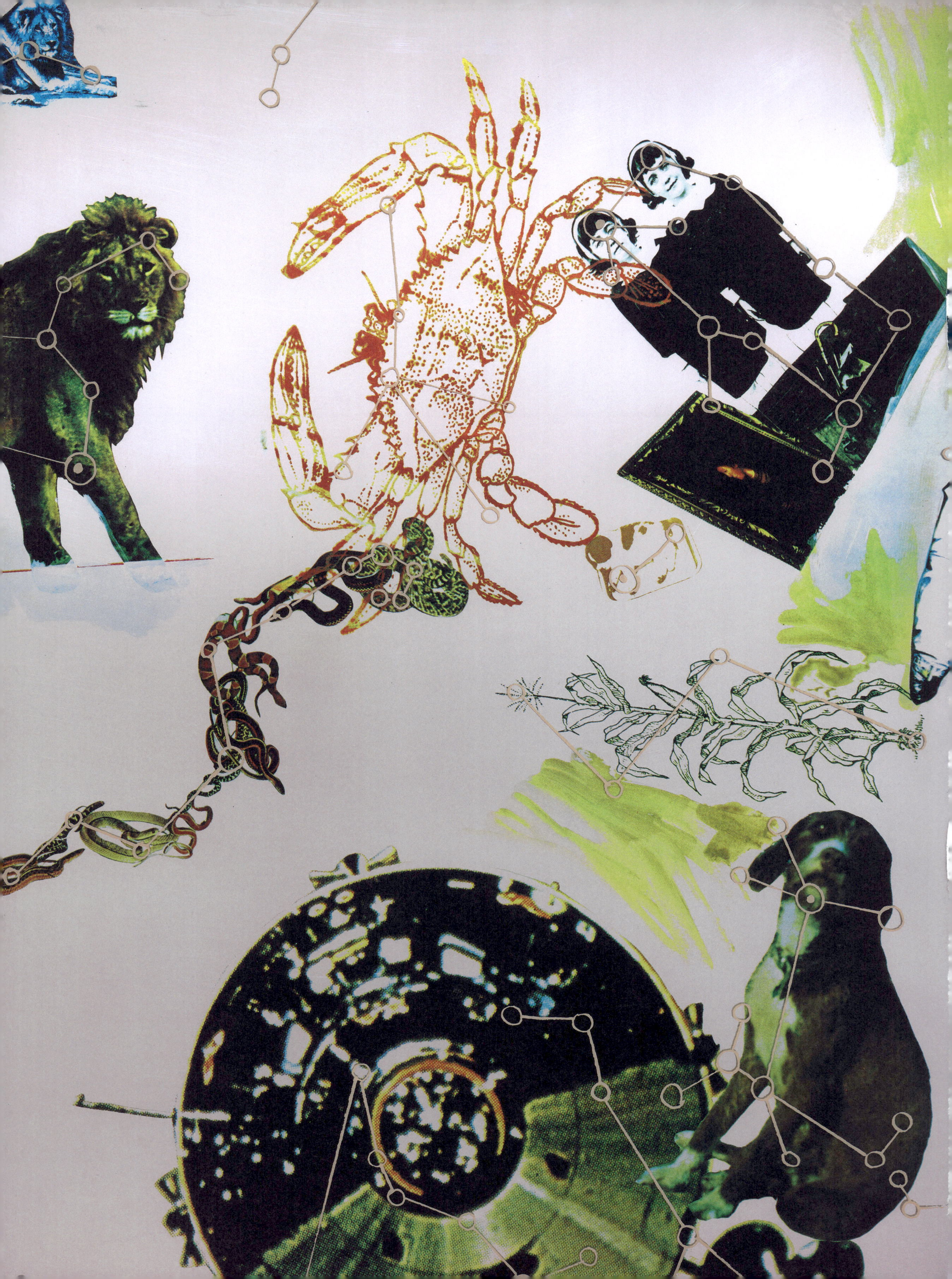